LATIN FOR THE NEW MILLENNIUM

STUDENT TEXT

Second Edition **LEVEL 1**

LATIN FOR THE NEW MILLENNIUM
Series Information

LEVEL ONE
Student Text, Second Edition

Student Workbook, Second Edition

College Exercise Book, Levels 1 and 2

Teacher's Manual, Second Edition

Teacher's Manual for Student Workbook, Second Edition

ENRICHMENT TEXTS
From Romulus to Romulus Augustulus:
Roman History for the New Millennium

The Original Dysfunctional Family:
Basic Classical Mythology for the New Millennium

LEVEL TWO
Student Text, Second Edition

Student Workbook, Second Edition

Teacher's Manual, Second Edition

Teacher's Manual for Student Workbook, Second Edition

ENRICHMENT TEXTS
From Rome to Reformation:
Early European History for the New Millennium

The Clay-footed SuperHeroes:
Mythology Tales for the New Millennium

LEVEL THREE
Student Text

Teacher's Manual

ENRICHMENT TEXTS
Latin 3: Select Latin Enrichment Readings

ELECTRONIC RESOURCES
www.lnm.bolchazy.com

www.bolchazy.com/ebooks.htm

Quia Question Bank

LATIN
FOR THE NEW MILLENNIUM

STUDENT TEXT

1

Second Edition **LEVEL 1**

Milena Minkova and Terence Tunberg

Bolchazy-Carducci Publishers, Inc.
Mundelein, Illinois USA

Series Editor: LeaAnn A. Osburn

SECOND EDITION

Volume Editor: Donald E. Sprague

Contributing Editors: Laurel Draper, Karen Lee Singh

FIRST EDITION

Volume Editors: Elisa C. Denja, LeaAnn A. Osburn

Contributing Editors: Timothy Beck, Judith P. Hallett, Laurie Haight Keenan, Karen Lee Singh, Donald E. Sprague, Rose Williams, Vicki Wine

Historical Timeline: Jayni Reinhard

Cover Design & Typography: Adam Phillip Velez

Cover Illustration: Roman Forum © Bettmann/CORBIS

Other Illustrations: Photography Credits appear on pp. 443–446

Cartography: Mapping Specialists

Indexing: Michael Hendry

Proofreader: Gary Varney

Latin for the New Millennium
Student Text, Level 1
Second Edition

Milena Minkova and Terence Tunberg

Bolchazy-Carducci Publishers, Inc.
1570 Baskin Road
Mundelein, Illinois 60060
www.bolchazy.com

Printed in Canada
2020
by Friesens

ISBN 978-0-86516-807-7

Library of Congress Cataloging-in-Publication Data

Names: Minkova, Milena, author. | Tunberg, Terence, author.
Title: Latin for the new millennium : student text, level 1 / Milena Minkova and Terence Tunberg.
Description: Second edition. | Mundelein, Illinois USA : Bolchazy-Carducci Publishers, Inc., 2017.
Identifiers: LCCN 2016034073 | ISBN 9780865168077 (hardbound : alk. paper)
Subjects: LCSH: Latin language--Readers. | Latin language--Grammar.
Classification: LCC PA2095 .L3448 2017 | DDC 478.6/421--dc23 LC record available at https://lccn.loc.gov/2016034073

LIST OF MAPS

FOREWORD

The *aurea mediocritās* of Latin textbooks has arrived! Not a grammar-translation nor a reading approach book, *Latin for the New Millennium* is a blend of the best elements of both.

The key to *Latin for the New Millennium*, Level 1, is the emphasis on reading Latin at the beginning of each chapter and using conversational Latin at the end of each chapter, or, as the authors indicate in the Preface, "it (Latin) offers you the linguistic key to the minds that shaped European (and therefore American) culture from the time of the Romans to the modern scientific revolution . . . In this book you will learn about the language by using it, step by step."

The reading passages at the opening of each chapter are based on Latin literature and proceed in chronological order from Plautus to Boethius. Each reading is supported by prereading and facing page vocabulary. Grammar is introduced using sentences already seen in the reading passage and, *mīrābile dictū*, there are plenty of exercises. The Vocabulary to Learn, chosen from the adapted reading passage, thus contains some literature-based words and is reiterated consistently in the exercises and other short reading passages.

Something not seen in most Latin textbooks is the conversational dialogue at the end of each chapter. This will pique the student's interest in the Latin version of modern-day activities and meet certain classical language standards directly. The authors, Milena Minkova and Terence Tunberg, professors at the University of Kentucky at Lexington, are the directors of the hugely popular *Conventiculum Lexintoniense*, the annual summer program that has been running for more than ten years. They are also on the faculty of the *Conventiculum Bostoniense*, a similar program that draws participants to experience conversational Latin in different geographical settings. At the 2007 American Classical League Institute at Vanderbilt University, I participated in a conversational Latin workshop presented by Minkova and Tunberg. Though the participants were seasoned Latin teachers, most were experiencing for the first time the tried and true methods these two experts were using to inspire us to speak Latin. By the end of the workshop, we could converse in familiar Latin phrases and saw how useful this could be for our own students. Tunberg's and Minkova's leadership in these summer programs made them uniquely well suited to design the conversational dialogues in *Latin for the New Millennium* and the copious oral exercises that are contained only in the Teacher's Manual, thus allowing teachers to pick and choose which exercises best meet the needs of their own students.

This book with its range of offerings will appeal to all types of language students and will allow teachers to bring the many facets of the Roman and post-Roman world into the classroom. How wonderful it is to see a passage of adapted Plautus in Chapter 2, a prose adaptation of Catullus's *passer* poem in Chapter 7, of Horace's satire on the boor in Chapter 13, and even of Tacitus's description of the great fire in Rome in Chapter 17. Roman culture is embodied in each of these passages, thus meeting another classical language standard. Accompanying each passage is a quotation or motto, connected to the passage or chapter.

All of this said, *Latin for the New Millennium* is student friendly. Study tips, rhymes, and mnemonics abound in each chapter and little sections called "By the Way" offer additional information for those who always want to know more.

The unit review sections are truly gems! After three chapters, a Latin review chapter provides not just the complete list of Vocabulary to Learn and plentiful exercises but often another piece of adapted literature to read—snippets of Martial or Cicero and more.

But this is not all. A section called "Considering the Classical Gods" offers high-interest readings in both English and Latin on the pantheon of classical gods. Another section, entitled "Connecting with the Ancient World," provides in English additional information on a particular aspect of Roman life contained within the unit.

Capping each review unit is a distinctive essay that explores Roman and modern topics, each written by a university scholar. From the University of Massachusetts to Stanford University, and many places in between, these professors have contributed their special expertise on subject matter related to the chapters. I know of no other book that does this!

There are many useful photographs and maps appropriately placed throughout. The reproductions of fine art and photographs of archaeological sites provide a visual learning experience as well. Needless to say, there are appendices on grammar and syntax and English to Latin and Latin to English glossaries with an added section on various mottoes.

The authors, editors, consultants, and pilot teachers have done a superior job of organizing this book for maximum usefulness and effectiveness. This unique series will include the following: Level 1 Student Text, Level 1 Student Workbook, Level 1 Teacher's Manual, and Level 1 Workbook Teacher's Manual; Level 2 Student Text, Level 2 Student Workbook, Level 2 Teacher's Manual, and Level 2 Workbook Teacher's Manual.* Many online and electronic resources will also accompany this series.

Latin for the New Millennium has been thoughtfully designed for and with the twenty-first century student in mind. Please join me in heralding the appearance of this unique new series that will improve and enhance the study of Latin for the twenty-first century.

PAUL PROPERZIO
Boston Latin Academy
2008

---

* Editor's Note: When Bolchazy-Carducci Publishers' late president and founder, Ladislaus J. Bolchazy, PhD, conceived of the *Latin for the New Millennium* series, based on the company's success producing textbooks for Latin 3 and Latin 4, he envisioned the series only having Levels 1 and 2. However, feedback from teachers and school districts indicated the need for a Level 3. Thus, *Latin for the New Millennium*, Level 3, and its Teacher's Manual were launched in 2012. *Latin 3: Select Latin Enrichment Readings* followed in 2013. The adoption of *Latin for the New Millennium* at colleges and universities led to the publication of the *College Exercise Book*, Levels 1 and 2 in 2012.

Learning Latin helps you learn English and other languages better, and, perhaps even more importantly, it offers you the linguistic key to the minds that shaped European (and therefore American) culture from the time of the Romans to the modern scientific revolution. Latin was the language these people used to express themselves and to record their ideas in permanent form across so many centuries. In this book you will learn about the language by using it, step by step.

CHAPTER COMPONENTS

READING PASSAGES

Each chapter begins with a Reading Passage and notes on the facing page that will help you understand any linguistic elements you have not previously seen. These notes feature vocabulary words in an easy to follow alphabetical listing, providing you the exact meaning needed to understand the reading passage but not the full lexical entries at this point. By reading and seeing these new elements in their natural context, often you will need no explanation to understand how they function, because they appear with words you already know. The Reading Passages are adapted from authentic works of Latin literature, and they are presented in chronological order. As you complete each chapter, you will be tracing the story of Latin as a literary language and the stories of the authors who used it. In addition, you will learn about Roman culture over the periods of time in which the featured reading of each chapter was produced.

VOCABULARY TO LEARN

The Vocabulary to Learn repeats some words encountered in the Reading Passage for each chapter, but in this section the words are listed by parts of speech instead of alphabetically and here the full lexical entry is given. These are words you will need to memorize in order to recognize and use them throughout the remainder of the book.

DERIVATIVES

In order to aid you in recognizing connections between Latin words and the English words derived from or related to them, a derivative exercise follows each Vocabulary to Learn.

At the end of each chapter, a set of English words derived from the chapter's Latin Vocabulary to Learn words is presented.

LANGUAGE FACTS AND EXERCISES

In the body of each chapter you will find simple explanations of the Language Facts featured in the chapter reading passage, along with many different exercises that allow you to *use* all the information you are learning. By doing the exercises in each chapter and in the student workbook, you will not only be reading and writing Latin, you'll be speaking it! Some exercises involve oral exchanges with the teacher and with other students. Because Latin communicates thought, it is a living thing. Therefore, a person who gains an active working knowledge in the language, along with a reading ability, is more likely to progress quickly to a deeper understanding of the language and the enjoyment of its literature. If you have an oral facility and can write in a language, you will not need to be reminded about forms and grammatical rules so often. In this book you will acquire that active facility as a basic part of learning the language.

CONVERSATIONAL LATIN

Toward the end of each chapter there is a Latin dialogue in which a group of modern students are the participants. They discuss, in Latin, situations often encountered in our daily lives. In these dialogues, you will find a bridge between our lives and the thoughts of the ancient, medieval, or Renaissance authors who wrote in Latin—a bridge constructed of the same basic language, Latin.

OTHER FEATURES

In each chapter you will find other interesting matter that will help you learn and enjoy Latin.

- **Memorābile Dictū** The first page of each chapter features a famous saying labeled *Memorābile Dictū* (A Memorable Thing to Say), a Latin phrase so well known that it has become an often repeated proverb or quotation. Learning each famous saying will increase your understanding not just of Latin, but of the thoughts and ideas that were important to Romans and have continued to be an integral part of modern life.

- **Study Tips** Each chapter contains sayings, rhymes, mnemonic devices, verses, or other information that will help you remember the various things you are learning.

- **By the Way** You will see this phrase repeated throughout every chapter. When you see this label, you will know that additional information is being presented.

REVIEW COMPONENTS

At the conclusion of every set of three chapters, there is a review containing various components:

VOCABULARY TO KNOW

This is a complete list of all the Vocabulary to Learn words presented in the three chapters, arranged by parts of speech.

EXERCISES

Here you will see many new exercises that will help you review and reinforce the material in the three preceding chapters. In the review exercise section there is often an additional reading passage to help you understand more about Latin literature and its heritage today.

CLASSICAL MYTHOLOGY

This section, entitled *Considering the Classical Gods*, includes passages on mythology, one in English and one in Latin, which tell some of the principal stories about the Greek and Roman gods. These stories reflect many of the main themes seen in literature and art from classical to modern times.

ASPECTS OF ROMAN LIFE

Next you will find a reading in English on an important aspect of Roman daily life. This section, entitled *Connecting with the Ancient World*, will present additional information on a topic encountered in the previous chapters.

EXPLORING ROMAN AND MODERN LIFE

Following the section on daily life, there will be a short essay in English that compares and contrasts some aspect of Roman and American life and illustrates a way in which Latin is a part of our life today. Each of these essays has been written by a university scholar with special expertise in this field of study.

MĪRĀBILE AUDĪTŪ

Each review chapter concludes with a list of Latin quotations, mottoes, phrases, or abbreviations used in English. These sayings relate to one of the unit topics.

The Latin language and Roman culture have not only inspired writers throughout the ages and influenced modern life but have also left their presence in art and archaeology. In this volume, reproductions of paintings, drawings, sculpture, mosaics, frescoes, and other artifacts from antiquity through the present abound with depictions of and references to the stories and lives of the Romans. Likewise, views of archaeological sites remind us of what Rome and its area of influence was like in ancient times. The illustrations throughout the text support the written word in visual form, thus offering you a vivid recollection of the chapter content.

Each author of this book has written different sections of the textbook but both authors have benefited, throughout the composition of the textbook, from continuous mutual advice and support.

M. M. and T. T.
2017

Visit www.lnm.bolchazy.com to see the electronic resources that accompany *Latin for the New Millennium.*

AUTHORS

MILENA MINKOVA

MA and PhD, Christian and Classical Philology, Pontifical Salesian University, Rome, Italy; MA and PhD, Classics, University of Sofia, Bulgaria

Professor of Classics, University of Kentucky, Lexington, Kentucky

Milena Minkova has studied, conducted research, and taught in Bulgaria, Switzerland, Germany, Italy, the Vatican City, and the USA. Minkova has authored three book monographs: *The Personal Names of the Latin Inscriptions from Bulgaria* (Peter Lang, 2000); *The Protean Ratio* (Peter Lang, 2001); and *Introduction to Latin Prose Composition* (Bolchazy-Carducci, 2007, reprint; Wimbledon, 2001). She has also published numerous articles on Latin medieval philosophy (most recently on twelfth century Renaissance), Latin literature in its continuity, Latin composition, and Latin pedagogy. Minkova has recently prepared a *College Exercise Book* based on *Latin for the New Millennium* (Bolchazy-Carducci, 2012).

TERENCE TUNBERG

BA and MA, Classics, University of Southern California; Postgraduate researcher, and doctoral student, Medieval Studies, University of London, England; PhD, Classical Philology, University of Toronto, Canada

Professor of Classics, University of Kentucky, Lexington, Kentucky

Terence Tunberg has taught in Belgium and Canada, as well as in the USA. He is a specialist in Latin composition, and an expert in the history of the approaches to writing Latin prose from antiquity to early modern times. Tunberg's works include an edition of a collection of medieval Latin speeches, commentaries on Latin works, and numerous studies of the history of imitation in Latin writing. His newest book elucidates the various functions of conversational Latin discourse in the culture of the humanists of the Renaissance and early modern period. In addition, he has for nearly two decades offered summer seminars designed to introduce people to the use of spoken Latin.

JOINT PUBLICATIONS BY THE AUTHORS

Minkova and Tunberg have together coauthored the following books: *Readings and Exercises in Latin Prose Composition* (Focus, 2004); *Reading Livy's Rome: Selections from Livy, Books I– VI* (Bolchazy-Carducci, 2005); *Mater Anserina: Poems in Latin for Children* (Focus, 2006); and *Latin for the New Millennium*, Level 2 (Bolchazy-Carducci, 2017). They are the directors of the Institute for Latin Studies at the University of Kentucky, in which students study the history of Latin from ancient to modern times, and take part in seminars in which Latin is the working language of all activities. Both Minkova and Tunberg are elected fellows of the Rome-based *Academia Latinitati Fovendae*, the primary learned society devoted to the preservation and promotion of the use of Latin.

EDITORS, CONSULTANTS, AND PILOT TEACHERS

VOLUME EDITORS

FIRST EDITION

Elisa C. Denja
Editor, Bolchazy-Carducci Publishers
Baker Demonstration School, Emerita
Evanston, Illinois

LeaAnn A. Osburn
Editor, Bolchazy-Carducci Publishers
Barrington High School, Emerita
Barrington, Illinois

SECOND EDITION

Donald E. Sprague
Editor, Bolchazy-Carducci Publishers
Professor of Humanities, Retired
Kennedy-King College
City Colleges of Chicago, Illinois

BOARD OF CONSULTANTS

FIRST EDITION

Virginia Anderson
Latin Teacher
Illinois Virtual High School
Barrington Middle School, Emerita
Barrington, Illinois

Jill M. Crooker
Latin Teacher
Pittsford-Mendon High School, Emerita
Pittsford, New York

Judith Peller Hallett
Professor of Classics
University of Maryland
College Park, Maryland

Sherwin D. Little
1–12 Foreign Language Program Leader
Indian Hill High School
Cincinnati, Ohio

Sherrilyn Martin
Chair, Department of Foreign Languages
Keith Country Day School
Rockford, Illinois

Mary Pendergraft
Professor of Classical Languages
Wake Forest University
Winston-Salem, North Carolina

John Traupman
Professor of Classics
St. Joseph's University, Emeritus
Philadelphia, Pennsylvania

Cynthia White
Associate Professor of Classics
University of Arizona
Tucson, Arizona

Rose Williams
McMurry College, Emerita
Abilene High School, Emerita
Abilene, Texas

Donna Wright
Latin Teacher
Lawrence North and Lawrence Central High
   Schools
Indianapolis, Indiana

PILOT TEACHERS

FIRST EDITION

Jeremy M. Walker
Latin Teacher
Crown Point High School
Crown Point, Indiana

Lanetta Warrenburg
Latin Teacher
Elgin High School
Elgin, Illinois

VOLUME EDITORS

FIRST EDITION

ELISA C. DENJA

BA Marygrove College, Detroit, Michigan; MA Columbia University; MA Loyola University Chicago

Elisa Denja taught Latin at North Chicago High School and Baker Demonstration School in Evanston, Illinois, for many years while concurrently teaching classical mythology at Loyola University Chicago and in the gifted-distance learning program at Northwestern University. Elisa was awarded the Illinois Latin Teacher of the Year award in 1992 and the Illinois Lifetime Achievement Award in 2007.

LEAANN A. OSBURN

BA Monmouth College, Illinois; MA Loyola University Chicago

While teaching Latin for many years at Barrington High School in Barrington, Illinois, LeaAnn served as both vice-president and president of the Illinois Classical Conference. LeaAnn received the Illinois Latin Teacher of the Year award in 1989, the Illinois Lt. Governor's Award in 1990, and the Classical Association of the Middle West and South Good Teacher Award in 1996, the Illinois Classical Conference Lifetime Achievement Award in 2008, and the American Classical League *Emerita* Award in 2012.

SECOND EDITION

DONALD E. SPRAGUE

BA Williams College, Massachusetts; MPS Loyola University Chicago

Donald Sprague also studied at the Intercollegiate Center for Classical Studies in Rome. He taught Latin and Greek, founded the Honors Program, established a summer study tour of Italy and Greece, and served as an administrator for many years at Loyola Academy in Wilmette, Illinois. He regularly develops and leads adult education tours of Roman sites. He served as treasurer of the Illinois Classical Conference for fourteen years and two terms as president of the Chicago Classical Club. In 1990, Sprague received the Illinois Latin Teacher of the Year award and the Illinois Lt. Governor's Award. Sprague taught the humanities and ethics as an adjunct professor at Kennedy-King College, one of the City Colleges of Chicago, from 2005 to 2016.

MARY PENDERGRAFT

AB, PhD University of North Carolina, Chapel Hill

After teaching at UNC-Greensboro and Duke University, Mary Pendergraft began teaching classics full-time at Wake Forest. Mary is a former President of the North Carolina Classical Association and participated in the focus group that wrote the North Carolina Standard Course of Study for Latin. Pendergraft served as Chief Reader for Advanced Placement Latin from 2007 to 2011. She was the recipient of the American Classical League's *Emerita* Award in 2011 and of a Classical Association of the Middle West and South *Ovatio* in 2014.

JOHN TRAUPMAN

BA Moravian College; MA, PhD Princeton University

John Traupman is professor emeritus from St. Joseph's University in Philadelphia where he taught for thirty-eight years. Among his many awards, John received the Distinguished Teaching Award from St. Joseph's University in 1982, a certificate of appreciation from the Pennsylvania Department of Education in 1990, and the Special Award from the Classical Association of the Atlantic States in 1996. John Traupman is especially well-known as the author of *Conversational Latin for Oral Proficiency* and *The New College Latin and English Dictionary.*

CYNTHIA WHITE

BA Chestnut Hill College; MA Villanova University; PhD Catholic University of America

Cynthia White is the Director of the Undergraduate Latin Program and supervises teacher training and K–12 Latin Teacher Certification at the University of Arizona. She regularly teaches at the *Istituto Internazionale di Studi Classici di Orvieto*, the Classics Department's Study Abroad Program in Orvieto, Italy, and has studied in Rome with the Papal Latinist Reginald Foster, O.D.C.

ROSE WILLIAMS

BA Baylor University; MA University of North Carolina, Chapel Hill

In addition to postgraduate work in Latin and Humanities at the University of Dallas and the University of Texas at Arlington, on a Rockefeller Grant Rose Williams did research at the Bodleian Library, Oxford University in England and at the University of Pisa. She taught Latin for over thirty years at both the high school and the university levels in Texas and is the author of some thirty books about the classics.

DONNA WRIGHT

BA, MA Ball State University

After teaching Latin at Carmel High School, Donna Wright currently teaches at both Lawrence North and Lawrence Central High Schools in Indianapolis, Indiana. She has been an active member of the Indiana Classical Conference, being named Creative Latin Teacher of the Year in 1976. She has also been active in the American Classical League, sponsoring a Junior Classical League chapter, and leading Italy trips for nearly twenty years. Donna also served as an officer, speaker, and board member of Pompeiiana, Inc.

PILOT TEACHERS

FIRST EDITION

JEREMY M. WALKER

AB Wabash College; MA Indiana University

Jeremy Walker has taught Latin at Crown Point High School in Crown Point, Indiana, since 1995. He has served as the Co-Chair of the Indiana Junior Classical League and Membership and Public Relations Chair of the National Junior Classical League. In addition to studying in Italy at the Intercollegiate Center for Classical Studies and in Greece at the American School for Classical Studies, he was president of the Indiana Classical Conference. In 2003, Jeremy was recognized as the Latin Teacher of the Year in Indiana, and in 2004 was recognized by the Indiana State Teachers Association as a Torch of Knowledge Recipient.

LANETTA WARRENBURG

BA Indiana University; MAT Indiana University-Purdue University, Indianapolis

Lanetta Warrenburg has taught high school English and Latin for thirty-three years at schools in Indiana and Illinois. Her last twenty-four years of teaching Latin were at Elgin High School in Elgin, Illinois. While teaching Latin there, she served as the Illinois Classical Conference chairperson for Chicago Classics Day, as co-chair for the Illinois Certamen League since 1993, and as state chair for the Illinois Junior Classical League from 1999 to 2001. Lanetta was honored as the Illinois Latin Teacher of the Year in 2001 and was president of the Chicago Classical Club from 2005 to 2007.

INTRODUCTION

ALPHABET

The Latin alphabet was derived from the Etruscan alphabet some time before the seventh century BCE. The Etruscans were a people in pre-Roman Italy.

Their alphabet owes much to the Greek alphabet. In turn, the Greek alphabet was derived from the Phoenician alphabet. Phoenician traders had spread their system of writing throughout the Mediterranean region. The Phoenician alphabet itself can be traced to the North Semitic alphabet, which was used in Syria and Palestine as early as the eleventh century BCE, and is considered to be the earliest fully developed alphabetic writing system.

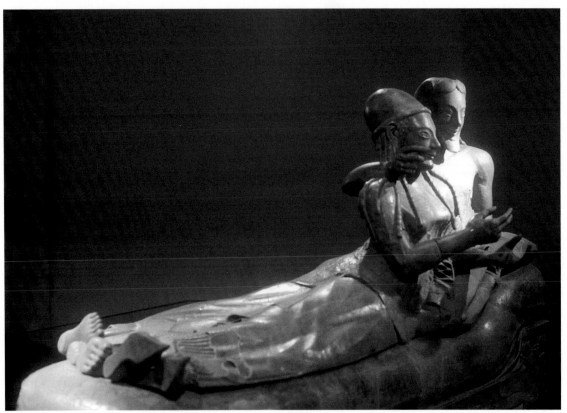

An Etruscan couple reclining on a funerary sarcophagus. Archaeologists have recovered a treasure trove of everyday objects from Etruscan tombs. The Etruscans buried these items so that the deceased could use them in the afterlife.

Look at the English alphabet in the left column, and at the Latin alphabet in the right one. The Latin alphabet is accompanied by the names of the Latin letters (in parentheses).

English Alphabet		Latin Alphabet		
Uppercase	Lowercase	Uppercase	Lowercase	Letter Name
A	a	A	a	(a "ăh")
B	b	B	b	(be "bay")
C	c	C	c	(ce "cay")
D	d	D	d	(de "day")
E	e	E	e	(e "ĕh")
F	f	F	f	(ef)
G	g	G	g	(ge "gay")
H	h	H	h	(ha "hah")
I	i	I	i	(i "ee")
J	j			
K	k	K	k	(ka "kah")
L	l	L	l	(el)
M	m	M	m	(em)
N	n	N	n	(en)
O	o	O	o	(o "ŏh")
P	p	P	p	(pe "pay")
Q	q	Q	q	(qu "koo")
R	r	R	r	(er)
S	s	S	s	(es)
T	t	T	t	(te "tay")
U	u	U	u	(u "oo")
V	v	V	v	(u consonant)
W	w			
X	x	X	x	(ix "eex")
Y	y	Y	y	(upsilon)
Z	z	Z	z	(zeta "dzayta")

The English alphabet is derived directly from the Latin alphabet. This accounts for the great similarities between the two alphabets. There are 26 letters in the English alphabet and 24 in the Latin. The differences are the following:

- The letter *W, w* (which is the doubled letter *v*) is missing in the Latin alphabet.

- The letter *J, j* is a more recent invention. In fact, it appears in Latin texts written during the Middle Ages and the Renaissance, as well as in many modern editions of ancient Latin texts. It is used to indicate the semi-vowel *i*, sometimes called consonantal *i*. The consonantal *i* is the *i* at the beginning of a word before a vowel, or *i* between two vowels. According to this method, for example, *Iūlius* is written *Jūlius*, and *Āiax* is written *Ājax*. In this book, the letter *J, j* will not be used.

- The distinction between the vowel *U, u* and the consonant *V, v* also belongs to later times. Initially, there was only one letter *V, u* used for both the vowel and the consonant, e.g., *Vrbs*, "The City" (i.e., Rome), or *uictor*, "the winner." However, in accord with the prevailing practice of expressing the vowel with *U, u*, and the consonant with *V, v*, in this book the two letters will be distinguished.

The Latin words *senātus, rēgēs, ūlla, gentēs,* and *prīmus* are engraved on this stone.

Sign from Pompeii carved on stone with Latin letters.

PRONUNCIATION OF LATIN

VOWELS

There are six vowels in Latin and their pronunciation is as follows:

Long Vowel Sound	Short Vowel Sound
ā is pronounced as in "father": *ōrātor* "orator"	*a* is pronounced as in "alike": *amō* "love"
ē is pronounced like the *a* in "rave": *nēmō* "nobody"	*e* is pronounced as in "pet": *bene* "well"
ī is pronounced like the double *e* in "seen": *līmes* "boundary"	*i* is pronounced as in "pit": *nihil* "nothing"
ō is pronounced as in "stove": *videō* "(I) see"	*o* is pronounced as in "often": *rosa* "rose"
ū is pronounced as in "moon": *ūnus* "one"	*u* is pronounced as in "put": *tum* "then"
ȳ comes from Greek and is pronounced in length somewhere between the *i* in "hit" and the *u* in "mute": *Pȳramus* "Pyramus"	*y* comes from Greek. Its sound, whether long or short, lies in between the sounds of *i* and *u* much as in the French "sûr," but the sound of short *y* is less drawn out than that of long *y*: *lyricus* "lyrical"

BY THE WAY

Everywhere in this book long vowels are indicated by macrons, i.e., **ā, ē, ī, ō, ū, ȳ,** while above the short vowels there are no signs. Sometimes two words differ from each other only in the length of the vowel. For example, *mālum* with a long *a* means "apple," while *malum* with a short *a* means "bad thing."

▶ EXERCISE 1

Repeat these words aloud after your teacher pronounces them.

1. alō	7. lēnis	13. probō	19. sūtor
2. alumnus	8. sēdēs	14. nota	20. ūsus
3. rāna	9. iter	15. pōnō	21. syllaba
4. rādō	10. timeō	16. dōnum	22. Pȳrēnē
5. teneō	11. nītor	17. ululō	
6. petō	12. mīrus	18. lupus	

DIPHTHONGS

Diphthongs are two vowels combined in one syllable and pronounced together as one sound. There are six diphthongs in Latin:

- *ae* much like the *y* in "sky": *laevus* "left"
- *au* pronounced as *ou* in "our": *aurum* "gold"
- *ei* pronounced as *ei* in "feign": *oiei!* "alas!"
- *eu* pronounced *eoo*, much as if in the two words "gray blue" you were to subtract the "gr-" and the "bl-" and combine the two vowel sounds: *Eurōpa* "Europe"
- *oe* pronounced as *oy* in "boy": *proelium* "battle"
- *ui* pronounced nearly like "we": *hui!* "oh!"

It is believed that quite early, still in ancient times, the diphthongs *ae* and *oe* began to be pronounced as *e*. If you encounter them written *aē* or *aë*, and *oē* or *oë*, this means that they are not diphthongs and the letters should be pronounced separately: *āēr, poēta.*

The diphthongs are always long.

▶ EXERCISE 2

Repeat these words after your teacher pronounces them.

1. aestās	7. seu	13. aēneus
2. aequō	8. moenia	14. poēma
3. raeda	9. neu	15. hei
4. laudō	10. poena	16. huic
5. aut	11. neuter	
6. aula	12. Poenus	

CONSONANTS

- **c** is pronounced as in "come": *clārus* "bright," *censeō* "(I) deem," *cārus* "dear."

- When **b** is followed by **s,** as in *urbs* "city," the sound of **b** approaches that of **p**: a sound we might represent as *urps*.

- **g** is pronounced as in "get": *gaudium* "joy," *gignō* "(I) beget, (I) bear," *grātia* "favor, agreeableness."

- Some think that the Romans of Cicero's time (first century BCE) pronounced the two consonants **ng** as **ngn**: for example, the adjective *magnus* "great" would have been pronounced in a way that we might represent as *mangnus*.

- **k** is a very rare consonant. In fact, it appears only in two words: *Kalendae* "the first day of every month in the Roman calendar," and in the personal name *Kaeso*.

- **q** appears always in combination with **u** and the combination **qu** is pronounced as in "queen": *quattuor* "four."

- **v** has a sound similar to **w** (as in the word "wife"): *videō* "I see."

- The consonant **u** in the combination **su** sounds like the English **w** in the following four words: *suēscō* "(I) become accustomed"; *Suēvī*, a name of a German tribe; *suādeō* "(I) advise"; *suāvis* "sweet."

- The letter **r** is trilled slightly. The sound has no exact equivalent in English, but is heard in many other European languages. The best way to make this sound is to pronounce **r** as in "rope," but vibrate the end of the tongue slightly as you say it.

- **x** is a double consonant (equivalent to **cs** or **gs**) that sounds much like the **x** in "six."

- **z** is another double consonant (equivalent to **dz**) and sounds almost like **z** in "zebra." It begins with a slight **d** sound first, so in pronouncing this letter you should hear **dz**.

- **ph** sounds like **p** in "pen," but with the addition of a slight breath of air represented by the **h**; **th** sounds like **t** as in "Tom," but with the addition of a slight extra breathing represented by the **h**; **ch** sounds nearly like the combination **kh.** These consonants are borrowed from Greek and appear in Greek words: *zephyrus* "western breeze," *chorus* "chorus," *theātrum* "theatre." When **p** and **t** are not accompanied by **h**, this slight aspiration is absent.

- When consonants are doubled, as in the verb *aggredior*, the consonantal sound is lengthened slightly.

▶ EXERCISE 3

Repeat these words after your teacher pronounces them:

1. cibus
2. capiō
3. cumulus
4. crēscō
5. gemma
6. Gallus
7. glōria
8. Zeus
9. bibliothēca
10. philosophia
11. zōna
12. theōrēma
13. phasēlus
14. charta
15. cēlō
16. antīquus

ACCENT

A Latin word is made up not just of letters, but also of syllables. A Latin word has as many syllables as it has vowels or diphthongs (a diphthong works like a single vowel, since it is made up of two vowels pronounced together [see diphthongs, above]).

You will need to know the following terms, when learning about accent.

- ultima — the last syllable in a word
- penult — the second-to-last syllable in a word
- antepenult — the third-to-last syllable in a word

So, in the word *ze-phy-rus* the vowel *u* is the ultima, *y* is the penult, and *e* is the antepenult.

RULES ABOUT THE STRESS ACCENT IN LATIN

1. The stress accent in Latin falls on either the penult or the antepenult.

2. The accent falls on the penult, if the penult is long. If the penult is short, the accent falls on the antepenult.

3. How to determine whether the penult is long or short.

   a. If the penult contains a long vowel (or any diphthong), the penult itself is long. You often need to learn whether the vowel in the penult is long or short as a basic element in learning a new word. A macron above the vowel will tell you that the vowel is long, while the absence of a macron will indicate a short vowel. Pronouncing the word can help you remember the vowel lengths. For example, *vi-de-ō* "I see" is pronounced *vi´deō*; while *au-rō-ra* "dawn" is pronounced *aurō´ra*; and *po-pu-lus* "people" is pronounced *po´pulus*.

   b. If the vowel in the penult is followed by two or more consonants, the penult is long, **no matter whether the vowel in the penult is long or short**, and the accent necessarily falls on the penult. For example, *do-cu-men-tum* "document" is pronounced *documen´tum*.

BY THE WAY

The consonant *x* is double (*cs* or *gs*) and counts as two consonants when determining whether the penult is long.

   c. There is one exception to 'b' above. Sometimes, even when there are two consonants between the penult and the ultima, they still do not determine that the penult is long. This happens when the two consonants are a mute and a liquid.

   The mutes are *p, b, d, t, g, c.*

   The liquids are *l, r.*

So, in the word *pal-pe-bra* "eyelid," the antepenult is accented (*pal´pebra*); the vowel of the penult is short, since it is followed by a mute and a liquid. Of course, rule 'a' still applies: in the word *the-ā-trum* "theatre," the penult is accented (*theā´trum*), since it is naturally long, something we learn from the macron.

▶ EXERCISE 4

Repeat each sentence aloud after your teacher reads it. Pay attention to the pronunciation and stress accent of each word.

What it is Like to Live Over a Bathhouse!
(Adapted from Seneca, *Moral Letter* 56)

Ecce undique clāmor sonat! Suprā ipsum balneum habitō! Prōpōne nunc tibi omnia genera vōcum odiōsa! Fortiōrēs exercentur et manūs plumbō gravēs iactant, cum aut labōrant aut labōrantem imitantur. Gemitūs audiō, quotiēns spīritum remīsērunt. Sunt quoque ūnctōrēs et tractātōrēs. Audiō crepitum manuum umerōs ferientium: sonus quoque ictuum mūtātur: nunc enim manus pervenit plāna, nunc concava. Audiō clāmōrēs, sī fūr est in balneō dēprehēnsus.

Look, there is noise sounding all around! I live above the bathhouse itself! Imagine to yourself now all the hateful types of voices! The stronger ones exercise themselves and swing their hands loaded with lead weights, while they work out—or imitate a person working out. I hear moans, every time they let go a <pent-up> breath. There are also anointers and masseurs. I hear the slap of hands hitting shoulders and the sound of the blows changes: for sometimes the hands come flat, sometimes cupped. I hear shouting, if a thief is caught in the bathhouse.

The Celts worshipped Sul, the goddess of the only natural hot springs in England. The Romans built a bath and temple complex to Sul-Minerva and named the location Aquae Sulis (Waters of Sul), today's Bath.

OVERVIEW OF ROMAN HISTORY

According to legend, Romulus and his twin brother Remus were set adrift on the Tiber River. A she-wolf nursed the boys until a shepherd rescued them. Upon reaching manhood, in 753 BCE, the twins founded a new city near the place where they had been found by the she-wolf, on the basis of an *augustō auguriō*, "a favorable sighting of birds." But Romulus killed Remus in a dispute over who would rule the new city and became its first king.

A view of the Tiber River as it flows through the city of Rome. To the left is
Castello Sant'Angelo, the fortified Mausoleum of Diocletian.

Six other kings ruled after Romulus: Numa Pompilius, Tullus Hostilius, Ancus Martius, Tarquinius Priscus, Servius Tullius, and Tarquinius Superbus (Tarquin the Proud). After the last of these seven kings was overthrown in 509 BCE, Rome became a republic, with a representative form of government headed by two consuls, elected annually. By 451 BCE, the first corpus of Roman law, known as the Twelve Tables, was created.

In the last century BCE, the Roman Republic was shaken apart by a series of civil wars. By 31 BCE an autocratic regime headed earlier by Julius Caesar and later by his great-nephew Octavian brought the Republic to an end. The years from 27 BCE—when Octavian assumed the title of *prīnceps*, "chief citizen," as well as the name Augustus—to around 180 CE are known as the early principate, or empire. During this era Rome extended her boundaries to the British Isles in the north, North Africa in the south, Spain in the west, and the Tigris and Euphrates rivers in the east.

From 180 CE onward, in the period known as the late empire, the Roman state experienced severe economic problems and frequent invasions by Germanic tribes. Responding to the pressure of the first wave of migrations, as well as internal political unrest and economic difficulties, the emperor Diocletian (ruled 284–305 CE) had already divided the Roman Empire into an eastern and western half, each under its own emperor—an attempt to make the vast Roman state more manageable.

This political division of the empire actually mirrored a cultural division too: the main language of the West was Latin, while the main language of the East was Greek. Shortly afterward the emperor Constantine (ruled 312–337 CE) established a new capital for the Eastern empire at Byzantium, which he renamed Constantinople ("the city of Constantine," today called Istanbul). But even after this reorganization, the imperial government ultimately proved incapable of stemming the tide of the migrations, in part because the Roman army was too widely extended and could not be in so many places at once. Indeed many of the invaders were given the status of *foederātī* or "treaty troops." In effect, they were allowed to occupy segments of the empire in return for protecting it. So when Alaric, King of the Visigoths sacked Rome in 410 CE, he actually had a title as a commander in the Roman army!

Rome was sacked again in 455 CE by the Vandals, who had already occupied the Roman province of North Africa. The pillaging of the city of Romulus by the invaders made a profound impression on contemporaries, and to this day the term "vandalism" is a word in several languages for wanton destruction. While the Eastern empire (always more stable and economically prosperous than the West) continued to exist until 1453 CE, the Western empire was extinct as a political entity by 476 CE. In its place were Germanic kingdoms and tribes: Angles and Saxons in Britain, Visigoths in Spain, Ostrogoths in Italy, Franks and Burgundians in Gaul—to name only the major groups. The combination of these new societies with the previous inhabitants, who had been Romanized to varying degrees, would one day provide the basis for the cultures of modern Europe.

But the end of the ancient Roman Empire in the West was **not** the end of Latin. On the contrary, during the next 1200 years Latin not only flourished as the major literary language in the territories of the former Western Roman Empire, the use of Latin was extended to regions the Romans had never occupied, including Ireland, Scandinavia, and even the New World.

BEGINNINGS OF LATIN LITERATURE

Very few complete works of Latin literature produced before the mid-second century BCE (i.e., before 150 BCE) have survived. One reason for this loss was the tremendous popularity of the works produced in the following century by such authors as Cicero, Vergil, and Ovid. Their writings were so widely read and copied in subsequent centuries that the authors preceding them were gradually neglected.

Among the major figures of early Latin literature was a freed slave from the Greek city of Tarentum named Livius Andronicus, who lived from 284 to 204 BCE. He was known for his adaptations of Greek drama for Roman audiences, and his translation of Homer's *Odyssey* into Latin verse.

THE ROMAN WORLD

BRITANNIA

GERMĀNIA

EURŌPA

GALLIA

ALPĒS MONTĒS

Verōna
Patavium
Padus
Mantua
Rubicō
APPENNINUS MŌNS
Mare Hādriāticum
ETRŪRIA
ITALIA
Tiberis
Tarquiniī
Rōma
CORSICA
Pompēiī
Brundisi
Alba Longa
Vesuvius Mōns
Neāpolis
Stabiae
Tarentu
HISPĀNIA
SARDINIA
Mare Tyrrhēnum
M
Īon

▲ *Aetna Mōns*
SICILIA
Syrācūsae

Hippō
Rēgius
Carthāgō

NUMIDIA
AFRICA
PRŌVINCIA
Mare

A F R I C A

PERSIA →

Pontus Euxīnus

BĪTHȲNIA

PONTUS

ĀSIA

THRĀCIA

Bȳzantium/
Constantīnopolis

ĀSIA PRŌVINCIA

...ACEDONIA

▲ Olympus Mōns

Trōia/Īlium

Thermopylae

Mare Aegaeum

Antiochīa

SYRIA

...ACA

Delphī

GRAECIA

Athēnae

Babylōn

Sparta

DĒLOS

CYPRUS

CRĒTA

Internum

Alexandrēa

AEGYPTUS

The Romans regarded Ennius (ca. 239–169 BCE) as the father of Latin literature. He wrote many kinds of literary works, including plays. His *Annālēs*, an epic poem about the early history of Rome, was particularly renowned, and perhaps the primary epic read in Roman schools before the time of Vergil. Only fragments of his writings remain.

One of Ennius's contemporaries was the famed Cato the Censor, also known as Cato the Elder (234–149 BCE), a rigidly conservative Roman senator. Most of his treatise on agriculture, called *Dē agrī cultūrā*, survives. It is the oldest work of Latin prose; among Cato's recommendations here are that field slaves be treated similarly to beasts of burden. Cato is also remembered for his statement *Carthāgō dēlenda est*, "Carthage must be destroyed," evidence for the Roman fear of the Carthaginians. The Romans fought three wars, known as the Punic Wars, against the Carthaginians. The first ended before Cato was born; in the second, against Hannibal, Cato served with military distinction; the third ended in 146 BCE, as Cato had demanded, with the destruction of Carthage. On this occasion the victorious Romans were said to have plowed salt into the Carthaginian soil.

Discussions about later authors and adaptations from their writings will be presented chronologically in the chapters of this book.

Roman ruins at Carthage in Africa.

CHAPTER 1

Parts of Speech; Nouns: Number, Gender, Case (Nominative and Accusative); First Declension Nouns

Oil painting of Romulus and Remus with the she-wolf. Peter Paul Rubens (1577–1640).

MEMORĀBILE DICTŪ

SPQR: Senātus Populusque Rōmānus.
"The Senate and the People of Rome."

These four letters form what is known as an acronym, one that symbolized supreme power in ancient Rome.

READING

This story describes how Rome was said to have been founded in 753 BCE. King Numitor of Alba Longa was overthrown by his cruel and ambitious brother Amulius, who not only seized the throne, but so feared that one of Numitor's male descendants might have a legitimate claim on it that he made Numitor's daughter Rhea Silvia a priestess of the goddess Vesta. These priestesses were not allowed to marry during their childbearing years.

RŌMULUS ET REMUS

1   Mārs est deus. Mārs Rhēam Silviam amat. Itaque Rhēa Silvia duōs
     filiōs habet: Rōmulum et Remum. Amūlius Rhēam Silviam vinculīs
     claudit. Amūlius Rōmulum et Remum in aquam pōnit. Lupa ad aquam
     ambulat. Lupa Rōmulum et Remum bene cūrat et amat. Rōmulus et
5   Remus crēscunt. Posteā Rōmulus et Remus Rōmam aedificant.

Famous bronze statue housed in Rome's Capitoline Museum depicts the she-wolf and the twins.

READING VOCABULARY

ad aquam – to the water

aedificant – build

*amat** – loves

*ambulat** – walks

Amūlius – Amulius

*aquam** – water

*bene** – well

claudit – locks up

crēscunt – grow up

*cūrat** – takes care of, cares for

deus – god

duōs – two

*est** – is

*et** – and

fīliōs – sons

habet – has

in aquam – into the water

*itaque** – and so

*lupa** – she-wolf

Mārs – Mars, the god of war

pōnit – puts

*posteā** – afterward, later

Remum – Remus

Remus – Remus

Rhēa Silvia – Rhea Silvia

Rhēam Silviam – Rhea Silvia

*Rōmam** – Rome

Rōmulum – Romulus

Rōmulus – Romulus

vinculīs – with chains

*Words marked with an asterisk will need to be memorized later in the chapter.

COMPREHENSION QUESTIONS

1. Whose sons are Romulus and Remus?

2. What did Amulius do?

3. Who saved the life of Romulus and Remus?

4. What did Romulus and Remus do?

LANGUAGE FACT I

PARTS OF SPEECH

The *parts of speech* used in a Latin sentence determine its meaning, just as in English. While the noun and the verb are the two most important, other common parts of speech are listed below.

Noun: a person, place, thing, idea, action, or quality. Examples: "Romulus," "river," "courage."

Pronoun: a word that stands in place of a noun that has been previously mentioned or is clear from context. Examples: "I," "she," "him," "it."

Adjective: a word that limits or defines a noun or a pronoun. Examples: "little," "strong."

Adverb: a word that limits or defines verbs, adjectives, or (other) adverbs. Examples: "very," "quietly."

Verb: a word that describes an action or state of being. Examples: "go," "stay," "was."

Preposition: a word that begins a prepositional phrase, such as "in," "to," "on," "for," "by," "with." A prepositional phrase is a preposition joined to a noun. Examples: "in the morning," "with a sharp pencil."

Conjunction: a word that connects words, phrases, clauses, and sentences. Examples: "and," "but," "although."

Interjection: a word that expresses emotion. Example: "wow!"

▶ EXERCISE 1

Review the meanings and identify the parts of speech of the following words. The Reading Vocabulary may be consulted.

1. filiōs
2. bene
3. aedificant
4. ad
5. ambulat

6. et
7. lupa
8. claudit
9. Rōmam
10. amat

VOCABULARY TO LEARN

NOUNS

agricola, agricolae, *m.* – farmer

aqua, aquae, *f.* – water

āthlēta, āthlētae, *m.* – athlete

fīlia, fīliae, *f.* – daughter

lupa, lupae, *f.* – she-wolf

nauta, nautae, *m.* – sailor

poēta, poētae, *m.* – poet

puella, puellae, *f.* – girl

Rōma, Rōmae, *f.* – Rome

terra, terrae, *f.* – land

VERBS

amat – he/she/it loves

ambulat – he/she/it walks

cūrat – he/she/it takes care of, cares for

est – he/she/it is

ADVERBS

bene – well

posteā – afterward

CONJUNCTIONS

et – and

itaque – and so

Aqueducts carried water (*aqua*) to the cities in the Roman world. This aqueduct built in 19 BCE, which stretched across the Gard River, was named the Pont du Gard and brought water to the city of Nîmes in France in ancient times.

BY THE WAY

Each *noun* given in the vocabulary has two forms. The second form is the genitive singular.

A *derivative* is an English word rooted in a Latin word. The English derivative is similar in meaning and form to its Latin source.

STUDY TIP

An English derivative often can help you remember what a Latin word means.

▶ EXERCISE 2

Find the English derivatives based on the Vocabulary to Learn in the following sentences. Write the corresponding Latin word.

1. She shows a considerable filial respect toward her father.

2. Agriculture is a science of cultivating the land.

3. The ship is equipped with all the necessary nautical instruments.

4. We saw all kinds of fish in the aquarium.

5. This is an all-terrain vehicle.

6. When will the athletic competition start?

7. She has a truly poetic nature.

LANGUAGE FACT II

NOUNS: NUMBER, GENDER, CASE (NOMINATIVE AND ACCUSATIVE)

Nouns in Latin show number, gender, and case.

Number: Latin nouns are either singular or plural in number. Number is shown in different ways by different types of nouns, but some ending-patterns are for singular forms, and other ending-patterns are for plural forms.

Gender: Every noun, likewise, is either masculine, feminine, or neuter in gender. You must learn the gender of each noun. In the Vocabulary to Learn lists, the gender is indicated by the common abbreviations *m.* (masculine), *f.* (feminine), or *n.* (neuter).

Case: Latin nouns must have an ending-pattern that displays case. This is quite different from English, in which case is indicated by word position, and not by endings (although case markers are preserved in certain pronouns, such as "he" and "him"). A noun's case reveals what function the noun has in the sentence. There are five common cases: nominative, genitive, dative, accusative, and ablative. Two less frequently used cases are called the vocative and the locative.

STUDY TIP

An easy way to remember the names of the five common cases is to use this mnemonic device:

Never	**N**ominative
Give	**G**enitive
Dogs	**D**ative
Any	**A**ccusative
Abuse	**Ab**lative

Nominative: The nominative case identifies the subject. The subject is a noun or a pronoun that performs the action or exists in a state of being. In the sentence "William is reading," the word "William" is the subject.

> Example: *Mārs . . . amat.* Mars loves . . .

> The noun subject of the verb "love" is the god Mars.

Find more examples of nominatives and their verbs from the reading passage at the beginning of the chapter.

The nominative case *also* identifies the predicate nominative. In the sentence "William is a student," the predicate nominative is "a student." A predicate nominative completes the meaning of the verb "to be." Look at this example from the reading:

> Example: *Mārs est deus.* Mars is a god.

> *Mārs* is the subject and *deus* is a predicate nominative.

Accusative: The fourth case listed is called the accusative; the genitive, dative, and ablative cases will be discussed in later chapters. The accusative case points out the noun (or pronoun) that is the direct object. Remember: direct objects receive the action of the verb. In the sentence "I am writing a letter," the direct object is "a letter."

> Example: *Mārs Rhēam Silviam amat.* Mars loves Rhea Silvia.

> The direct object of "love" is the noun *Rhēam Silviam.*

Find more examples of accusatives and their verbs from the reading passage at the beginning of the chapter.

▶ EXERCISE 3

a. Identify whether the nouns in bold in these sentences are subjects, direct objects, or predicate nominatives. The Reading Vocabulary may be consulted.

b. Label each sentence as *vērum* (true) if it agrees or *falsum* (false) if it disagrees with the Latin reading passage at the beginning of the chapter.

Example: Amūlius est **deus**.
Predicate nominative   falsum

1. **Rhēa Silvia** Rōmulum et Remum cūrat.
2. Amūlius **Rōmulum** et **Remum** bene cūrat.
3. Amūlius **lupam** vinculīs claudit.
4. **Mārs** Rōmulum et Remum in aquam pōnit.
5. Lupa **Rhēam Silviam** cūrat.
6. **Amūlius** ad aquam ambulat.

The power of the city of Rome, founded according to legend by Romulus, is symbolized by these four letters that are prominently displayed in various places within the city.

LANGUAGE FACT III
FIRST DECLENSION NOUNS

A *declension* is a group of nouns that show a certain pattern of word endings. There are five different declensions in Latin. In the reading about Romulus and Remus, these are the forms belonging to the first declension:

Rhēam Silviam   Rhēa Silvia   aquam   lupa   Rōmam

Notice that the text says *Rhēa Silvia* when she is the subject, and *Rhēam Silviam* when she is the direct object.

The first declension is composed of words that characteristically have the vowel **a** at or near the end of the word: *lupa*.

Below is the pattern that first declension nouns follow to show case and number. Memorize the Latin words in order from the nominative singular down to the ablative singular, and then from the nominative plural down to the ablative plural.

Remember that the endings for a whole group of nouns follow this pattern. Once you learn this pattern, you can recognize the case and number of all the words belonging to this declension.

In this chapter, you have begun to learn about the nominative and accusative cases. The other cases will be explained in later chapters.

First Declension

Singular			Plural		
Nominative	lup**a**	the she-wolf	Nominative	lup**ae**	the she-wolves
Genitive	lup**ae**	of the she-wolf	Genitive	lup**ārum**	of the she-wolves
Dative	lup**ae**	to/for the she-wolf	Dative	lup**īs**	to/for the she-wolves
Accusative	lup**am**	the she-wolf	Accusative	lup**ās**	the she-wolves
Ablative	lup**ā**	by/with the she-wolf	Ablative	lup**īs**	by/with the she-wolves

Dative and ablative plural of the words *fīlia*, "daughter," and *dea*, "goddess" is **fīliābus** and **deābus**. This is to distinguish these forms from the corresponding forms of *fīlius*, "son," and *deus*, "god."

STUDY TIP

Notice that the ablative singular ending *–ā* has a long mark (macron) above it: this is the only difference between the nominative and ablative singular endings.

Notice that the dative and ablative plural endings are identical.

Here are more words belonging to the first declension:

puella – girl   *fīlia* – daughter   *terra* – land

Most first declension words are feminine in gender, but a few (usually ones that indicate masculine occupations in ancient times) are masculine. Examples are *poēta*, "poet"; *agricola*, "farmer"; *nauta*, "sailor"; *āthlēta*, "athlete."

▶ EXERCISE 4

Identify the case of each singular noun. Then change each form into plural. For some, more than one answer is possible.

Example: fīlia
nominative   fīliae

1. puellae
2. nautam
3. terram
4. agricola

5. aquae
6. puellā
7. āthlētā

One of the mosaics on the floor of the beautiful nineteenth-century Galleria Vittorio Emanuele II
in Milan depicts Rome personified with the she-wolf and Romulus and Remus.

▶ EXERCISE 5

Identify the case of each plural noun. Then change each form into the singular. For some, more than one answer is possible.

Example: puellās
accusative   puellam

1. fīliae
2. terrīs
3. nautārum
4. lupae

5. aquīs
6. poētārum
7. agricolae

BY THE WAY

In all declensions, endings are added to the base of a noun. It is important to know that the base of a noun is found by removing the ending from its genitive singular form. For example, the genitive singular of *puella* is *puellae*. If you remove the *–ae* from *puellae*, what remains is the base of the word, namely *puell–*. For this reason, learning the genitive singular is as important as knowing the nominative singular of the noun.

STUDY TIP

Always learn the genitive together with the nominative, because from the genitive you will know to which declension a word belongs!

A wall painting depicting a Roman farmer (*agricola*) with his sheep.

▶ EXERCISE 6

Translate from Latin into English, and from English into Latin. The most common Latin word order is:

subject – direct object – verb.

1. Agricola terram amat.
2. The athlete loves water.
3. Nauta filiam amat.
4. The poet loves Rome.
5. Agricola terram cūrat.
6. The she-wolf cares for (is taking care of) the girl.

BY THE WAY

Even though the most common word order is subject – direct object – verb, remember that endings—not word order!—determine which word is the subject and which is the direct object.

TALKING

When we meet one person, we greet her/him with *salvē!* When we meet two or more people, we greet them with *salvēte!* When we bid goodbye to one person, we say *valē!* When we bid goodbye to two or more people, we say *valēte!*

Here are various ways to ask "how are you?" or "how are you doing?":

> *Quōmodo valēs?* or *Quōmodo tē habēs?* or *Quid agis?*
> "How are you?"

Here is a range of possible answers:

> *bene* "well"
> *pessimē* "very bad"
> *optimē* "great"
> *melius* "better"
> *mediocriter* "so-so" or "not too bad"
> *meliusculē* "a little better"
> *male* "bad"

SAYING HELLO

Marīa, Helena et Christīna sunt (*are*) discipulae (*students*).

Marīa: Salvēte, Helena et Christīna!

Christīna: Salvē, Marīa!

Helena: Salvē, Marīa!

Marīa: Quōmodo valēs, Helena? Quōmodo valēs, Christīna?

Helena et Christīna: Bene. Quōmodo tū (*you*) valēs, Marīa?

Marīa: Pessimē.

Helena et Christīna: Cūr? (*Why?*)

Marīa: Timeō linguam Latīnam (*I fear the Latin language*).

Helena: Ego (*I*) linguam Latīnam amō.

Christīna: Et ego linguam Latīnam amō!

DERIVATIVES

agricola – agriculture, agricultural

aqua – aquarium, aquatic, aqueduct, aqueous, ewer, sewage, sewer

āthlēta – athlete, athletic

fīlia – affiliation, filiate, affiliate, hidalgo, filial, filicide

lupa – lupine, lupus

nauta – nautical

poēta – poet, poetic, poetry

puella – puerile

Rōma – Roman, Romance (languages), Romanesque, Romania

terra – terrace, inter, disinter, subterranean, terrestrial, terrier, territory, terrain

amat – amateur, amiable, amicable, amity, amorous, enemy, enmity, inimical, paramour, Amy

ambulat – amble, ambulance, ambulatory, perambulator, preamble

cūrat – accurate, assure, curate, curio, curiosity, ensure, insecure, insurance, manicure, procure, proctor, proxy, reassure, scour, sinecure, sure

bene – benefit, benediction, benefactor, benevolent, benign

posteā – posterity, postern, posthumous, postwar, preposterous, puny, postpone

CHAPTER 2

First and Second Conjugation Verbs; Principal Parts; Properties of Verbs: Number, Person, Tense, Stem; The Infinitive; Subject and Verb Agreement

This wall painting from Pompeii shows three actors on a stage. At the left is an actor wearing a slave's mask. At the right are two actors, usually men, portraying females.

MEMORĀBILE DICTŪ

Inter sacrum saxumque.

"Between a rock and a hard place," literally "between the sacrificial animal and the rock." (Plautus, *Captives* 617)

This expression was used by the Roman comic playwright Plautus in his comedies *The Captives* and *Casina* to indicate a difficult situation for which there seems to be no solution. Characters in many of Plautus's comedies find themselves in such difficult circumstances.

READING

The major Latin literary works from prior to 100 BCE are comedies by two Roman dramatists, Titus Maccius Plautus (ca. 254–184 BCE) and Publius Terentius Afer (called Terence in English), who died in 159 BCE. Plautus is said to have written approximately 130 plays. Only twenty-one, however, still survive. He modeled these plays on Greek comedies written in the fourth and third centuries BCE by various Athenian writers.

Still, Plautus writes for a contemporary Roman audience of all social backgrounds, ranging from slaves to the political elite. His comedies allude to current Roman events, and are noteworthy for their inventive and playful use of the Latin language. Here is an excerpt from his *Menaechmī*.

A merchant from Syracuse (a city on the island of Sicily) has two identical twin sons. When they reach the age of seven, he takes one of them, named Menaechmus, on a business trip. The boy gets lost in a crowd and is adopted by local residents. The remaining twin, Sosicles, is renamed Menaechmus in memory of his lost brother. After this Menaechmus-Sosicles grows up, he travels without knowing it to the town where his twin brother resides. A long series of misunderstandings occurs. Menaechmus's friends and family think Menaechmus-Sosicles is Menaechmus, while Messenio, the slave of Menaechmus-Sosicles, assumes that Menaechmus is his master. Because the two men are identical twins, the misunderstandings are not surprising, but because neither twin knows of the other's existence they involve numerous complications. Confusion comes to a head when the two Menaechmi finally meet, each still unaware that the other exists. The slave Messenio is present at this meeting, realizes that the two young men are identical in appearance, and gives voice to his surprise.

DĒ MENAECHMĪS

1   Messeniō: Prō Iuppiter! Quid videō?

Menaechmus Sōsiclēs: Quid vidēs?

Messeniō: (*pointing at Menaechmus*) Hic fōrmam tuam habet.

Menaechmus Sōsiclēs: Quam fābulam mihi nārrās?

5   Messeniō: Fābulās nōn nārrō. Tū vidēre dēbēs.

Menaechmus Sōsiclēs: Papae! (*addressing Menaechmus*) Quōmodo
tē vocant?

Menaechmus: Menaechmum mē vocant.

Menaechmus Sōsiclēs: Fābulās nārrās! Mē quoque Menaechmum
vocant.

Messeniō: Sunt sīcut duae guttae aquae!

10   Menaechmus Sōsiclēs: Quam patriam habēs?

Menaechmus: Sum Syrācūsānus.

Menaechmus Sōsiclēs: Ego quoque ibi habitō. Itaque tū es frāter meus. Salvē, mī frāter! Diū tē exspectō.

Menaechmus: Salvē, mī frāter! Dēbēmus nunc cum patre habitāre.

READING VOCABULARY

cum patre – with father

*dēbēmus – we ought, must

dēbēs – ought, must

dē Menaechmīs – about the Menaechmi <brothers>

*diū – for a long time

duae guttae aquae – two drops of water

ego – I

es – are

*exspectō – I am waiting for

*fābula, fābulae, *f.* – story

*fōrma, fōrmae, *f.* – form, appearance

frāter meus – my brother

gutta, guttae, *f.* – drop

habēs – do you have

*habet – has

habitāre – to live

*habitō – live, dwell

hic – this (man)

ibi – there

mē – me

Menaechmī – plural of Menaechmus

Menaechmum – Menaechmus

mī frāter – my brother

mihi – to me

nārrās – are you telling, you are telling

*nārrō – I do tell

*nōn – not

*nunc – now

papae! – wow!

*patria, patriae, *f.* – fatherland

prō Iuppiter! – by Jove!

quam – what?

quid – what?

quōmodo – how?

quoque – also

salvē! – hello!

sīcut – as

*sum – I am

sunt – they are

Syrācūsānus – from Syracuse

tē – you

tū – you

tuam – your

*videō – do I see

vidēre – to see

vidēs – do you see

*vocant – do they call, they call

*Words marked with an asterisk will need to be memorized.

COMPREHENSION QUESTIONS

1. What happens between the two Menaechmi?

2. Who is the first to notice the similarity between the two Menaechmi?

3. What serves as a confirmation that the two Menaechmi are brothers?

4. What is the Menaechmi brothers' intention for the future?

LANGUAGE FACT I

FIRST AND SECOND CONJUGATION VERBS; PRINCIPAL PARTS

A *conjugation* is a class of verbs that all follow a certain pattern. There are four conjugations in Latin. In this chapter, you will learn only about the first and second conjugations.

You recognize a verb's conjugation from its *principal parts*, especially from the second principal part.

The principal parts of a verb provide stems for different verb forms. This chapter will concentrate on the first and second principal parts—most verbs have four. You will learn more about the third and fourth principal parts in later chapters.

The *first principal part* is the first person singular of the present active tense verb form. In the case of the English verb "do," the first person singular of the present active tense would be "I do."

The *second principal part* is the infinitive. In English, the infinitive is formed by adding the word "to" to the basic form of the verb: so for the verb "do" the infinitive is "to do."

nārrō ("I tell"), **nārrāre** ("to tell"), nārrāvī, nārrātum

habeō ("I have"), **habēre** ("to have"), habuī, habitum

Look at the second principal part of the verbs listed above. Note that the second principal part ends in a vowel + *–re*. The vowel that precedes the *–re* reveals the conjugation to which the verb belongs. The long vowel *–ā–* shows that *nārrāre* is a first conjugation verb; the long vowel *–ē–* in *habēre* shows that it is a second conjugation verb.

STUDY TIP

You can easily remember that the vowel *a* is in the first conjugation and the vowel *e* is in the second conjugation, if you know this little rhyme:

A comes before *E*
Even Alphabetical-**ly.**

▶ EXERCISE 1

Determine the conjugation of each verb by looking at the vowel in the second principal part.

1. videō, vidēre, vīdī, vīsum

2. habitō, habitāre, habitāvī, habitātum

3. nārrō, nārrāre, nārrāvī, nārrātum

4. dēbeō, dēbēre, dēbuī, dēbitum

5. cūrō, cūrāre, cūrāvī, cūrātum

6. exspectō, exspectāre, exspectāvī, exspectātum

VOCABULARY TO LEARN

NOUNS

fābula, fābulae, *f.* – story

fōrma, fōrmae, *f.* – form, appearance

patria, patriae, *f.* – fatherland

VERBS

ambulō, ambulāre, ambulāvī, ambulātum – to walk

amō, amāre, amāvī, amātum – to love

cūrō, cūrāre, cūrāvī, cūrātum – to care for, to take care of

dēbeō, dēbēre, dēbuī, dēbitum – ought, must, should; to owe

exspectō, exspectāre, exspectāvī, exspectātum – to wait for, to await, to expect

habeō, habēre, habuī, habitum – to have

habitō, habitāre, habitāvī, habitātum – to live, to dwell

nārrō, nārrāre, nārrāvī, nārrātum – to tell

parō, parāre, parāvī, parātum – to prepare, to get ready

sum – I am

teneō, tenēre, tenuī, tentum – to hold

videō, vidēre, vīdī, vīsum – to see

vocō, vocāre, vocāvī, vocātum – to call

ADVERBS

diū – for a long time

nōn – not

nunc – now

▶ EXERCISE 2

Find the English derivatives based on the Vocabulary to Learn in the following sentences. Write the corresponding Latin word.

1. I read a long narrative about World War II.

2. Have you worked with Habitat for Humanity?

3. The results exceeded our expectations.

4. This seems fabulous!

5. We are watching a video about the field trip.

6. This group is rather vocal about their rights.

7. Are you paying by credit or debit?

8. Everybody started singing a patriotic song.

9. The preparations for the festival were moving at full speed.

10. The octopus has long tentacles.

11. We heard the siren of an ambulance.

LANGUAGE FACT II
PROPERTIES OF VERBS: NUMBER, PERSON

Number: Latin verbs are either singular or plural in number (depending on the number of the subject noun).

Person: Latin verbs, like verbs in English, may be in the first, second, or third person. The person represents the identity of the subject. The first person is "I" or "we." The second person is "you" (singular or plural). The third person is "s/he/it" or "they."

Six endings in Latin indicate what person is performing the action of the verb. They are in the chart below and must be learned along with the corresponding English pronoun.

Verb Endings				
	Singular		**Plural**	
First person	–ō or –m	I	–mus	we
Second person	–s	you	–tis	you
Third person	–t	s/he/it	–nt	they

BY THE WAY

You have seen the first person singular ending –*m* in the word *sum* ("I am"). The first person singular ending –*ō* is seen more commonly on Latin verbs than the ending –*m.*

▶ EXERCISE 3

Identify the person and number of each verb.

Example: aedificant
third person plural

1. nārrās
2. vidēs
3. aedificat
4. habēs
5. dēbēs
6. dēbēmus
7. vocant
8. amat

LANGUAGE FACT III
PROPERTIES OF VERBS: TENSE, STEM

Tense: A verb indicates the time when the action occurs. There are six tenses in Latin, but in this chapter you will be focusing only on the present tense, which shows action happening now.

Stem: The present stem conveys the basic meaning of a word. Find the present stem by removing the –*re* from the second principal part.

To form the present tense of a Latin verb, the personal endings for this tense are added to the present stem of the verb. This is called conjugating the verb in the present tense. Remember: the predominant vowel in the first conjugation is an $-\bar{a}-$ and in the second conjugation an $-\bar{e}-$.

First Conjugation: Present Active

parō, parāre		Singular		Plural
First person	parō	I prepare	parā**mus**	we prepare
Second person	parā**s**	you prepare	parā**tis**	you prepare
Third person	para**t**	s/he/it prepares	para**nt**	they prepare

Second Conjugation: Present Active

teneō, tenēre		Singular		Plural
First person	teneō	I hold	tenē**mus**	we hold
Second person	tenē**s**	you hold	tenē**tis**	you hold
Third person	tene**t**	s/he/it holds	tene**nt**	they hold

BY THE WAY

Note that Latin pronouns such as *ego* (I) or *tū* (you) are optional, while the personal endings that indicate the pronoun subject are required. Verb forms in Latin are a "package deal" because in one word they include both the meaning of the verb and the subject pronoun.

Translating Latin verbs into English: There are three ways to translate a Latin present tense verb into English. Here are some examples from both first and second conjugation verbs.

> parō: I prepare; I do prepare; I am preparing
> parās: you prepare; you do prepare; you are preparing
> parat: s/he/it prepares; s/he/it does prepare; s/he/it is preparing
>
> tenēmus: we hold; we do hold; we are holding
> tenētis: you hold; you do hold; you are holding
> tenent: they hold; they do hold; they are holding

▶ EXERCISE 4

Give three English translations for each present tense verb.

Example: teneō
I hold/I do hold/I am holding

1. vocās
2. videt
3. exspectant
4. cūrāmus
5. dēbētis
6. habeō

▶ EXERCISE 5

Choose one of three ways to translate each singular Latin verb and write the plural Latin form of each.

Example: exspectās
you wait for *or* do wait for *or* are waiting for   exspectātis

1. vidēs
2. dēbet
3. ambulat
4. habeō
5. tenēs
6. amō
7. habitat

▶ EXERCISE 6

Choose one of three ways to translate each plural Latin verb and write the singular Latin form of each.

Example: parant
they prepare *or* do prepare *or* are preparing   parat

1. habitāmus
2. amāmus
3. tenent
4. nārrant
5. habētis
6. vidēmus
7. exspectātis

LANGUAGE FACT IV

THE INFINITIVE

In the opening of the chapter reading, Messenio addresses his master: *Tū vidēre dēbēs.* "You ought to see." At the end of the same passage Menaechmus tells his brother: *Dēbēmus nunc cum patre habitāre.* "We ought to live with (our) father now."

In English, an infinitive is a verb form preceded by the word "to." In Latin, an infinitive (second principal part) is the verb form that ends with the letters –*re*. The infinitive is unlimited by a specific person: when you say "to read," you are not specifying any person doing the reading—you are just describing the action itself.

Greek mask of comedy.

First conjugation infinitives have the vowel *–ā–* before *–re,* while second conjugation verbs have the vowel *–ē–* before *–re.*

> First conjugation infinitive: **parā-re**
>
> Second conjugation infinitive: **tenē-re**

▶ EXERCISE 7

Translate the infinitive and indicate whether it belongs to the first or second conjugation.

Example: amāre
to love   first conjugation

1. ambulāre
2. habēre
3. nārrāre
4. exspectāre
5. dēbēre
6. vidēre

LANGUAGE FACT V
SUBJECT AND VERB AGREEMENT

The verb *agrees* in number with the subject. This means that if the noun subject is singular, the verb is singular. Likewise, if the noun subject is plural, the verb must be plural.

> Examples:
> *Puella fābulam nārrat.*
> The girl tells a story.

The verb *nārrat* has the third person singular ending *–t,* since the noun subject *puella* is singular (as the nominative singular ending *–a* shows).

> *Puellae fābulās nārrant.*
> The girls tell stories.

The verb *nārrant* has the third person plural ending *–nt,* since the noun subject *puellae* is plural (as the nominative plural ending *–ae* shows).

▶ EXERCISE 8

Make the verbs agree with the subjects in the following sentences. The Reading Vocabulary may be consulted.

Example: Messeniō Menaechmum _____ (vidēre).
Messeniō Menaechmum videt.

1. Menaechmus Sōsiclēs et Messeniō Menaechmum _____ (vidēre).

2. Menaechmus-Sosicles tells Messenio: "Tū fābulās _____ (nārrāre)."

3. Messenio asks Menaechmus: "Quōmodo ego et Menaechmus Sōsiclēs tē vocāre _____ (dēbēre)?"

4. Menaechmus answers: "Tū et Menaechmus Sōsiclēs mē Menaechmum vocāre _____ (dēbēre)."

5. After Menaechmus-Sosicles asks: "Quam patriam habēs?" Menaechmus exclaims: "Quam patriam ego _____ (habēre)? Sum Syrācūsānus."

The Hellenistic era Theatre of Ephesus, which today is in Turkey, was built in the third century BCE into a hillside in the Greek manner. It was enlarged during Roman times in the first and second centuries CE and is said to have accommodated 25,000 spectators.

▶ EXERCISE 9

Translate into Latin.

1. We ought to wait.

2. You all ought to tell a story.

3. Now they see the fatherland.

4. I take care of the daughter.

▶ EXERCISE 10

Label each sentence as *vērum* (true) if it agrees or *falsum* (false) if it disagrees with the Latin reading passage at the beginning of the chapter.

1. Menaechmus et Menaechmus Sōsiclēs sunt sīcut duae guttae aquae.

2. Menaechmus Sōsiclēs nōn est Syrācūsānus.

3. Menaechmus est Syrācūsānus.

4. Messeniō et Menaechmus sunt sīcut duae guttae aquae.

The Romans endowed the North African city of Sabratha with magnificent public buildings. The most renowned is the theatre, probably built during the reign of the emperor Commodus (161–192 CE), with its three orders of columns of the *scenae frons* and other elaborate sculptural decoration.

TALKING

In the chapter reading, you encountered the expression:

> *Quōmodo tē vocant?* "How do they call you?"
> *Mē vocant Menaechmum.* "They call me Menaechmus."

There are various ways of asking someone's name in Latin:

> *Quod nōmen est tibi?* "What is your name?"
> *Mihi nōmen est Marīa.* "My name is Mary."

> *Quod vērō nōmen tibi est?* "And what is your name?"
> *Mihi nōmen est Mārcus.* "My name is Mark."

> *Quō nōmine appellāris?* "By what name are you called?"
> *Laura appellor.* "I am called Laura."

This is a list of some common Roman first names for males and their abbreviations:

A. = Aulus	C. = Gāius	L. = Lūcius
M. = Mārcus	P. = Pūblius	Q. = Quīntus
Ser. = Servius	Sex. = Sextus	T. = Titus

For information about names for females, see p. 107.

The Roman naming system consisted of *praenōmen* (first name), *nōmen* (family name), and *cōgnōmen* (surname/nickname).

In the name *Titus Maccius Plautus*: *Titus* is the first name, *Maccius* is the family name, and *Plautus* is a surname (it literally means "flat-footed").

In the chapter reading, Menaechmus was asked *Quam patriam habēs?* "What fatherland do you have?" and he answered *Syrācūsānus sum*, "I am from Syracuse."

There are several ways of asking where someone is from in Latin:

> *Cūiās es?* "Where are you from?"
> *Cūiātēs estis?* "Where are you all from?"
> *Unde es ortus/orta?* "Where do you come from (male/female)?"
> *Unde estis ortī/ortae?* "Where do you all come from (male/female)?"

Here are some possible answers:

> *Ortus/orta sum ex Cīvitātibus Foederātīs Americae Septentriōnālis. Americānus/Americāna sum.* "I come from the USA. I am an American (male/female)."

Ortus/orta sum ex Californiā, ex Texiā, ex Ohiō, ex Kentukiā, ex Massacusētā, ex Flōridā, ex Novā Caesareā, ex Carolīnā Septentriōnālī, ex Virginiā, ex Indiānā. "I come from California, Texas, Ohio, Kentucky, Massachusetts, Florida, New Jersey, North Carolina, Virginia, Indiana."

Ortus/orta sum urbe (from the city of) *Novō Eborācō, Bostōniā, Chicāgiā/Sicāgō, Angelopolī, Detroitō, Novā Aurēliā, Atlantā, Philadelphiā, Vasintōniā.* "I come from New York, Boston, Chicago, Los Angeles, Detroit, New Orleans, Atlanta, Philadelphia, Washington, DC."

GETTING ACQUAINTED

Mārcus est discipulus novus. (*Mark is a new student.*)

Marīa: Salvēte! Quōmodo valētis?

Helena et Christīna: Bene valēmus.

Mārcus: Salvēte!

Marīa: Salvē! Quod nōmen est tibi?

Mārcus: Mihi nōmen est Mārcus. Quōmodo tē vocant?

Marīa: Mē vocant Marīam. Cūiās es?

Mārcus: Ortus sum ex Californiā! Cūiās tū es?

Marīa: Ego sum Americāna.

Mārcus: Ego quoque (*also*) sum Americānus. At unde es orta? (*But where do you come from?*)

Marīa: Orta sum urbe Vasintōniā.

Helena: Et ego sum orta urbe Vasintōniā.

Christīna: Et ego sum orta urbe Vasintōniā.

Mārcus: Certē (*certainly*). Schola nostra est Vasintōniae. (*Our school is in Washington, DC.*)

DERIVATIVES

fābula – fable, fabulous

fōrma – conform, cuneiform, deformity, formal, formation, formula, inform, platform, reformatory, transformation, uniform, vermiform

patria – patriot, patriotic

ambulō – See *ambulat* p. 13.

amō – See *amat* p. 13.

cūrō – See *cūrat* p. 13.

dēbeō – debit, debt, due, duly, duty, endeavor

exspectō – expect, expectant, expectation

habeō – habit, ability, prohibitive, inhibition, rehabilitation

habitō – habitat, inhabitant

nārrō – narrate, narration, narrator

parō – emperor, imperative, imperious, inseparable, parachute, parade, parapet, parasol, pare, prepare, rampart, repair, separate, sever

sum – absent, essence, interest, quintessence, present

teneō – abstain, contain, contents, contentment, continent, continual, countenance, entertain, impertinence, lieutenant, maintenance, pertinacity, rein, retinue, tenacious, tenant, tenement, tennis, tenet, tenor, tenure

videō – advice, advise, envious, evident, improvise, imprudent, interview, invidious, invisible, jurisprudence, preview, provision, proviso, purvey, revise, surveyor, television, vision, visit, vista, visual

vocō – advocate, avow, convocation, equivocal, invoke, irrevocable, provocative, revoke, vocation, vocative, vouch

nōn – nonchalant, nonconformist, nonentity, nonpareil, nonsense, umpire

The choreographer and actors are detailed in this mosaic from the House of the Tragic Poet in Pompeii.

MEMORĀBILE DICTŪ

Homō sum: hūmānī nihil ā mē aliēnum putō.

"I am a human being: I think that nothing human is foreign to me." (Terence, *The Self-Tormentor* 77)

This saying became proverbial, furnishing evidence for Terence's intense interest in human character.

READING

Terence, or Publius Terentius Afer, was born in North Africa between 195 BCE and 185 BCE. He came to Rome as a slave, received a good education, and was freed. He and Plautus are among the most ancient Roman writers whose works have come to us in non-fragmentary form, and their works are the earliest complete examples of Latin comedy. Six of Terence's comedies have been preserved. Terence died in Greece probably in 159 BCE, where he had traveled because of his studies.

Like Plautus, Terence based his comedies on earlier Greek models, but made many changes to these "originals": stating his own views about comedy-writing in the prologues of his plays, emphasizing the humanity of his individual characters, and using refined, elegant language that contrasts with Plautus's distinctive, colloquial, and often bawdy Latin.

Terence loves moral problems that are universal, common to all cultures and ages. That is why his comedies have continuously remained popular until the present day.

The central conflicts between characters in Terence's *Adelphoi*, a comedy whose Greek title means "The Brothers," remain relevant today. The brothers referred to in the title are Demea, a conservative farmer, who believes in imposing rigid limits and tight controls on his children, and Micio, a liberal city-dweller with a more permissive approach to child-rearing. Demea has two sons: Ctesipho, who lives with his father, and Aeschinus, who has been adopted by his uncle Micio. Demea, however, has begun to regret his decision, because he suspects that Micio has allowed Aeschinus to adopt an undisciplined and wild lifestyle. When he pays an unexpected visit to Micio's household, however, Demea runs into Ctesipho, who is spending time with his brother there. Demea insists on exercising his fatherly authority and tries to take Ctesipho away with him. But he has not anticipated being greeted at the door by the trusted slave Syrus.

DĒ DUŌBUS FRĀTRIBUS

1   Dēmea: (*knocking at the door*) Heus, mī fīlī!!!

Syrus and Ctesipho are inside the house.

Syrus: Quis vocat? Quis est hic vir?

Ctēsiphō: Pater mē vocat. Valdē timeō.

5   Syrus: Nōn dēbēs timēre. Dēbēs habēre bonum animum.

Syrus answers the door.

Syrus: Quis es tū?

Dēmea: Salvē, mī bone vir! Ego sum Dēmea, pater Aeschinī et
    Ctēsiphōnis. Habitō in agrīs. Fīlium meum nunc vidēre dēbeō.

10   Syrus: Num ego fīlium tuum habeō? Aeschinus nōn est domī.

Dēmea: Estne domī Ctēsiphō?

Syrus: Nōn est. Fīliōs tuōs ego nōn habeō.

Dēmea: Estne frāter meus domī?

Syrus: Nōn est.

15 Dēmea: Ubi est Ctēsiphō?

Syrus: Ctēsiphō est cum amīcō.

Dēmea: Ubi habitat amīcus?

Syrus: Prīmum ambulās in viā, deinde in clīvō, deinde vidēs rīvum. Ibi est porta et casa. Ctēsiphō est in casā cum amīcō.

Having sent Demea away on a "wild goose chase," Syrus returns inside to report his success to Ctesipho.

READING VOCABULARY

Aeschinī et Ctēsiphōnis – of Aeschinus and Ctesipho

***amīcus** – friend

***animum** – spirit, soul, mind

bonum – good

***casa, casae,** *f.* – little house, cottage

Ctēsiphō, Ctēsiphōnis, *m.* – Ctesipho

***cum amīcō** – with a friend

dē duōbus frātribus – about two brothers

***deinde** – then

Dēmea, *m.* – Demea

***domī** – at home

***ego** – I

es – are

estne? – is?

***fīliōs tuōs** – your sons

fīlium meum – my son

fīlium tuum – your son

frāter meus – my brother

heus! – hey!

hic – this

ibi – there

***in agrīs** – in the fields, in the countryside

in casā – in the cottage

in clīvō – on the hill

in viā – on the road

mē – me

mī bone vir! – my good fellow!

mī fīlī! – my son!

nōn est – he is not

num? – do I? (negative answer implied)

pater – father

porta, portae, *f.* – gate

prīmum – first

quis? – who?

***rīvum** – brook, stream

salvē! – hello!

sum – am

***timeō** – to fear, to be afraid

***tū** – you

ubi – where

***valdē** – very, exceedingly

***via, viae,** *f.* – road

***vir** – man

*Words marked with an asterisk will need to be memorized.

COMPREHENSION QUESTIONS

1. What is the main purpose of Demea's visit?

2. Is Ctesipho happy about his father's visit?

3. What is Syrus's attitude toward Demea?

4. What is the reason for Syrus's behavior toward Demea?

5. What makes Demea go away?

The town of Bosra in Syria was conquered by Trajan's armies in 106 CE. Built in the freestanding Roman style rather than built into a hillside in the Greek manner, the stage and part of the seating area are shown.

LANGUAGE FACT I

SECOND DECLENSION MASCULINE –*US* NOUNS

In Chapter 1 you learned the first declension, with its characteristic vowel *ā.* In the chapter reading passage above, there are several forms with the characteristic vowel *ō* or *u: animum, fīlium, fīliōs, amīcō, amīcus, clīvō, rīvum.*

Nouns that end –*us* in the nominative singular and –*ī* in the genitive singular belong to the second declension. Most of the second declension nouns are masculine with a few feminine and neuter exceptions.

Second Declension Masculine –us Nouns					
		Singular			**Plural**
Nominative	amīc**us**	the friend	amīc**ī**	the friends
Genitive	amīc**ī**	of the friend, friend's	amīc**ōrum**	of the friends, friends'
Dative	amīc**ō**	to/for the friend	amīc**īs**	to/for the friends
Accusative	amīc**um**	the friend	amīc**ōs**	the friends
Ablative	amīc**ō**	by/with the friend	amīc**īs**	by/with the friends

STUDY TIP

Notice that the second declension forms look identical in the genitive singular and nominative plural, in the dative and ablative singular, and in the dative and ablative plural. Even though these forms are spelled the same, you can tell the cases apart in context based on their very different functions in the sentence.

▶ EXERCISE 1

Identify the case and number of each noun. For some, more than one answer is possible.

Example: animum
accusative singular

1. fīlium
2. fīliōs
3. amīcō
4. amīcōs
5. animō
6. rīvōrum
7. fīliī
8. animīs

VOCABULARY TO LEARN

NOUNS

ager, agrī, *m.* – field
amīcus, amīcī, *m.* – friend
animus, animī, *m.* – spirit, soul, mind
casa, casae, *f.* – little house, cottage
domī – at home
fīlius, fīliī, *m.* – son
puer, puerī, *m.* – boy
rīvus, rīvī, *m.* – brook, stream
via, viae, *f.* – road
vir, virī, *m.* – man

PRONOUNS

ego – I
tū – you

VERB

timeō, timēre, timuī, —— – to fear, to be afraid

ADVERBS

deinde – then
valdē – very, exceedingly

PREPOSITIONS

cum + *ablative* – with
in + *ablative* – in, on

The sign "——" indicates that the verb has no fourth principal part.

▶ EXERCISE 2

Find the English derivatives based on the Vocabulary to Learn in the following sentences. Write the corresponding Latin word.

1. Better selflessness than egotism.

2. Many small farmers are interested in the new agrarian laws.

3. Being violent is not a sign of virility.

4. You should be more amicable with your colleagues!

5. Let us not be timid, but act with bravery!

6. I flew to Europe via Chicago.

7. Joy and hope animated his face.

8. Do not meddle in the domestic affairs of the others!

9. This is a puerile, not an adult behavior.

▶ EXERCISE 3

Give the forms indicated in parentheses and an English translation that shows the case, number, and meaning of each noun.

Example: filia (genitive singular)
filiae   of the daughter *or* daughter's

1. rīvus (dative singular)
2. patria (genitive singular)
3. fīlius (nominative plural)
4. animus (ablative singular)
5. fōrma (accusative singular)
6. terra (ablative plural)

LANGUAGE FACT II

SECOND DECLENSION MASCULINE *–ER, –IR* NOUNS

In the chapter reading, you can see the word *ager* in the phrase *in agrīs* "in the fields, in the countryside." Some second declension nouns end *–er* in the nominative singular, instead of *–us*. These nouns decline like *amīcus* in all cases except the nominative singular.

Second Declension Masculine *–er* Nouns				
	Singular		**Plural**	
Nominative	ager	the field	agrī	the fields
Genitive	agrī	of the field, field's	agrōrum	of the fields, fields'
Dative	agrō	to/for the field	agrīs	to/for the fields
Accusative	agr**um**	the field	agrōs	the fields
Ablative	agrō	by/with the field	agrīs	by/with fields

Notice that *ager* loses its –*e*– in all cases but the nominative singular. Nouns like *ager* should be distinguished from a closely related type of second declension –*er* noun that keeps the –*e*– in all cases, such as *puer*.

Second Declension Masculine –*er* Nouns				
Singular			**Plural**	
Nominative	puer	the boy	puerī	the boys
Genitive	puerī	of the boy, boy's	puer**ō**rum	of the boys, boys'
Dative	puer**ō**	to/for the boy	puerīs	to/for the boys
Accusative	puer**um**	the boy	puer**ō**s	the boys
Ablative	puer**ō**	by/with the boy	puerīs	by/with the boys

STUDY TIP

In order to know what pattern a word ending in –*er* should follow, look closely at the genitive singular. If the –*e*– from the nominative **is not** present in the genitive (as in *ager, agrī*), it will not be present in any of the other cases. If, however, the –*e*– from the nominative **is** present in the genitive (as in *puer, puerī*), it will be present in all the other cases as well.

A distinct second declension noun is *vir* (man), which you encountered in the reading. This noun has the unique nominative singular ending –*ir*.

BY THE WAY

All words in –*er* and –*ir* of the second declension are masculine without exception.

Second Declension Masculine –*ir* Nouns				
Singular			**Plural**	
Nominative	vir	the man	virī	the men
Genitive	virī	of the man, man's	vir**ō**rum	of the men, men's
Dative	vir**ō**	to/for the man	virīs	to/for the men
Accusative	vir**um**	the man	vir**ō**s	the men
Ablative	vir**ō**	by/with the man	virīs	by/with the men

STUDY TIP

The spelling of an English derivative often shows whether the –*e*– remains in the stem. For example, the spelling of the English word "agrarian" shows that the –*e*– has dropped from the base Latin word *ager*. Likewise, the English derivative "puerile" reveals that *puer* keeps its –*e*–.

Second Declension Noun Types				
Noun Type	Words in –us	Words in –er	Words in –er	Words in –ir
Nominative	amīcus	ager	puer	vir
Genitive	amīcī	agrī	puerī	virī
Other cases	amīcō amīcum amīcō . . .	agrō agrum agrō . . .	puerō puerum puerō . . .	virō virum virō . . .

▶ EXERCISE 4

Identify the case and number of each noun. Then change each form into the singular if it is plural and into the plural if it is singular. For some, more than one answer is possible.

Example: fīliī
genitive singular   fīliōrum   nominative plural   filius

1. agrīs
2. lupārum
3. amīcō

4. virōs
5. rīvī
6. animōrum

▶ EXERCISE 5

Give the forms indicated in parentheses and an English translation of the changed form that shows its case, number, and meaning.

Example: puer (genitive plural)
puerōrum   of the boys

1. ager (ablative plural)
2. puer (dative singular)
3. vir (dative plural)

4. puella (genitive singular)
5. fīlius (genitive plural)
6. animus (accusative singular)

LANGUAGE FACT III

GENITIVE CASE

In the chapter reading, Demea presents himself to the slave who opens the door: *Ego sum Dēmea, pater Aeschinī et Ctēsiphōnis.* "I am Demea, father of Aeschinus and Ctesipho." The forms *Aeschinī* and *Ctēsiphōnis* are genitive. The name *Aeschinus* declines like *amīcus* (Aeschinus, Aeschinī, m.).

A noun in the genitive usually modifies another noun. The genitive often shows possession. A noun in the genitive case usually can be translated using the English word *of*, as in *of the girl*, or by using an apostrophe, as in *girl's*. In the plural, the genitive can be translated as in *girls'* with an **s'**, or by using *of* with a phrase like *of the girls*.

This Roman mosaic of the masks of comedy and tragedy is housed in the Capitoline Museum in Rome.

BY THE WAY

The first declension uses the same ending for the genitive singular and nominative plural: *–ae*. The second declension also uses the same ending for genitive singular and nominative plural: *–ī*.

▶ EXERCISE 6

Underline the genitive in each sentence, and then translate each sentence.

1. Fīlia agricolae āthlētam amat.

2. Fīlius poētae fābulās amat.

3. In casā amīcōrum habitāmus.

4. Puerī fōrmam lupae timent.

5. Animus nautae terram exspectat.

6. Fābulās poētārum nārrāmus.

7. Agrōs patriae amātis.

LANGUAGE FACT IV

VOCATIVE CASE

In the chapter reading, Demea shouts, *mī fīlī*, "my son," and calls Syrus *mī bone vir*, "my good fellow." These forms are in the vocative case. The vocative case is used to address someone.

The vocative case is usually identical in form to the nominative, except for the vocative singular of second declension nouns of the type ending in *–us*. These nouns have the vocative singular ending *–e*.

> **Example:**
> Nominative: amī**cus**   Vocative: amī**ce**

Vocative Case, First and Second Declensions			
	First Declension	**Second Declension Masculine –us Nouns**	**Second Declension Masculine –er, –ir Nouns**
Singular	puella	amīce	ager, puer, vir
Plural	puellae	amīcī	agrī, puerī, virī

BY THE WAY

The Latin word for "son," *fīlius*, has an irregular vocative *fīlī*, as do all second declension nouns that end in *-ius*. The irregular vocative of *meus*, "my," is *mī*.

▶ EXERCISE 7

Complete each sentence with the correct form of the word in parentheses.

Example: Dēmea _____ (fīlius) vocat.
Dēmea fīlium vocat.

1. Syrus is asking Demea: "Quis es tū, _____ (amīcus)?"

2. Demea is answering: "Habitō in _____ (agrī)."

3. Syrus is saying to Demea: " _____ (fīlius) nōn videō."

4. Dēmea dēbet ambulāre ad casam _____ (amīcus).

5. Fīlius nōn est cum _____ (amīcus).

The Theatre of Marcellus was built as a freestanding structure in the Roman style. Julius Caesar began the construction of this theatre in Rome. Augustus completed its construction in 13 BCE and dedicated it to his nephew and intended heir, Marcellus. This theatre held 20,000 seats and until its completion plays in Rome were held in temporary wooden structures.

LANGUAGE FACT V
PREPOSITIONAL PHRASES

In the chapter reading, Demea says: *Habitō in agrīs*, "I live in the countryside." When Demea asks about his son, the slave answers: *Ctēsiphō est cum amīcō*, "Ctesipho is with a friend." Then he gives Demea (false) directions: *ambulās in viā, deinde in clīvō*, "you walk on the road, then on the hill." Finally he repeats: *Ctēsiphō est in casā cum amīcō*, "Ctesipho is in (that) cottage with a friend."

This ancient Roman road, called the *Via Sacra*, leading toward the Arch of Titus in Rome, shows the enduring, yet worn nature of the polygonal blocks of stone that formed the top layer of Roman roads.

in agrīs,
cum amīcō,
in viā,
in clīvō,
in casā

are all prepositional phrases. A prepositional phrase is a preposition joined with a noun (that may have an adjective with it).

Prepositions are words (usually small words) that denote a relationship between a noun or a pronoun and another word. The word "preposition" comes from the Latin verb *praepōnere*, which means "to place in front." In Latin, the preposition usually precedes its object noun or pronoun. Prepositions require a particular **case** of the noun object.

Note that the preposition *in* used with the ablative case can mean "in" or "on," and the preposition *cum* used with the ablative means "with."

BY THE WAY

When you are talking about someone's home and you want to express "at home," you say *domī* without any preposition.

▶ EXERCISE 8

Supply the preposition that makes sense. Then translate the sentence.

Example: Ambulō _____ aquā.
Ambulō in aquā.   I am walking in the water.

1. Puer _____ puellā nautam exspectat.

2. _____ fābulā lupa puerōs cūrat.

3. Habitāmus _____ amīcīs.

4. Vir est _____ viā.

5. Lupa est _____ agrō.

▶ EXERCISE 9

Label each sentence as *vērum* (true) if it agrees or *falsum* (false) if it disagrees with the Latin reading passage at the beginning of the chapter.

1. Ctēsiphō est domī.

2. Ctēsiphō est in casā amīcī.

3. Syrus est pater Aeschinī et Ctēsiphōnis.

4. Syrus fābulās nārrat.

TALKING

Hoc est conclāve scholasticum. "This is the classroom."

Cōnsīdās in sellā! "Sit down in your seat!"

Cōnsīdātis in sellīs! "Sit down (plural) in your seats!"

Surgās et ad tabulam scriptōriam veniās. "Get up and come to the board."

In tabulā scriptōriā scrībō. "I am writing on the board."

Scrībō crētā. "I am writing with chalk."

Scrībō calamō coāctilī. "I am writing with a board marker."

Ēiice hoc in scirpiculum! "Throw this into the garbage can!"

Nōlī susurrāre! "Do not whisper!"

Nōlīte susurrāre! "Do not whisper (plural)!"

Favēte linguīs! "Silence!"

Licetne mihi īre ad locum secrētum (or lātrīnam)? "May I go to the bathroom?"

Licet/nōn licet. "You may/you may not."

Licetne habēre mappulam chartāceam (nāsutergium)? "May I have a kleenex?"

IN THE CLASSROOM

Magistra: (*teacher [female]*) Salvēte, discipulī! (*Hello, students!*)

Discipulī: (*students*) Salvē, magistra!

Mārcus: Heus (*hey*), Marīa, Helena! Estne magistra bona? (*Is the teacher good?*)

Magistra: Ssst! (*Shh!*) Favēte linguīs! Habēmus novum discipulum. Quod nōmen est tibi?

Mārcus: Nōmen mihi est Mārcus.

Magistra: Surgās et ad tabulam scriptōriam veniās. Dēclīnā (*decline*) "fīlius!"

Mārcus: (*TO MARIA*) Timeō! (*TO THE TEACHER*) Licetne mihi īre ad locum secrētum?

Magistra: Nōn licet. Dēbēs scrībere (*to write*). Ecce (*here is*) crēta.

DERIVATIVES

ager – agrarian, peregrination, pilgrim, pilgrimage, acre

amīcus – amicable, inimical

animus – animadversion, animosity, equanimity, magnanimity, magnanimous, pusillanimity, pusillanimous, unanimity, unanimous, unanimously

casa – casino

domī – domestic, domicile, domesticate, domestication, domain, dome

fīlius – See *fīlia* p. 13.

puer – See *puella* p. 13.

rīvus – derivation, derivative, derive, rival, rivalry, rivulet

via – convey, conveyance, convoy, conveyor, deviate, devious, envoy, impervious, invoice, obviate, obvious, previous, trivial, viaduct, voyage, voyager

vir – triumvirate, virile, virtual, virtue, virtuoso, virtuous

ego – egoism, egotism, egotistic

timeō – intimidate, timid, timidity, timorous

valdē – valid, validate, validity

cum – compose, comfort, concert, concord

in – incarcerate, intimidate, invaluable, inflammable

REVIEW 1: CHAPTERS 1–3

VOCABULARY TO KNOW

NOUNS

ager, agrī, *m.* – field

• **agricola, agricolae,** *m.* – farmer

amīcus, amīcī, *m.* – friend

animus, animī, *m.* – spirit, soul, mind

• **aqua, aquae,** *f.* – water

• **āthlēta, āthlētae,** *m.* – athlete

casa, casae, *f.* – little house, cottage

domī – at home

fābula, fābulae, *f.* – story

• **fīlia, fīliae,** *f.* – daughter

fīlius, fīliī, *m.* – son

fōrma, fōrmae, *f.* – form, appearance

lupa, lupae, *f.* – she-wolf

nauta, nautae, *m.* – sailor

patria, patriae, *f.* – fatherland

poēta, poētae, *m.* – poet

puella, puellae, *f.* – girl

puer, puerī, *m.* – boy

rīvus, rīvī, *m.* – brook, stream

Rōma, Rōmae, *f.* – Rome

terra, terrae, *f.* – land

via, viae, *f.* – road

vir, virī, *m.* – man

PRONOUNS

ego – I

tū – you

VERBS

ambulō, ambulāre, ambulāvī, ambulātum – to walk

amō, amāre, amāvī, amātum – to love

cūrō, cūrāre, cūrāvī, cūrātum – to care for, to take care of

dēbeō, dēbēre, dēbuī, dēbitum – ought, must, should; to owe

est – s/he/it is

exspectō, exspectāre, exspectāvī, exspectātum – to wait for, to await, to expect

habeō, habēre, habuī, habitum – to have

habitō, habitāre, habitāvī, habitātum – to live, to dwell

nārrō, nārrāre, nārrāvī, nārrātum – to tell

parō, parāre, parāvī, parātum – to prepare, to get ready

sum – I am

teneō, tenēre, tenuī, tentum – to hold

timeō, timēre, timuī, —— – to fear, to be afraid

videō, vidēre, vīdī, vīsum – to see

vocō, vocāre, vocāvī, vocātum – to call

ADVERBS

bene – well

deinde – then

diū – for a long time

nōn – not

nunc – now

posteā – afterward

valdē – very, exceedingly

PREPOSITIONS

cum + *ablative* – with

in + *ablative* – in, on

CONJUNCTIONS

et – and

itaque – and so

▶ EXERCISE 1

Decline the following nouns.

1. *terra, terrae*, f. – land

2. *rīvus, rīvī*, m. – stream

3. *socer, socerī*, m. – father-in-law

4. *liber, librī*, m. – book

▶ EXERCISE 2

Conjugate the following verbs. Give the Latin infinitive with its meaning for each verb.

Example: amō, amāre, amāvī, amātum

amāre – to love

amō	amāmus
amās	amātis
amat	amant

1. *habeō, habēre, habuī, habitum*

2. *exspectō, exspectāre, exspectāvī, exspectātum*

3. *dēbeō, dēbēre, dēbuī, dēbitum*

4. *cūrō, cūrāre, cūrāvī, cūrātum*

▶ EXERCISE 3

Fill in the blanks with the correct form of the words in parentheses and translate each sentence.

Example: _____ et _____ videō. (ager) (rīvus)
Agrum et rīvum videō.   I see the field and the river.

1. _____ nārrāmus. (fābula [in plural])

2. Tū amīcum _____. (vidēre)

3. Nōn sum _____. (poēta)

4. Dēbēmus filium _____. (cūrō)

5. _____ nōn timeō. (lupa)

6. Fīlius nōn est _____. (nauta)

▶ EXERCISE 4

Choose the appropriate word from the list below to complete the sentence and translate the passage.

cum	et	habeō
dēbet	fīlium	in
est	fīlius	valdē

Dēmea _____ vocat. Syrus Dēmeam convenit (*meets*) _____ dīcit (*says*): "Fīlius nōn est hīc (*here*)." Ctēsiphō autem (*however*) audit (*hears*) et Dēmeam_____ timet. Syrus dīcit: "Fīliōs tuōs (*your*) ego nōn teneō. Fīliōs tuōs ego nōn _____." Dēmea rogat (*asks*): "Ubi (*where*) _____ Ctēsiphō? Ubi est _____?" Syrus dīcit: "Ctēsiphō est _____ casā _____ amīcō." Itaque Dēmea ad (*to*) amīcum ambulāre _____.

▶ EXERCISE 5

In each pair of nouns, change the second one into the genitive, using the number indicated in parentheses. Translate each phrase.

Example: ager amīcus (plural)
ager amīcōrum   the field of the friends *or* the friends' field

1. animī poēta (plural)
2. aqua āthlēta (singular)
3. terra fīlia (plural)
4. patria puer (plural)
5. amīcus fīlius (singular)
6. fōrma rīvus (plural)

This fresco from the House of the Banker, probably Lucius Caecilius Iucundus, in Pompeii depicts the type of writing utensils that might be used by educated Roman adults and writers like Martial. The scrolls are housed in a typical cylindrical container and a writing tablet is shown.

▶ EXERCISE 6

Translate the following Latin text.

This short poem was written by Marcus Valerius Martialis, known to us as Martial, who lived ca. 40–102 CE. Born in Spain, he specialized in the literary form of the epigram. Martial's epigrams are renowned for their pointed wit, and for the vivid picture of Roman society that they paint.

The Latin text of this epigram has not been modified or simplified, but presented in the very words that Martial wrote twenty centuries ago.

Nōn amo tē, Sabidī, nec possum dīcere quārē.
　Hoc tantum possum dīcere: nōn amo tē. (Martial 1.32)

hoc – this
nec = **et nōn**
possum dīcere – I can say
quārē – why

Sabidius, Sabidiī, *m.* – a personal name, Sabidius
tantum (*adv.*) – only
tē – you (*accusative singular*)

Martial's epigram is the source of the satirist Thomas Brown's famous poem:

> I do not like thee, Doctor Fell,
> The reason why, I cannot tell;
> But this I know, and know full well,
> I do not like thee, Doctor Fell.

CONSIDERING THE
CLASSICAL GODS

MARS

In the initial Chapter 1 reading, Mars was introduced as the father of Romulus and Remus, the legendary founders of Rome. From an early period, the god Mars was identified with the Greek divinity Ares, who was the son of Zeus, king of the gods, and his wife Hera. Ares, the god of war, was not attractively depicted in Greek mythology. A number of Greek authors portray him as often unsuccessful in battle, and engaging in embarrassing behavior. It is worth noting, therefore, that Zeus's unions with goddesses other than his wife created such impressive divinities as Athena, Apollo, Artemis, and the Muses, but his marriage to Hera produced a son who commanded far less respect.

Yet for the Romans, an extremely military-minded people, Ares, under the name of Mars, ranked as one of the most important and inspiring gods. His name was connected with the origins of their city. Chariot races were held in his honor, and his altar was located in the "field of Mars," the Campus Martius, where military exercises were regularly performed. The wolf was his sacred animal. During the census, the counting of citizens that took place in Rome at five-year intervals, the Roman people gathered around Mars's altar in the Campus Martius and offered him a special sacrifice of a pig, a sheep, and an ox to guarantee the continued military success of the Roman people. The Temple of Mars Ultor was built by Augustus to honor the god after the Battle of Philippi (42 BCE), in which he avenged the assassination of his adoptive father Julius Caesar.

The deities Mars and Venus, who were reported to have had an affair, are on this Roman fresco from the House of Marcus Lucretius Frontinus in Pompeii.

JUPITER (JOVE)

In the reading for Chapter 2, the slave cries out *Prō Iuppiter!* "By Jove!" It was a frequent practice to invoke the god Jupiter as a witness to oaths, or merely in simple exclamations. The Latin name for Jupiter, *Iuppiter*, literally means "sky-father." Jupiter's Greek counterpart is called Zeus, a name that also is associated with the sky.

Like Zeus, Jupiter is the greatest god in the Olympian pantheon, sovereign over heaven and earth, who wields a mighty thunderbolt and causes lightning to strike. Every god on Mt. Olympus is his child or sibling. He himself is the son of the Titans Cronus—whom the Romans called Saturn—and Rhea. Cronus, who had previously overthrown his own father Uranus, feared a similar fate from his own offspring and thus devoured each of his children as soon as they were born.

Featuring a portrayal of the head of Zeus, this ancient Greek bronze coin dates from the third century BCE.

But Rhea outsmarted her husband when she gave birth to her last child, and handed him a stone wrapped in baby clothes, saving Jupiter in the process. Later, Jupiter rescued his brothers and sisters from inside their father's body. Although Jupiter married one of these sisters, whom the Romans called Juno, he had love affairs with many other goddesses and many mortal females. The moons circling the planet Jupiter are named after some of these women.

JUNO

Jupiter's wife is Juno, the name given by the Romans to the Greek goddess Hera. Even though she wields power as queen of heaven, she is tormented by jealousy of Jupiter's lovers, and by hatred of the offspring produced

The marriage of Jupiter and Juno on Mt. Ida, portrayed on this fresco from Pompeii.

by these unions. Juno is the patron divinity of women, and especially of marriage. The Romans called her by distinctive names that indicated her various functions. *Iūnō Lūcīna*, "Juno who brings to light," was her name as the protector of childbirth. *Iūnō Monēta* (from *moneō, monēre, monuī, monitum*, "to warn") was Juno in her role as giver of advice. A mint was established in the Temple of Juno Moneta at Rome, where coins were made. From this place comes our English word for "money"; indeed, by the time Rome became an empire, the Latin word *monēta, -ae, f.* had come to mean "coined money" or "currency."

Hera's temple in Paestum in southern Italy dates from the fifth century BCE. The Doric-styled temple features thirty-six fluted columns.

READ THE FOLLOWING PASSAGE

Iuppiter et Iūnō fīlium habent. Fīlius est Mārs. Mārs pugnās valdē amat et pugnās semper parat. Mārs vītam virōrum nōn cūrat. Itaque Graecī eum nōn amant. In quādam pugnā virī deum vulnerant. Deus fugit et Graecī rīdent.

deus, deī, *m.* – god	**quādam** – a certain
eum – him	**rīdent** – laugh
fugit – runs away, flees	**semper** (*adv.*) – always
Graecus, Graecī, *m.* – Greek	**vīta, vītae,** *f.* – life
pugna, pugnae, *f.* – battle	**vulnerō, vulnerāre, vulnerāvī, vulnerātum** – to wound

The Greek and Roman gods and goddesses were said to live on the cloudy peaks of Mt. Olympus in Greece.

CONNECTING WITH THE ANCIENT WORLD

SLAVERY IN ANCIENT ROME

In the readings for Chapters 2 and 3, slaves play a large role in the dialogue. Roman comedy, from which these two reading passages are taken, often features slaves who take charge and solve problems—a comic inversion, perhaps, of the way Roman society actually was. Slavery was extremely visible in ancient Rome, and assumed many forms. Ancient slavery was by no means identical to slavery in more recent periods and countries, such as colonial America. The Romans did not reduce a single race or culture to slavery; rather, slaves came from all over the ancient Mediterranean world, and typically fell into servile status by capture in war. The prices of slaves depended greatly on their qualifications. Many slaves were skilled and educated, often more so than their masters. Slave dealers (*mangōnēs*) both sold and rented out slaves at public auctions. White chalk on the feet indicated that the slave was imported. A tag around the neck gave the slave's name, nationality, and a description of his character, a guarantee for the buyer that he was making a good purchase.

The top relief is of a Roman butcher shop, while the bottom relief at the left shows two slaves carrying an amphora, and the bottom relief at the right depicts a woman selling herbs. From the second century CE.

The experience of slavery differed for different individuals. House slaves might be educated and assigned to train the master's children, or to act as literary or business assistants to the master himself; such slaves might be treated much like personal friends. Tiro, Cicero's secretary, friend, and former slave, invented a system of shorthand to facilitate taking notes. At the other end of the spectrum, however, slaves who worked in the fields and mines might have existences no better than those endured by beasts of burden. Slavery was ordinarily a hereditary condition; children of a slave mother would remain slaves. However, slaves might liberate themselves by accumulating savings (*pecūlium*) and buying their freedom, or be liberated by their masters as a reward for good service (*manūmissiō*). Freedmen were granted citizenship and so were any subsequent children born to them. The playwright Terence himself was a freed slave, who apparently enjoyed close ties to his master. Maltreatment of slaves appears to have been common and those who tried to escape could be whipped, branded with the letters FUG (*fugitīvus*, runaway) on their forehead, or made to wear an inscribed metal collar. The condition of slaves, however, improved somewhat as a result of laws passed during the early imperial period.

Roman workers, probably slaves, are building a wall under the direction of an overseer in this fragment from a painting.

This second century CE Roman mosaic portrays slaves preparing for a festival. The mosaic was found in Carthage.

Each year around the time of the winter solstice in December, the Romans celebrated a festival called *Sāturnālia*. Some say that this happy holiday was the best day of the year. Rules of social conduct and distinctions of social class were reversed on that day, and slaves not only behaved as if they were masters but also acted disrespectfully toward their own masters.

EXPLORING ROMAN COMEDY

ROMAN PRODUCTIONS AND MODERN RENDITIONS

While Roman armies were struggling in Spain and Italy with Hannibal (220–200 BCE), in the city people were developing theatrical forms adapted from Greece, and particularly Roman Comedy offered rich distraction from the anxieties of war. There were two holidays that gave the ordinary people an opportunity for free entertainment at comedies, to laugh away their cares, and to identify with clever slaves who could outwit and out-talk their masters and bring a complex plot to a "happy ending." One of these holidays came in March, as spring was starting: it was called the *Megalēnsia* and honored the goddess Cybele. The other was the Roman Games or *Lūdī Rōmānī,* celebrated in September in the fall. The plays were chosen in competition by junior officials called aediles and staged at public expense. We know the names of several early comic poets (the plays were in verse), but the works of only two have survived: Plautus and Terence.

A theatre mask of comedy from the second century BCE.

Plautus (about 254–184 BCE) freely adapted Greek comedies and added song (*cantica*) and dance to the more sober and "artistic" originals. This combination of dialogue (*diverbia*) interspersed with song is reminiscent of the Gilbert and Sullivan operettas. In the *Menaechmī* there are five such song interludes. Plautus's Latin was colloquial; he made fun of the Greek plots, and he only pretended to be showing a Greek production. The fun for him and the audience came in the obvious Romanization and Latinization of non-Roman situations and half-Roman characters. The crowds loved this kind of theatrics, so much so that we still have twenty-one of his comedies, which were studied and imitated by the first writers of the Italian Renaissance and then by European dramatists like Shakespeare and Molière. The plot lines of Shakespeare's *The Comedy of Errors* are likewise built on coincidences and complications.

One of the most successful modern adaptations of a Plautine comedy is *A Funny Thing Happened on the Way to the Forum* (1966). A combination of two plays (*Pseudolus* and *Mīles Glōriōsus*), this entertaining theatrical play, later made into a movie, combines the favorite characteristics of Roman comedy: disguises, lovers at a loss, deception, slapstick, the clever slave, recognition and recovery, and a happy, if not realistic, ending.

Every time the plot of an ancient play like the *Menaechmī* contains twins, there is an automatic opportunity for one twin accidentally to substitute for the other in good or bad luck, until finally they recognize each other. In the Chapter 2 passage chosen from the *Menaechmī*, the twin brothers work out their identity and decide to return home to Sicily.

Even more recently, the movie *The Parent Trap*, first produced in 1968 and later remade in a modern version in 1998, is another example of mistaken identity and role reversal whereby twin girls try to make their parents reunite rather than rewed. Part of the plot of this movie was reworked into the 2002 TV show *So Little Time*, the second TV show in which the Olson twins starred. Likewise in the TV show *Sister, Sister* the twins Tia and Tamera Mowra were separated at birth but at age fourteen met by chance in a Detroit department store. Thus modern TV situation comedies and theatre plays owe much to the continuous comic tradition that runs from Plautus to today.

Terence's dates are uncertain, but we are told that he started life in Rome as a slave, gained his freedom as a young man, and staged his six comedies from 165 to 160 BCE. He too used Greek originals, but he adapted them with different methods and goals than Plautus. He did not try to make his plays more funny and animated than the Greek, and he often focused on the human

This well-preserved theatre built during Roman times is in Caesarea, a town in Israel and capital of the Roman province of Judaea. After this city had been under the control of Cleopatra, Augustus returned it to Herod the Great who named it in honor of Caesar Augustus.

emotions felt by the characters. The Chapter 3 selection from the *Adelphoi* (*Brothers*) would seem from its title to offer humorous opportunities to Terence. Demea, the father of Aeschinus and Ctesipho, has let his brother Micio adopt Aeschinus. The two sons and Micio conspire to fool him and pursue their own pleasures, but that is not so funny now, because Demea is really fond of Ctesipho and anxious to bring him up well. And he disapproves of the way Micio is raising Aeschinus, who in fact has gotten his girlfriend pregnant and not consulted either father about his responsibilities. So we watch a scene here where the slave Syrus is having fun deceiving Demea about where Ctesipho is and what he is doing. Yet what is "fun" for Syrus is sad for Demea, and the audience sees both the fun and the sadness and tends to feel sorry for Demea. This is not simply a trite situation comedy. Both sets of brothers are differentiated by Terence, not exploited for ridiculous games. An audience would come away from a play like this, after two hours, either bored stiff or talking over the moral themes of the comedy: they would not simply be tickled and guffawing at Syrus's confident deceptions. Terence won great success with the crowd that attended his *Eunuch*. On the other hand, he could not hold the audience for either of the first two performances of his *Mother-in-Law*. The *Brothers* was staged at the expense of his friend Scipio Africanus, to honor Scipio's father on the occasion of his death in 160 BCE.

The comedies of Terence were much admired for their moral sentiments, the realistic characters, and the urbane Latin that they spoke; and as a result the plays made him a "school author" throughout antiquity and then in the Renaissance. He had an early admirer and imitator in the nun Hrotswitha of Gandersheim, who wrote six pious plays in his manner in the tenth century. Dante quoted and admired Terence; so did Petrarch, who even wrote a biography of him and left an annotated manuscript of the comedies in Florence. In Florence in 1476, the first Terentian play to be staged since antiquity was the *Andria*. In the fifteenth century, continuing to be a "school author," Terence inspired most of the Latin comedies that the humanists attempted. He was read and admired throughout Europe. Molière staged a version of the *Phormio* in 1671.

To conclude, Plautus was more popular with audiences and continues to be performed and performable today, but Terence dominated Roman and Renaissance culture as a "school author." He won the respect of teachers, orators, and religious leaders (like Luther) until late in the nineteenth century. The twentieth century saw Plautus reclaiming dominance (in spite of the adaptation in 1930 of *The Woman of Andros* [*Andria*] by Thornton Wilder), but there are signs in this new millennium that students of Latin comedy are beginning to see that Terence and Plautus each has dramatic and literary merits. The two of them together combine into a superior variety of eminent comedy.

WILLIAM S. ANDERSON
Professor of Classics Emeritus
University of California Berkeley
Berkeley, California

MĪRĀBILE AUDĪTŪ

PHRASES AND QUOTATIONS
RELATING TO THE COMIC TRADITION

PHRASES AND QUOTATIONS

- Drāmatis persōnae. "Characters in a play." An expression indicating the actors in a drama.

- Exit. Exeunt. "S/he exits <the scene>. They exit <the scene>." A way to indicate in a script that an actor or a group of actors are leaving the scene.

- Mīles glōriōsus. "A bragging soldier." This title of a comedy by Plautus also describes a common figure in Roman comedy.

- Nōdum in scirpō quaeris. "You seek a knot in the bulrush, i.e., you find a difficulty where there is none." (Plautus, *Menaechmī* 2.1.22; Terence, *The Woman of Andros* 5.4.38)

- Plaudite, ācta est fābula. "Applaud, the play is over." A typical expression said to the Roman audience at the end of a play. The words "ācta est fabula" were allegedly pronounced by Augustus on his deathbed. Suetonius, in *The Life of Augustus* 99, writes that just before dying the emperor asked whether he had played well his role in the comedy of life.

This theatre, with its *scenae frons*, lies in Gerasa, now Jerash, situated just north of Jordan, conquered by Rome in 63 BCE, annexed as a Roman province first of Syria and later of Arabia.

CHAPTER 4

Second Declension Neuter Nouns; Dative Case (Indirect Object); First and Second Declension *–us, –a, –um* Adjectives; Agreement of Nouns and Adjectives

King Pyrrhus of Epirus fought against Rome twice in the third century BCE. At the top left of the picture is Pyrrhus's name and at the top right the Latin word *rēx*, "king," and the letters "Epi," which stand for Epirus.

MEMORĀBILE DICTŪ

Aurī sacra famēs.

"Accursed hunger for gold." (Vergil, *Aeneid* 3.57)

Vergil's words have become proverbial as a concise phrase condemning the insatiable human appetite for money.

READING

Perhaps the greatest of all Roman writers of prose was Mārcus Tullius Cicero (106–43 BCE). Cicero was a great statesman, active in politics (in fact, he was eventually killed upholding the cause of the Roman Republic against the absolute rule of powerful dictators in the series of civil wars that shook the Roman state in the last century BCE). He was famous as an orator, and wrote numerous speeches, many of which have survived.

Cicero wrote many letters, which tell us a great deal about the social and political life of his day. He was also a philosopher and the author of many philosophical works, which, though not very original, are highly polished and well designed to transmit Greek philosophical ideas to a Roman audience.

The passage you will now read comes from Cicero's philosophical essay *Dē officiīs* ("On Duties"), where Cicero discusses the relationship between what is morally right (*honestum*) and what is expedient (*ūtile*). In Book 3.86, he relates an event that occurred more than two centuries earlier.

While Rome had not yet conquered all of Italy in the early third century BCE, it was already the dominant power in the Italian peninsula. Alarmed at Rome's expansionism, the Greek city of Tarentum in the south of Italy made an alliance with Pyrrhus, King of Epirus (a region just west of Macedonia), a kinsman of Alexander the Great and no less greedy for military glory. Pyrrhus's military forces met those of Rome twice, in 280 and 279 BCE. The Greek armies were victorious in both battles. But Pyrrhus had lost so many men each time that he was unable to stop the Romans, and he ultimately had to abandon his ambitions in Italy. To this very day, we call a victory won at an unacceptable price a "Pyrrhic victory." Here is Cicero's version of what occurred just before the Romans met the army of Pyrrhus in open battle.

PROFUGA PRAEMIUM VULT

1   Pyrrhus, rēx praeclārus, bellum cum Rōmānīs gerit. Terram in Italiā habēre vult. Profuga ē castrīs Pyrrhī clam fugit et in castra Rōmānōrum ambulat. Nōn timet profuga, sed Fābricium vidēre vult. Fābricius est cōnsul et dux Rōmānōrum. "Dēbēs magnum praemium mihi dare,"
5   inquit profuga; "sī praemium mihi dās, habeō in animō clam intrāre in Pyrrhī castra et Pyrrhum venēnō necāre." Fābricius autem victōriam dolō habēre nōn vult, sed bellō iūstō. Itaque virōs armātōs vocat. Praemium nōn dat profugae, sed vincula. Iubet virōs armātōs cum profugā ad Pyrrhī castra ambulāre et profugam vīnctum Pyrrhō dare.

READING VOCABULARY

*ad + *accusative* – into, toward, to

*armātus, armāta, armātum – armed

*autem – however

bellō iūstō – through open warfare

*bellum, bellī, *n.* – war

*castra, castrōrum, *n. pl.* – camp (*note this noun is one of several that have only plural forms, with a singular meaning*)

clam (*adv.*) – secretly

cōnsul, *m.* – consul

*dō, dăre, dedī, dătum – to give

dolō – through treachery

*dolus, dolī, *m.* – trickery, deception

dux, *m.* – leader, general

*ē (ex *before a vowel*) + *ablative* – from, out of

Fābricius, Fābriciī, *m.* – Fabricius

fugit – flees

gerit – wages

*in + *accusative* – into, to

inquit – says

*intrō, intrāre, intrāvī, —— – to enter

Italia, Italiae, *f.* – Italy

*iubeō, iubēre, iussī, iussum + *accusative* + *infinitive* – to order somebody to do something

*iūstus, iūsta, iūstum – legitimate, open, just

*magnus, magna, magnum – large, great, important

mihi (*dative case*) – to me

necō, necāre, necāvī, necātum – to kill

*praeclārus, praeclāra, praeclārum – famous, distinguished

*praemium, praemiī, *n.* – reward

profuga, profugae, *m.* – deserter

Pyrrhus, Pyrrhī, *m.* – Pyrrhus

rēx, *m.* – king

*Rōmānus, Rōmāna, Rōmānum – Roman (Rōmānī *in the masculine plural means "the Romans"*)

*sed (*conj.*) – but

sī (*conj.*) – if

venēnō – by poison

*venēnum, venēnī, *n.* – poison

victōria, victōriae, *f.* – victory

vīnctus, vīncta, vīnctum – bound, chained

*vinculum, vinculī, *n.* – chain, fetter

vult – he wants, wishes

*Words marked with an asterisk will need to be memorized.

COMPREHENSION QUESTIONS

1. With whom are the Romans at war?

2. What does Pyrrhus want in Italy?

3. When the deserter comes to the Roman camp, whom does he need to see?

4. What is the deserter's plan?

5. Why doesn't Fabricius accept the deserter's proposal?

LANGUAGE FACT I

SECOND DECLENSION NEUTER NOUNS

Since Chapter 3 you have already become acquainted with the second declension. You learned the declension of the masculine nouns in **–us**, exemplified by *amīcus* (the largest group of second declension nouns) as well as the declensions of *ager, puer,* and *vir.*

In the text above, you saw another type of second declension noun. These are neuter nouns in **–um**: *bellum, praemium, venēnum, vinculum.* The noun *castra, –ōrum* belongs to the same group, but occurs only in the plural.

These words are declined in the same way as *amīcus* with two exceptions: their nominative, accusative, and vocative are identical to one another; and the ending for the nominative and accusative (and vocative) plural is **–a**.

Second Declension Neuter Nouns				
	Singular		**Plural**	
Nominative	bell**um**	the war	bell**a**	the wars
Genitive	bell**ī**	of the war	bell**ōrum**	of the wars
Dative	bell**ō**	to/for the war	bell**īs**	to/for the wars
Accusative	bell**um**	war	bell**a**	the wars
Ablative	bell**ō**	by/with/from war	bell**īs**	by/with/from wars
Vocative	bell**um**	o, war	bell**a**	o, wars

BY THE WAY

All neuter words in Latin, of whatever declension, always have identical nominative, accusative, and vocative forms, and the *plural* nominative, accusative, and vocative always end in **–a**.

▶ EXERCISE 1

Identify the case and number of each noun. For some, more than one answer is possible.

Example: venēna
nominative or accusative plural

1. praemiīs
2. āthlēta
3. castra
4. vinculōrum
5. dolum
6. fīliī
7. praemiī

VOCABULARY TO LEARN

NOUNS

bellum, bellī, *n.* – war

castra, castrōrum, *n. pl.* – camp

dolus, dolī, *m.* – trickery, deception

praemium, praemiī, *n.* – reward

venēnum, venēnī, *n.* – poison

vinculum, vinculī, *n.* – chain, fetter

ADJECTIVES

armātus, armāta, armātum – armed

bonus, bona, bonum – good

iūstus, iūsta, iūstum – legitimate, open, just

magnus, magna, magnum – large, great, important

malus, mala, malum – bad

praeclārus, praeclāra, praeclārum – famous, distinguished

Rōmānus, Rōmāna, Rōmānum – Roman

VERBS

dō, dăre, dedī, dătum – to give (*note the unusual short stem vowel in this first conjugation verb*)

**intrō, intrāre, intrāvī, —— ** – to enter

iubeō, iubēre, iussī, iussum + *accusative* + *infinitive* – to order somebody (*acc.*) to do something (*inf.*)

PREPOSITIONS

ad + *accusative* – ~~into~~ toward, to

ē (ex) + *ablative* – from, out of

in + *accusative* – into, ~~to~~ against

CONJUNCTIONS

autem – however

sed – but

A Roman legionary, during the time of the Roman wars with Dacia. This is a relief from Trajan's column, which was built by Apollodorus of Damascus at the command of the Roman Senate and was completed in 113 CE. The column was constructed in honor of Trajan's victory over the Dacians and stands in the Forum of Trajan in Rome.

▶ EXERCISE 2

Find the English derivatives based on the Vocabulary to Learn in the following sentences. Write the corresponding Latin word.

1. These youths are rather bellicose and always fighting.
2. A jussive mood of the verb is a form that conveys an order.
3. This product is premium quality.
4. The venom of the snake was fatal.
5. I received a bonus at the end of the year.
6. The army is ready for a battle.
7. Where is the main entrance?
8. She is a very sweet person, totally devoid of malice.

LANGUAGE FACT II

DATIVE CASE (INDIRECT OBJECT)

In the Latin reading passage you read these sentences and phrases:

> *Dēbēs magnum praemium mihi dare . . .*
> You ought to give me a great reward . . .

> *Sī praemium mihi dās . . .*
> If you give me a reward . . .

> *Praemium nōn dat profugae, sed vincula . . .*
> He does not give a reward to the deserter, but chains . . .

> *Iubet virōs armātōs . . . profugam vīnctum Pyrrhō dare . . .*
> He orders the armed men to give the chained deserter to Pyrrhus . . .

In each of these sentences the nouns in the accusative case (*praemium, vincula, profugam, vīnctum*) are direct objects—they indicate the entity directly acted upon by the verb.

The nouns in the dative case (*mihi, profugae, Pyrrhō*) indicate the indirect object, i.e., the entity indirectly affected by the verb.

Use the words "to" or "for" to express the indirect object in English.

BY THE WAY

Indirect objects often occur in sentences that include a verb that means "give," "show," "tell," or a synonym or antonym of one of these verbs.

▶ EXERCISE 3

Fill in the blanks with the dative case of the words in parentheses.

Example: Cōnsul praemium _____ dat. (vir)
Cōnsul praemium virō dat.

1. Fābricius praemium _____ nōn dat. (profuga)

2. Profuga venēnum _____ dare vult. (Pyrrhus)

3. Dux Rōmānōrum vincula _____ parat. (profuga)

4. Fābricius profugam _____ dat. (armātī virī)

▶ EXERCISE 4

Fill in the blanks with the dative case of the words in parentheses and translate each sentence.

Example: Fābulās _____ nārrat. (fīlia)
Fābulās fīliae nārrat.   S/he tells stories to the daughter.

1. Venēnum _____ damus. (lupae)

2. Aquam _____ parātis. (āthlētae)

3. Praemia _____ dēbētis. (nautae)

4. Terram _____ dant. (agricolae)

5. Casam _____ parāmus. (puer et puella)

Modern actors dressed in ancient Roman military and other official garb. Legionaries, ordinary soldiers, served in a legion, usually a group of soldiers about 4,000–6,000 strong. These men served under the direction of a centurion but an *imperātor* or *dux* was in command of the entire legion.

LANGUAGE FACT III

FIRST AND SECOND DECLENSION –*US*, –*A*, –*UM* ADJECTIVES; AGREEMENT OF NOUNS AND ADJECTIVES

Look closely at the following four phrases taken from the passage about Fabricius at the beginning of the chapter: *rēx praeclārus* ("renowned king"), *magnum praemium* ("large reward"), *virōs armātōs* ("armed men"), *profugam vīnctum* ("chained deserter").

In each instance, a noun is modified by an adjective that describes the noun. An adjective *always* agrees with its noun in case, number, and gender. There are different types of adjectives. In this chapter you will learn adjectives with a masculine form ending in –*us*, a feminine form ending in –*a*, and a neuter form ending in –*um*, e.g., *iūstus, iūsta, iūstum*.

The masculine form is declined like *amīcus*, the feminine form is declined like *lupa*, and the neuter form is declined like *bellum*: i.e., the endings are identical to those you have learned for nouns of the first (feminine) and second (masculine/neuter) declensions.

First and Second Declension –*us*, –*a*, –*um* Adjectives

Singular

	Masculine	Feminine	Neuter
Nominative	iūst**us**	iūst**a**	iūst**um**
Genitive	iūst**ī**	iūst**ae**	iūst**ī**
Dative	iūst**ō**	iūst**ae**	iūst**ō**
Accusative	iūst**um**	iūst**am**	iūst**um**
Ablative	iūst**ō**	iūst**ā**	iūst**ō**
Vocative	iūst**e**	iūst**a**	iūst**um**

Plural

	Masculine	Feminine	Neuter
Nominative	iūst**ī**	iūst**ae**	iūst**a**
Genitive	iūst**ōrum**	iūst**ārum**	iūst**ōrum**
Dative	iūst**īs**	iūst**īs**	iūst**īs**
Accusative	iūst**ōs**	iūst**ās**	iūst**a**
Ablative	iūst**īs**	iūst**īs**	iūst**īs**
Vocative	iūst**ī**	iūst**ae**	iūst**a**

Two frequently used adjectives of this type:

> *bonus, bona, bonum* – good
> *malus, mala, malum* – bad

BY THE WAY

An adjective agrees with its noun in case, number, and gender—regardless of the declension to which the noun belongs. So "the just sailor" is *nauta iūstus*, **not** *nauta iūsta*, because the noun *nauta* has a masculine gender.

▶ EXERCISE 5

Make *magnus, magna, magnum* agree with **each** noun in the following sentences and translate the changed sentence.

Example: Ad castra ambulāmus.
Ad magna castra ambulāmus.   We are walking to the large camp.

1. In castrīs sum.
2. Fīliōs habēmus.
3. Bellum valdē timēmus.
4. Praemia dēbēs.
5. Casam poētae cūrāmus.
6. Agricola ad rīvum ambulat.

▶ EXERCISE 6

Change the noun-adjective pair into the singular if it is plural and into the plural if it is singular. For some, more than one answer is possible.

Example: virōrum Rōmānōrum
virī Rōmānī

1. iūstō praemiō
2. agrīs magnīs
3. bella mala
4. nautae armātī
5. poētae praeclārō
6. vincula mala

▶ EXERCISE 7

Translate into English.

1. Dēbēmus nunc praemium exspectāre.
2. Fābricius dolum nōn amat: victōriam iūstam amat.
3. In castra Rōmānōrum nōn ambulāmus.
4. Nōn bellum, sed venēnum timēmus.
5. Amīcum iubēs Rōmānīs praeclārīs magna praemia dare.
6. Amīcōs bonōs habētis.

► EXERCISE 8

Fill in the blanks with the accusative case of the words in parentheses, keeping the same number, and translate each sentence.

Example: Virīs armātīs _____ nōn datis. (praemia)
Virīs armātīs praemia nōn datis.   You are not giving rewards to the armed men.

1. Ad patriam _____ vocāmus. (poētae)
2. _____ agricolīs nōn damus. (agrī magnī)
3. _____ Rōmānīs parō. (praemium iūstum)
4. Bellō nōn dolō _____ habēmus. (victōria iūsta)

► EXERCISE 9

Label each sentence as *vērum* (true) if it agrees or *falsum* (false) if it disagrees with the Latin reading passage at the beginning of the chapter. The Reading Vocabulary may be consulted.

1. Pyrrhus dolum parat.
2. Fābricius magnum praemium habēre vult.
3. Pyrrhus bellum cum Rōmānīs gerit.
4. Profuga Fābricium necāre vult.
5. Fābricius victōriam iūstam habēre dēbet.
6. Rōmānī profugae praemium dant.
7. Profuga est in vinculīs.

A modern re-enactor displays the helmet and body armor of a Roman soldier. A meritorious soldier could rise to the rank of centurion, a non-commissioned officer who usually directed about eighty men from a legion in war.

TALKING

cūr – why

Hoc est pēnsum domesticum. "This is the homework assignment."

locus Cicerōnis – a passage of Cicero

in crāstinum – for tomorrow

ita vērō – yes indeed

Locum in diem crāstinum parāre dēbēmus. "We must prepare the passage for tomorrow."

lexicum, lexicī, n. – dictionary

Licet vōbīs lexicum īnspicere. "You may (i.e., it is permitted for you to) consult a dictionary."

minimē – no

quis – who

DISCUSSING HOMEWORK

Remember that questions are introduced by the little word -ne attached to another word.

Marīa: Habēmusne pēnsum in crāstinum?

Helena: Ita vērō. Dēbēmus parāre locum Cicerōnis.

Marīa: Estne locus magnus?

Christīna: Nōn est nimis (*too*) magnus.

Mārcus: Quis erat Cicero? (*Who was Cicero?*)

Christīna: Cicero erat philosophus (*philosopher*).

Marīa: Cūr verba (*words*) philosophōrum legere (*read*) dēbēmus? Philosophī dē vērā vītā (*about true life*) nōn nārrant.

Helena: Cicero vēram (*true*) fābulam nārrat dē (*about*) Fābriciō. Fābricius victōriam dolō habēre nōn vult, sed bellō iūstō.

Mārcus: Haec (*this*) fābula nōn est vēra. Virī magnī victōriam etiam (*even*) dolō habēre volunt (*want*).

Helena: Fābricius autem nōn sōlum (*only*) est magnus, sed etiam (*also*) iūstus et praeclārus. Virī iūstī victōriam dolō habēre nōn dēbent.

Christīna: Et nōs pēnsum parāre dēbēmus.

DERIVATIVES

bellum – belligerent, bellicose, duel, rebel, rebellion, revel, revelry

castra – castle, château, chatelaine, forecastle

dolus – sedulous

praemium – premium

venēnum – venom, venomous

armātus – armature

bonus – bonus, boon, bounty, bonbon, debonair

iūstus – adjust, injustice, justification, unjust

magnus – magnanimous, magnate, magnify, magnificent, magnitude

malus – malediction, dismal, malaria, malady, Maleficent, malefactor, malevolent, malice, malign, malignant, malnutrition, maltreat

Rōmānus – Roman, romanize, romanization, Romance

dō – addition, betray, data, dative, dice, donation, dowry, edit, endow, extradite, render, rendezvous, rent, sacerdotal, surrender, tradition, traitor, treason, vendor

iubeō – jussive

ad – adhere, admit, admire, admonition, adjacent, adjourn

ex – exit, emit, exclaim, evident, evict, eject

in – See p. 42.

CHAPTER 5

First and Second Conjugation Verbs: Present Tense Passive, Present Passive Infinitive; Ablative of Agent; First and Second Declension *–er* Adjectives

The portrait of a couple on this wall painting from Pompeii is a reminder of Cicero's letters to his wife Terentia.

MEMORĀBILE DICTŪ

STVBEEV

"If you are well, it is well; I am well."

The Romans could send a letter as short as these seven letters, which stand for *"Sī tū valēs, bene est; ego valeō."*

READING

Cicero left a large collection of letters, which tell us a great deal about him as a private person. They not only illustrate the family life of an upper-class Roman of the last century BCE, but also reveal much about the psychology of Cicero as an individual. When Cicero was sent into exile to Greece by his political enemies, he wrote letters full of laments, resentment, and despair. In many of them, though, we detect tender love for his wife Terentia and for his children. Such a letter is presented below.

When the early Renaissance Italian author Petrarch (1304–1374) discovered Cicero's correspondence, he was dismayed to find that Cicero, whom he had earlier known only from his speeches and philosophical essays, was, as a private individual, subject to powerful emotions and plagued by human feelings. Although Cicero had been dead for centuries, Petrarch responded by writing Cicero a letter of his own, full of harsh criticism.

CICERO TERENTIAE SALŪTEM PLŪRIMAM DĪCIT

1   Epistulam tuam, mea Terentia, nunc teneō. Epistulam tamen tuam nōn
     sōlum cum gaudiō, sed etiam cum lacrimīs legō. Nam longē ā patriā,
     longē ā familiā sum miser. Dē tē, dē fīliā et dē fīliō semper cōgitō.
     Animus dolet. Mala cōnsilia ā malīs virīs contrā mē parantur et
5   auxilium mihi ā bonīs virīs darī dēbet. Tē, Terentia mea, valdē amō et
     ā tē epistulās longās exspectō. Sī epistulās tuās legō, tē in animō meō
     videō. Tē ipsam, fīlium, fīliam pulchram bene cūrāre dēbēs. Valē!

READING VOCABULARY

*ā (ab *before a vowel*) + *ablative* – by, from

*auxilium, auxiliī, *n.* – help

Cicero, *m.* – Cicero

*cōgitō, cōgitāre, cōgitāvī, cōgitātum – to think

*cōnsilium, cōnsiliī, *n.* – plan, advice

contrā + *accusative* – against

darī dēbet – has to be given

*dē + *ablative* – about, concerning, down from

*doleō, dolēre, doluī, —— – to feel pain, to hurt

*epistula, epistulae, *f.* – letter

*familia, familiae, *f.* – family, household

gaudiō – with joy

*gaudium, gaudiī, *n.* – joy

*lacrima, lacrimae, *f.* – tear

lacrimīs – with tears

legō – I read

*longē (*adv.*) – far

*longus, longa, longum – long

mē (*accusative*) – me

meus, mea, meum – my

mihi – to me

*miser – wretched, sad, miserable

*nam (*conj.*) – for, in fact

*nōn sōlum . . . , sed etiam . . . – not only . . . , but also
. . .

parantur – are being prepared

*parō – to design (*you already know the meanings "to
prepare, to get ready"*)

*pulchram (*accusative singular feminine*) – beautiful

salūtem plūrimam dīcit + *dative* – s/he greets
(someone) (*a standard formula for beginning a letter).
Literally it means "(s/he) says (i.e., wishes) very much
health (the best of health) to . . ."*

*semper (*adv.*) – always

sī (*conj.*) – if

sum – I am

*tamen (*conj.*) – nevertheless

tē (*accusative* and *ablative*) – you

tē ipsam (*accusative*) – yourself

Terentia, Terentiae, *f.* – Terentia

tuus, tua, tuum – your

valē! – goodbye!

*Words marked with an asterisk will need to be
memorized.

COMPREHENSION QUESTIONS

1. Where is Cicero while writing the letter?

2. How many family members does Cicero mention in his letter and who are they?

3. What is Cicero afraid of?

4. How does Cicero feel (according to his own words), when he reads Terentia's letter?

5. What does Cicero ask Terentia to do?

LANGUAGE FACT I

FIRST AND SECOND CONJUGATION VERBS: PRESENT TENSE PASSIVE

In the reading passage you saw the form *parantur*, which you undoubtedly recognized from the forms of the verb *parō, parāre*. Its ending, however, is different from the endings that you already know. This form belongs to the **passive** voice.

Voice: the voice of the verb shows whether the subject is doing the action or is receiving the action.

> **Active voice:** the subject is doing the action.
> Example: *Malī virī mala cōnsilia parant.*
> Bad men are designing bad plans.

> **Passive voice:** the subject is not doing the action, but receiving the action.
> Example: *Mala cōnsilia ā malīs virīs parantur.*
> Bad plans are being designed by bad men.

To form the present passive tense of a Latin verb, the personal endings of the passive voice (see below) are added to the stem of the verb in all persons except the first singular in which the passive ending *-r* should be added to the active first singular form.

Passive Endings

	Singular		Plural	
First person	**–r**	I	**–mur**	we
Second person	**–ris**	you	**–minī**	you
Third person	**–tur**	s/he/it	**–ntur**	they

BY THE WAY

The personal endings for the present passive of first and second conjugation verbs are identical. Just as in the active voice, the only difference between the two conjugations appears in the stem vowel. Remember: the predominant vowel in the first conjugation is a long *–ā–* and in the second conjugation a long *–ē–*.

First Conjugation: Present Passive

	Singular		Plural	
First person	pa**ror**	I am prepared	parā**mur**	we are prepared
Second person	parā**ris**	you are prepared	parā**minī**	you are prepared
Third person	parā**tur**	s/he/it is prepared	para**ntur**	they are prepared

Second Conjugation: Present Passive					
		Singular		**Plural**	
First person	teneor	I am held	tenēmur	we are held
Second person	tenēris	you are held	tenēminī	you are held
Third person	tenētur	s/he/it is held	tenentur	they are held

▶ EXERCISE 1

Identify the person and number of each verb and change into the passive voice.

Example: tenēs
second person singular   tenēris

1. vident
2. vocat
3. iubēmus
4. cūrātis

5. amō
6. dēbent
7. dās
8. exspectat

VOCABULARY TO LEARN

NOUNS

auxilium, auxiliī, *n.* – help
cōnsilium, cōnsiliī, *n.* – plan, advice
epistula, epistulae, *f.* – letter
familia, familiae, *f.* – family, household
gaudium, gaudiī, *n.* – joy
lacrima, lacrimae, *f.* – tear

ADJECTIVES

longus, longa, longum – long
miser, misera, miserum – wretched, sad, miserable
pulcher, pulchra, pulchrum – beautiful, nice

VERBS

cōgitō, cōgitāre, cōgitāvī, cōgitātum – to think
doleō, dolēre, doluī, —— – to feel pain, to be hurt
parō – to design (*you already know the meanings "to prepare, to get ready"*)

ADVERBS

longē – far
semper – always

PREPOSITIONS

ā (ab) + *ablative* – by, from, away from
dē + *ablative* – about, concerning, down from

CONJUNCTIONS

nam – for, in fact
nōn sōlum . . . , sed etiam . . . – not only . . . , but also
. . .
tamen – however

▶ EXERCISE 2

Find the English derivatives based on the Vocabulary to Learn in the list below. Write the corresponding Latin word.

misery   mini-series   malicious   malignant   mall
auxiliary   auction   counsel   constitution   pulchritude
pool   lacrosse   longitude   doll

▶ EXERCISE 3

Complete each sentence with the correct form of the word in parentheses and translate.

Example: Venēnum ā malīs virīs _____. (parō)
Venēnum ā malīs virīs parātur.   Poison is being prepared by bad men.

1. Epistula Terentiae ā Cicerōne (*ablative*, _____. (teneō)
2. Cicero est _____ et Terentia est _____. (miser)
3. Bona cōnsilia ā bonīs virī _____. (parō)
4. Epistulae longae ā Cicerōne (*ablative*) _____ spectō)
5. Terentia in animō Cicerōnis (_____. (videō)

Bust of Cicero from the second century CE.

LANGUAGE FACT II

FIRST AND SECOND CONJUGATION VERBS: PRESENT PASSIVE INFINITIVE

In the reading passage there is a new form of the infinitive: *darī* ("to be given").

> *Auxilium ā bonīs virīs darī dēbet.*
> Help ought to be given by good men.

The present passive infinitive functions in a sentence just like the active infinitive, except that its meaning is passive.

Remember that the infinitive is a verb unlimited by a specific person. In English, the passive infinitive is expressed by putting the English verb form that usually (but not always) ends in *–ed* after the words "to be."

Compare the following active and passive infinitives in English:

Active:	Passive:
to love	to be loved
to warn	to be warned
to sing	to be sung
to hold	to be held

In Latin, the passive infinitive of the first two conjugations is formed by adding the ending *–rī* to the stem vowel of the verb.

Present Passive Infinitive

> *parārī* – to be prepared
> *tenērī* – to be held

Compare the present active and present passive infinitives.

	Present Active Infinitive	Present Passive Infinitive
First conjugation	parāre – to prepare	parārī – to be prepared
Second conjugation	tenēre – to hold	tenērī – to be held

▶ EXERCISE 4

Change all the active infinitives into the passive and translate the passive infinitives.

Example: parāre
parārī   to be prepared

1. cōgitāre
2. vocāre
3. habēre
4. amāre

5. dēbēre
6. vidēre
7. exspectāre
8. nārrāre

LANGUAGE FACT III

ABLATIVE OF AGENT

Look at this sentence from the reading passage:

> Mala cōnsilia ā malīs virīs contrā mē parantur et auxilium mihi ā bonīs virīs darī dēbet.
>
> Bad plans are being designed against me by bad men, and help ought to be given to me by good men (good men have to help me).

With the passive voice, the person who does the action is in the ablative case following the preposition *ā* or *ab*. This ablative is translated with the preposition "**by**."

If the same statement is made in the **active** voice, the ablative of agent becomes the nominative subject and the passive subject becomes the accusative direct object:

> Malī virī mala cōnsilia contrā mē parant et virī bonī auxilium mihi dare dēbent.
>
> Bad men design bad plans against me and good men ought to give me help.

STUDY TIP

Remember the three P's for the ablative of agent: Preposition, Person, Passive.

▶ EXERCISE 5

Change the active verbs into the passive and indicate the doer of the action with an ablative of agent. Translate the changed sentence. The Reading Vocabulary may be consulted.

Example: Puer puellam vocat.

Puella ā puerō vocātur.   The girl is being called by the boy.

1. Vir epistulam tenet.
2. Vir puellam amat.
3. Puer āthlētam nōn videt.
4. Terentia fīlium et fīliam cūrat.
5. Vir agricolae miserō auxilium dat.
6. Nauta fīlium cūrat.
7. Vir cōnsilia bona parat.
8. Fēmina cōnsilia mala timet.
9. Āthlēta praemia praeclāra exspectat.
10. Poētae fābulās longās nārrant.
11. Puer puellam vocat.
12. Puella epistulam habet.

LANGUAGE FACT IV
FIRST AND SECOND DECLENSION –*ER* ADJECTIVES

In the previous chapter you have seen the adjective *iūstus, iūsta, iūstum,* which matches the forms of nouns in the first and second declensions. Adjectives have all three genders because they **agree** in **case**, **number**, and **gender** with any noun they modify. Notice this sentence from the reading passage:

> *Tē ipsam, fīlium, fīliam pulchram bene cūrāre dēbēs.*
> You must take good care of yourself, of (our) son, of (our) beautiful daughter.

The adjective *pulchram* is feminine, singular, and accusative because it agrees with one of the direct objects of the sentence, *fīliam*—also feminine, singular, and accusative.

The adjective *pulcher, pulchra, pulchrum* has endings just like *iūstus, iūsta, iūstum,* except in the masculine nominative singular. It illustrates a sub-type of first and second declension adjectives, in which the masculine nominative singular ends in –*er,* but the –*e*– disappears in all other forms (much as in the noun *ager, agrī*).

First and Second Declension –*er* Adjectives

Singular

	Masculine	Feminine	Neuter
Nominative	pulcher	pulchra	pulchrum
Genitive	pulchrī	pulchrae	pulchrī
Dative	pulchrō	pulchrae	pulchrō
Accusative	pulchrum	pulchram	pulchrum
Ablative	pulchrō	pulchrā	pulchrō
Vocative	pulcher	pulchra	pulchrum

Plural

	Masculine	Feminine	Neuter
Nominative	pulchrī	pulchrae	pulchra
Genitive	pulchrōrum	pulchrārum	pulchrōrum
Dative	pulchrīs	pulchrīs	pulchrīs
Accusative	pulchrōs	pulchrās	pulchra
Ablative	pulchrīs	pulchrīs	pulchrīs
Vocative	pulchrī	pulchrae	pulchra

Another type of first and second declension –*er* adjective keeps the –*e*– in its stem. An example you encountered in Cicero's letter is *miser, misera, miserum*, meaning "wretched." *Miser* can be compared with the noun *puer*, because in both the –*e*– remains present in all forms.

First and Second Declension –*er* Adjectives

Singular

	Masculine	Feminine	Neuter
Nominative	miser	misera	miser**um**
Genitive	miserī	miserae	miserī
Dative	miserō	miserae	miserō
Accusative	miser**um**	miser**am**	miser**um**
Ablative	miserō	miserā	miserō
Vocative	miser	misera	miser**um**

Plural

	Masculine	Feminine	Neuter
Nominative	miserī	miserae	misera
Genitive	miser**ōrum**	miser**ārum**	miser**ōrum**
Dative	miserīs	miserīs	miserīs
Accusative	miser**ōs**	miser**ās**	misera
Ablative	miserīs	miserīs	miserīs
Vocative	miserī	miserae	misera

BY THE WAY

The examples *pulcher, pulchra, pulchrum* and *miser, misera, miserum* show that you have to look to the nominative singular form of the feminine (and neuter) to see whether the base keeps its –*e*–. The spelling of English derivatives of –*er* words will also help you remember whether the Latin word keeps the –*e*–. For example, "pul**ch**ritude," "mi**ser**y."

STUDY TIP

In –*er* adjectives and nouns sometimes the word keeps the –*e*– and sometimes sets it free.

▶ EXERCISE 6

Make the adjective agree with the noun and translate the new phrase.

Example: cōnsilia (malus)
cōnsilia mala

1. lacrimīs (miser)
2. viam (longus)
3. āthlētārum (pulcher)
4. virō (iūstus)
5. poētā (armātus)
6. patriā (pulcher)
7. vinculōrum (miser)
8. puerī (miser)
9. familiīs (bonus)
10. animus (magnus)

This sign, attributed to Ciero (*sic*), in Latin *ut conclāve sine librīs, ita corpus sine animā*, may or may not actually be his words but are generally credited to him. It is the motto of the San Francisco Public Library.

▶ EXERCISE 7

Label each sentence as *vērum* (true) if it agrees or *falsum* (false) if it disagrees with the Latin reading passage at the beginning of the chapter. The Reading Vocabulary may be consulted.

1. Epistula ā filiā Terentiae tenētur.
2. Cicero gaudium nōn habet.
3. Cicero Terentiam valdē amat.
4. Cicero malam filiam et malum filium habet.
5. Auxilium bonōrum virōrum ā Cicerōne (*by Cicero*) exspectātur.
6. Mala cōnsilia contrā Cicerōnem (*accusative of Cicero*) nōn parantur.
7. Terentia longās epistulās dare nōn dēbet.
8. Fīlius et filia ā Terentiā cūrārī dēbent.

TALKING

Quid agis? "What are you doing?"

Quod est mūnus tuum? "What is your job?"

Discipulus sum. "I am a student (male)."

Discipula sum. "I am a student (female)."

Magister sum. "I am a teacher (male)."

Magistra sum. "I am a teacher (female)."

Quod mūnus habēre vīs? "What job do you want to have?"

Volō fierī . . . "I want to become . . ."

mūnus, n. – job

negotiātor/negotiātrix – businessman/businesswoman

custōs pūblicus – police officer

iūriscōnsultus, iūriscōnsultī, m./*iūriscōnsulta, iūriscōnsultae,* f. – lawyer

medicus, medicī, m./*medica, medicae,* f. – doctor (male/female)

artifex, m./f. – artist

DISCUSSING OCCUPATIONS

Marīa: Volō fierī iūriscōnsulta. Nam pater (*father*) est iūriscōnsultus. Iūriscōnsultī magnam pecūniam (pecūnia, pecūniae, f. – *money*) habent.

Christīna: Ego fierī volō medica. Nōn sōlum iūriscōnsultī, sed etiam medicī magnam pecūniam habent. Medicī tamen virīs et fēminīs (fēmina, fēminae, f. – *woman*), puerīs et puellīs auxilium semper dant. Ego volō cūrāre puerōs et puellās.

Helena: Ego dē pecūniā nōn cōgitō. Ego sum artifex et dē arte (*art*) cōgitō. Quod mūnus tū, Mārce, habēre vīs?

Mārcus: Ego sum āthlēta. Pater autem est astronauta (*astronaut*). In Californiā in caelō volābat (*flew in the sky*). Nunc Vasintōniae (*in Washington, DC*) habet mūnus in regimine pūblicō (*government*).

Puellae: Papae! (*Wow!*)

DERIVATIVES

auxilium – auxiliary

cōnsilium – counsel, counselor

epistula – epistle, epistolary

familia – family, familiar

gaudium – gaudy, joy, enjoy, joyous, rejoice

lacrima – lachrymal, lachrymose

longus – elongate, longevity, longitude, lunge, oblong, prolong, purloin

miser – commiserate, miserable, misery, miser

pulcher – pulchritude, pulchritudinous

cōgitō – cogitate, cogitation

doleō – condolence, doleful, dolorous, Dolores, indolence, indolent

parō – prepare, preparatory

semper – sempiternal, semper paratus, semper fidelis

ab – abduct, abridge, abdicate

dē – deduct, depress, depend, depict

Present Tense and Present Infinitive of *Sum* and *Possum*; Complementary Infinitive with *Possum*, *Dēbeō*, *Soleō*; Transitive and Intransitive Verbs

In Bellini's opera *Norma*, composed in the nineteenth century, the main character was Norma, a high priestess of the Druids and a leader to her people who were in a struggle against the occupying Romans. Norma, however, has secretly borne children to the Roman pro-consul. In this scene, Norma confesses her guilt to the Druids.

MEMORĀBILE DICTŪ

Iacta ālea est.

"The die is cast." (Suetonius, *The Life of Julius Caesar* 33)

These words were reportedly said by Julius Caesar when he crossed the Rubicon River into Italy with his victorious armies after his conquest of Gaul, disregarding the Senate's order to disband his forces. The saying has become symbolic of the state of mind of a person who has made a fateful decision and is prepared to accept the outcome.

READING

Together with Mārcus Tullius Cicero, Gāius Iūlius Caesar (100–44 BCE) is a chief author of the classical epoch of Roman literature.

Two principal works of Caesar survive: one is his account of his own conquest of Gaul (*Dē bellō Gallicō*, "On the Gallic War"), the region that English speakers now call France; the other is his description of the civil conflicts in which he was the leader of the anti-senatorial faction (*Dē bellō cīvīlī*, "On the Civil War"). Though Caesar emerged victorious, and in virtual control of the Roman state, he was murdered by his enemies at the Theatre of Pompey, where the Senate was meeting, on the famous Ides of March, 44 BCE. Caesar's works are a gold mine of information about the late Roman Republic, and especially the impressive Roman military machine. He was also an excellent observer of the customs and habits of other peoples. In the passage below he describes the Druids, the high priests who constituted a ruling class in the Celtic society of the Gauls.

DĒ DRUIDIBUS

1   Inter Gallōs sunt virī magnī quī vocantur Druidēs. Sacra Gallōrum ā
    Druidibus cūrantur. Druidēs ā Gallīs valdē timentur: nam auctōritātem
    magnam habent, et dē virīs bonīs et malīs iūdicāre solent. Praemia et
    poenae ā Druidibus dantur. Vīta Gallōrum ā Druidibus cūrātur.

5   Propter Druidum scientiam magnam multī puerī cum Druidibus diū
    manent. Puerī ā Druidibus discunt: Druidēs puerōs docent. Druidēs
    dē sacrīs scientiam magnam habent, sed librōs et litterās nōn amant.
    Nam sacra Gallīs videntur esse magna, sī in tenebrīs iacent. Itaque sacra
    Gallōrum nōn litterīs, sed memoriā servantur. Druidēs scientiam

10 magnam memoriā servāre possunt. Itaque dum Druidēs exempla
    docent et fābulās nārrant, puerī memoriam firmant.

READING VOCABULARY

auctōritātem (*accusative singular feminine*) – authority

discunt – (they) learn

***doceō, docēre, docuī, doctum** – to teach (*sometimes both the thing taught and the person being taught are in the accusative case*)

Druidēs, *m. pl.* – the Druids

Druidibus (*ablative case*) – Druids

Druidum (*genitive case*) – Druids

***dum** (*conj.*) – while

***exemplum, exemplī,** *n.* – example

***firmō, firmāre, firmāvī, firmātum** – to strengthen

Gallī, Gallōrum, *m. pl.* – the Gauls

***iaceō, iacēre, iacuī,** ⸺ – to lie down, to be inert

inter + *accusative* – among

***iūdicō, iūdicāre, iūdicāvī, iūdicātum** – to judge

***liber, librī,** *m.* – book

***littera, litterae,** *f.* – letter of the alphabet; *pl.* literature, letter (epistle)

***maneō, manēre, mānsī, mānsum** – to remain

***memoria, memoriae,** *f.* – memory

***multus, multa, multum** – much, many

poena, poenae, *f.* – punishment

***possum, posse, potuī,** ⸺ – to be able, can

***propter** + *accusative* – because of, on account of

quī (*masculine nominative pl.*) – who

sacra, sacrōrum, *n. pl.* – religious rites

scientia, scientiae, *f.* – knowledge

***servō, servāre, servāvī, servātum** – to save, to preserve

sī – if

***soleō, solēre, solitus sum** + *infinitive* – to be accustomed

***sum, esse, fuī,** ⸺ – to be

sunt (*third person singular of* sum) – there are

***tenebrae, tenebrārum,** *f. pl.* – shadows, darkness

videntur – *note that often (as here) the passive of* videō *means "to seem"*

***vīta, vītae,** *f.* – life

*Words marked with an asterisk will need to be memorized.

COMPREHENSION QUESTIONS

1. Why do the Gauls fear the Druids?

2. Why do many boys among the Gauls attach themselves to the Druids?

3. Why do the Druids make little use of books and writing?

4. How are the sacred rites of the Gauls preserved?

5. What faculty/skill must the students of the Druids develop with special care?

LANGUAGE FACT I

PRESENT TENSE AND PRESENT INFINITIVE OF *SUM*

In the passage at the beginning of this chapter, you met the word *sunt*, which means "they are." This is the present tense, third person plural of the verb "to be."

The forms of the verb "to be" are *sum, esse, fuī, ——.*

In previous chapters you have met other forms of this verb: *est*, "s/he/it is"; and *sum*, "I am."

In Latin, as in many languages, this verb is irregular. But in Latin, as in other languages, you cannot go far without knowing this very important verb. Here are the forms of *sum* in the present indicative, followed by the present infinitive:

Present Tense of *sum*				
		Singular		**Plural**
First person	sum	I am	sumus	we are
Second person	es	you are	estis	you are
Third person	est	s/he/it is / there is	sunt	they are / there are

Present Infinitive of *sum*
esse   to be

▶ EXERCISE 1

Translate into English. The Reading Vocabulary may be consulted.

1. Druidēs sunt virī magnī.

2. Estis Druidēs: exempla bona docētis et fābulās nārrātis.

3. Nōn sumus Druidēs.

4. Vir iūstus sum.

5. Ego autem sum magnus āthlēta.

6. Tū nōn es āthlēta; tu es poēta.

7. Liber est bonus.

VOCABULARY TO LEARN

NOUNS

exemplum, exemplī, *n.* – example

liber, librī, *m.* – book

littera, litterae, *f.* – letter of the alphabet; *pl.* literature, letter (epistle)

memoria, memoriae, *f.* – memory

tenebrae, tenebrārum, *f. pl.* – shadows, darkness

vīta, vītae, *f.* – life

ADJECTIVE

multus, multa, multum – much, many

VERBS

doceō, docēre, docuī, doctum – to teach

firmō, firmāre, firmāvī, firmātum – to strengthen

iaceō, iacēre, iacuī, —— – to lie down, to be inert

iūdicō, iūdicāre, iūdicāvī, iūdicātum – to judge

maneō, manēre, mānsī, mānsum – to remain

possum, posse, potuī, —— – to be able, can

servō, servāre, servāvī, servātum – to save, to preserve

soleō, solēre, solitus sum + *infinitive* – to be accustomed

sum, esse, fuī, —— – to be

ADVERB

saepe – often

PREPOSITION

propter + *accusative* – because of, on account of

CONJUNCTION

dum – while

Latin letters are engraved on this marble slab from Pompeii.

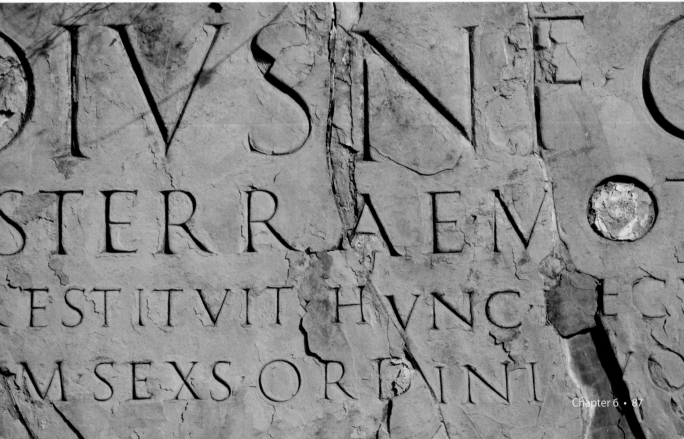

▶ EXERCISE 2

Find the English derivatives based on the Vocabulary to Learn in the following sentences. Write the corresponding Latin word. For some, there is more than one derivative in the sentence.

1. Please send this letter with a delivery confirmation.

2. She works in the conservation department of the museum.

3. We must hear what the essence of the problem is.

4. The garage is adjacent to the main building.

5. This is the largest library in the country.

6. In the past, many people did not go to school and remained illiterate.

7. Have you read the memorandum?

8. One multivitamin a day is recommended for good health.

9. I have a permanent license to park here.

10. There is a very potent agent in this prescription, which can be dangerous in an overdose.

11. They immediately checked for his vital signs in the hospital.

LANGUAGE FACT II

PRESENT TENSE AND PRESENT INFINITIVE OF *POSSUM*

In the text at the beginning of the chapter you also see *possum*, another important irregular verb:

> *Druidēs scientiam magnam memoriā servāre possunt.*
>
> The Druids are able to preserve a large body of knowledge by means of memory.

The verb *possum* means "I can" or "I am able." Notice that in this sentence *possum* is joined with the infinitive of another verb (*servāre*): in a moment, you will take a closer look at this tendency of *possum* to join up with an infinitive.

Julius Caesar's head along with his name in Latin letters on a modern postage stamp from Italy.

Here are the forms of the present indicative of *possum* and its infinitive:

Present Tense of *possum*

		Singular			Plural
First person	possum	I can, am able		possumus	we can, are able
Second person	potes	you can, are able		potestis	you can, are able
Third person	potest	s/he/it can, is able		possunt	they can, are able

Present Infinitive of *possum*

posse   to be able

STUDY TIP

The forms of the verb *possum* are nothing more than the root *pot-* (meaning "power-ful") with the forms of *sum* added to it, with **t** changing to **s** before another **s**.

▶ EXERCISE 3

Fill in the blanks with the correct form of *possum*. The subjects are indicated in parentheses. Translate the sentences. The Reading Vocabulary may be consulted.

Example: (Ego) iūdicāre nōn _____.
(Ego) iūdicāre nōn possum.   I cannot judge.

1. (Nōs/we) Puerōs docēre _____
2. (Tū) Scientiam magnam habēre _____
3. (Ego) Memoriam firmāı _____
4. (Illī/they) Sacra Gallōrum cūrāre nōn _____
5. (Ille/he) Druidēs (accusative) amāre nōı _____
6. (Tū) Druidēs timēre _____

▶ EXERCISE 4

Translate into English.

1. Nōn dēbētis tenebrās timēre

2. Memoriam firmāre et servāre possum

3. Litterās in librīs servāre solēmus.

4. Virī bonī bona exempla dare possunt.

5. Semper cōgitāre dēbētis.

6. Virī armātī patriam cūrāre dēbent.

7. Fābulās longās nārrāre soleō.

8. Vīta nōn sōlum lacrimās, sed etiam gaudia dare solet.

9. Rōmam vidēre dēbēs.

LANGUAGE FACT III

COMPLEMENTARY INFINITIVE WITH *POSSUM, DĒBEŌ, SOLEŌ*

Some Latin verbs, such as *possum*, do not usually appear by themselves.

The most common of these verbs are:

> *possum* – "I am able" (to do something)
> *dēbeō* – "I ought" (to do something)
> *soleō* – "I am accustomed" (to do something)

Such verbs often form phrases with a *complementary* infinitive that "fills out" their meaning.

There are clear examples of such phrases in the passage at the front of this chapter:

> *Druidēs . . . dē virīs bonīs et malīs iūdicāre solent.*
> The Druids are accustomed to make judgment about good and bad men.

> *Druidēs scientiam magnam memoriā servāre possunt.*
> The Druids are able to preserve a large body of knowledge by means of memory.

BY THE WAY

Verbs (like *possum*, *dēbeō*, and *soleō*) that take a complementary infinitive can appear with either an active or passive infinitive.

For example: *Puella puerō librum dare potest*, "The girl can give the book to the boy," in the passive voice becomes *Liber puerō ā puellā darī potest*, "The book can be given to the boy by the girl."

► EXERCISE 5

Translate into Latin.

1. We are accustomed to preserve (our) books.

2. You (plural) ought not to fear the Druids (*Druidēs*).

3. Memory can be strengthened.

4. Stories are usually (are accustomed to be) told by the Druids (*Druidibus*).

5. We can have the rewards: rewards can be given by the Druids.

6. Boys ought to be taught.

LANGUAGE FACT IV

TRANSITIVE AND INTRANSITIVE VERBS

The verbs *sum* and *possum* have no passive forms because they are *intransitive*.

An intransitive verb describes a state of being or an action that takes no direct object (coming, going, and the like). Here are some other intransitive verbs, in addition to those you have already learned: *ambulō* ("walk"), *iaceō* ("lie down"), and *maneō* ("remain").

A *transitive* verb, by contrast, is a verb that takes a direct object and so can be used in the passive voice. Such verbs include: *dō* ("give"), *habeō* ("have"), *videō* ("see").

Julius Caesar writing his commentaries on the Gallic War (*Dē bellō Gallicō*) and on the Civil War (*Dē bellō cīvīlī*).

▶ EXERCISE 6

Identify the transitive and intransitive verbs in the following sentences and translate into English.

1. Epistulam puellae teneō.
2. In familiā sunt memoriae pulchrae.
3. Virī magnī saepe in vinculīs iacent.
4. Auxilium ā bonīs virīs datur.
5. Fīliam et fīlium valdē amō.
6. Amīcus in memoriā semper manet.

▶ EXERCISE 7

Change the following sentences into the passive if the verb is active, and into the active if the verb is passive. Translate the changed sentence.

Example: Puer ā puellā exspectātur.
Puella puerum exspectat.   The girl expects the boy.

1. Auxilium ā bonīs amīcīs datur.
2. Puella fābulam nārrat.
3. Familia ā puerīs amātur.
4. Poētae litterās iūdicant.
5. Mala cōnsilia ā Rōmānīs nōn parantur.

▶ EXERCISE 8

Read and understand the following sentences, then label each one as *vērum* (true), or *falsum* (false). The Reading Vocabulary may be consulted.

1. Inter Gallōs sacra ā Druidibus cūrantur.
2. Druidēs vītam Gallōrum cūrant.
3. Puerī Gallōrum nōn diū cum Druidibus manēre solent.
4. Druidēs sacra Gallōrum librīs et litterīs servāre solent.
5. Puerī ā Druidibus docentur.
6. Gallī memoriam firmāre possunt et dēbent.

The women of Gaul during Caesar's invasion of their country. August Barthelemy Glaize (1807–1893).

TALKING

probātiō, f. – exam

exāmen, n. – exam

probātiuncula, probātiunculae, f. – quiz

Tollite calamōs. "Take up your pens."

In chartā vacuā scrībite. "Write on an empty piece of paper."

In chartā versā. "On the back of the paper."

In chartā rēctā. "On the front of the paper."

Probātiōnem subībis, subībitis "You/you (plural) will take an exam."

Notam optimam accipiēs. "You will get an excellent grade."

Nōlim in probātiōne cadere! "I don't want to fail the exam!"

PREPARING FOR A TEST

Magistra: Probātiunculam hodiē (*today*) subībitis.

Christīna: Cūr (*why*) probātiunculam hodiē subīre (*to take*) dēbēmus?

Magistra: Quia (*because*) scientiam (*knowledge*) memoriā servāre dēbētis. Nōnne litterās Latīnās (*Latin*) amās? (Nōnne amās? – *Don't you love?*)

Christīna: Litterās Latīnās amō.

Magistra: Itaque locum Caesaris (*passage of Caesar*) discere (*to learn*) dēbēs.

Christīna: In illō (*that*) locō Caesaris sunt multa verba (*words*) nova (*new*). Druidēs nōn sumus. Gallī nōn sumus. Scientiam magnam et multa verba memoriā servāre nōn solēmus.

Magistra: Locum Caesaris iam (*already*) memoriā tenēs! Es discipula (*student*) bona! Estisne (*are you . . . ?*), discipulī, nunc parātī (*prepared*)?

Discipulī: Parātī sumus.

Magistra: Tollite calamōs. In chartīs vacuīs scrībite. In chartā versā nōmina vestra (*your names*) scrībite.

DERIVATIVES

exemplum – example, exemplary, exemplify, exemption, sample

liber – libel, libretto, library, librarian

littera – alliteration, illiteracy, illiterate, letter, literacy, literal, literature, obliterate

memoria – memorial, memory, memoir, memorable, remember, commemorate, immemorial

tenebrae – tenebrous, tenebrific

vīta – vital, vitality, vitamin, victual(s)

multus – multiple, multiplier, multiplication, multitude, multitudinous

doceō – docile, doctorate, doctrine, document, doctor, documentary

firmō – affirm, confirm, farm, farmer, firm, firmament, infirm, infirmary, infirmity

iaceō – adjacent, gist, joist

iūdicō – judge, judgment, judicial, judicious, prejudice

maneō – manor, manorial, manse, mansion, menagerie, menial, permanence, permanent, remain, remnant

possum – possible, possibility, puissance, impossible

servō – conservation, conservative, conservatory, observe, preservation, reservation, reserve, reservoir

soleō – insolence, insolent, obsolete, obsolescent

sum – entity, omnipresent, presentation, present, represent. See also p. 28.

REVIEW 2: CHAPTERS 4–6

VOCABULARY TO KNOW

NOUNS

auxilium, auxiliī, *n.* – help

bellum, bellī, *n.* – war

castra, castrōrum, *n. pl.* – camp

cōnsilium, cōnsiliī, *n.* – plan, advice

dolus, dolī, *m.* – trickery, deception

epistula, epistulae, *f.* – letter

exemplum, exemplī, *n.* – example

familia, familiae, *f.* – family, household

gaudium, gaudiī, *n.* – joy

lacrima, lacrimae, *f.* – tear

liber, librī, *m.* – book

littera, litterae, *f.* – letter of the alphabet; *pl.* literature, letter (epistle)

memoria, memoriae, *f.* – memory

praemium, praemiī, *n.* – reward

tenebrae, tenebrārum, *f. pl.* – shadows, darkness

venēnum, venēnī, *n.* – poison

vinculum, vinculī, *n.* – chain, fetter

vīta, vītae, *f.* – life

ADJECTIVES

armātus, armāta, armātum – armed

bonus, bona, bonum – good

iūstus, iūsta, iūstum – legitimate, open, just

longus, longa, longum – long

magnus, magna, magnum – large, great, important

malus, mala, malum – bad

miser, misera, miserum – wretched, sad, miserable

multus, multa, multum – much, many

praeclārus, praeclāra, praeclārum – famous, distinguished

pulcher, pulchra, pulchrum – beautiful, nice

Rōmānus, Rōmāna, Rōmānum – Roman

VERBS

cōgitō, cōgitāre, cōgitāvī, cōgitātum – to think

dō, dāre, dedī, dātum – to give

doceō, docēre, docuī, doctum – to teach

doleō, dolēre, doluī, —— – to feel pain, to be hurt

firmō, firmāre, firmāvī, firmātum – to strengthen

iaceō, iacēre, iacuī, —— – to lie down, to be inert

intrō, intrāre, intrāvī, —— – to enter

iubeō, iubēre, iussī, iussum + *accusative* + *infinitive* – to order somebody to do something

iūdicō, iūdicāre, iūdicāvī, iūdicātum – to judge

maneō, manēre, mānsī, mānsum – to remain

parō – to design (*you already know the meanings "to prepare, to get ready"*)

possum, posse, potuī, —— – to be able, can

servō, servāre, servāvī, servātum – to save, to preserve

soleō, solēre, solitus sum + *infinitive* – to be accustomed

sum, esse, fuī, —— – to be

ADVERBS

longē – far

saepe – often

semper – always

PREPOSITIONS

ā (ab) + *ablative* – by, from, away from

ad + *accusative* – into, toward, to

dē + *ablative* – about, concerning, down from

ē (ex) + *ablative* – from, out of

in + *accusative* – into, to, against

propter + *accusative* – because of, on account of

CONJUNCTIONS

autem – however

dum – while

nam – for, in fact

nōn sōlum . . . , sed etiam . . . – not only . . . , but also . . .

sed – but

tamen – however

▶ EXERCISE 1

Decline the following nouns.

1. *exemplum, exemplī,* n. – example

2. *gaudium, gaudiī,* n. – joy

▶ EXERCISE 2

Conjugate the following verbs in the passive voice. Give the Latin passive infinitive with its meaning for each verb.

1. *servō, servāre, servāvī, servātum*

2. *firmō, firmāre, firmāvī, firmātum*

3. *doceō, docēre, docuī, doctum*

4. *habeō, habēre, habuī, habitum*

▶ EXERCISE 3

Fill in the blanks with the correct form of the adjectives in parentheses and translate each sentence.

Example: Virōs _____ vidēre possum. (armātus)
Virōs armātōs vidēre possum.   I am able to see armed men.

1. Dē praemiō _____ cōgitāre possumus. (magnus)

2. Familiae _____ auxilium damus. (miser)

3. Praemium virīs _____ datur. (bonus)

4. Dē fīliā _____ semper cōgitō. (pulcher)

5. Virī _____ memoria librīs servātur. (iūstus)

6. Rōmānōrum _____ vīta litterīs servārī potest. (praeclārus)

Weapons and utensils
from the late republican era of
ancient Rome. These are the types of
weapons with which Roman soldiers
of that time would have been armed.

▶ EXERCISE 4

Change the following active sentences into the passive by using the ablative of agent. Translate the changed sentence.

Example: Fābricius virō praemium nōn dat. (Fābricius, Fābriciī, m.)
Virō praemium ā Fābriciō nōn datur.   A reward is not being given to the man by Fabricius.

1. Vir Rōmānus epistulam Terentiae nunc tenet. (Terentia, Terentiae, f.)

2. Fābricius virōs armātōs vocat.

3. Virī malī mala cōnsilia parant.

4. Puerī memoriam firmant.

5. Virī praeclārī patriae auxilium dant.

6. Virī iūstī patriam cūrant.

▶ EXERCISE 5

Translate the verbs in parentheses and change the present tense verb to a complementary infinitive. Translate the changed sentence.

Example: Agrum amīcīs damus. (we can)
Agrum amīcīs dare possumus.   We can give the field to (our) friends.

1. Propter memoriam multa exempla servantur. (they can)

2. Exempla animum firmant. (they are accustomed)

3. Praemium virō nōn datis. (you [plural] ought)

4. Epistulās Terentiae exspectō. (I am accustomed)

5. Poētae praeclārī sumus. (we can)

6. Puerōs docent. (they are accustomed)

▶ EXERCISE 6

After translating this passage, list on paper all the transitive and intransitive verbs.

The following passage is adapted from Cicero's speech *Prō Archiā*. Here Cicero argues that the Greek poet Archias is entitled to Roman citizenship because of his literary merits, extolling the study of literature as well as the special talents of Archias himself.

In librīs sunt exempla multa et bona. Propter litterās bona exempla in tenebrīs nōn iacent. Exempla dantur ā virīs iūstīs quōrum (*whose*) vīta librīs servātur. Dum patriam cūrō, virōs praeclārōs videō, quōrum memoria litterīs tenētur. Propter litterās virī iūstī et bonī et praeclārī in vītā manent et mē vocant. Auxilium et cōnsilia litterīs dantur. Animus litterīs semper firmātur. Litterae nōbīscum (*with us*) domī sunt, sunt nōbīscum in agrīs, manent nōbīscum in viā . . .

Transitive verbs: **Intransitive verbs:**

The remains in the Roman Forum of the Basilica of Maxentius, marked by the three arches seen in the picture. This basilica, built between 308 and 312 CE, served, like most basilicas during ancient Roman times, as a courthouse and meeting hall. Today the word "basilica" usually refers to a church in which the architectural plan is similar to the ones used in ancient basilicas.

CONSIDERING THE CLASSICAL GODS

As you learned in Review 1, Jupiter and Juno were children of Rhea and Cronus, who had four more children: Neptune, Pluto, Vesta, and Ceres. All six of these children are regarded as the generation of older Olympian gods. The three male siblings divided the universe among themselves, with Jupiter taking the heaven, Neptune the ocean, and Pluto the underworld.

The famous Trevi Fountain in Rome with a statue of Neptune in its central niche.

NEPTUNE

Neptune, who was known by the Greeks as Poseidon, was the brother of Zeus, lord of the seas. Neptune also controlled earthquakes on land. He is often represented with his three-pronged trident. Neptune was said to inhabit the ocean with his wife Amphitrite, an Oceanid, one of the daughters of the Ocean himself. The depths of the ocean were reported to house many sea creatures. Among them were nymphs called Nereids and the "old man of the sea," named Proteus, who was able to change his form constantly. According to legend, Neptune, together with the mortal Cleito, sired the royal dynasty of the blessed island Atlantis. Ancient tales about the disappearance of this island, an event that ancient authors connect with the spread of human vice, continue to fascinate contemporary archaeologists who still search for it in various underwater locales.

PLUTO AND THE UNDERWORLD

The Greeks imagined a world of three stories: the plain of the earth, surrounded by the river of the ocean; the vault of heaven, which, on the cloudy peaks of Mt. Olympus, was the abode of the gods; and the gloomy region of the underworld where dead souls dwelt. They also conceptualized a place even deeper than the underworld itself: a black pit beneath it called Tartarus, where the special enemies of the gods were imprisoned.

It was believed by the Greeks that when people died, their souls descended to the underworld. Near its entrance awaited Charon, a greedy old man who transported the souls in a ferry across the river Acheron (or Styx) to the underworld itself. Since Charon required a fee for this ride, it was customary to place a coin under the tongue of a dead person. The soul of a person who could not pay, or who had not received a proper burial, would wander perpetually without rest.

The ruler of the underworld was Hades, or Pluto, the brother of Jupiter and Neptune. Pluto is represented as a stubborn old man, whose hat could make him invisible, just as the approach of

An elaborate fountain with the god Neptune at its center marks the entrance to Neptune Park at Santa Lucia Hill in Santiago, Chile.

death itself is often invisible. Pluto was thought to reign in the kingdom of the shadows with his wife Proserpina, called Persephone in Greek.

While the souls of most humans, both good and evil, dwelt more or less in the same part of the underworld and endured a similar shadowy existence, a few notorious wrongdoers were doomed to an eternity of punishment. Among them was Tantalus, condemned to stand in a pool of water, with luscious fruits hanging over his head. Whenever he wanted to eat or

Charon rowing his skiff across the river Acheron (or Styx) in the underworld.

drink, the tree with the fruits moved its branches upward, and the water in the pool receded, thereby "tantalizing" him with perpetual thirst and hunger. Similarly, Sisyphus was condemned to roll a boulder to the top of a mountain, only to see it roll back every time he pushed it to the peak. The crimes of these unfortunate individuals involved challenging the power of the gods and attempting to exceed human limitations.

VESTA

In ancient Roman culture, Vesta was the goddess of the hearth and the household, identified with the Greek goddess Hestia. Yet Hestia was a minor deity in the Greek pantheon and had no place among the Olympian gods. By way of contrast, Vesta and her cult were extremely important in Roman society, for she was regarded as embodying the sanctity of family and home. Vesta had a round temple in the heart of Rome, one of the earliest Roman buildings to survive intact.

The Vestal Virgins lived in a large imposing house in the Roman Forum itself. The pool in the photograph is part of the peristylium complex of their house. Just beyond the house the three columns in a row are remnants of the Temple of Castor and Pollux while the white building to the right is the reconstructed Temple of Vesta.

Her temple contained a sacred flame, symbolic of the hearth, which was carefully tended so it would never be extinguished. A group of priestesses known as Vestal Virgins were in charge of the flame and temple. Girls of good character having both parents living qualified as candidates to enter the service of Vesta. They were chosen by the Pontifex Maximus (highest priest) at no later than the age of ten, and had to swear that they would remain virgins for the next thirty years. Anyone who let the sacred fire go out was beaten, and a violation of the vow of chastity was punished by being buried alive. The Vestals were highly respected, given many privileges, and were very influential when intervening on someone's behalf.

CERES

Ceres is the Latin name given to the Greek Olympian goddess Demeter, and she was thought to be a sister of Jupiter and Juno. The English word "cereal" is derived from her name, and a stalk of grain was her symbol. She was a goddess of vegetation, of the earth's creative power, and of agriculture. She is also depicted as suffering painfully over her separation from her daughter, Proserpina. Ancient authors relate that Pluto, the ruler of the underworld, abducted Proserpina when she was picking flowers with other young girls in Sicily, and made her his wife and queen over the dead. For many days Ceres wandered the earth, searching for her daughter in vain, and consumed by deep grief. Finally, the Sun God, who had witnessed Proserpina's abduction, pitied Ceres and told her where her daughter had been taken. Although it was too late for Ceres to get Proserpina

back, for she had eaten some pomegranate seeds in the underworld, a compromise was arranged whereby Proserpina would spend part of each year with her mother, and part with her husband. According to classical mythology, Proserpina's return to her mother brings spring and the rebirth of vegetation, but autumn and the death of the earth's greenery results when she descends back to Hades. In this way the ancients used the myth of Ceres and Proserpina to explain the origin of the seasons.

Greece, ever proud of its ancient heritage, issued a stamp to celebrate the 5th Symposium of the European Conference of Transport Ministers that met in Athens in 1973. The stamp shows Triptolemus riding a chariot and holding a sheaf of wheat.

READ THE FOLLOWING PASSAGE

Cerēs in terrīs ambulat. Cerēs Proserpinam fīliam vidēre nōn potest et Proserpinam quaerit. Proserpina tamen ā Plutōne in tenebrīs tenētur. Animus deae valdē dolet. Dea terram cūrāre nōn potest et terra est misera.

Tum Iuppiter iubet: "Proserpina per sex mēnsēs in terrā manēre dēbet et per sex mēnsēs in tenebrīs."

Cerēs terram per sex mēnsēs cūrat et terra est pulchra. Dum autem filia est cum Plutōne, terra ā deā nōn cūrātur.

Cerēs, *f.* – Ceres
dea, deae, *f.* – goddess
per sex mēnsēs – for six months
Plutōne (*ablative*) – Pluto

Proserpina, Proserpinae, *f.* – Proserpina
quaerit – seeks
tum (*adv.*) – then

ROMAN MARRIAGE

In Chapter 5 you read correspondence between members of a Roman family in the form of a letter from Cicero to his wife Terentia. The Latin word *familia*, from which we derive "family," encompassed not only what we call the nuclear family, headed by the father, or *paterfamiliās* (*familiās* is an archaic form of *familiae*), but also the slaves that they owned. In the privileged households that Roman sources most often describe marriages were arranged for Roman girls in their early teens to young men in their early twenties. When a *paterfamiliās* promised his daughter to a bridegroom, she was said to have become *spōnsa*, "engaged," from the verb *spondeō*, "to promise solemnly." A man who became engaged (*spōnsus*) sent his betrothed a ring, which—like all Roman rings—was worn on the finger next to the little finger of the left hand.

A bride gets ready for her wedding in this fresco from the Villa of the Mysteries in Pompeii, first century CE.

Setting a date for the wedding had its complications, since the ceremonies could not take place during the many Roman festivals, or in the month of May (which was said to bring bad luck). The traditional and most strict form of a Roman marriage was called the *cōnfārreātiō*, which included a ritual consecrating of a special bread—*fār* is a kind of grain—to Jupiter. This most solemn event took place in the presence of the Pontifex Maximus and ten witnesses. Another ritual was called *coēmptiō*, i.e., "buying," which probably reflected the financial arrangements entailed in funding a marriage. *Coēmptiō* was one method by which a Roman wife came under the legal control of her husband, which the Romans called *manus*, "hand." Another was through the process of *ūsus*, in which the wife remained married to her husband for a continuous year.

Various Latin literary works portray the members of a Roman wedding party carrying torches and shouting obscene verses, which were supposed to promote fertility. The bride wore a long white robe and a bright saffron veil. A hair-net and shoes were of the same color. Her hair was fashioned like that of the

Vestal Virgins with three curls hanging down on each side of the face. The Roman historian Livy (*Ab Urbe Conditā* 1.9) explains the practice of shouting "Talassiō" in his account of how the earliest Romans acquired brides by inviting the neighboring Sabines to a festival, and then abducting their daughters. According to his narrative, one of the Romans abandoned his efforts to seize a particular woman when he heard this phrase: it means "she is reserved for Talassius," the name of another, presumably wealthier and more powerful, man.

After the wedding, once the groom carried the bride over the threshold, under one form of Roman marriage she passed from her father's into her husband's control; the technical expression for this form of marriage was *cum manū, manus* being the Latin term for "hand" or "control." Married Roman women were called *mātrōnae*, which means "women entitled to be mothers of legitimate children." Compared to women in Greek society, particularly those in fifth-century BCE Athens, Roman women had a good deal of autonomy in social and economic matters.

The rape of the Sabine women in a painting attributed to the Dutch painter Theodoor van Thulden (1606–1669).

Connecting with the Ancient World • 105

EXPLORING ROMAN FAMILIES

PARENTS AND CHILDREN THEN AND NOW

In the modern world, there are many laws that protect children from neglect and compel parents to look after their offspring. Fathers and mothers must provide financial support and cannot just abandon babies on the steps of a church or in an alleyway. Parenthood is easy to prove with documents like birth certificates and DNA evidence. But in the ancient world, children were not kept from harm by the state; indeed, they were entirely at the mercy of their fathers, who could choose whether or not to raise them and who could retain complete control over their children, even in adulthood.

When a Roman child was born in the parents' house, the baby was laid at the feet of the father, who would show his acceptance of the child as his own by picking the infant up. If he chose to reject the child, he had no further responsibility; the child might have been fortunate enough to have been raised by the slaves in the household or unlucky enough to be left to die on a wooded hillside outside of the city. There were no formal accommodations, like orphanages or adoptive homes, for unwanted babies, although surely sometimes arrangements must have been made with childless couples. While today citizenship is automatically granted to all people born in the United States, only children born to Roman citizen parents, both father and mother, and accepted by their fathers were Roman citizens from birth.

This funerary bust from Palmyra, Syria, features a husband holding a scroll, and his wife with a spindle and distaff in her hands. The inscription is in Greek.

Much time and effort is spent today deciding on names for babies. Books and websites are dedicated to the possibilities, and every relative and friend has a suggestion to offer. But a Roman baby had no name at first and was called *pūpa* or *pūpus*, girl or boy baby, until the eighth or ninth day after birth (eight for girls; nine for boys). Many babies did not live to see their naming day; in fact, without the type of healthcare the modern world has developed with vaccinations and antibiotics, more than thirty percent of Roman babies died before they were a year old, and children had only a fifty percent chance of living to the age of ten. But if the child did survive to see the *diēs lustricus*, the family gathered to bestow its name and to give the baby *crepundia*, little metal trinkets strung as a necklace that the child would wear around the neck and whose rattling would amuse the infant and might even serve as identification if the child should become lost. No fingerprints or GPS sneakers for the Romans! On this day a child also began to wear a *bulla* (which means "bubble" in Latin), a round locket that contained an amulet to protect the child from evil spirits. If the family was wealthy, the *bulla* would be made of gold, and it clearly marked the child of an important father, and so someone not to be harmed without penalty. Children of the lower classes wore *bullae* made of leather. A boy was also protected by the *genius* (guardian spirit) of the *gēns* (clan), a part of which was born with him and stayed with him for life; in fact, his birthday would be celebrated as a festival of his *genius* to whom offerings of food and drink and flowers would be made to insure his continued presence. A similar spirit called a *Iūnō* watched over a girl.

The firstborn boy of an upper class family would have been given the same three names as his father—a *praenōmen*, the clan name (or *nōmen*) and a *cognōmen*, but all girls were named the feminine form of their clan name—Iūlia, Cornelia, Claudia. Following this tradition, Mārcus Tullius Cicero named his daughter Tullia and his son Mārcus Tullius Cicero. Formal distinctions were made between daughters with the use of *maior* and *minor* for·two girls and *prīma*, *secunda*, *tertia*, etc. for more than two; day-to-day confusion must have been avoided by the use of nicknames for the girls and for the son who shared the name of the *paterfamiliās*, just as today a boy named for his father might be called Junior or Buddy.

While Roman parents did have ultimate responsibility for a child's welfare, in a wealthy family daily care was seen to by the child's *nūtrix*, or nurse, who often knew the child better than its parents and was considered a part of the *familia*, much like a nanny might be today. Indeed, the word *familia* in Latin indicates many more people than a modern American family, which generally includes only parents and children, although sometimes grandparents or other blood relatives may live in the same house and share in caring for the children. But a Roman *familia* also consisted of the household slaves, both adults and children owned by the *paterfamiliās*, and perhaps even some of his freedmen.

Young children spent their time at home, learning to read and write along with the other children of the household, both slave and free, and playing with toys, dolls, balls, hoops, dice, and gaming boards or pet dogs, birds, or even monkeys. Cats as pets were late arrivals in Rome (first century CE), following the conquest of Egypt, where they were revered. Roman mothers oversaw this early training, particularly moral instruction, and they made sure that their children were not exposed to any evils that might corrupt their characters.

Sculpture of the head of a young Roman boy.

When boys were seven years old, it was time for more formal education. Unlike modern times when many countries offer education for all children at no charge, Roman schooling was available only to those who could afford to pay the fees, in the same way that parents must now pay tuition if they wish to send their children to private schools. Only boys went to school, but since at seven a boy was too young to go off into the world alone, his parents assigned him a *paedagōgus* (from the Greek word παιδαγωγός meaning "child-guider") who would take him to and from school and oversee his studies. Even though the *paedagōgus* was a slave, he could punish his charge for failing to pay attention! Once a boy had honed his skills in reading, writing, and arithmetic—the same subjects taught today in elementary schools—he began to study history, philosophy, literature, and rhetoric, all things he would need to know to have a successful political career. Science and mathematics were not part of a Roman education, since these subjects were used only by workmen doing physical labor—constructing buildings, ships, roads, etc.—none of which was considered a suitable career for a well-to-do Roman man. When not in school, a Roman boy spent time with his father, watching how he conducted business and dealt with his clients.

This plaster cast preserves the first century CE body of a young man who had worked as a muleteer. Tradition holds that he was found near an entrance gate to Pompeii. The plaster cast of his crouching figure was moved to a building along the forum which protects a variety of finds like the amphorae that surround him.

While educational and career opportunities for women in the United States are virtually the same as those for men, there are many countries even today in which such equality is far from reality. Roman girls had few educational opportunities since they were required to remain at home and learn household management from their mothers—weaving and overseeing the work of the family's slaves. In much the same way, children of the lower classes were trained in whatever trade their parents practiced—as farmers or bakers or fish sellers—and probably began working at the family business as soon as they were physically able to do so. Indeed, all Roman children, wealthy or poor, followed the same life path as their parents, much as in modern times when children are often groomed to work in and eventually take over family businesses.

Childhood for girls often ended rather quickly, since they could marry as early as twelve years of age, although they were more likely to be fourteen or fifteen. A *paterfamiliās* chose his son-in-law, based on the economic or political advantage a union between his household and that of the groom might bring him. On her wedding day, a girl removed her *bulla* and dedicated it along with her toys, the symbols of childhood, to the *Larēs*, the household gods, and left her parents' house to become part of her husband's household (although during the empire, it was not unusual for a woman to remain a part of her father's *familia*, despite her marriage).

Another type of ceremony marked a boy's coming of age: his assumption of the *toga virīlis*. While it could come as early as the age of fourteen, most boys did not make the transition until the age of sixteen. In the morning on the appointed day, just as his married sister had done, a boy placed his *bulla* at the altar of the *Larēs* along with his *toga praetexta* (a bordered toga that marked him as a freeborn male child) and then assumed the white toga of a Roman citizen. A procession composed of family friends, clients, slaves, freedmen, and relatives then accompanied him to the Forum where his name was entered on the role of citizens, much like registering to vote today at the age of eighteen. Today, coming of age means financial and legal independence, but despite his new position as a fully recognized Roman man, a man's father continued to hold formal control over his son's life and finances (if he chose to exercise it) until the day he died, when his son finally assumed the role of *paterfamiliās* of his own household.

Jacqueline Carlon
Associate Professor of Classics
University of Massachusetts
Boston, Massachusetts

MĪRĀBILE AUDĪTŪ

PHRASES, MOTTOES, AND ABBREVIATIONS RELATING TO LIFE IN THE TWENTY-FIRST CENTURY

PHRASES

- Annuit coeptīs. "He has nodded favorably on our beginnings." Taken from Vergil's *Georgics*, this inscription is found on the one dollar bill.

- Caveat ēmptor. "Let (may) the buyer beware!" A common warning in commerce.

- Dē factō. "In practice."

- In vitrō. "In a glass."

- Quid prō quō? "What for what?" A favor for a favor, "tit for tat."

- Sine quā nōn. A shorter phrase expressing the concept of *condiciō sine quā nōn*, "a necessary condition," and literally meaning "without which not."

- Status quō. "The condition in which <things are now>."

- Tempus fugit. "Time flees." An inscription often found on clocks.

- Urbī et Orbī. "To the City <of Rome> and to the World." The title of the Pope's address to the world on Easter and Christmas.

- Vice versā. "Conversely," "the opposite."

MOTTOES

- Semper parātus. "Always ready." Motto of the US Coast Guard.

Notice on the one dollar bill the Great Seal of the United States, which contains on top of the eye above the pyramid the Latin phrase *Annuit Coeptīs* and below the pyramid another set of Latin words, *Novus Ordō Saeclōrum*, or "A New Order of Ages."

Written on a blackboard, this Latin phrase that means "Let the buyer beware" should be heeded by all who are about to purchase something.

ABBREVIATIONS

- @ The symbol @, which is used in e-mail addresses, comes from the Latin medieval abbreviation of *apud*, "at," "at the home of."

- etc. An abbreviation for *et cētera*, "and other things."

- P.S. An abbreviation for *post scrīptum*, "written afterward or below," an item added below the signature to a letter.

This symbol, once used only occasionally in financial matters, is now commonplace and seen in e-mail addresses regularly.

CHAPTER 7

Third Declension Masculine and Feminine Nouns; Indirect Statement: Accusative and Infinitive

Sir Lawrence Alma-Tadema (1836–1912) is renowned for painting classical subjects. He painted the oil *Catullus Reading his Poems at Lesbia's House* in 1870.

MEMORĀBILE DICTŪ

Ōdī et amō.

"I hate and I love." (Catullus 85)

The Roman poet Catullus wrote these contradictory words in line one of poem 85 to express his conflicted and painful feelings about his beloved.

READING

Gāius Valerius Catullus (who lived from approximately 84 to 54 BCE) is one of the greatest Latin poets, and the best known among the neoteric, or "new" poets of the first century BCE. They modeled their works and literary personalities on those of Greek writers from the Hellenistic era (third and second centuries BCE). Among them is Callimachus, best remembered for the phrase *Mega biblion, mega kakon,* "a big book is a big evil."

Catullus also places a distinctive stamp on what he writes by giving voice to his own emotions, frankly and often bawdily. Many of his poems treat his passionate and often painful love affair with a woman whom he calls "Lesbia," in homage to the literary achievements and sensibilities of the sixth century BCE Greek female poet Sappho. The name "Lesbia" is evidently a metrically equivalent pseudonym for Clodia, a Roman matron from a politically powerful family.

Several historical figures from the turbulent period in which he lived—Caesar and Cicero among them—figure in Catullus's poems, both those in lyric meters and those in the elegiac couplet.

His elegies greatly influenced the love poetry of Propertius, Tibullus, and Ovid, who wrote during the principate of Augustus (27 BCE–14 CE), and whose work in turn had a major impact on the romantic poetry of the Middle Ages. Like Catullus, they characterize erotic passion as a form of enslavement, referring to the female beloved with the term *domina,* meaning "mistress of slaves." So, too, they emphasize the obstacles to the fulfillment of their desires, ranging from jealous husbands and rivals to locked doors and other forms of physical separation.

DĒ AMŌRE

1   Puella mea passerem habet. Ō, passer, dēliciae meae puellae! Cum
     passere puella mea lūdit, passerem tenet, passerī digitum dat, digitus
     ā passere mordētur. Puella nārrat sē passerem amāre. Puella passerem
     plūs quam oculōs amat. Nam passer est mellītus. Catullus videt
5   passerem esse semper in gremiō puellae. Passer ad dominam semper
     pīpiat. Catullus tamen vult cum puellā esse et ā puellā amārī. Itaque
     Catullus passerī invidet. Tū, puella, Catullum amāre dēbēs, nōn
     passerem. Senēs autem sevērī putant puellam Catullum amāre nōn
     dēbēre. Verba senum, puella, ūnīus assis aestimāre possumus. Nam vīta
10   nōn est longa.

READING VOCABULARY

ā passere (*ablative singular*) – by the sparrow

*aestimō, aestimāre, aestimāvī, aestimātum – to regard, esteem

*aestimō ūnīus assis – I do not care a bit (as, assis, *m. is the Latin word for a small copper coin*)

*amor, amōris, *m.* – love

Catullus, Catullī, *m.* – Catullus

*dēliciae, dēliciārum, *f. pl.* – delight, pet

*digitus, digitī, *m.* – finger

*domina, dominae, *f.* – mistress

*gremium, gremiī, *n.* – lap

*invideō, invidēre, invīdī, invīsum + *dative* – to envy someone

lūdit – plays

mellītus, mellīta, mellītum – sweet as honey

*meus, mea, meum – my

mordeō, mordēre, momordī, morsum – to bite

nārrat sē passerem amāre – tells that she loves the sparrow

ō (*interjection*) – oh!

*oculus, oculī, *m.* – eye

*passer, passeris, *m.* – sparrow

passerī (*dative singular*) – to the sparrow

pīpiō, pīpiāre, ——, —— – to chirp

plūs quam – more than

putant puellam . . . dēbēre – think that the girl should . . .

*putō, putāre, putāvī, putātum – to think, consider

*sē (*reflexive pronoun, accusative*) – she/he (*in an indirect statement*)

senēs (*nominative plural*) – old men

*senex, senis, *m.* – old man

senum (*genitive plural*) – of the old men

*sevērus, sevēra, sevērum – serious, strict, severe

*verbum, verbī, *n.* – word

videt passerem esse – sees that the sparrow is

vult – wants

*Words marked with an asterisk will be need to be memorized.

COMPREHENSION QUESTIONS

1. How does the poet feel about the girl's pet bird? Why?

2. Who is in the way of the poet's and the girl's love?

3. What is the poet's reason for his impatience to enjoy love?

LANGUAGE FACT I

THIRD DECLENSION MASCULINE AND FEMININE NOUNS

You have already learned the ending patterns of nouns belonging to the first and second declensions. In the reading passage for this chapter, you saw nouns belonging to the third declension. Their forms are new and distinctive: for example, *amōre*, *passerem*, *senum*.

For a noun of the third declension **there is no difference in the case endings between masculine and feminine nouns**. Therefore, the gender of each new noun of this type must be learned along with its meaning.

Third Declension Masculine and Feminine Nouns				
	Singular		**Plural**	
Nominative	passer	the sparrow	passer**ēs**	the sparrows
Genitive	passer**is**	of the sparrow	passer**um**	of the sparrows
Dative	passer**ī**	to/for the sparrow	passer**ibus**	to/for the sparrows
Accusative	passer**em**	the sparrow	passer**ēs**	the sparrows
Ablative	passer**e**	by/with the sparrow	passer**ibus**	by/with the sparrows
Vocative	passer	o, sparrow	passer**ēs**	o, sparrows

STUDY TIP

The nominative singular form of third declension nouns follows no regular pattern, but the stem is easy to find: look at the genitive singular form and remove the ending *-is*. For this reason the genitive singular and the nominative singular should always be learned together.

▶ EXERCISE 1

Find all the third declension nouns in the Latin reading passage. Identify the case and number of each form. If the same noun occurs more than once, write it only once.

VOCABULARY TO LEARN

NOUNS

amor, amōris, *m.* – love

dēliciae, dēliciārum, *f. pl.* – delight, pet

digitus, digitī, *m.* – finger

domina, dominae, *f.* – mistress

gremium, gremiī, *n.* – lap

oculus, oculī, *m.* – eye

passer, passeris, *m.* – sparrow

senex, senis, *m.* – old man

soror, sorōris, *f.* – sister

verbum, verbī, *n.* – word

PRONOUN

sē (*reflexive pronoun, accusative*) – s/he (her/himself)/ they (themselves) *in an indirect statement*

ADJECTIVES

meus, mea, meum – my (*a possessive adjective*)

sevērus, sevēra, sevērum – serious, strict, severe

VERBS

aestimō, aestimāre, aestimāvī, aestimātum – to regard, esteem

aestimō ūnīus assis – I do not care a bit

invideō, invidēre, invīdī, invīsum + *dative* – to envy someone

putō, putāre, putāvī, putātum – to think, consider

A coin called an *as* was among those that held the least value for Romans. Nero's head is on one side of this coin.

▶ EXERCISE 2

Find the English derivatives based on the Vocabulary to Learn in the following sentences. Write the corresponding Latin word.

1. The whole dinner was delicious.

2. Throughout my college years, I was always a member of the same sorority.

3. Senior citizens can purchase tickets at a discount price.

4. The story is about an amorous relationship.

5. We are equipped with digital technology.

6. Can I have an estimate for this repair?

7. This is the dominion of a dark power.

8. We have a verbal agreement.

9. Don't be so severe with me!

10. I bought myself a new computer.

▶ EXERCISE 3

Decline the following noun.

1. *soror, sorōris*, f. – sister

▶ EXERCISE 4

Translate into Latin.

1. I have beautiful sisters.
2. Many are the tears of love.
3. We do not fear peace.
4. The girl is being taken care of by the sister.
5. The poet envies the sparrow.
6. The old men envy the poet.
7. The poet tells the old men a story.

STUDY TIP

Note that the rules of agreement for nouns and adjectives apply to any noun, regardless of declension: any adjective modifying a noun of the third declension will agree with the noun in case, number, and gender.

▶ EXERCISE 5

Make the adjective agree with the noun and translate the phrase into English.

1. praemium (magnus)
2. sorōribus (pulcher)
3. amōrī (miser)
4. senis (armātus)
5. lacrimās (multus)
6. senum (sevērus)
7. passerēs (miser)
8. senex (iūstus)

LANGUAGE FACT II

INDIRECT STATEMENT: ACCUSATIVE AND INFINITIVE

In the chapter reading you notice some sentences with a new construction.

> *Catullus videt passerem esse semper in gremiō puellae.*
> Catullus sees that the sparrow is always on the girl's lap.

In Latin, **verbs of saying** (e.g., *nārrō* "I report [that] . . ."), **thinking** (e.g., *putō* "I think [that] . . ."), and **observing** (e.g., *videō* "I see [that] . . .") appear with a construction called an **indirect statement**. While a *direct* statement is an exact quotation of someone's perceptions, thoughts, or words, an *indirect* statement indirectly reports these thoughts or words. In English, the conjunction "that" commonly follows such verbs. Classical Latin, however, has no conjunction equivalent to "that." Instead, the subject of the indirect statement becomes the **accusative** (not nominative), and the verb of the indirect statement becomes an **infinitive**.

Look more closely at the previous example. The direct statement would be:

> *Passer est semper in gremiō puellae.*
> The sparrow is always on the girl's lap.

After the main verb *videt* (a verb of observing) introduces the statement indirectly, the nominative subject of the direct statement (*passer*) becomes the accusative subject of the indirect statement (*passerem*), and the verb *est* becomes the infinitive *esse*.

> *Catullus videt passerem esse semper in gremiō puellae.*
> Catullus sees that the sparrow is always on the girl's lap.

If the **subject of the infinitive** is also the **subject of the main verb**, then the accusative *sē* (called a reflexive pronoun because it refers back to the subject) is used as the subject in the indirect statement. For a good example of this, look at another sentence from the chapter reading:

> *Puella nārrat sē passerem amāre.*
> The girl reports that she (herself) loves the sparrow.

The direct statement would be:

> *Passerem amō.*
> I love the sparrow.

In this sentence, the first person subject of the direct statement becomes third person (just as in English) and is expressed as accusative *sē*, which is translated "s/he/they (herself/himself/themselves)." The verb of the direct statement then becomes an infinitive.

If there is a **predicate nominative** in the direct statement, this predicate becomes **accusative** too, in agreement with the subject of the indirect statement. Look at this sentence:

The dove was a bird sacred to Venus, goddess of love. A mosaic from Pompeii.

> *Puella putat passerem esse mellītum.*
> The girl thinks that the sparrow is sweet as honey.

The direct statement would be:

> *Passer est mellītus.*

The predicate nominative *mellītus* becomes accusative *mellītum* in the indirect statement.

BY THE WAY

In a direct statement, the subject of a verb is often expressed in Latin by the verb ending alone (e.g., *damus* for "we give"). But in an indirect statement the accusative subject (e.g., *sē*) is typically expressed in Latin. Why? The answer is simple: the infinitive lacks personal endings, so another word is needed to express the subject!

Find one more indirect statement in the Latin reading passage.

▶ EXERCISE 6

Translate into English. The Reading Vocabulary may be consulted.

1. Catullus videt passerem ā puellā amārī.
2. Poēta nārrat passerem digitum puellae mordēre.
3. Catullus nārrat sē passerī invidēre.
4. Puella putat sē passerem plūs quam Catullum amāre.
5. Catullus putat sē puellam plūs quam oculōs amāre.
6. Catullus putat vītam nōn esse longam.

Sparrows and other small birds in ancient times, like now,
can be quite tame and become like a pet.

▶ EXERCISE 7

Change the following direct statements into indirect statements using the accusative and infinitive construction. The Reading Vocabulary may be consulted.

Example: Puella nārrat: "Passer digitum mordet."
Puella nārrat passerem digitum mordēre

1. Vir cōgitat: "Oculī puellae sunt pulchrī."
2. Poēta nārrat: "Puella ā familiā amātur."
3. Catullus videt: "Puella dēliciās amat."
4. Puella putat: "Passer est pulcher."
5. Poēta cōgitat: "Doleō."
6. Senēs nārrant: "Vīta nōn est semper pulchra."
7. Poēta et puella putant: "Malae fābulae ā senibus nārrantur."

▶ EXERCISE 8

Translate the Latin sentences into English, and the English sentences into Latin.

1. Puer putat puellam esse sevēram.
2. The girl thinks that love is joy.
3. Senex nārrat vītam esse miseram.
4. The poet tells that the war is long.
5. Domina videt poētam exspectāre.
6. The farmer sees that the she-wolf takes care of the boys.
7. Āthlēta cōgitat sē praemia amāre.
8. The sailor thinks that the fatherland is calling.

TALKING

Ēsuriō. "I am hungry."

Bene tibi sapiat! Bene vōbīs sapiat! "Bon appetit!" (singular and plural)

Quid comedēs . . . ? "What are you going to eat . . . ?"

Vīsne comedere (+ accusative)? "Do you want to eat . . . ?"

Vīsne bibere (+ accusative)? "Do you want to drink . . . ?"

Volō comedere . . . "I want to eat . . ."

Da mihi, quaesō (a word in accusative) "Give me, please, . . ."

Grātiās tibi agō! "Thank you."

Libenter! "Not at all, gladly done."

Quōmodo sapit? "How does it taste?"

Bene. Optimē. Male. "Well. Excellent. Bad."

Sum bene sagīnātus/sagīnāta. "I ate well (male/female)."

cibus, cibī, m. – food

Mexicānus, Mexicāna, Mexicānum – Mexican

sapidus, sapida, sapidum – delicious

pānis, pānis, m. – bread

Romans often bought food or beverages from establishments like this *thermopōlium* in Herculaneum. They would line up at the fast-food counter to make their purchases quickly.

pānis īnfersus – sandwich

lac, lactis, n. – milk

īsicium, īsiciī, n. *Hamburgēnse* – hamburger

pōtiō, pōtiōnis, f. *Arabica* – coffee

carō, carnis, f. – meat

piscis, piscis, m. – fish

māla, mālōrum, n. pl. *terrestria* – potatoes

lactūca, lactūcae, f. – lettuce

acētāria, acētāriōrum, n. pl. – salad

pasta, pastae, f. – pasta

placenta, placentae, f. *Neāpolītāna* – pizza

mālum, mālī, n. – apple

banāna, banānae, f. – banana

crūstulum, crūstulī, n. – cookie

thermopōlium, thermopōliī, n. – cafeteria

IN THE CAFETERIA

Mārcus: Salvē, Marīa!

Marīa: Salvē, Mārce!

Mārcus: Quid comedēs? Vīsne comedere banānam?

Marīa: Volō comedere nōn sōlum banānam, sed etiam īsicium Hamburgēnse. Nam valdē ēsuriō. Quid tū comedēs?

Mārcus: Ego volō comedere pānem īnfersum.

Christīna et Helena: Salvēte, Mārce et Marīa!

Christīna: (*TO THE WAITER*) Da mihi, quaesō, placentam Neāpolītānam. Grātiās tibi agō.

Mārcus: Quōmodo placenta Neapolitāna sapit?

Christīna: Bene. Quōmodo pānis īnfersus sapit?

Mārcus: Optimē. Cibus est sapidissimus (*very delicious*). Sum bene sagīnātus.

Helena: Nārrās, Mārce, cibum esse sapidissimum. Sed ego volō comedere cibum Mexicānum. Placentam Neāpolītānam et īsicium Hamburgēnse ūnīus assis aestimō.

Marīa: Hīc (*here*) nōn est cibus Mexicānus.

Helena: Tum tantum crūstula comedere volō. Nam crūstula valdē amō.

Mārcus: (*TO HIMSELF*) Ego tē, Helena, amō. Volō (*I want*) tē esse meam puellam . . .

DERIVATIVES

amor – See *amat* p. 13.

dēliciae – delectable, delicious, delight, dilettante

digitus – digit, digital

domina – dame, damsel, Donna, madam, mademoi-selle, Madonna, granny; also see *domī* p. 42.

oculus – antler, binoculars, inoculate, eyelet, inveigle, monocle

senex – messieurs, monsieur, seigneur (French), señor, señora, señorita (Spanish), signor, signora, signorina (Italian), senate, senile, seniority, sir, sire, surly

soror – sorority, sororicide, cousin

verbum – adverb, proverb, verb, verbal, verbiage, verbose, verbatim

meus – me

sevērus – asseveration, perseverance, persevere, severe

aestimō – aim, aimless, esteem, estimate, inestimable

invideō – invidious, envious, envy

putō – account, amputate, computation, computer, count (verb), deputation, deputy, discount, disputable, disreputable, impute, imputation, indisputable, reputation

Third Conjugation Verbs: Present Tense Active and Passive, Present Active and Passive Infinitive; Ablatives of Manner, Instrument, Separation, Place from Which, Place Where; Accusative of Place to Which

This head is a detail from the fifth century BCE statue of Themistocles.

MEMORĀBILE DICTŪ

Melius in umbrā pugnābimus!

"We will fight better in the shade!" (Frontinus, *Stratagems* 4)

When King Xerxes of Persia invaded Greece in 480 BCE, he was defeated by the Athenians both on the sea and then on land. But this would not have occurred so quickly if not for the Spartan king Leonidas. Warned that the Persians would shoot so many arrows that they would blot out the sunlight, Leonidas replied with this phrase. His tiny band of men held off the Persians in Thermopylae's narrow pass, until an informant showed the Persians a path behind the Greeks' position. Surrounded, the three hundred Spartans died, fighting to the last man.

READING

Cornēlius Nepos (ca. 100–ca. 25 BCE) wrote a book of short biographies about famous Greeks, and some Romans, entitled *Dē virīs illūstribus* ("About famous men"). Nepos's style is simple, and his open-minded attitude is apparent in the preface to *Dē virīs illūstribus*, in which he refuses to condemn certain Greek customs that were not approved of by the Romans.

Here is a passage adapted from Nepos's life of Themistocles, the Athenian leader whose cunning strategy not only helped to advance Athens to leadership in the Greek world in the fifth century BCE, but also helped the united forces of the Greek cities to defeat the immense invasion of Greece by the Persian king Xerxes in 480 BCE. Xerxes had come to Greece with so many soldiers that legend says they drank the rivers dry . . .

THEMISTOCLĒS GRAECŌS SERVAT

1   Themistoclēs est Athēniēnsium dux et homō valdē callidus. Xerxēs rēx
Persārum contrā Graecōs bellum cum magnā industriā parāre dīcitur.
Xerxēs multōs mīlitēs et multās nāvēs habet et cum multīs virīs armātīs
ad Graeciam nāvigat. Athēniēnsēs bellum timent et ōrācula Pȳthiae
5   petere dēcernunt. Pȳthia Delphīs habitat et cōnsilia Apollinis
hominibus dat. Pȳthia haec verba Athēniēnsibus in templō Delphicō
dīcit: "Athēniēnsēs mūrīs ligneīs servārī possunt." Sōlus Themistoclēs
sē cōnsilium Apollinis intellegere putat. Mūrōs ligneōs esse nāvēs dīcit.
Athēniēnsēs verba Themistoclis esse bona putant. Ā terrā suā fugiunt,
10   sed multās nāvēs aedificant. Tunc nāvēs Persārum magnā fortitūdine
oppugnant et Persās vincunt. Athēniēnsēs timōre līberantur.

READING VOCABULARY

aedificō, aedificāre, aedificāvī, aedificātum – to build

Apollō, Apollinis, *m.* – Apollo

Athēniēnsēs – the Athenians

Athēniēnsium (*genitive plural*) – of the Athenians

callidus, callida, callidum – clever, cunning

***contrā** + accusative* – against

***dēcernō, dēcernere, dēcrēvī, dēcrētum** – to decide, determine (*often + infinitive*)

Delphicus, Delphica, Delphicum – belonging to Delphi, Delphic

Delphīs – at Delphi

***dīcō, dīcere, dīxī, dictum** – to say

***dux, ducis,** *m.* – leader, general

***fortitūdō, fortitūdinis,** *f.* – courage

fugiunt – they flee

Graecia, Graeciae, *f.* – Greece

Graecus, Graeca, Graecum – Greek (**Graecī, Graecōrum,** *m. pl.* – the Greeks)

haec (*neuter plural*) – these

***homō, hominis,** *m.* – man (*i.e.,* human being); *pl.* people

industria, industriae, *f.* – industry, care

***intellegō, intellegere, intellēxī, intellēctum** – to understand

***līberō, līberāre, līberāvī, līberātum** (+ *accusative* + *ablative*) – to free (*someone from something*)

ligneus, lignea, ligneum – wooden

***mīles, mīlitis,** *m.* – soldier

mūrus, mūrī, *m.* – wall

nāvēs, *f.* (*nominative and accusative plural*) – ships

***nāvigō, nāvigāre, nāvigāvī, nāvigātum** – to sail, voyage

oppugnō, oppugnāre, oppugnāvī, oppugnātum – to attack

***ōrāculum, ōrāculī,** *n.* – oracle

Persae, Persārum, *m.* – the Persians

***petō, petere, petīvī, petītum** – to seek, head for, go to, rush at

Pȳthia, Pȳthiae, *f.* – the Pythian priestess, *responsible for uttering the ambiguous oracles at the shrine of Apollo at Delphi, in Greece*

***rēx, rēgis,** *m.* – king

sōlus, sōla, sōlum – sole, only

suā – their own (*agreeing with* terrā)

***templum, templī,** *n.* – temple

Themistoclēs, Themistoclis, *m.* – Themistocles

***timor, timōris,** *m.* – fear

***tunc** (*adv.*) – then

***vincō, vincere, vīcī, victum** – to conquer, defeat

Xerxēs, Xerxis, *m.* – Xerxes, *the great king of the Persians, who invaded Greece in 480 BCE*

*Words marked with an asterisk will need to be memorized.

COMPREHENSION QUESTIONS

1. What are Xerxes's intentions?

2. What do the Athenians do before undertaking anything against Xerxes?

3. Why is Pythia's answer enigmatic?

4. Was Pythia's advice effective?

LANGUAGE FACT I

THIRD CONJUGATION VERBS: PRESENT TENSE ACTIVE AND PASSIVE, PRESENT ACTIVE AND PASSIVE INFINITIVE

Look at the verbs in the Latin reading passage. You will notice that some forms—*dīcitur, petere, dēcernunt, dīcit, intellegere, vincunt*—do not follow the patterns of the first and second conjugations. These verbs belong to the third conjugation.

Remember: the stem of first conjugation verbs ends in –*ā*–, and the stem of second conjugation verbs ends in –*ē*–. The stem of the third conjugation ends in –*e*–, which changes to –*i*– in front of –*s*, –*t*, –*m,* and to –*u*– in front of –*nt*. The first person singular passive is formed by adding –*r* to the first person singular active.

Here are the present active and passive forms of the third conjugation:

Third Conjugation: Present Active				
	Singular		**Plural**	
First person	pet**ō**	I seek	peti**mus**	we seek
Second person	peti**s**	you seek	peti**tis**	you seek
Third person	peti**t**	s/he/it seeks	petu**nt**	they seek

Present Active Infinitive	
pet**ere**	to seek

Third Conjugation: Present Passive				
	Singular		**Plural**	
First person	pet**or**	I am sought	peti**mur**	we are sought
Second person	pet**eris**	you are sought	peti**minī**	you are sought
Third person	peti**tur**	s/he/it is sought	petu**ntur**	they are sought

Present Passive Infinitive	
pet**ī**	to be sought

Note that the present passive infinitive of the third conjugation verbs is quite new: the ending –*ī* is attached to the stem minus the –*e*.

STUDY TIP

Note that the *e* before the infinitive ending –*re* in the second conjugation is long (*ē*), but the *e* before the infinitive ending –*re* in the third conjugation is short (*e*).

► EXERCISE

Translate into Latin.

1. it is thought
2. we are prepared
3. you (plural) are ordered
4. to become accustomed
5. you judge
6. we teach
7. they understand
8. they are sought
9. you (plural) conquer
10. to be regarded

VOCABULARY TO LEARN

NOUNS

dux, ducis, *m.* – leader, general

fortitūdō, fortitūdinis, *f.* – courage

homō, hominis, *m.* – man (*i.e.,* human being); *pl.* people

mīles, mīlitis, *m.* – soldier

ōrāculum, ōrāculī, *n.* – oracle

rēx, rēgis, *m.* – king

templum, templī, *n.* – temple

timor, timōris, *m.* – fear

VERBS

dēcernō, dēcernere, dēcrēvī, dēcrētum – to decide, determine (*often + infinitive*)

dīcō, dīcere, dīxī, dictum – to say

intellegō, intellegere, intellēxī, intellēctum – to understand

līberō, līberāre, līberāvī, līberātum (+ *accusative* + *ablative*) – to free someone from something

nāvigō, nāvigāre, nāvigāvī, nāvigātum – to sail, voyage

petō, petere, petīvī, petītum – to seek, head for, go to, rush at

vincō, vincere, vīcī, victum – to conquer, defeat

ADVERB

tunc – then

PREPOSITION

contrā + *accusative* – against

▶ EXERCISE 2

Match the English word with the corresponding Latin word.

duchy	līberō
fortitude	nāvigō
human	petō
decree	contrā
dictum	intellegō
intelligent	dēcernō
liberated	dīcō
navigation	timor
petition	rēx
contrary	ōrāculum
military	mīles
oracular	homō
regal	dux
timorous	fortitūdō

▶ EXERCISE 3

Conjugate the following verb in the active and passive voice. Give the active and passive infinitives.

1.   *intellegō, intellegere, intellēxī, intellēctum*

LANGUAGE FACT II

ABLATIVES OF MANNER, INSTRUMENT, SEPARATION, PLACE FROM WHICH

Go back again to the reading passage at the beginning of this chapter and notice the way the ablative case is used in these passages:

A. *Xerxēs rēx Persārum contrā Graecōs bellum cum magnā industriā parāre dīcitur.*
Xerxes, king of the Persians, is said to prepare war against the Greeks with great care.

Tunc nāvēs Persārum magnā fortitūdine oppugnant.
Then, with great courage, they attack the ships of the Persians.

In both these sentences an ablative noun describes the way in which an action took place. This is called the **ablative of manner**. The preposition *cum* is very frequently used with this meaning of the ablative: in fact *cum* is always used if the noun is not modified by an adjective (e.g., *cum fortitūdine*), and the preposition is optional if the noun does have an adjective agreeing with it, as in the two previous examples.

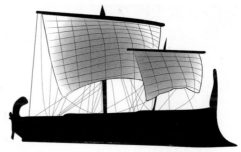

A drawing of a Greek warship.

B. *Athēniēnsēs mūrīs ligneīs servārī possunt.*
The Athenians can be saved by means of wooden walls.

Here, *with no preposition*, the **ablative of instrument** (also called the **ablative of means**) describes the means or instrument by or with which an action is performed.

Note the difference between this ablative and the **ablative of agent,** which indicates by what *person* something is done. An ablative of agent *always* follows the preposition *ā/ab*.

C. *Athēniēnsēs timōre līberantur.*
The Athenians are freed from fear.

This type of ablative, the **ablative of separation,** is used with verbal expressions of freeing, lacking, and separation. The ablative of separation usually appears without a preposition, but sometimes the prepositions *ā/ab, dē,* or *ē/ex* are used. Active transitive verbs that take the ablative of separation can take an accusative object as well: e.g., *Athēniēnsēs timōre līberō* (I am freeing the Athenians [accusative] from fear [ablative]). The ablative of separation is closely related in meaning and use to the **ablative of place from which**; the latter, however, almost always appears with a preposition: e.g., *Ā terrā suā fugiunt . . .* (They flee from their land . . .).

BY THE WAY
Because these closely related ablatives describe the circumstances attending/accompanying the action of the verb, they can be called "adverbial," and are all examples of the ablative functioning as the "adverbial" case. The meanings implied in the ablative are more or less conveyed by the English prepositions "by," "with," and "from."

Leonidas and his three hundred men at Thermopylae, by the neoclassical painter Jacques-Louis David (1748–1825).

▶ EXERCISE 4

Change each sentence by putting the noun in parentheses into the ablative case, keeping the same number. A preposition may or may not be needed. Translate the sentence and identify the type of ablative in each sentence. The Reading Vocabulary may be consulted.

Example: Graecī servantur. (dux)

Graecī ā duce servantur.   ablative of agent   The Greeks are being saved by the general.

1. Praemium meum exspectō. (gaudium)

2. Multōs miserōs senēs vidēre possum. (oculī meī)

3. Nautae fābulam nārrant. (lacrimae multae)

4. Persās exspectāre possumus. (fortitūdō)

5. Animus magnus nōn vincitur. (tenebrae)

6. Iūstī hominēs līberārī dēbent. (vincula)

7. Ad castra ambulāmus. (casa)

▶ EXERCISE 5

Translate into Latin.

1. We seek the oracles with joy.

2. You are not freed from war.

3. We teach the boys and girls by means of rewards.

4. The wretched people are being held by chains.

5. You are expecting the soldiers of the Persians with great fear.

LANGUAGE FACT III

ABLATIVE OF PLACE WHERE; ACCUSATIVE OF PLACE TO WHICH

You know the ablative of "place from which." Now consider how to indicate "place where" and "place to which." In fact you already have an idea how this is done, since expressions of these relationships have appeared in your readings without comment. Look again at these sentences from the passage at the beginning of this chapter:

> *Xerxēs . . . cum multīs virīs armātīs ad Graeciam nāvigat.*
> Xerxes with many armed men is sailing to Greece.

"Place to which" is expressed by the accusative case, usually with the prepositions *ad* or *in*.

STUDY TIP

Note that the word "to" is used in English with more than one meaning. This word is found where Latin would use the dative of indirect object, as in the sentence "I give the book **to** the boy." But "to" is also used to indicate motion toward a place, as in the sentence "I walk **to** the temple." This distinction in meaning should be kept in mind.

> *Pȳthia haec verba Athēniēnsibus in templō Delphicō dīcit.*
> The Pythian priestess says these words to the Athenians in the Delphic temple.

"Place where" is expressed by the **ablative case** with the preposition *in*.

A reproduction of the face of the Delphic Sibyl, called Pythia. The original picture was painted on the Sistine Chapel ceiling by Michelangelo.

BY THE WAY

You will notice the rule for "place where" requiring a preposition is not followed in the sentence *Pȳthia Delphīs habitat* (The Pythian priestess lives at Delphi). Phrases involving certain geographic locations constitute an exception, which you will study later on.

The remains of a round temple, a "tholos," dedicated to Athena in her sanctuary at Delphi.

▶ EXERCISE 6

Fill in the blanks with the appropriate preposition and the appropriate case of the word in parentheses. The preposition is not in parentheses and needs to be added based on context. Then translate the sentences.

1. Nautae _____ (patria) nāvigant.

2. _____ (pulchra casa) habitāmus.

3. _____ (casa) venīmus.

4. Mīlitēs _____ (castra) manent.

5. Agricola _____ (agrī) ambulat.

6. Virī armātī dolō _____ (castra Rōmānōrum) intrant.

7. Dux _____ (templum) manet; deinde _____ (templum) venit et _____ (castra) ambulat.

▶ EXERCISE 7

Translate the following questions. Then choose the best answer for each and translate. The Reading Vocabulary may be consulted.

1. Quō (to/toward what place) ambulant Athēniēnsēs?

    Ad templum Delphicum ambulant Athēniēnsēs.

    Ex templō Delphicō ambulant Athēniēnsēs.

    In templō Delphicō ambulant Athēniēnsēs.

2. Quō (to/toward what place) rēx Persārum nāvigat?

    Ē Graeciā rēx Persārum nāvigat.

    Ad Graeciam rēx Persārum nāvigat.

    In Graeciā rēx Persārum nāvigat.

3. Unde (from where) rēx Persārum nāvigat?

    Ad Āsiam (Āsia) rēx Persārum nāvigat.

    Ex Āsiā rēx Persārum nāvigat.

    In Āsiā rēx Persārum nāvigat.

4. Ubi (where) bellum exspectant Athēniēnsēs?

    In castrīs bellum exspectant Athēniēnsēs.

    Ex castrīs bellum exspectant Athēniēnsēs.

    Ad castra bellum exspectant Athēniēnsēs.

5. Ubi manēre nōn possunt Athēniēnsēs?

    In terrā manēre nōn possunt Athēniēnsēs.

    Ad terram manēre nōn possunt Athēniēnsēs.

    Ē terrā manēre nōn possunt Athēniēnsēs.

6. Quō (to/toward what place) Athēniēnsēs nāvigant?

    In marī (the sea) Athēniēnsēs nāvigant.

    Ē terrā Athēniēnsēs nāvigant.

    Ad nāvēs Persārum Athēniēnsēs nāvigant.

TALKING

merenda, merendae, f. – snack

merendō, merendāre – to have a snack

pila, pilae, f. – ball

tabula (tabulae, f.) *subrotāta* – skateboard

tēlevīsiō, tēlevīsiōnis, f. – television

tēlevīsōrium, tēlevīsōriī, n. – television set

pēnsum domesticum perficere – to do homework

pilā lūdere – to play ball

Quid post merīdiem faciēs? "What are you going to do in the afternoon?"

tabulā subrotātā vehī – to ride a skateboard

tēlevīsiōnem spectāre – to watch TV

tēlevīsōrium accendere – to turn on the TV

tēlevīsōrium exstinguere – to turn off the TV

Vīsne + infinitive "Do you want . . . ?"

Volō + infinitive "I want to . . . ."

AFTER SCHOOL ACTIVITIES

Marīa: Salvē, Mārce! Quid post merīdiem faciēs?

Mārcus: Tabulā subrotātā vehī volō. Quid tū faciēs?

Marīa: Pēnsum domesticum perficere dēbeō.

Christine approaches.

Mārcus: Salvē, Christīna! Quid post merīdiem faciēs?

Christīna: Tēlevīsiōnem spectāre volō.

Mārcus: Vīsne mēcum (*with me*) tabulā subrotātā vehī? Tēlevīsōrium accendere posteā (*afterward*) poteris (*you will be able*).

Christīna: Ita vērō! (*Yes indeed!*) Volō tēcum (*with you*) tabulā subrotātā vehī.

Helen approaches.

Mārcus: Salvē, Helena! Quid post merīdiem faciēs?

Helena: Pilā lūdere volō, deinde merendāre.

Mārcus: Vīsne mēcum et cum Christīnā tabulā subrotātā vehī? Pilā lūdere et merendāre posteā poteris.

Helena: Ita vērō! Volō vōbīscum (*with you*) tabulā subrotātā vehī. Et quid tū, Marīa, faciēs?

Marīa: Pēnsum domesticum perficere dēbeō.

Helena: Heu! Heu! (*Oh! Oh!*) Dēbēs nōbīscum (*with us*) tabulā subrotātā vehī! Pēnsum domesticum perficere posteā poteris.

Marīa: Ita vērō! Bene dīcis. Pēnsum domesticum perficere posteā poterō (*I will be able*). Ubi (*where*) sunt tabulae subrotātae?

DERIVATIVES

dux – conductor, doge, ducal, ducat, duchess, duchy, duke

fortitūdō – fortitude

homō – homage, homicide, human, humane, humanist, humanitarian, inhuman, superhuman

mīles – militant, militarist, militate, militia

ōrāculum – oracle, oracular

rēx – realm, regal, regicide, reign, royal, royalty, viceroy

templum – contemplate, contemplation, temple

timor – timorous

dēcernō – decree

dīcō – addiction, benediction, condition, contradict, dictate, diction, ditty, indictment, malediction, predict, verdict

intellegō – intellect, intellectual, intelligence, intelligent, intelligentsia, unintelligible

līberō – liberal, liberality, liberation, liberty, libertine, livery, deliver, delivery

nāvigō – navigable, navigate, navigator

petō – appetite, appetizer, compete, competence, competition, impetus, impetuous, impetigo, perpetual, perpetuity, petition, petulance, repeat, repetition

vincō – convict, convince, invincible, vanquish, victorious, victory

contrā – contrary, contrast, counter, country, encounter

Fourth Conjugation Verbs: Present Tense Active and Passive, Present Active and Passive Infinitive; Third Declension Neuter Nouns; Third Declension *I*-Stem Nouns

An iconic painting by Cesare Maccari (1840–1919) of Cicero denouncing Catiline in the Senate House.

MEMORĀBILE DICTŪ

Ō tempora, ō mōrēs!

"O, the times, o, the customs!" (Cicero, *Against Catiline* 1.1)

Cicero exclaimed these words in perhaps his most famous speech, in which he denounced Catiline—Lūcius Sergius Catilīna—for having conspired to overthrow the Roman Republic.

READING

Gāius Sallustius Crispus (86–35/34 BCE), whom we call Sallust, is the first great Roman historian writing in Latin whose works survive. He wrote *Dē coniūrātiōne Catilīnae* ("About the Plot of Catiline") and *Bellum Iugurthīnum* ("The Jugurthine War"). Catiline was a bankrupt Roman politician who conspired to overthrow the Republic. Jugurtha was a usurper of the kingdom of Numidia in North Africa supported by bribed Roman officials. Sallust thought the main source of these upheavals was the decline of Roman morality in the mid-first century BCE. He bitterly describes Rome as "a city for sale and doomed to quick destruction, if it should ever find a buyer."

The following text is an adaptation from Sallust's book about Catiline. The conspirators had planned uprisings and massacres in Rome, supported by their revolutionary army camped in Etruria. Catiline tries to cover up the plot, but he encounters an unexpectedly vigorous accuser . . .

DĒ CONIŪRĀTIŌNE CATILĪNAE

1   Urbs permovētur. In locum pācis et gaudiī veniunt timor et trīstitia. Hominēs miserī ambulant, nēminī crēdunt, valdē timent. Clāmōrēs mulierum in urbe audiuntur.

    Animus Catilīnae mala cōnsilia parat. Catilīna tamen in cūriam

5   intrat, sellam petit, sē tamquam bonus vir gerit. Tunc Mārcus Tullius Cicerō cōnsul longam et lūculentam ōrātiōnem in cūriā habet. Cicerō magnā fortitūdine nārrat Catilīnam esse virum malum et cīvibus Rōmānīs mortem parāre. Cicerō dīcit sē posse armīs Rōmānōs servāre et Catilīnam ab urbe Rōmā sēmovēre. Catilīna audit et terram spectat.

10   Tandem Catilīna dīcit patrēs nōn dēbēre verba Cicerōnis audīre. Patrēs tamen verba Cicerōnis audiunt et urbem servāre dēcernunt.

Finally Catiline fled from Rome to his army in Etruria. The army was defeated and Catiline was killed in the battle.

READING VOCABULARY

*arma, armōrum, *n. pl.* – weapons

*audiō, audīre, audīvī, audītum – to hear, listen

Catilīna, Catilīnae, *m.* – Catiline

*cīvis, cīvis, *m./f.* – citizen

clāmor, clāmōris, *m.* – shout, cry

coniūrātiō, coniūrātiōnis, *f.* – plot

*cōnsul, cōnsulis, *m.* – consul

*crēdō, crēdere, crēdidī, crēditum + *dative* – to believe somebody

cūria, cūriae, *f.* – senate (building)

*gerō, gerere, gessī, gestum – to carry; sē gerit – s/he behaves

locus, locī, *m.* – place

lūculentus, lūculenta, lūculentum – splendid

Mārcus Tullius Cicero (Cicerōnis, *m.*) – Marcus Tullius Cicero

*mors, mortis, *f.* – death

*mulier, mulieris, *f.* – woman

nēminī – nobody (with *credō*)

*ōrātiō, ōrātiōnis, *f.* – speech; ōrātiōnem habeō – make a speech

pater, patris, *m.* – father, senator (*senators were called fathers because they were originally the "elders" of the leading families*)

*pāx, pācis, *f.* – peace

permoveō, permovēre, permōvī, permōtum – to perturb

sella, sellae, *f.* – seat, chair

sēmoveō, sēmovēre, sēmōvī, sēmōtum – to remove

spectō, spectāre, spectāvī, spectātum – to look at

tamquam (*adv.*) – as if

*tandem (*adv.*) – at last

trīstitia, trīstitiae, *f.* – sadness

*urbs, urbis, *f.* – city (*usually the city of Rome*)

*veniunt – come

*Words marked with an asterisk will need to be memorized.

COMPREHENSION QUESTIONS

1. What was the situation in Rome during the times Sallust is describing?

2. What were Catiline's intentions?

3. By whom was Catiline discredited?

4. Why was it not easy to discredit Catiline?

LANGUAGE FACT I

FOURTH CONJUGATION VERBS: PRESENT TENSE ACTIVE AND PASSIVE, PRESENT ACTIVE AND PASSIVE INFINITIVE

In the narrative about Catiline there are a number of verbs belonging to the third conjugation: e.g., *crēdunt, petit, gerit, dīcit*. Notice also the form *audit*, which seems similar to the third conjugation verbs, but actually belongs to the fourth. If you look at the infinitive *audīre*, and the forms *audiunt* and *audiuntur*, you will understand that this certainly is not a third conjugation verb.

Here are the present active and passive voices of the fourth conjugation, using the verb *audīre* as an example:

Fourth Conjugation: Present Active				
	Singular		**Plural**	
First person	audiō	I hear	audīmus	we hear
Second person	audīs	you hear	audītis	you hear
Third person	audit	s/he/it hears	audiunt	they hear

Present Active Infinitive
audīre   to hear

Fourth Conjugation: Present Passive				
	Singular		**Plural**	
First person	audior	I am heard	audīmur	we are heard
Second person	audīris	you are heard	audīminī	you are heard
Third person	audītur	s/he/it is heard	audiuntur	they are heard

Present Passive Infinitive
audīrī   to be heard

STUDY TIP

The fourth conjugation is formed as usual by adding the personal endings to the verb stem. The linking vowel –*u*– appears only in the third person plural, just as in the third conjugation.

The verbs of the fourth conjugation are not very numerous, especially compared with the third and first conjugations. Here are three more important verbs:

scio, scīre, scīvī, scītum – to know
sentiō, sentīre, sēnsī, sēnsum – to feel, realize
veniō, venīre, vēnī, ventum – to come

▶ EXERCISE 1

Find one more fourth conjugation verb in the Latin reading passage. Identify the person and number and whether the form is active or passive.

VOCABULARY TO LEARN

NOUNS

animal, animālis, *n.* – animal
arma, armōrum, *n. pl.* – weapons
caput, capitis, *n.* – head
cīvis, cīvis, *m./f.* – citizen
cōnsul, cōnsulis, *m.* – consul
corpus, corporis, *n.* – body
exemplar, exemplāris, *n.* – example
mare, maris, *n.* – sea
mors, mortis, *f.* – death
mulier, mulieris, *f.* – woman
ōrātiō, ōrātiōnis, *f.* – speech; **ōrātiōnem habeō** – make a speech
pāx, pācis, *f.* – peace
tempus, temporis, *n.* – time
urbs, urbis, *f.* – city (*usually the city of Rome*)

VERBS

audiō, audīre, audīvī, audītum – to hear, listen
crēdō, crēdere, crēdidī, crēditum + *dative* – to believe somebody
gerō, gerere, gessī, gestum – to carry; **sē gerit** – s/he/it behaves
scio, scīre, scīvī, scītum – to know
sentiō, sentīre, sēnsī, sēnsum – to feel
veniō, venīre, vēnī, ventum – to come

ADVERB

tandem – at last

Roman body armor.

▶ EXERCISE 2

Find the English derivatives based on the Vocabulary to Learn in the following sentences. Write the corresponding Latin word.

1. There was a heated debate about capital punishment.
2. We insist on keeping our civil rights.
3. What is the meaning of this gesture?
4. The audience received the speaker enthusiastically.
5. He is always buying on credit.
6. I could only find a temporary position.
7. Corporal punishment is banished from our schools.
8. He behaved with exemplary courage.
9. The rate of mortality has dropped significantly.
10. There is urban poverty in this area of the country.
11. Our troops are better armed than our adversaries.
12. You need to apply for a visa at the consulate.
13. This agency works for the protection of animals.
14. Science has made vast improvements in our lives.
15. Let us go to the marina and watch the boats!
16. Cicero was famous for his oratory.
17. The letter I received from my friend was very sentimental.

▶ EXERCISE 3

Translate into English.

1. scītur
2. venīre
3. sciunt
4. sciuntur
5. venīmus
6. scīminī
7. scit
8. scīrī

▶ EXERCISE 4

Fill in the blanks in the second sentence by using the verb from the first sentence, but change the form to complete the meaning. Translate the changed sentence. The Reading Vocabulary may be consulted.

Example: Hominēs clāmōrēs mulierum audiunt. Clāmōrēs mulierum _____.
Clāmōrēs mulierum audiuntur.   Women's cries are being heard.

1. Catilīna Cicerōnem audit. Cicero ā Catilīna _____.

2. Mulierēs timōrem sentiunt. Timor ā mulieribus _____.

3. Patrēs in cūriam veniunt. Patrēs in cūriam _____ solent.

4. Patrēs verba Cicerōnis audīre dēbent. Verba Cicerōnis ā patribus _____ dēbent.

5. Sciō Catilīnam esse malum hominem. Patrēs _____ Catilīnam esse malum hominem.

The Senate House (the Curia) built by Julius Caesar and dedicated to him after his assassination by his great-nephew Augustus was destroyed by fire in the second century CE. The emperor Diocletian commissioned a new senate house that was built with brick on the very same spot in the Forum. This is the building in the left foreground of the picture.

LANGUAGE FACT II
THIRD DECLENSION NEUTER NOUNS

In Chapter 7 you learned about third declension nouns, either masculine or feminine, that follow the pattern of *passer, passeris*. These words have an irregular nominative, and so the genitive provides their stem.

There are also neuter nouns that belong to this pattern; you have already encountered one of them, *tempora,* in the famous saying at the beginning of the chapter.

These neuter nouns follow the third declension pattern of masculine and feminine nouns with one general exception, which you have already learned in Chapter 4: namely, that the nominative, accusative, and vocative of neuter nouns are always the same; and that the ending for the nominative, accusative, and vocative plural is always *–a*. This general rule applies to all neuter nouns, whatever their declension.

Third Declension Neuter Nouns				
	Singular		Plural	
Nominative	tempus	the time	tempora	the times
Genitive	temporis	of the time	temporum	of the times
Dative	temporī	to/for the time	temporibus	to/for the times
Accusative	tempus	the time	tempora	the times
Ablative	tempore	by/with the time	temporibus	by/with the times
Vocative	tempus	o, time	tempora	o, times

▶ EXERCISE 5

Make the adjective agree with the noun in case, number, and gender and translate each phrase.

Example: animālia (magnus)
magna animālia   big animals

1. timōrēs (malus)

2. ducī (sevērus)

3. corporis (pulcher)

4. tempus (longus)

5. corporibus (multus)

6. in ōrātiōne (meus)

LANGUAGE FACT III

THIRD DECLENSION *I*–STEM NOUNS

The following pattern is usually called "third declension *i*–stem" because the vowel –*i*– precedes a few of the standard endings of the third declension. In this sub-class of third declension nouns, the –*um* ending (genitive plural) becomes –*ium* and the –*a* ending (neuter nominative, accusative, and vocative plural) becomes –*ia*.

Three types of words are classified as third declension *i*–stem:

1. Masculine and feminine nouns with the **same** number of syllables in the nominative and genitive.

   In the chapter reading you have encountered *cīvis, cīvis*, m./f., a word with the same number of syllables in the nominative and in the genitive:

Third Declension *i*–stem Nouns				
(same number of syllables in nominative singular and genitive singular)				
	Singular		**Plural**	
Nominative	cīvis	the citizen	cīvēs	the citizens
Genitive	cīvis	of the citizen	cīvium	of the citizens
Dative	cīvī	to/for the citizen	cīvibus	to/for the citizens
Accusative	cīvem	the citizen	cīvēs	the citizens
Ablative	cīve	by/with the citizen	cīvibus	by/with the citizens
Vocative	cīvis	o, citizen	cīvēs	o, citizens

2. Masculine and feminine third declension nouns that have only one syllable in the nominative singular, usually ending in –*s* or –*x*, and have two consonants before the –*is* ending of the genitive singular.

   In the Latin reading passage you encountered the *i*-stem noun *urbs, urbis*, f., which has a one-syllable nominative and a genitive ending preceded by two consonants.

Third Declension *i*–stem Nouns				
(one syllable in nominative singular; the base from the genitive singular ends in two consonants)				
	Singular		**Plural**	
Nominative	urbs	the city	urbēs	the cities
Genitive	urbis	of the city	urbium	of the cities
Dative	urbī	to/for the city	urbibus	to/for the cities
Accusative	urbem	the city	urbēs	the cities
Ablative	urbe	by/with the city	urbibus	by/with the cities
Vocative	urbs	o, city	urbēs	o, cities

3. Neuter nouns that end in the nominative singular in *–ar*, *–al*, and *–e*. These words have the *–ium* genitive ending and the *–ia* nominative, accusative, and vocative plural ending, but the ablative singular ends in *–ī*.

Such are the words *exemplar, exemplāris, n.*, "example," *animal, animālis, n.*, "animal," and *mare, maris, n.*, "sea."

Third Declension *i*–stem Nouns
(neuters in *–al*, *–ar*, *–e*)

	Singular			Plural	
Nominative	mar**e**	the sea		mar**ia**	the seas
Genitive	mar**is**	of the sea		mar**ium**	of the seas
Dative	mar**ī**	to/for the sea		mar**ibus**	to/for the seas
Accusative	mar**e**	the sea		mar**ia**	the seas
Ablative	mar**ī**	by/with the sea		mar**ibus**	by/with the seas
Vocative	mar**e**	o, sea		mar**ia**	o, seas

View of the Mediterranean Sea (*Mare Internum*) from an Italian coastal town.

STUDY TIP

The only difference between third declension *i*–stem nouns and other third declension nouns is the additional vowel –*i*– in the genitive plural ending –*ium* and in the ending –*ia* for the neuter plural nominative, accusative, and vocative endings, as well as the ablative ending –*ī* instead of –*e* for neuter nouns like *mare, exemplar,* and *animal.*

▶ EXERCISE 6

Change the singular forms into plural and the plural forms into singular. For some, more than one answer is possible. Translate the changed form.

Example: exemplar
exemplāria   examples

1. maribus
2. animālis
3. urbibus

4. exemplārī
5. cīvēs
6. mortium

▶ EXERCISE 7

Fill in the blanks with the correct form of the words in parentheses and translate each sentence. The Reading Vocabulary may be consulted.

Example: _____ mala veniunt. (tempus)
Tempora mala veniunt.   Bad times come.

1. Hominēs _____ intellegunt. (timor)
2. Catilīna in cūriam _____. (ambulō)
3. Cicero _____ Catilīnam arma parāre. (sciō)
4. Cicero dīcit Catilīnam contrā cōnsulem Rōmānum _____. (sentiō)
5. Verba Cicerōnis ā patribus _____. (exspectō)
6. Catilīna est _____ malī hominis. (exemplar)
7. Patrēs _____ Cicerōnem bene dīcere. (nārrō)

TALKING

amictōrium, amictōriī, n. – scarf

brācae Genāvēnsēs – jeans (trousers made with fabric from the city of Genova/Genoa)

brācae, brācārum, f. pl. – trousers

calceāmenta āthlētica, calceāmentōrum āthlēticōrum, n. pl. – sneakers

calceāmenta, calceāmentōrum, n. pl. – shoes

camīsia, camīsiae, f. – shirt, blouse

castula, castulae, f. – skirt

digitābula, digitābulōrum, n. pl. – gloves

Exue tunicam. "Take off (your) coat."

Gestābō + accusative . . . "I will wear . . ."

gestō, gestāre + accusative – I am wearing

Indue camīsiam. "Put on (your) shirt."

Lēvigā brācās. "Iron (your) trousers."

perspicillum fuscātum, perspicillī fuscātī, n. – sunglasses

perspicillum, perspicillī, n. – glasses

pilleus, pilleī, m. – cap

Pōne calceāmenta. "Take off (your) shoes."

Pōne pilleum. "Take off (your) hat."

Quid gestābis? "What are you going to wear?"

stola, stolae, f. – dress

subūcula, subūculae, f. – T-shirt

Sūme calceāmenta. "Put on (your) shoes."

Sūme pilleum. "Put on (your) hat."

tībiālia, tībiālium, n. pl. – socks

tunica, tunicae, f. – coat

umbella, umbellae, f. – umbrella

Velim gestāre + accusative . . . "I would like to wear . . ."

vestis, vestis, f. – dress, garment

GETTING DRESSED FOR A PARTY

Marīa: Quid hodiē (*today*) gestābis, Christīna?

Christīna: Castulam et camīsiam pulchram gestābō. Quid tū gestābis, Marīa?

Marīa: Ego brācās Genāvēnsēs velim gestāre.

Helena: Brācae Genāvēnsēs nōn sunt valdē pulchrae.

Marīa: Quid gestābis tū, Helena?

Helena: Ego stolam gestāre velim.

Marīa: Venietne ad cōnvīvium Mārcus? (*Is Marcus coming to the party?*)

Christīna: Ita. (*Yes.*)

Marīa: Nunc intellegō . . . Putō Mārcum Helenam amāre et ā Helenā amārī. Indue, Helena, vestem et tū, Christīna, indue castulam et camīsiam pulchram. Ego autem meās brācās Genāvēnsēs gestāre velim et calceāmenta āthlētica.

Helena: Bene. Nunc parārī dēbēmus. Venītisne? (*Are you coming?*)

DERIVATIVES

animal – animal

arma – alarm, armada, armadillo, armament, armistice, armor, army, firearm

caput – achieve, biceps, cabbage, cad, cadet, capital, Capitol, capitulate, captain, cattle, chapter, chattel, chef, chief, handkerchief, kerchief, mischief, mischievous, precipice, precipitation, recapitulate

cīvis – citadel, citizen, city, civilian, civilization, civilize

cōnsul – consular, consulate, consulship

corpus – corporal, corporation, corporeal, corps, corpse, corpulent, corpuscle, corsage, corset, incorporate

mare – marinate, marine, maritime, rosemary, submarine

mors – immortal, mortality, mortally, mortgage, mortification

mulier – muliebrity

ōrātiō – oration, oratorio, oratory, peroration

pāx – appease, pacific, pacifist, pay, payable, peace, taxpayer

tempus – contemporary, extempore, tempest, tempestuous, tempo, temporal, temporary, tense (noun)

urbs – suburb, urban, urbane, urbanity, interurban

audiō – audible, audience, audit, obey, disobedient, obeisance, inaudible

crēdō – accredit, credence, credible, credit, credulous, credentials, creed, grant, incredible, miscreant

gerō – belligerent, congestion, digest, digestion, gerund, gesture, jest, register, suggest

sciō – conscience, conscientious, conscious, nice, omniscience, plebiscite, prescient, science, subconscious

sentiō – assent, consent, dissent, insensible, nonsense, resent, scent, sensation, sensory, sensuous, sentence, sententious, sentient, sentiment

veniō – advent, adventitious, adventure, avenue, circumvent, convene, convenient, convent, covenant, event, inconvenient, intervene, invent, parvenue, prevent, revenue, souvenir, venture

REVIEW 3: CHAPTERS 7–9

VOCABULARY TO KNOW

NOUNS

amor, amōris, *m.* – love

animal, animālis, *n.* – animal

arma, armōrum, *n. pl.* – weapons

caput, capitis, *n.* – head

cīvis, cīvis, *m./f.* – citizen

cōnsul, cōnsulis, *m.* – consul

corpus, corporis, *n.* – body

dēliciae, dēliciārum, *f. pl.* – delight, pet

digitus, digitī, *m.* – finger

domina, dominae, *f.* – mistress

dux, ducis, *m.* – leader, general

exemplar, exemplāris, *n.* – example

fortitūdō, fortitūdinis, *f.* – courage

gremium, gremiī, *n.* – lap

homō, hominis, *m.* – man (*i.e.,* human being); *pl.* people

mare, maris, *n.* – sea

mīles, mīlitis, *m.* – soldier

mors, mortis, *f.* – death

mulier, mulieris, *f.* – woman

oculus, oculī, *m.* – eye

ōrāculum, ōrāculī, *n.* – oracle

ōrātiō, ōrātiōnis, *f.* – speech; **ōrātiōnem habeō** – make a speech

passer, passeris, *m.* – sparrow

pāx, pācis, *f.* – peace

rēx, rēgis, *m.* – king

senex, senis, *m.* – old man

soror, sorōris, *f.* – sister

templum, templī, *n.* – temple

tempus, temporis, *n.* – time

timor, timōris, *m.* – fear

urbs, urbis, *f.* – city (*usually the city of Rome*)

verbum, verbī, *n.* – word

PRONOUNS

sē (*reflexive pronoun, accusative*) – s/he (him/herself)/ they (themselves) *in an indirect statement*

ADJECTIVES

meus, mea, meum – my (*a possessive adjective*)

sevērus, sevēra, sevērum – serious, strict, severe

VERBS

aestimō, aestimāre, aestimāvī, aestimātum – to regard, esteem

aestimō ūnīus assis – I do not care a bit

audiō, audīre, audīvī, audītum – to hear, listen

crēdō, crēdere, crēdidī, crēditum + *dative* – to believe somebody

dēcernō, dēcernere, dēcrēvī, dēcrētum – to decide, determine (*often* + *infinitive*)

dīcō, dīcere, dīxī, dictum – to say

gerō, gerere, gessī, gestum – to carry; **sē gerit** – s/he/it behaves

intellegō, intellegere, intellēxī, intellēctum – to understand

invideō, invidēre, invīdī, invīsum + *dative* – to envy someone

līberō, līberāre, līberāvī, līberātum + *accusative* + *ablative* – to free someone from something

nāvigō, nāvigāre, nāvigāvī, nāvigātum – to sail, voyage

petō, petere, petīvī, petītum – to seek, head for, go to, rush at

putō, putāre, putāvī, putātum – to think, consider

sciō, scīre, scīvī, scītum – to know

sentiō, sentīre, sēnsī, sēnsum – to feel

veniō, venīre, vēnī, ventum – to come

vincō, vincere, vīcī, victum – to conquer, defeat

ADVERBS

tandem – at last

tunc – then

PREPOSITION

contrā + *accusative* – against

▶ EXERCISE 1

Conjugate the following verbs in the present active and passive voice and give the present active and passive infinitives.

1. *gerō, gerere, gessī, gestum*

2. *crēdō, crēdere, crēdidī, crēditum*

Conjugate the following verb in the active voice. Give the active infinitive for the verb.

3. *veniō, venīre, vēnī, ventum*

▶ EXERCISE 2

Decline the following nouns.

1. *cōnsul, cōnsulis,* m. – consul

2. *caput, capitis,* n. – head

3. *fortitūdō, fortitūdinis,* f. – courage

4. *nox, noctis,* f. – night

5. *rēte, rētis,* n. – net, internet

▶ EXERCISE 3

Change the direct statements into indirect statements. Translate the indirect statements.

Example: Pulchram mulierem amō.   Catullus dīcit _____
Catullus dīcit sē pulchram mulierem amāre.   Catullus says that he loves a beautiful woman.

1. Passer est dēliciae mulieris.

   Poēta dīcit _____

2. Verba senum sevērōrum ūnīus assis aestimō.

   Catullus sentit _____

3. Amor semper vincit.

   Catullus scit _____

4. Nāvēs Graecōs servāre possunt.

     nāvis, nāvis, *f.* – ship   **Graecus, Graecī,** *m.* – Greek

    Pȳthia scit _____

5. Verba Pȳthiae intellegō.

    Themistoclēs sentit _____

6. Graecī nāvigāre dēbent.

    Themistoclēs scit _____

7. Catilīna mortem cīvium petit.

    Cicero intellegit _____

8. Rōma ā Catilīnā līberārī dēbet.

    Cicero scit _____

9. Cōnsul pācem servāre potest.

    Hominēs audiunt _____

▶ EXERCISE 4

Fill in the blanks with the correct form of the words in parentheses. For some, a preposition may be needed. Translate each sentence.

Example: Cīvēs possunt _____ servārī. (cōnsul)
Cīvēs possunt ā cōnsule servārī.   The citizens can be saved by the consul.

1. _____ dē Catilīnā cōgitāmus. (timor)
2. Catilīna _____ vincī potest. (arma)
3. Virī et mulierēs _____ ambulāre dēbent et nāvigāre. (mare)
4. _____ in agrōs veniunt. (urbs)
5. Passer _____ puellae manet. (gremium)

▶ EXERCISE 5

Translate into Latin.

1. I see with my eyes.

2. We ought to be freed from fear.

3. You should come to the city.

4. You (plural) decide to remain in the city.

5. I hear the words with love.

6. The example ought to be given by the king and by the leaders.

▶ EXERCISE 6

Translate into English.

Catullus sentit sē esse miserum. Nam puella amōrem servāre nōn vult. Catullus dēbet intel-legere amōrem servārī nōn posse. Amor in animō puellae nōn manet. Puella Catullum nōn petit. Puella verba Catullī audīre nōn vult. Puella bāsia Catullō dare nōn vult. Itaque Catullus animum firmāre dēbet et ā puellā ambulāre.

bāsium, bāsiī, *n.* – kiss

vult – wants

APOLLO

You have already learned about the older generation of Olympian gods. Let us now turn to the younger Olympians, all of them children of Zeus. Apollo, as he is called in both Greek and Latin, represents the Greek ideal of physical beauty and emotional tranquility: possessing a perfectly proportioned body and rational intellect. He is identified with the sun and with the arts. Apollo is the leader of the nine Muses, who preside over each of these arts: Clio over History; Euterpe over Lyric Poetry; Thalia over Comedy; Melpomene over Tragedy; Terpsichore over Dance; Erato over Erotic Poetry; Polyhymnia over Songs; Urania over Astronomy; and Calliope over Epic Poetry.

Apollo and his twin sister Artemis, known to the Romans as Diana, were the children of Zeus and the goddess Leto. In her capacity as goddess of childbirth and their father's wife, Juno tried to prolong Leto's birth pangs, but eventually, after nine days of labor, she delivered the twins on the island of Delos, which became an important religious center. Its name, which means "bright," is connected with Apollo's role as the god of the sun.

Apollo is often represented with a bow and a lyre, and is also the god of prophecy and healing. The most important oracle in Greece, at Delphi, was associated with his worship. There, his priestess, known as the Pythia, would sit on a tripod and chew bay leaves, working herself into an inspired state from which she would utter obscure prophetic pronouncements. You may remember those prophecies from the reading about the Athenian leader Themistocles. Apollo's son Aesclepius, or Aesculapius in Latin, was the god of medicine.

Replica of a bronze statue of Apollo on the east side of the Temple of Apollo in Pompeii.

Despite his physical beauty, Apollo is not, like his father Jupiter, remembered for his successes in love. Indeed, the best-known story about his romantic interests concerns his unreciprocated desire for the nymph Daphne, whom the gods turned into a laurel tree to spare her from Apollo's embraces. But he remains closely linked with the idea of the rational intellect: the US space expeditions to the moon bear his name.

The ruins at Delos, a site sacred to Apollo.

The Italian Renaissance artist Antonio del Pollaiolo (1431–1498) captures the beginning of Daphne's transformation into the laurel tree.

READ THE FOLLOWING PASSAGE

Cassandra est fīlia rēgis Trōiānī. Apollō Cassandram amat, sed ā Cassandrā nōn amātur. Apollō Cassandrae dōnum dat, sī Cassandra Apollinem amāre vult. Dōnum est hoc: Cassandra futūra scīre potest. Cassandra dōnum habet, sed tandem Apollinem nōn amāre dēcernit. Tunc Apollō aliud dōnum Cassandrae dat. Aliud dōnum est hoc: hominēs Cassandrae nōn crēdunt.

Graecī equum ligneum parant et Trōiānīs dant. Tunc Cassandra dīcit Graecōs Trōiānīs mortem parāre. Trōiānī tamen Cassandram nōn audiunt. Equus urbem Trōiānōrum intrat et cum equō mors ad Trōiānōs venit.

aliud (*neuter*) – another
Apollō, Apollinis, *m.* – Apollo
Cassandra, Cassandrae, *f.* – Cassandra
dōnum, dōnī, *n.* – gift
equus, equī, *m.* – horse
futūra, futūrōrum, *n. pl.* – future
Graecus, Graecī, *m.* – Greek

hoc – this
ligneus, lignea, ligneum – wooden
sī (*conj.*) – if
Trōiānus, Trōiāna, Trōiānum – Trojan
Trōiānus, Trōiānī, *m.* – Trojan
vult – wants

Doric-style Temple of Apollo in Corinth, Greece.

CONNECTING WITH THE ANCIENT WORLD

ROMAN ATTIRE

In Chapter 9 and in the essay "Exploring Roman Families," you were introduced to some names for articles of clothing in Latin. Roman clothes were usually woven from wool, and the process of weaving itself—the spinning of woolen fleece into thread, and the production of cloth from the thread—was viewed not only as women's work, but also as the most distinctive and important female activity. An early Roman tombstone inscription praises its occupant with the words *Domum servāvit, lānam fēcit*, "She sustained the household, she made wool." Wealthier Roman women had female slaves to help with the weaving, and such fabrics as cotton, silk, and linen were eventually used to clothe the Romans as well.

Like much else in the ancient Roman world, clothing was a marker of social status. Both men and women wore a simple garment known as a *tunica* under their clothing. On top of the *tunica*, Roman married women wore a *stola*, a long sleeveless robe of undyed wool.

Roman males of the citizen class, however, wore the *toga virīlis*, "dress of manhood," a white garment without any decoration, which they received on the day when their families celebrated their entrance into adulthood. The *toga* was

This fresco from Herculaneum shows a man wearing a toga.

a large piece of heavy woolen cloth, not pinned or fastened in any way, but gracefully draped around the torso. Men who wore the *toga* sometimes kept it from unfolding by pressing their left arm against their body.

While, as many ancient Roman statues attest, the toga symbolized the majesty and dignity of the Roman citizen, it did not permit strenuous physical activity. Those holding high political office wore a *toga* with a large purple margin called the *toga praetexta*. Those who sought political office dressed in a *toga candida*, made of snowy white wool; it is from this garment that we derive our English word "candidate." Triumphant military leaders would wear gold-embroidered garments called *togae pictae*. To clean these garments, the Romans had extensive dry-cleaning facilities, staffed by cleaners called *fullōnē*s.

Roman men wore their hair short, and were clean-shaven. During the imperial period, statues and other works of art portray men with increasingly complicated hairstyles as well as beards. Women always appear to have arranged their hair in elaborate styles; as time went by many also wore wigs and used hairpins. Much evidence suggests that Roman women adorned themselves with different kinds of jewelry, although men usually limited their ornamentation to a signet ring.

These busts show the varying hairstyles of Roman men and women.

EXPLORING ROMAN GOVERNMENT

POLITICS IN GREECE, ROME, AND THE UNITED STATES

Athens in the fifth and fourth centuries BCE and Rome in the third, second, and first centuries BCE are the two best-known, and most influential, ancient examples of popular government. The Athenian democracy (*dêmokratia* meaning "power of the people" in the sense of "the capacity of the people to do things") and the Roman Republic (*rēs pūblica* meaning "the public thing" in the sense of "that which is publicly shared") have some important features in common. Both systems were developed as alternatives to government in which all power was concentrated in the hands of an individual: a king or tyrant. When compared to tyranny and monarchy, ancient Greek democracy and Roman republicanism are, therefore, rightly understood as sharing a common set of core values. Most fundamentally, in democratic Athens and republican Rome it was, in principle, the collective will of the citizens (in Athens: *ho dêmos tôn Athênaiôn*; in Rome: *senātus populusque Rōmānus*) that decided policy—not the individual will of an autocrat.

Yet in both Athens and Rome, only adult men were allowed to be active citizens. Women (along with slaves and many free men who had not been granted citizenship) were denied participation rights much like American women who did not have the right to vote until the suffrage movement eventually brought about the passage of the nineteenth amendment in 1919 and its ratification in 1920.

Neither Athens nor Rome employed the familiar modern political principles of representation or separation of powers; neither had a well-developed conception of human rights. This concept was, however, a major issue in the Lincoln-Douglas debates. Presidential candidate Lincoln supported the belief that all men, even slaves, had the "inalienable rights of life, liberty, and the pursuit of happiness." Martin Luther King Jr. in his famous "I Have a Dream" speech anticipates the day when there will be equality among all people.

Athens and Rome, like the United States much later, developed sophisticated sets of political institutions that encouraged public deliberation: that is to say, important policies were made and carried out only after a range of policies had been considered and discussed. As a result, public speeches remained a genuinely important part of political life and political leaders were often skilled orators. Demosthenes, the most famous of the Athenian orators, spoke vehemently against Philip II of Macedon who was planning the conquest of the Greek states. Centuries later in Rome, the well-known orator Cicero delivered several orations against Mark Antony. These were called "Philippics" after Demosthenes's speeches against Philip II. Even today very bitter opposition speeches are known as "Philippics." In the history of the United States oratory also plays a distinct role. Modern political candidates are expected to give public speeches and debate each other on a regular basis. This system of public deliberations in ancient Greece and Rome allowed for competition among would-be leaders, contests that were decided by voting and elections. In these systems there was a rotation of leadership, but also some provision for continuity. In both Athens and Rome, the political system was complemented by a system of justice that (again in principle) arbitrated disputes and punished criminal behavior on the basis of established law. While both Athenians and Romans spoke with reverence of their ancient lawgivers and the traditional political practices of the past (Athens: *patria politēia*; Rome: *mōs maiōrum*), in fact both systems evolved over time; new institutions and practices were developed in response to new challenges just as in the United States the Bill of Rights and amendments to the Constitution were developed. While Athens made a greater point of free speech, a freedom guaranteed in the United States by the First Amendment, in both Athens and Rome critical dissent by individuals against public decisions was possible and both societies supported a flourishing tradition of political philosophy.

There are, however, substantial differences between the democratic Athenian and republican Roman systems of government. Some of the differences can be explained by scale: Although Athens was among the largest of the Greek city-states, by the third century BCE Rome was already vastly larger than Athens. By the first century BCE, the scale difference was profound. By this time the population of Roman citizens was measured in the millions. By contrast, Athens, at its height, measured its citizen population in the tens of thousands. This scale difference came about because of very different policies on citizen naturalization: Rome was once no larger than Athens, but continually enlarged its citizenship. Roman allies, conquered peoples, even former slaves, found it fairly easy to become Roman citizens. The Athenians, by contrast, jealously guarded citizenship and only occasionally naturalized those who had not been born to Athenian parents. In America, citizenship is a product of birth or naturalization. The limited size of the Athenian citizen population is a primary reason for Athens's eventual failure. Faced by a demographic crisis at the end of the fifth century BCE and by the threat of growing Macedonian power fifty years later, the Athenians consistently refused to follow the advice of politicians who urged enfranchising resident foreigners and freeing slaves in order to expand the citizen body. When, in the later fourth century BCE, the decisive battles were fought, there were not enough Athenians on the battlefield to stop the highly trained and well-led Macedonians.

The scale difference made the experience of popular politics very different in the two societies. In Athens ordinary (male) citizens really did control the government. A citizen, whether rich or poor, whether highly educated or unschooled, expected to vote directly on legislation in the Assembly (*ekklêsia*). A large percentage of all citizens over age 30 had extensive public experience as jurors in the People's Courts, on boards of responsible magistrates, and by serving for a year on the agenda-setting Council of 500 (*boulê*). By contrast, important public offices in Rome were, for the most part, monopolized by a relatively small elite of wealthy and well-connected families. Much of the real work of the government was done at the direction of the Senate. The Senate was a very hierarchical institution, dominated in practice by a handful of highly influential Romans who were invariably former high magistrates (consuls and praetors). The Senate was formally limited to a consultative role, but its advice was typically respected and closely followed—both by individual magistrates and by the voting assemblies. Unlike Athenians, Roman citizens voted on legislative proposals not as individuals, but as members of very large voting-bloc groups. Voting assemblies were divided into "centuries" (in the *Comitia Centuriāta*) or tribes (in the *Comitia Tribūta*). The unequal size and social composition of the voting blocs ensured that, in ordinary circumstances, a wealthy and well-connected minority was able to control the outcome.

Popular government worked well for Athens and Rome. Both democratic Athens and republican Rome were very successful in their own contexts. For most of the 180 years (ca. 507–322 BCE) of its democratic history Athens was the richest, most powerful, and overall most prominent of the ca. 1000 classical Greek city-states. Under its republican government Rome came to dominate not only Italy but the entire Mediterranean region, including the Greek city-states. Although the two best-known popular governments of antiquity were overall successful, both were subject to political pathologies. In the Athenian case the democratic government was dangerously prone to over-ambitious projects and snap judgments. These bad political choices included decisions to launch imperialistic wars (notably, the expedition to Sicily in the later years of the Peloponnesian War) that, by the end of the fifth century BCE led to catastrophic losses of men, economic crisis, and ultimately to civil war. Another well-known, over-quick judgment, carried out after democracy had been restored in the aftermath of the civil war, was the legal conviction and execution of the philosopher Socrates (399 BCE). To their credit, the Athenians never repeated that mistake (Plato and Aristotle flourished in democratic Athens), and the restored democracy instituted legal reforms intended to limit the tendency of the citizen Assembly to make over-hasty judgments.

Political crises in Rome were precipitated by resistance to the Senate's monopoly of power and by increasingly dangerous conflicts between highly ambitious leaders (Marius, Sulla, Pompey, and Caesar are examples) who did not willingly relinquish power at the end of their terms of public service. Their ambitions were fed by the chance of converting independent citizens into obedient clients. Rome's successful wars of expansion had helped to create a large class of impoverished citizens, whose only hope of getting ahead was to join the army. The Roman legionary soldiers increasingly owed their loyalty to their commanders, such as the well-known devotion of Marius's soldiers to him rather than to the political system that offered them neither meaningful chances for political participation nor any meaningful share of the great wealth of empire. The widespread willingness of highly trained Roman citizen-soldiers to follow their commanders into battle with fellow citizens, in violation of Roman constitutional law, was the fuel that fed a long generation of nightmarish civil wars, including the war of Caesar against Pompey and that of Octavian against Antony. The final result was the collapse of the Republic at the end of the first century BCE and the creation of the imperial principate by the first Roman emperor, Augustus. With this change the long history of popular government in antiquity ended—the political forms of republic and democracy would not reappear in human history until the Renaissance (the northern Italian city-state republics of, for example, Florence and Genoa); democracy was not revived as a term for a legitimate national government until the eighteenth and nineteenth centuries, in western Europe and the United States.

JOSIAH OBER
Professor of Classics and Political Science
Stanford University
Stanford, California

PHRASES AND MOTTOES RELATING TO GOVERNMENT AND DEMOCRACY

PHRASES

- Ē plūribus ūnum. "One \<whole\> out of more \<elements\>." This Latin phrase expresses the essence of the federal spirit as conceived by the founding fathers: a group of self-governing units, all parts of an indissoluble whole. It appears on the Great Seal of the United States, as well as on the one-dollar bill.

- Ex officiō. "By virtue of office" held by a particular individual.

The motto of the United States, *Ē Plūribus Ūnum*, can be seen on the reverse side of a penny.

Ē Plūribus Ūnum is shown on this postage stamp.

On the one dollar bill, the reverse side of the Great Seal of the United States is shown with the phrase *Ē Plūribus Ūnum* on banners on both sides of the eagle's head.

MOTTOES

- Audēmus iūra nostra dēfendere. "We dare to defend our rights." Motto of the state of Alabama.

- Ense petit placidam sub lībertāte quiētem. "He seeks with a sword a quiet rest under freedom." Motto of the state of Massachusetts.

- Iūstitia omnibus. "Justice to all people." Motto of the District of Columbia.

- Montānī semper līberī. "The people of the mountains are always free." Motto of the state of West Virginia.

- Salūs populī suprēma lēx estō! "Let the salvation of the people be a supreme law!" Motto of the state of Missouri.

- Sīc semper tyrannīs. "Thus always <it happens> to tyrants." Motto of the state of Virginia. These Latin words aptly describe the outcome of Catiline's plot against the Roman state but are found depicted on the Great Seal of the Commonwealth of Virginia as a female figure representing Virtus stepping on a fallen tyrant.

A Latin motto on the state seal of Massachusetts.

Sīc semper tyrannīs, the motto of Virginia, is on its state seal.

CHAPTER 10

Third Conjugation *–iō* Verbs: Present Tense Active and Passive, Present Active and Passive Infinitive; Third Declension Adjectives; Substantive Adjectives

A modern reconstruction of the Trojan Horse, standing at the archaeological site of Troy in modern-day Turkey.

MEMORĀBILE DICTŪ

Quidquid id est, timeō Danaōs et dōna ferentēs!

"Whatever it is, I fear the Greeks even bringing gifts!" (Vergil, *Aeneid* 2.49)

This is the exclamation that the poet Vergil places in the mouth of the Trojan priest Laocoön, who tries in vain to dissuade the Trojans from bringing into their city the huge wooden horse left, apparently as a gift, by the departing Greeks.

READING

Publius Vergilius Maro (70–19 BCE) wrote perhaps the greatest work of Latin literature: the *Aeneid*, an epic poem in twelve books that celebrates the origins of Rome. In the first six books, Vergil narrates the journey of the mythic Trojan hero Aeneas through the Mediterranean Sea after the destruction of Troy by the Greeks. Its second six books tell of how Aeneas and his Trojan exiles settle in Italy. There the gods ordain that the blending of the Trojans with the local Italian inhabitants produce the people who will one day become the Romans.

Vergil wrote the *Aeneid* as a Roman equivalent of Homer's monumental Greek epic poems, the *Iliad* and the *Odyssey*, to recognize the emperor Augustus's achievements. Chief among them was bringing an end to Rome's civil wars.

The *Aeneid* became the standard Latin poetic text read by schoolboys for centuries to come, not only during the Roman Empire, but also in the Middle Ages and Renaissance, and into later times.

The following passage is adapted from the beginning of the second book of the *Aeneid*. It is the story related by Aeneas himself about the Greek stratagem that caused the fall of Troy. The Greeks had been besieging Troy without success for nine years, trying to recover Helen, Spartan king Menelaus's wife, who had been abducted by the Trojan prince Paris. Finally, the crafty Greek warrior Odysseus—known in Latin as "Ulixes" and English as "Ulysses"—devised the plan for the Trojan Horse that brought the Greeks victory.

DĒ EQUŌ TRŌIĀNŌ

1   Graecī verba Ulixis audiunt et cōnsilia capiunt. Magnus equus ligneus ā
Graecīs aedificātur. Mīlitēs fortēs in equō occultantur. Mala et Trōiānīs
fūnesta ā mīlitibus Graecīs in equō occultātīs parantur. Tunc equus ad
urbis portam movētur. Trōiānī equum vident et dīcunt sē bellum nōn
5   nunc timēre: equum esse dōnum; Graecōs equum deīs dare. At Trōiānī
nōn sunt fēlīcēs. Nam Graecōs abesse crēdunt, nec dē perīculō scīre
cupiunt. Nunc equus in urbe est. Graecī in equō occultātī noctem et
tenebrās exspectant. Nox venit. Graecī armātī ex equō in urbem exeunt.
Trōiānī imparātī contrā hostēs parātōs et ācrēs pugnāre dēbent. Urbs
10 Trōiānōrum servārī nōn potest. Trōia armīs Graecōrum et flammīs
dēlētur. Paucī fugere possunt.

READING VOCABULARY

absum, abesse, āfuī, —— – to be absent, away (*this verb is composed of* ab *and* sum)

*ācer, ācris, ācre – keen, fierce

ācrēs (*masculine plural*) – fierce

*aedificō, aedificāre, aedificāvī, aedificātum – to build

at – but

*capiō, capere, cēpī, captum – to take, adopt, capture; **cōnsilia capere** – to make plans

*cupiō, cupere, cupīvī, cupītum – to desire, want

*dēleō, dēlēre, dēlēvī, dēlētum – to destroy

*deus, deī, *m.* – god

*dōnum, dōnī, *n.* – gift

*equus, equī, *m.* – horse

exeunt – exit, go out

*fēlīx, fēlīcis – fortunate, happy

*flamma, flammae, *f.* – flame

*fortis, forte – brave, strong

*fugiō, fugere, fūgī, —— – to flee, run away

fūnestus, fūnesta, fūnestum + *dative* – fatal, deadly (for somebody)

Graecus, Graeca, Graecum (*adjective*) – Greek

Graecus, Graecī, *m.* – Greek

*hostis, hostis, *m.* – enemy

imparātus, imparāta, imparātum – unprepared

ligneus, lignea, ligneum – wooden

mala – bad things

*moveō, movēre, mōvī, mōtum – to move

*nec (*conj.*) – and not, nor

*nox, noctis, *f.* – night

occultātus, occultāta, occultātum – hidden

occultō, occultāre, occultāvī, occultātum – to hide, conceal

parātus, parāta, parātum – prepared

*paucī, paucae, pauca – few

*perīculum, perīculī, *n.* – danger

porta, portae, *f.* – gate

*pugnō, pugnāre, pugnāvī, pugnātum – to fight

Trōia, Trōiae, *f.* – Troy

Trōiānus, Trōiāna, Trōiānum (*adjective*) – Trojan

Trōiānus, Trōiānī, *m.* (*noun*) – Trojan

Ulixes, Ulixis, *m.* – Odysseus, Ulysses (*Latin*)

*Words marked with an asterisk will need to be memorized.

COMPREHENSION QUESTIONS

1. What was Odysseus's plan?

2. What did the Trojans think about the horse?

3. What happened during the night?

LANGUAGE FACT I

THIRD CONJUGATION –*IŌ* VERBS: PRESENT TENSE ACTIVE AND PASSIVE, PRESENT ACTIVE AND PASSIVE INFINITIVE

In the chapter reading passage you see the verb forms *capiunt* and *cupiunt*. Seeing the vowel –*i*–, you might think that they belong to the fourth conjugation. In fact, these forms belong to a special group of third conjugation verbs whose first principal part ends in –*iō*. These third conjugation –*iō* verbs are distinguished from other verbs of the third conjugation by the additional letter –*i*– that appears before some of the endings. The verb *capiō* ("to take," "to capture") is an example of this class of verb. Notice that the infinitive *capere* has the same form as other third conjugation infinitives (as does the form *fugere* that you encountered in the reading above).

Third Conjugation –*iō*: Present Active

	Singular		Plural	
First person	cap**iō**	I take	cap**imus**	we take
Second person	cap**is**	you take	cap**itis**	you take
Third person	cap**it**	s/he/it takes	cap**iunt**	they take

Present Active Infinitive

cap**ere**   to take

Third Conjugation –*iō*: Present Passive

	Singular		Plural	
First person	cap**ior**	I am taken	cap**imur**	we are taken
Second person	cap**eris**	you are taken	cap**iminī**	you are taken
Third person	cap**itur**	s/he/it is taken	cap**iuntur**	they are taken

Present Passive Infinitive

cap**ī**   to be taken

STUDY TIP

Third conjugation –*iō* verbs are identical to fourth conjugation verbs in their first person singular forms, active and passive (–*iō* and –*ior*), and their third person plural forms, active and passive (–*iunt*, –*iuntur*).

▶ EXERCISE 1

Translate into English.

1. cupimur
2. cupiunt
3. fugis
4. cupere
5. fugimus
6. cupior
7. cupiminī
8. fugitis

VOCABULARY TO LEARN

NOUNS

deus, deī, *m.* – god
dōnum, dōnī, *n.* – gift
equus, equī, *m.* – horse
flamma, flammae, *f.* – flame
hostis, hostis, *m.* – enemy
nox, noctis, *f.* – night
perīculum, perīculī, *n.* – danger

ADJECTIVES

ācer, ācris, ācre – keen, fierce
celeber, celebris, celebre – renowned, well-known, crowded
fēlīx, fēlīcis – fortunate, happy
fortis, forte – brave, strong
paucī, paucae, pauca (*in plural*) – few

VERBS

aedificō, aedificāre, aedificāvī, aedificātum – to build
capiō, capere, cēpī, captum – to take, adopt, capture; **cōnsilia capere** – to make plans
cupiō, cupere, cupīvī, cupītum – to desire, want
dēleō, dēlēre, dēlēvī, dēlētum – to destroy
fugiō, fugere, fūgī, —— – to flee, run away
moveō, movēre, mōvī, mōtum – to move
pugnō, pugnāre, pugnāvī, pugnātum – to fight

CONJUNCTION

nec – and not, nor

▶ EXERCISE 2

Find the English derivatives based on the Vocabulary to Learn in the following sentences. Write the corresponding Latin word.

1. Bats are nocturnal creatures.

2. Celebrities win votes too easily in our political system.

3. Despite the paucity of defenders, the fort held out until relief came.

4. Driving in a dense fog can be very perilous.

5. Gasoline is extremely flammable.

6. In many parts of the country equine sports are still popular.

7. In the second draft of the chapter, many lines were deleted by the author.

8. Many of those who did not lose their lives in the battle were captured.

9. On the accession of a new emperor, Roman soldiers used to receive a donation to keep them loyal.

10. Sometimes simple fortitude is the best remedy for adversity.

11. That lawyer has a pugnacious personality.

12. The cupidity of some politicians is simply amazing.

13. The fugitives hid in the forest and in barns during the day and traveled by night.

14. The governor encountered a very hostile reception in that city.

15. The motion picture industry is still thriving.

16. The outcome was felicitous: I got the job!

17. The post office is an imposing edifice.

▶ EXERCISE 3

Fill in the blanks by changing the verb from the first sentence to complete the meaning of the second sentence. Translate the changed sentence. The Reading Vocabulary may be consulted.

Example: Graecī cōnsilia capiunt. Cōnsilia ā Graecīs _____.

Cōnsilia ā Graecīs capiuntur.   Plans are made by the Greeks.

1. Ulixes dīcit: "Magnum equum ligneum aedificāre cupiō." Graecī dīcunt: "Nōs (we) magnum equum ligneum aedificāre _____."

2. Trōiānī contrā hostēs ācrēs cōnsilia capiunt. Trōiānī contrā hostēs ācrēs cōnsilia _____ dēbent.

3. Cōnsilia contrā Graecōs capiō. Cōnsilia ā mē (by me) contrā Graecōs _____.

4. Paucī Trōiānī fugiunt. Dīcō paucōs Trōiānōs _____.

5. Ex urbe Trōiānōrum fugimus. Ego ex urbe Trōiānōrum _____.

After the ruse of the Trojan Horse allowed the Greeks inside the city, they burned Troy. On his way home to Ithaca, Odysseus had himself tied to the mast of his ship in order to be able to hear the songs of the dangerously enchanting Sirens.

LANGUAGE FACT II

THIRD DECLENSION ADJECTIVES

In the passage at the beginning of the chapter, you met some words (*fortēs, fēlīcēs, ācrēs*) that clearly belong to the third declension, based on their endings. They are not nouns but adjectives.

Adjectives are used to modify or describe nouns:

> **Mīlitēs fortēs** *in equō occultantur.*
> Brave soldiers are hidden in the horse.

Adjectives of the third declension follow three different patterns. Their differences are seen in the nominative singular.

1. Adjectives with three distinct nominative singular endings (masculine, feminine, and neuter). The genitive is the same as the feminine nominative form.

   > *ācer, ācris, ācre* – keen, fierce

2. Adjectives with two distinct nominative singular endings (one for masculine and feminine, and one for neuter). The genitive singular is the same as the masculine and feminine nominative singular forms.

   > *fortis, forte* – brave, strong

3. Adjectives with one shared nominative singular ending showing masculine, feminine, and neuter gender. Because the nominative form is irregular, these adjectives must be learned with their genitive form.

   > *fēlīx, fēlīcis* – fortunate, happy

STUDY TIP

The genitive singular ending of all third declension adjectives is the same.

Third Declension Three Nominative Ending Adjectives

Singular

	Masculine	Feminine	Neuter
Nominative	ācer	ācris	ācre
Genitive	ācris	ācris	ācris
Dative	ācrī	ācrī	ācrī
Accusative	ācrem	ācrem	ācre
Ablative	ācrī	ācrī	ācrī
Vocative	ācer	ācris	ācre

Plural

	Masculine	Feminine	Neuter
Nominative	ācrēs	ācrēs	ācria
Genitive	ācrium	ācrium	ācrium
Dative	ācribus	ācribus	ācribus
Accusative	ācrēs	ācrēs	ācria
Ablative	ācribus	ācribus	ācribus
Vocative	ācrēs	ācrēs	ācria

Third Declension Two Nominative Ending Adjectives

Singular

	Masculine and Feminine	Neuter
Nominative	fortis	forte
Genitive	fortis	fortis
Dative	fortī	fortī
Accusative	fortem	forte
Ablative	fortī	fortī
Vocative	fortis	forte

Plural

	Masculine and Feminine	Neuter
Nominative	fortēs	fortia
Genitive	fortium	fortium
Dative	fortibus	fortibus
Accusative	fortēs	fortia
Ablative	fortibus	fortibus
Vocative	fortēs	fortia

Third Declension One Nominative Ending Adjectives

Singular

Masculine, Feminine, and Neuter

Nominative	fēlīx	⟶
Genitive	fēlīcis	⟶
Dative	fēlīcī	⟶
Accusative	fēlīcem	fēlīx (neuter)
Ablative	fēlīcī	⟶
Vocative	fēlīx	⟶

Plural

Masculine, Feminine, and Neuter

Nominative	fēlīcēs	fēlīcia (neuter)
Genitive	fēlīcium	⟶
Dative	fēlīcibus	⟶
Accusative	fēlīcēs	fēlīcia (neuter)
Ablative	fēlīcibus	⟶
Vocative	fēlīcēs	fēlīcia (neuter)

BY THE WAY

Aside from the nominative singular forms of these adjectives, all the other case endings follow the general pattern of third declension nouns. But one special point should be noticed carefully: the endings of third declension adjectives are the same as those of the *i*–stem neuter third declension nouns (*–ium* for the genitive plural, *–ī* for the ablative singular *of all genders*, and *–ia* for the neuter nominative, accusative, and vocative plural).

STUDY TIP

The three-ending adjectives walk in three columns: masculine, feminine, and neuter. The two-ending adjectives walk in two columns: masculine and feminine together, and neuter by itself. The single-ending adjectives walk together, until they come to the accusative singular, or to the nominative, accusative, and vocative plural. Then the neuter separates into its own column.

▶ EXERCISE 4

Keeping the same case, number, and gender, replace the adjective with the one in parentheses.
Translate the changed phrase.

Example: cīvibus iūstīs (fēlīx)
cīvibus fēlīcibus

1. verba magna (celeber)
2. dominārum pulchrārum (fēlīx)
3. duce sevērō (miser)
4. cīvis malī (fortis)
5. verba bona (ācer)
6. hostī iūstō (fēlīx)
7. mīlitum armātōrum (fortis)

▶ EXERCISE 5

Translate into English.

1. Urbem celebrem hostēs dēlent.
2. Hostēs fortēs timēmus.
3. Vir fēlīx mulierem fēlīcem amat.
4. Rēx amōre ācrī capitur.
5. Hominēs sentiunt mortem esse ācrem.
6. Perīcula ā mīlitibus fortibus nōn timentur.
7. Castra fortia aedificantur.
8. Multī poētam celebrem audiunt.

▶ EXERCISE 6

Translate into Latin. The Reading Vocabulary may be consulted.

1. We do not hear the fierce enemies in the horse.
2. You (singular) do not think the Trojans are fortunate.
3. The Greeks capture the city of the Trojans.
4. They are not thinking about the fierce soldiers.
5. We see the city of fortunate citizens.
6. I do not desire the gift of the Greeks.
7. I am captured by the enemies of the brave Trojans.

LANGUAGE FACT III

SUBSTANTIVE ADJECTIVES (ESPECIALLY NEUTER PLURAL)

In the text at the beginning of the chapter, you read this sentence:

> *Mala et Trōiānīs fūnesta ā mīlitibus Graecīs in equō occultātīs parantur.*
> Bad things and things deadly for the Trojans are prepared by the Greek soldiers hidden in the horse.

Mala is the neuter nominative plural of the adjective *malus*. Likewise, *fūnesta* is the neuter nominative plural of the adjective *fūnestus*.

As this sentence shows, an adjective can sometimes be used by itself, without any noun form. It can be used this way in each of the three genders: in the masculine or feminine, it supposes an implied "man" or "woman," while used in the neuter, it supposes an implied "thing."

So, *bonus* by itself would mean "a good man," *bona* by itself would mean "a good woman" (or "good things," if neuter plural), and *bonum* by itself would mean "a good thing." A frequent use of these **substantive adjectives** is in the **neuter plural**; the noun "things" is always implied with such adjectives. Note that a masculine plural substantive adjective may refer to people collectively, both male and female (e.g., *bonī*, "good people").

▶ EXERCISE 7

Translate into English.

1. Pulchra nōn semper servāmus.
2. Fortēs nōn semper vincunt.
3. Fēlīcēs timōre līberantur.
4. Multī iūsta petunt.
5. Bonī gaudium, malī timōrem sentiunt.
6. Fēlīcia et pulchra petimus, mala timēmus.

▶ EXERCISE 8

Choose the best answer for each of the following questions and translate. The questions pertain to the Latin reading passage. The Reading Vocabulary may be consulted.

1. Cūius (whose) cōnsiliō equus ligneus aedificātur?

    Trōiānorum cōnsiliō equus ligneus aedificātur.

    Deōrum cōnsiliō equus ligneus aedificātur.

    Ulixis cōnsiliō equus ligneus aedificātur.

2. Cūr (why) Trōiānī equum nōn timent?

    Trōiānī bellum nōn timent.

    Trōiānī equum esse dōnum crēdunt.

    Trōiānī sē nōn esse fēlīcēs crēdunt.

3. Cūr Trōiānī nōn sunt fēlīcēs?

    Trōiānī equum vident.

    Equus ad urbem movētur.

    Trōiānī Graecōs abesse crēdunt, sed Graecī nōn absunt.

4. Quālēs (what sort of) mīlitēs in equō occultantur?

    Multī mīlitēs in equō occultantur.

    Paucī mīlitēs in equō occultantur.

    Mīlitēs ācrēs in equō occultantur.

5. Cūr Trōiānī vincuntur?

    Graecī armātī ex equō in urbem exeunt.

    Equus ligneus ad urbis portam movētur.

    Graecī tenebrās exspectant.

An imperial era mosaic showing Vergil, author of the *Aeneid*. The eighth line of the *Aeneid* (*Mūsa, mihi causās memorā*) can be seen on the scroll on his lap. To the right and the left of Vergil are the muse of history, Clio, and the muse of tragedy, Melpomene.

TALKING

ante + accusative – before

bene māne – early in the morning

bibō, bibere, bibī, —— – to drink

būtȳrum, būtȳrī, n. – butter

comedō, comedere, comēdī, —— – to eat

difficilis, difficile – difficult

dormiō, dormīre, dormīvī, —— – to sleep

excitō, excitāre, excitāvī, excitātum – to wake up

exeunte hebdomade – on the weekend

expedītē – quickly and easily

hōrologium excitātōrium, n. – alarm clock

ientāculum, ientāculī, n. – breakfast

ientō, ientāre, ientāvī, ientātum – to have breakfast

in studia incumbere – to study

māne – in the morning

omnis, omne – each, every, (in plural) all

ōvum, ōvī, n. – egg

pānis tostus – toast

pōmum, pōmī, n. – fruit

probātiō, probātiōnis, f. – exam

probātiōnem superāre – to pass an exam

pūncta superaddita (plural) – extra points

quandō? – when?

Quota hōra est? "What time is it?"

schola Latīna – Latin class

sērō – late

sīc – so

surgō, surgere, surrēxī, surrēctum – to get up

vesperī – in the evening

vultisne . . . ? – do you (plural) want . . . ?

THE MORNING BEFORE A TEST

Christīna: Quandō, Mārce, surgere solēs?

Mārcus: Sī (*if*) scholās adīre (*attend classes*) dēbeō, bene māne surgō. Tunc hōrologiō excitātōriō excitor. Semper autem cupiō sērō et diū dormīre. Exeunte hebdomade diūtius (*longer*) dormīre possum.

Christīna: Quandō, Marīa, surgere solēs?

Marīa: Semper bene māne surgō.

Christīna: Ego quoque (*also*) bene māne surgere cupiō. Tunc ientāculum bonum parāre possum. Ientāculum amō.

Helena: Ego quoque ientāculum amō. Quāle (*what sort of*) ientāculum parās? Quid (*what*) comedis?

Christīna: Pōma et ōva et pānem tostum cum būtȳrō comedō. Quota hōra nunc est?

Mārcus: Hōra nunc est octāva (*eight o'clock*).

Christīna: Ientāculum bonum nunc parāre cupiō. Ientāre ante scholam Latīnam possumus. Vultisne mēcum (*with me*) ientāre?

Mārcus, Helena: Maximē! (*Yes indeed!*)

Marīa: Tēcum (*with you*) ientāre cupiō, sed in studia incumbere dēbeō. Itaque expedītē ientāre dēbeō. In scholā Latīnā erit (*will be*) crās (*tomorrow*) probātiō. Itaque nōn sōlum vesperī, sed etiam māne in studia incumbō. Parārī dēbeō.

Christīna: Parārī dēbēmus, sed nōn nimium (*too much*) parārī.

Marīa: Nimium parārī nōn possum.

Christīna: Sed magistra (*teacher*) est iūsta. Probātiō nōn erit difficilis. Sīc dīcit magistra.

Mārcus: Sī omnēs probātiōnem superāmus, decem (*ten*) pūncta nōbīs (*to us*) omnibus superaddita dantur. Pūncta superaddita sunt dōna!

Marīa: Dē verbīs Vergiliī poētae cōgitō. In Aenēide (*the* Aeneid) Trōiānus dīcit "Quidquid id est, timeō Danaōs et dōna ferentēs."

Christīna: Timēre nōn dēbēs! Magistra est amīca (*friend*), nōn hostis!

DERIVATIVES

deus – adieu, deify, deist, deity

dōnum – donate, donation, dower

equus – equestrian, equine, equestrienne

flamma – aflame, flamboyant, flame, inflame, inflammable, inflammation, flammable, inflammatory

hostis – host, hostile, hostility, hostage

nox – equinox, nocturnal, nocturne

perīculum – imperil, peril, perilous

ācer – acrid, acrimonious, eager, vinegar

celeber – celebrate, celebration, celebrity

fēlīx – felicitous, felicity, felicitation

fortis – comfort, discomfort, effort, enforce, force, fort, forte, fortification, fortress, pianoforte, reinforce, unforced

paucī – paucity

aedificō – edification, edifice, edify

capiō – accept, anticipate, cable, capable, capacious, caption, captive, catch, chase, conceit, conceivable, concept, deceit, deceiver, deception, emancipation, exception, incapable, inception, incipient, intercept, misconception, municipal, occupancy, participant, participle, perceive, precept, prince, principal, principality, principle, purchase, receipt, reception, recipe, recipient, recover, recuperate, susceptible

cupiō – concupiscence, covet, covetous, cupidity

dēleō – indelible, delete, deleterious, deletion

fugiō – centrifugal, fugitive, fugue, refuge, subterfuge

moveō – automobile, commotion, emotion, locomotion, mob, mobile, moment, momentary, momentous, motif, motion, motive, motor, move, movie, mutineer, mutinous, promote, remote, remove

pugnō – impugn, pugnacious, repugnant

Imperfect Tense Active and Passive of All Conjugations; Imperfect Tense of *Sum* and *Possum*; Enclitics (*–que* and *–ne*)

Oil painting of Aeneas and Dido hunting, by the Flemish painter Jan Miel (1599–1663).

MEMORĀBILE DICTŪ

Tantae mōlis erat Rōmānam condere gentem!

"It was so much toil to found the Roman race!" (Vergil, *Aeneid* 1.33)

So exclaims the poet Vergil in the *Aeneid*. Throughout the epic, he justifies this assertion by describing the troubles the poem's hero Aeneas meets. Many Romans in Vergil's time saw the stable government established by Augustus, the first Roman emperor, as the ultimate political achievement—in contrast to the preceding civil wars. Yet Vergil never shrinks from making his readers feel the personal and political sufferings experienced by the Trojan exiles who were believed to have been the ancestors of the historical Romans.

READING

In the previous chapter you read part of Aeneas's account of how the wooden horse enabled the Greek invaders to capture Troy. After the horrific destruction of the city, Aeneas and his fellow survivors of Troy sail in search of a new home. Eventually they land at the North African city of Carthage, where Aeneas is welcomed at the court of Queen Dido. Book 4 of the *Aeneid* tells how the two embark upon a love affair that ends tragically.

After Dido's brother had murdered her husband, the king of Tyre in what is now Lebanon, she fled to North Africa, founded a new city, and swore never to love again. But after she meets Aeneas, she confesses to her sister Anna *āgnōscō . . . veteris vestīgia flammae*, "I recognize the traces of an old flame . . . ." Our English phrase for a former love interest, "old flame," may derive from Latin passages, such as this one, that represent passion as fire, although Dido is here referring to a totally new love interest. Read what this flame brought to Dido.

DĒ DĪDŌNE RĒGĪNĀ

1   Dīdō rēgīna amōre ārdēbat. Nam Aenēam valdē amābat.

Aenēās et Dīdō in silvā ambulant. Tempestās magna venit. Dum tonat et pluit, Aenēās et Dīdō in spēluncā manent. Aenēās sē ā Dīdōne amārī intellegit dīcitque sē quoque Dīdōnem amāre. Posteā Aenēās et

5   Dīdō Carthāgine saepe ūnā cōnspiciēbantur. Tunc propter amōrem Aenēās Dīdōque erant fēlīcēs. Sed Iuppiter rēx deōrum Mercurium ad Aenēam mittit. Mercurius Aenēam iubet Dīdōnem relinquere et terram novam petere.

Aenēās Dīdōnī dīcit sē manēre nōn posse. Dīdō putat Aenēam male

10   agere. Aenēās Dīdōnī crūdēlis esse vidētur. Sed Aenēās Dīdōnem relinquit et Italiam petit. Dīdō erat mulier fortis, sed dolōrem vincere nōn poterat. Vīta Dīdōnī mala esse vidēbātur mortemque petere cupiēbat.

READING VOCABULARY

Aenēās, Aenēae (*gen.*), **Aenēae** (*dat.*), **Aenēam/ān** (*acc.*), **Aenēā** (*abl.*) – Aeneas

*__**agō, agere, ēgī, āctum**__ – to drive, lead, do, behave

amābat – she loved (*imperfect tense*)

ārdēbat – was burning (*imperfect tense*)

*__**ārdeō, ārdēre, ārsī, ——**__ – to burn, be on fire

Carthāgine – at Carthage, in Carthage

cōnspiciēbantur – were observed (*imperfect tense*)

*__**cōnspiciō, cōnspicere, cōnspexī, cōnspectum**__ – to look at, observe

*__**crūdēlis, crūdēle**__ – cruel

cupiēbat – she wished (*imperfect tense*)

dīcitque – and says

Dīdō, Dīdōnis, *f.* – Dido

Dīdōque – and Dido

*__**dolor, dolōris,** *m.*__ – grief, pain

erant – were (*imperfect tense*)

erat – was (*imperfect tense*)

Italia, Italiae, *f.* – Italy

Iuppiter – Jupiter

male (*adv.*) – badly

Mercurius, Mercuriī, *m.* – Mercury

*__**mittō, mittere, mīsī, missum**__ – to send

mortemque – and death

*__**novus, nova, novum**__ – new

pluit – it is raining

poterat – was able (*imperfect tense*)

*__**-que**__ – and

*__**quoque** (*adv.*)__ – also

*__**rēgīna, rēgīnae,** *f.*__ – queen

*__**relinquō, relinquere, relīquī, relictum**__ – to leave behind, abandon

*__**silva, silvae,** *f.*__ – forest

*__**spēlunca, spēluncae,** *f.*__ – cave

*__**tempestās, tempestātis,** *f.*__ – storm

tonat – it is thundering

*__**ūnā** (*adv.*)__ – together

vidēbātur – seemed (*imperfect tense*)

*Words marked with an asterisk will need to be memorized.

COMPREHENSION QUESTIONS

1. What happened during the rainstorm near Carthage?

2. How long did the happiness of Aeneas and Dido last?

3. What was the duty Aeneas had to fulfill?

4. What happened to Dido after Aeneas's departure?

LANGUAGE FACT I

IMPERFECT TENSE ACTIVE AND PASSIVE OF ALL CONJUGATIONS

In the story about Aeneas and Dido, you have noticed some new verb forms:

> *amābat, ārdēbat, cōnspiciēbantur, cupiēbat, vidēbātur.*
> These forms belong to the imperfect tense.

The imperfect is used for a narrative in the past. It represents the action as continuous, and the completion of the action is not the primary object of attention. In fact, "imperfect" means "not completed, not perfect." Usually the imperfect is translated with the auxiliary verb "was": for example, "I was walking." In some contexts the phrases "used to" or "kept on" translate the imperfect: for example, "I used to travel" or "I kept on traveling." Sometimes the simple past can be used: for example, "I felt."

The common element in the formation of the imperfect is the syllable *–bā–* toward the end of the word. The imperfect stem is formed from the present stem of the verb in the following way:

1. For first, second, and third conjugation verbs, the syllable *–bā–* is added to the present stem:

   > amā-bā-
   > tenē-bā-
   > petē-bā-

   The *–e–* of the third conjugation stem becomes long.

2. For fourth conjugation verbs, the two syllables *–ēbā–* are added to the present stem:

   > *audī-ēbā-*

   Third conjugation *–iō* verbs resemble verbs of the fourth conjugation:

   > *capi-ēbā-*

   The endings are the same as in the present tense, except that the first person singular ending is *–m* instead of *–o*:

Active endings:		Passive endings:	
–m	*–mus*	*–r*	*–mur*
–s	*–tis*	*–ris*	*–minī*
–t	*–nt*	*–tur*	*–ntur*

BY THE WAY

Although the imperfect stem of all of the conjugations ends in a long *–ā–*, note that in some persons and numbers the vowel changes to a short *–a–* before the personal ending: in the active, first and third person singular and third person plural; in the passive, first person singular and third person plural.

First Conjugation: Imperfect Active

		Singular			Plural
First person	par**ābam**	I was preparing	par**ābāmus**	we were preparing
Second person	par**ābās**	you were preparing	par**ābātis**	you were preparing
Third person	par**ābat**	s/he/it was preparing	par**ābant**	they were preparing

First Conjugation: Imperfect Passive

		Singular			Plural
First person	par**ābar**	I was being prepared	par**ābāmur**	we were being prepared
Second person	par**ābāris**	you were being prepared	par**ābāminī**	you were being prepared
Third person	par**ābātur**	s/he/it was being prepared	par**ābantur**	they were being prepared

Second Conjugation: Imperfect Active

		Singular			Plural
First person	ten**ēbam**	I was holding	ten**ēbāmus**	we were holding
Second person	ten**ēbās**	you were holding	ten**ēbātis**	you were holding
Third person	ten**ēbat**	s/he/it was holding	ten**ēbant**	they were holding

Second Conjugation: Imperfect Passive

		Singular			Plural
First person	ten**ēbar**	I was being held	ten**ēbāmur**	we were being held
Second person	ten**ēbāris**	you were being held	ten**ēbāminī**	you were being held
Third person	ten**ēbātur**	s/he/it was being held	ten**ēbantur**	they were being held

Third Conjugation: Imperfect Active

		Singular			Plural
First person	pet**ēbam**	I was seeking	pet**ēbāmus**	we were seeking
Second person	pet**ēbās**	you were seeking	pet**ēbātis**	you were seeking
Third person	pet**ēbat**	s/he/it was seeking	pet**ēbant**	they were seeking

Third Conjugation: Imperfect Passive

		Singular			Plural
First person	pet**ēbar**	I was being sought	pet**ēbāmur**	we were being sought
Second person	pet**ēbāris**	you were being sought	pet**ēbāminī**	you were being sought
Third person	pet**ēbātur**	s/he/it was being sought	pet**ēbantur**	they were being sought

Fourth Conjugation: Imperfect Active

	Singular		Plural	
First person	audiēbam	I was hearing	audiēbāmus	we were hearing
Second person	audiēbās	you were hearing	audiēbātis	you were hearing
Third person	audiēbat	s/he/it was hearing	audiēbant	they were hearing

Fourth Conjugation: Imperfect Passive

	Singular		Plural	
First person	audiēbar	I was being heard	audiēbāmur	we were being heard
Second person	audiēbāris	you were being heard	audiēbāminī	you were being heard
Third person	audiēbātur	s/he/it was being heard	audiēbantur	they were being heard

Third Conjugation –iō verbs: Imperfect Active

	Singular		Plural	
First person	cōnspiciēbam	I was observing	cōnspiciēbāmus	we were observing
Second person	cōnspiciēbās	you were observing	cōnspiciēbātis	you were observing
Third person	cōnspiciēbat	s/he/it was observing	cōnspiciēbant	they were observing

Third Conjugation –iō verbs: Imperfect Passive

	Singular		Plural	
First person	cōnspiciēbar	I was being observed	cōnspiciēbāmur	we were being observed
Second person	cōnspiciēbāris	you were being observed	cōnspiciēbāminī	you were being observed
Third person	cōnspiciēbātur	s/he/it was being observed	cōnspiciēbantur	they were being observed

STUDY TIP

Remember: Those imperfect sheep always say "ba!"

▶ EXERCISE 1

Translate into English.

1. petēbātis
2. agēbāmin
3. relinquēba
4. cōgitābāmus
5. servābat
6. intellegēbās
7. dolēban
8. aestimāb
9. līberābāmu
10. veniēbam

VOCABULARY TO LEARN

NOUNS

dolor, dolōris, *m.* – grief, pain

rēgīna, rēgīnae, *f.* – queen

silva, silvae, *f.* – forest

spēlunca, spēluncae, *f.* – cave

tempestās, tempestātis, *f.* – storm

ADJECTIVES

crūdēlis, crūdēle – cruel

novus, nova, novum – new

VERBS

agō, agere, ēgī, āctum – to drive, lead, do, behave

ārdeō, ārdēre, ārsī, —— – to burn, be on fire

cōnspiciō, cōnspicere, cōnspexī, cōnspectum – to look at, observe

mittō, mittere, mīsī, missum – to send

relinquō, relinquere, relīquī, relictum – to leave behind, abandon

ADVERBS

ita – yes

minimē – no

quoque – also

ūnā – together

ENCLITIC PARTICLES

–ne – *added to the first word of a question*

–que – and

▶ EXERCISE 2

Find the English derivatives based on the Vocabulary to Learn in the following sentences. Write the corresponding Latin word.

1. An active life will keep you alive longer.

2. After the regicide a republic was established.

3. I heard his ardent confession of love.

4. His embarrassment was conspicuous and everybody could see it.

5. After a tempestuous love affair they settled to quieter life.

6. He is an agent of a foreign state.

7. I advise you to relinquish these plans completely and move on.

8. Novelty is always exciting.

9. The decision was unanimous.

10. We haven't had any missive from him since he was deployed for the mission.

11. After the surgery she has had a perpetually dolorous expression.

12. Matches were found in his room and he was accused of arson.

13. They were walking in the mysterious woods and wondering whether they would meet any sylvan deities.

▶ EXERCISE 3

Change the following imperfect active verbs into the imperfect passive, keeping the same person and number. Translate the passive forms.

Example: cōnspiciēbant
cōnspiciēbantur   they were being observed

1. capiēbam
2. līberābāmus
3. audiēbātis
4. timēbant
5. aestimābat
6. firmābāmus
7. crēdēbās

▶ EXERCISE 4

Change the verbs in the following passage to the imperfect tense, keeping the same person, number, and voice. Translate the changed passage.

Example: Domī maneō.
Domī manēbam.   I stayed at home. *or* I was staying at home. *or* I used to stay at home.

Aenēās et Dīdō in silvā ambulant. Aenēās sē ā Dīdōne amārī et sē quoque Dīdōnem amāre intel-legit. Sed tempestās ab Aeneā et Dīdōne timētur. In spēluncā manent. In spēluncā autem nōn timōrem sed gaudium sentiunt. Nam dē amōre cōgitant. Posteā saepe ūnā esse solent.

LANGUAGE FACT II

IMPERFECT TENSE OF *SUM* AND *POSSUM*

You have already met and learned the present indicative of the irregular and very often used verbs *sum* and *possum*. In the text at the beginning of the chapter, some new forms of these verbs appeared in the following sentences.

> *Tunc propter amōrem Aenēās Dīdōque erant fēlīcēs.*
> Then because of <their> love Aeneas and Dido were happy.

> *...dolōrem vincere nōn poterat.*
> ... <she> was not able to conquer <her> grief.

The new forms *erant* and *poterat*, from the verbs *sum* and *possum*, are in the imperfect tense. Remember that these verbs do **not** have a passive voice.

	Imperfect Tense of *sum*			
	Singular		**Plural**	
First person	eram	I was	erāmus	we were
Second person	erās	you were	erātis	you were
Third person	erat	s/he/it was	erant	they were

	Imperfect Tense of *possum*			
	Singular		**Plural**	
First person	poteram	I was able/could	poterāmus	we were able/could
Second person	poterās	you were able/could	poterātis	you were able/could
Third person	poterat	s/he/it was able/could	poterant	they were able/could

BY THE WAY

The forms of *possum* are almost the same as those of *sum*, with *pot–* added in front of the forms of *sum*. *Pot–* is a part of the adjective *potis*, which means "able, potent" (actually the English "potent" comes from the same root).

▶ EXERCISE 5

Translate into Latin.

1. (we) were able to *poterāmus*
2. (he) was *erat*
3. (I) was able to *poteram*
4. (they) were *erant*
5. (you [plural]) were *erātis*
6. (you) were able *poterās*
7. (s/he/it) was able *poterat*
8. (we) were *erāmus*

LANGUAGE FACT III

ENCLITICS (*–QUE* AND *–NE*)

An enclitic is attached to the word preceding it. You have already noticed one enclitic used repeatedly in the passage adapted from Vergil at the beginning of this chapter:

> *Aenēās sē ā Dīdōne amārī intellegit dīcit**que** sē quoque Dīdōnem amāre.*
> Aeneas realizes that he is loved by Dido, and he says that he also loves Dido.

> *Tunc propter amōrem Aenēās Dīdō**que** erant fēlīcēs.*
> Then because of <their> love Aeneas and Dido were happy.

> *Vīta Dīdōnī mala esse vidēbātur mortem**que** petere cupiēbat.*
> Life seemed to Dido to be bad, and she wished to seek death.

This is the enclitic *–que*, which means "and" (much like the conjunction *et*). Note that *–que* is always joined to the last of the two (or more) entities being joined.

You have also seen another enclitic in some exercises in previous chapters. This is *–ne*, which is added to the first word of any sentence to turn it into a question. Compare, for example, the two sentences below.

> *Mercurius Aenēam terram novam petere iubet.*
> Mercury orders Aeneas to seek a new land.

> *Mercurius**ne** Aenēam terram novam petere iubet?*
> Does Mercury order Aeneas to seek a new land?

The Latin word for "yes" is *ita*, and for "no" *minimē*.

Mercury (Hermes) wearing a traveler's hat (*petasus*) and carrying the caduceus.

Ruins of Carthage. When Aeneas left Carthage, Dido committed suicide. Many centuries later, the Romans destroyed the city of Carthage at the end of the Punic Wars.

THE TRAVELS OF AENEAS

EURŌPA

ĀFRICA

CORSICA

SARDINIA

ITALIA

Mare Hādriāticum

Mare Tyrrhēnum

Rōma* Alba Longa
Lāvīnium
Cāiéta
Cūmae
Sibylla

Scylla et
Charybdis

Tempestās ab
Iūnōne excitāta

Sepulcrum
Anchīsae

SICILIA

Cȳclops

Carthāgō

MELITA

*Mare
Īonium*

Mare Internum

GRAECIA

Būthrōtum

Actium

ITHACA

Harpȳiārum
Īnsula

Pontus
Euxīnus

THRĀCIA
Aenos

Trōia

Pergamum

*Mare
Aegaeum*

DĒLOS

CRĒTA

▶ EXERCISE 6

Read the following dialogue, which is written partly in English and partly in Latin. Translate the English parts into Latin, and the Latin parts into English. Use –*ne* for questions and –*que* for "and." Use the Reading Vocabulary; other words are explained below. The dialogue begins when Mercury, sent by Jupiter, appears before Aeneas.

Mercurius: Salvē! Esne Aenēās?

Aenēās: I am Aeneas. You seem to be very great! Are you a god?

Mercurius: Deus sum! Mercurius sum. Quid nunc parās?

Aenēās: Dido and I want to be king and queen in Carthage. I am building a cottage. Does the cottage seem beautiful?

Mercurius: Ita vērō! Sed cum Dīdōne manēre Carthāgineque habitāre nōn potēs.

Aenēās: Do you believe that love is bad? Do you understand that Dido and Aeneas must remain together?

Mercurius: Deī dē amōre hominum cōgitāre nōn solent. Amōrem Aenēae Dīdōnisque ūnīus assis aestimō! Aenēās Iovis verba audīre dēbet nec cum Dīdōne manēre!

Aenēās: Must I abandon Dido and sail to Italy?

Mercurius: Iuppiter tē iubet Dīdōnem relinquere Italiamque petere.

Aenēās: Jupiter is cruel! You are cruel! The gods are cruel!

Mercurius: Nōn deī, sed fāta sunt crūdēlia. Fāta dīcunt Aenēam Italiam petere dēbēre.

Aenēās: Must men be wretched?

Mercurius: Ita vērō. Posteā autem Aenēās erit celeber poētaque dīcet "Tantae mōlis erat Rōmānam condere gentem!"

condō, condere, condidī, conditum – to found	**ita vērō** – yes indeed
dīcet – will say (*future tense*)	**mōlēs, mōlis,** *f.* – weight, mass, trouble, effort
erit – will be (*future tense*)	**nec** – and not
fāta, fātōrum, *n. pl.* – the Fates	**quid . . . ?** – what . . . ?
gēns, gentis, *f.* – race, nation	**salvē!** – hello!
Iovis – of Jupiter (*genitive case of* Iuppiter)	**tantus, tanta, tantum** – so much, so great

TALKING

bene māne – early in the morning

excipiō, excipere, excēpī, exceptum – to pick up (someone in a vehicle)

iter faciō (facere, fēcī, factum) – I make a journey, travel

iter, itineris, n. – journey

pēs, pedis, m. – foot

prope (+ accusative) – near

raeda longa – bus

raeda, raedae, f. – car

birota, birotae, f. – bicycle

schola, scholae, f. – note that this word can mean both "school" and a particular "class." Later you will encounter some other words that mean just "school."

trāmen (trāminis, gen.) *subterrāneum* – subway train

TRAVELING TO SCHOOL

Mārcus: Diū pecūniam (*money*) servābam. Nam raedam habēre cupiēbam. Itaque raedam ēmī (*I bought*).

Christīna: Solēsne, Mārce, raedā tuā (*your*) ad scholam venīre?

Mārcus: Ita vērō. (*Yes indeed.*) Et in raedā mēcum (*with me*) venīre solet Helena. Quōmodo (*how*), Christīna, tū ad scholam venīre solēs?

Christīna: Raedā longā aut (*or*) trāmine subterrāneō ad scholam venīre soleō. Nam raedam nōn habeō, et ā scholā longē habitāmus. Cottīdiē (*every day*) iter longum facere dēbeō.

Mārcus: Quōmodo (*how*), Marīa, tū ad scholam venīre solēs?

Marīa: Birotā aut pedibus ad scholam venīre soleō. Nam prope scholam habitāmus. Itaque ad scholam aliquandō (*sometimes*) ambulāre possum. Cūr, Mārce, Helena tēcum (*with you*) semper ad scholam venit?

Mārcus: Ego et Helena iter ad scholam semper ūnā facere cupimus. Prīmum (*first*) iter ad casam Helenae faciō. Helena exspectat. Helenam excipiō. Deinde (*then*) iter ad scholam ūnā facimus.

DERIVATIVES

dolor – Delores, Dolores, dolorous

silva – Pennsylvania, savage, sylvan (silvan), silviculture, Silvanus

spēlunca – spelunk, spelunker

crūdēlis – cruel, cruelty

novus – innovation, novel, novelty, novice, novitiate, renovate, renovation

ārdeō – ardent, arson

cōnspiciō – conspicuous

mittō – admit, admission, commissary, commission, commit, committee, compromise, demise, dismiss, emissary, emission, intermission, manumission, mess, message, missile, mission, omit, permit, premise, promise, remission, remiss, submit, surmise, transmit

relinquō – relinquish, relic

minimē – minimal, minimum, minimize

CHAPTER 12

First, Second, and Third Person Personal Pronouns; First and Second Person Possessive Adjectives; Declension of *Vīs*

Mucius Scaevola with his right hand in the fire. Laurent Pecheux (1729–1821).

MEMORĀBILE DICTŪ

Fortēs fortūna adiuvat.

"Fortune helps the brave." (Terence, *Phormio* 203)

This famous phrase, which features a pun on two similarly sounding words, comes from the Roman playwright Terence.

READING

The Roman historian Titus Līvius (59 BCE–17 CE), known to us as Livy, was born in Patavium, today called Padua, in northern Italy, and apparently moved to Rome as a young man. While he seems to have held no official political positions, he developed a good relationship with the emperor Augustus, whose great-nephew, the future emperor Claudius (10 BCE–54 CE), he encouraged to write history.

Livy's own history of Rome took its title—*Ab Urbe Conditā*, "From the Founding of the City"—from the phrase that Romans used to calculate dates. Comprised of 142 books, it begins with Rome's origins prior to its foundation in 753 BCE and concludes in 9 BCE. Only Books 1–10 and 21–45 survive, some of these with substantial gaps in the texts.

In the opening books of his history, Livy highlights the courage and virtues of the earliest Romans, qualities that he believes gave rise to Rome's later greatness. At various points, in fact, he contrasts these values with what he perceives as the decadence of his own era, by which time the Roman Republic had become a vast, wealthy empire, with a government controlled by one man.

The following story from Book 2, chapter 12, of Livy's history is legendary, but describes events that were likely to have taken place around the end of the sixth century BCE. The Etruscans were besieging Rome. A young Roman man named Mucius volunteered to penetrate the enemy camp and assassinate the Etruscan king, Lars Porsenna. The plot failed, and Mucius was captured and dragged before the king. Although a helpless captive, Mucius displayed his defiance to Porsenna, through an act that explains why he was given the nickname "Scaevola," which means "left-handed."

DĒ MŪCIŌ SCAEVOLĀ

1 "Rōmānus sum" inquit Mūcius, "cīvis. Hominēs mē Mūcium vocant.
Tē hostem occīdere cupiēbam. Mīlitēs tuōs nōn timēbam. Nunc
mortem nōn timeō. Rōmānī vim hostium nōn timent. Multī sunt
Rōmānī mihi similēs et parātī id facere, quod ego facere nōn poteram.
5 Semper igitur cīvēs nostrōs timēre dēbēs. Bellum contrā nōs geris nōn
sōlum in castrīs, sed etiam domī, ubi hostēs occultī tē petunt." Rēx īrā
movētur. Iubet mīlitēs Etrūscōs ignēs prope Mūcium pōnere. Deinde
rēx, "Dīcisne mihi ex hostibus occultīs esse perīculum?" inquit. "Ego
dīcō tibi ex ignibus esse nunc perīculum! Ignēs nunc timēre dēbēs,
10 nisi nōmina hostium occultōrum mihi statim dīcis!" Mūcius autem

subitō dextram in ignem pōnit. Ibi manēbat nec dolōrem ostendēbat.
Attonitus rēx dextram Mūciī flammīs cōnsūmī videt. Tunc rēx Mūcium
līberāre dēcernit: nam intellegit eum esse valdē fortem iūdicatque
tantam fortitūdinem vincī nōn posse!

READING VOCABULARY

attonitus, attonita, attonitum – astounded

__cōnsūmō, cōnsūmere, cōnsūmpsī, cōnsūmptum__ –
   to consume

__dextra, dextrae__, *f.* – right hand

Etrūscus, Etrūsca, Etrūscum – Etruscan

eum – him (*masculine accusative singular*)

__faciō, facere, fēcī, factum__ – to do, make

__gerere bellum__ – to wage war

__ibi__ (*adv.*) – there

__id__ – that (*neuter accusative singular*)

igitur (*conj.*) – therefore

__ignis, ignis__, *m.* – fire

__inquit__ – says or said (*note that in classical Latin this
   verb is only used with direct speech*)

__īra, īrae__, *f.* – anger

mē – me (*accusative singular*)

mihi – me (*dative singular*)

Mūcius (Mūciī) Scaevola (Scaevolae), *m.* – Mucius
   Scaevola

nisi (*conj.*) – if not, unless

__nōmen, nōminis__, *n.* – name

__nōs__ – we (*accusative singular*)

__noster, nostra, nostrum__ – our

__occīdō, occīdere, occīdī, occīsum__ – to kill

occultus, occulta, occultum – hidden

__ostendō, ostendere, ostendī, ostentum__ – to show

parātus, parāta, parātum – prepared (*often
   + infinitive*)

__pōnō, pōnere, posuī, positum__ – to put, place

__prope__ + *accusative* – near

quod – which

__similis, simile__ + *genitive or dative* – like

__statim__ (*adv.*) – immediately

__subitō__ (*adv.*) – suddenly

__tantus, tanta, tantum__ – so great

tē – you (*accusative singular*)

tibi – you (*dative singular*)

__tuus, tua, tuum__ – your, yours

ubi – where

__vim__ – *accusative of* vīs, *meaning "force, strength"*

*Words marked with an asterisk will need to be
   memorized.

COMPREHENSION QUESTIONS

1. How does Mucius threaten Porsenna?

2. What is Mucius's reaction when Porsenna threatens him?

3. What does Porsenna do after Mucius's extraordinary action?

LANGUAGE FACT I

FIRST AND SECOND PERSON PERSONAL PRONOUNS

In the passage at the beginning of the chapter you notice a series of words in various cases meaning "me," "you," "us": *mē, tē, mihi, tibi, nōs*. The nominative singular *ego*, meaning "I," has already been introduced in the Vocabulary to Learn of Chapter 3, and the same is true of the nominative singular *tū*, which means "you."

Words of this type are pronouns; they take the place of nouns. In English, words like "she," "it," "they," "we," "you," and the like are pronouns. Here are the declensions of the first and second person personal pronouns, singular and plural.

First Person Pronoun

	Singular		Plural	
Nominative	ego	I	nōs	we
Genitive	meī	(to be discussed later)	nostrum/nostrī	(to be discussed later)
Dative	mihi	to/for me	nōbīs	to/for us
Accusative	mē	me	nōs	us
Ablative	mē	by/with me	nōbīs	by/with us

Second Person Pronoun

	Singular		Plural	
Nominative	tū	you	vōs	you
Genitive	tuī	(to be discussed later)	vestrum/vestrī	(to be discussed later)
Dative	tibi	to/for you	vōbīs	to/for you
Accusative	tē	you	vōs	you
Ablative	tē	by/with you	vōbīs	by/with you

BY THE WAY

In English, the second person pronoun "you" is the same in the singular and plural. In Latin, however, there is a separate form for the plural of the second person. Note that the gender distinction for "you" is apparent from the context.

► EXERCISE 1

Fill in the blanks with the correct form of the first or second person pronoun and translate both sentences. The verb in bold determines the person and number of the required personal pronoun.

Example: Dōnum _____ datur. Itaque dōnum mihi dare **dēbēs.**
Dōnum tibi datur.   A gift is being given to you.   Therefore you ought to give me a gift.

1. Dōna _____ datis. Itaque dōna vōbīs dare **dēbēmus.**

2. _____ valdē amāmus. Itaque nōs quoque amāre **dēbētis.**

3. _____ valdē amō. Itaque mē quoque amāre **dēbēs.**

4. Dē _____ semper cōgitās. Itaque dē tē semper cōgitāre **dēbēmus.**

5. Dē _____ semper cōgitātis. Itaque dē vōbīs semper cōgitāre **dēbeō.**

6. _____ **sumus** fēlīcēs. **Estisne** _____ fēlīcēs?

7. _____ **sum** fēlīx. **Esne** _____ fēlīx?

VOCABULARY TO LEARN

NOUNS

dextra, dextrae, *f.* – right hand

ignis, ignis, *m.* – fire

īra, īrae, *f.* – anger

nōmen, nōminis, *n.* – name

vīs, —, *f.; pl.* **vīrēs, vīrium** – force, strength

PRONOUNS

is, ea, id – s/he/it, this, that

nōs – we

vōs – you

ADJECTIVES

noster, nostra, nostrum – our

similis, simile + *genitive or dative* – like

tantus, tanta, tantum – so great

tuus, tua, tuum – your, yours

vester, vestra, vestrum – your, yours

VERBS

cōnsūmō, cōnsūmere, cōnsūmpsī, cōnsūmptum – to consume

faciō, facere, fēcī, factum – to do, make

inquit – s/he says or said (*note that in classical Latin this verb is only used with direct speech*)

occīdō, occīdere, occīdī, occīsum – to kill

ostendō, ostendere, ostendī, ostentum – to show

pōnō, pōnere, posuī, positum – to put, place

ADVERBS

ibi – there

statim – immediately

subitō – suddenly

PREPOSITION

prope + *accusative* – near

PHRASES

bellum gerō – to wage war

prō vīribus – with all one's might

▶ EXERCISE 2

Find the English derivatives based on the Vocabulary to Learn in the following sentences. Write the corresponding Latin word.

1. Please state only the facts.

2. Be less ostentatious and more simple in your manner!

3. He was proud of his social position.

4. We all are consumers of various goods.

5. A simile is a figure of speech that involves comparison.

6. The gladiator handled the sword with great dexterity.

7. The ignition system of that car needs to be replaced.

▶ EXERCISE 3

Change the singular sentences into plural and the plural into singular and translate the changed sentence.

Example: Dextrās nōbīs datis.
Dextram mihi dās.   You are giving me (your) right hand.

1. Nōs esse hostēs crēdunt.

2. Tē tempestatem cōnspicere cupiēbam.

3. Senex mihi similis nōn est.

4. Dē nōbīs mulierēs nōn cōgitant.

5. Dīcō tibi ē flammā esse perīculum.

6. Prope mē pōnitur ignis.

The right hand (*dextra*) from the colossal statue of the emperor Constantine.

LANGUAGE FACT II
THIRD PERSON PERSONAL PRONOUN *IS, EA, ID*

In the Latin reading passage you saw two other new pronoun forms in the following sentences.

> *Multī sunt Rōmānī mihi similēs et parātī **id** facere, quod ego facere nōn poteram.*
>
> There are many Romans like me and prepared to do **that** which I was not able to do (. . . prepared to do what I was not able to do).

> *Intellegit **eum** esse valdē fortem.*
>
> He understands that **he** (Mucius) is extremely brave.

The nominative singular forms of the third person pronoun in Latin are *is, ea, id*, in the masculine, feminine, and neuter respectively. These words are the equivalent of the English words "he," "she," "it." But sometimes the meaning of *is, ea, id* extends more widely and may be used as a kind of *demonstrative* to mean "this" or "that" (person or thing). Here are all the forms of this word:

Third Person Pronoun: *is, ea, id*			
Singular			
	Masculine	**Feminine**	**Neuter**
Nominative	is	ea	id
Genitive	eius	eius	eius
Dative	eī	eī	eī
Accusative	eum	eam	id
Ablative	eō	eā	eō
Plural			
	Masculine	**Feminine**	**Neuter**
Nominative	eī (iī)	eae	ea
Genitive	eōrum	eārum	eōrum
Dative	eīs (iīs)	eīs (iīs)	eīs (iīs)
Accusative	eōs	eās	ea
Ablative	eīs (iīs)	eīs (iīs)	eīs (iīs)

BY THE WAY

You may observe that *is, ea, id* follows mainly the first and the second declension, and in its dative singular has the ending of the third declension. However, the ending of the genitive singular matches none of the declensions we have seen so far. This is because *is, ea, id* belongs to a special declension shared by most pronouns. You will meet examples of this special pronominal declension again.

▶ EXERCISE 4

Change the nouns in parentheses to the correct corresponding form of *is, ea, id* and translate the changed sentence.

Example: Dextra (Mūciī) flammīs cōnsūmitur.
Dextra eius flammīs cōnsūmitur.   His right hand is being consumed by flames.

1. Dolōrem (mulierum) vidēmus.

2. Magna praemia (civibus) dantur.

3. Mūcius ē (rēgis) castrīs nōn fugit.

4. Mūcius (vītam) ā rēge nōn petēbat.

5. Mīles (bellum) nōn timēbat.

6. Lacrimīs (puellārum) movēbāmur.

7. Rēx (Mūciō) nōn crēdit.

8. Dē (patriā) saepe cōgitāmus.

9. Templum ā (duce) aedificātur.

The ancient Romans from early times to late imperial times built temples.
This temple (*templum*) was begun by the emperor Antoninus Pius in honor of his
deified wife, Faustina. After his death, the Romans dedicated the temple to both of them.

LANGUAGE FACT III
FIRST AND SECOND PERSON POSSESSIVE ADJECTIVES

Latin also has first and second person **possessive adjectives**. These words are like any other adjective, i.e., they agree in case, number, and gender with the noun they refer to, but they also show personal possession ("my," "your," "our," etc.).

Here are the first and second person possessive adjectives, singular and plural:

> **Possessive adjectives: first and second person**
> **meus, mea, meum** – my (declines like *bonus, bona, bonum*)
> **tuus, tua, tuum** – your (singular) (declines like *bonus, bona, bonum*)
> **noster, nostra, nostrum** – our (declines like *pulcher, pulchra, pulchrum*)
> **vester, vestra, vestrum** – your (plural) (declines like *pulcher, pulchra, pulchrum*)

Look closely at the following examples from the passage at the beginning of the chapter; you will see that these adjectives function just like other adjectives.

> *Mīlitēs tuōs nōn timēbam.*
> I was not afraid of your soldiers.

> *Semper igitur cīvēs nostrōs timēre dēbēs.*
> Therefore you must always fear our citizens.

Both possessive adjectives are in the accusative plural, because in each case the noun with which they agree is accusative plural.

▶ EXERCISE 5

Translate into Latin.

1. my son (nominative)

2. of my sons

3. to our daughter

4. our daughters (accusative)

5. by your word

6. your words (nominative)

7. with your (plural) horse

8. to your (plural) horses

▶ EXERCISE 6

Supply the correct form of the possessive adjective in parentheses and translate the completed sentence or phrase.

Example: īrae _____ (my)

īrae meae   to/for my anger   of my anger   my angers

1. nōminum _____ (your [plural])

2. Ā fīliō _____ equus dūcēbātur. (our)

3. Praemium _____ capis. (your)

4. Rēx _____ fīliās amābat. (my)

5. Hominēs terram _____ cōnspiciēbant. (our)

6. Nōn dēbēs dextram _____ in igne relinquere. (your)

LANGUAGE FACT IV

DECLENSION OF *VĪS*

You have already learned the third declension. There are, however, some irregular third declension nouns that must be learned individually because they have certain peculiarities. One of these nouns is *vīs*, which you have already met in the reading at the beginning of this chapter:

> *Rōmānī* **vim** *hostium nōn timent.*
> The Romans do not fear the force of enemies.

This common word means "force," or "violence," and sometimes (especially in the plural) "strength" or "energy." The plural can also denote "military forces." The phrase *prō vīribus* means "with all one's might" or "as best as one can."

Declension of *vīs*		
	Singular	**Plural**
Nominative	vīs	vīrēs
Genitive	-	vīrium
Dative	-	vīribus
Accusative	vim	vīrēs
Ablative	vī	vīribus

STUDY TIP

Be very careful never to confuse the word *vīs* (especially its plural forms) with the second declension noun *vir* ("man").

BY THE WAY

Vīs is called a defective noun because it has defects: i.e., it is missing some of its parts.

▶ EXERCISE 7

Translate into Latin. The Reading Vocabulary may be consulted.

1. Now I understand, Mucius (*Mūcī*), that your courage cannot be conquered by flames.

2. You want to think about my death, but you see my bravery.

3. These things (use a form of *is, ea, id*) seem to be dangers to you, king, but not to our Roman soldiers.

4. "You must," said the king, "immediately tell me the names of my enemies."

5. "In my city," said Mucius, "there are many (people) similar to me."

6. "You cannot understand," said Mucius, "the courage of our soldiers."

Soldiers formed an integral part of the life of Romans from the time of Mucius Scaevola to the imperial era. This stone relief is from the Antonine column that was built by the emperor Marcus Aurelius in honor of his predecessor Antoninus Pius.

TALKING

aestās, aestātis, f. – summer

annī tempus (*temporis,* n.) – season

annus, annī, m. – year

arbor, arboris, f. – tree

autumnus, autumnī, m. – autumn

caelum, caelī, n. – sky, weather

calor, calōris, m. – heat (often used in the plural when referring to climate)

folium, foliī, n. – leaf

fulgur, fulguris, n. – lightning

gemma, gemmae, f. – bud

hiems, hiemis, f. – winter

ningit (impersonal) – it snows

nix, nivis, f. – snow

nūbēs, nūbis, f. – cloud

nūbilus, nūbila, nūbilum – cloudy

placeō, placēre, placuī – to please (+ dative)

serēnus, serēna, serēnum – clear, bright

sūdus, sūda, sūdum – clear, bright

tempestās, tempestātis, f. – storm

tonitruum, tonitruī, n. – thunder

vēr, vēris, n. – spring

DISCUSSING THE WEATHER

Helena: Ningit hodiē (*today*). Nivēs nōn amō. Sī (*if*) ningit, domī manēre cupiō.

Marīa: Nivēs mihi placent. Bonum est in nivibus lūdere (*to play*). Quāle (*what sort of*) caelum tibi placet?

Helena: Caelum sūdum et serēnum mihi placet. Placet mihi aestās. Placent mihi calōrēs. Placet mihi mare. Nam aestāte (*during the summer*) prope mare lūdere possum. Placetne tibi, Mārce, aestās?

Mārcus: Aestās mihi placet. Omnia (*all*) annī tempora mihi placent. Quod (*what*) tempus tibi, Christīna, placet?

Christīna: Vēr mihi placet. Tunc caelum est serēnum, sed nūbilum. Nūbēs mihi pulchrae esse videntur. Gemmae quoque sunt vēre (*during the spring*) in arboribus.

Marīa: Vēr quoque mihi placet. Sed autumnum valdē amō. Tunc folia sunt pulchra: rubra (*red*) et flāva (*yellow*). Autumnō (*during the fall*) quoque sunt tempestātēs. Fēlīx sum, sī tonitrua audiō et fulgura videō.

DERIVATIVES

dextra – dexterity, ambidextrous

ignis – igneous, ignite, ignition, ignescent

īra – irascible, ire

nōmen – denomination, ignominious, misnomer, nominee, noun, pronoun, renown

vīs – inviolate, violation, violence

is, ea, id – identification, identical, identity

noster – nostrum

similis – assemble, assimilate, assimilation, dissemble, dissimilar, ensemble, resemblance, similar, simulation, simultaneous

cōnsūmō – consumer, consumption, consumptive

faciō – affair, affect, artificial, benefactor, beneficial, certificate, chauffeur, confection, confetti, counterfeit, deface, defeat, defect, deficit, difficult, edifice, efface, effect, facade, face, facet, facilitate, factious, factory, fashion, feasible, feat, feature, fetish, forfeit, imperfect, infection, Maleficent, manufacture, matter-of-fact, munificent, official, officious, olfactory, orifice, pacific, pluperfect, prefect, proficient, profit, prolific, ratification, refectory, sacrifice, scientific, significant, specific, soporific, suffice, superficial, surface, surfeit, terrific, versification

ostendō – ostensible, ostentatious, ostentation

pōnō – component, composition, compost, compound, deposit, depot, disposition, exponent, expound, imposition, imposter, juxtaposition, opponent, opposite, outpost, position, positive, post, postage, postilion, postpone, posture, preposition, proposition, provost, repository, supposition

statim – stat

prope – approach, approximate, propinquity, rapprochement, reproach

VOCABULARY TO KNOW

NOUNS

deus, deī, *m.* – god

dextra, dextrae, *f.* – right hand

dolor, dolōris, *m.* – grief, pain

dōnum, dōnī, *n.* – gift

equus, equī, *m.* – horse

flamma, flammae, *f.* – flame

hostis, hostis, *m.* – enemy

ignis, ignis, *m.* – fire

īra, īrae, *f.* – anger

nōmen, nōminis, *n.* – name

nox, noctis, *f.* – night

perīculum, perīculī, *n.* – danger

rēgīna, rēgīnae, *f.* – queen

silva, silvae, *f.* – forest

spēlunca, spēluncae, *f.* – cave

tempestās, tempestātis, *f.* – storm

vīs, ——, *f.; pl.* **vīrēs, vīrium** – force, strength

PRONOUNS

is, ea, id – s/he/it, this, that

nōs – we

vōs – you

ADJECTIVES

ācer, ācris, ācre – keen, fierce

celeber, celebris, celebre – renowned, well-known, crowded

crūdēlis, crūdēle – cruel

fēlīx, fēlīcis – fortunate, happy

fortis, forte – brave, strong

noster, nostra, nostrum – our

novus, nova, novum – new

paucī, paucae, pauca (*plural*) – few

similis, simile + *genitive or dative* – like

tantus, tanta, tantum – so great

tuus, tua, tuum – your, yours

vester, vestra, vestrum – your, yours

VERBS

aedificō, aedificāre, aedificāvī, aedificātum – to build

agō, agere, ēgī, āctum – to drive, lead, do, behave

ārdeō, ārdēre, ārsī, —— – to burn, be on fire

capiō, capere, cēpī, captum – to take, adopt, capture; **cōnsilia capere** – to make plans

cōnspiciō, cōnspicere, cōnspexī, cōnspectum – to look at, observe

cōnsūmō, cōnsūmere, cōnsūmpsī, cōnsūmptum – to consume

cupiō, cupere, cupīvī, cupītum – to desire, want

dēleō, dēlēre, dēlēvī, dēlētum – to destroy

faciō, facere, fēcī, factum – to do, make

fugiō, fugere, fūgī, —— – to flee, run away

inquit – s/he says or said (*note that in classical Latin this verb is only used with direct speech*)

mittō, mittere, mīsī, missum – to send

moveō, movēre, mōvī, mōtum – to move

occīdō, occīdere, occīdī, occīsum – to kill

ostendō, ostendere, ostendī, ostentum – to show

pōnō, pōnere, posuī, positum – to put, place

pugnō, pugnāre, pugnāvī, pugnātum – to fight

relinquō, relinquere, relīquī, relictum – to leave behind, abandon

ADVERBS

ibi – there

ita – yes

minimē – no

quoque – also

statim – immediately

subitō – suddenly

ūnā – together

PREPOSITION

prope + *accusative* – near

CONJUNCTION

nec – and not, nor

ENCLITIC PARTICLES

–ne – *added to the first word of a question*
–que – and

PHRASES

bellum gerō – to wage war
prō vīribus – with all one's might

▶ EXERCISE 1

Decline the following phrases.

1. *dōnum tuum*

2. *hostis noster*

3. *rēgīna crūdēlis*

4. *equus celeber*

▶ EXERCISE 2

Conjugate the following verb in the present active and passive voice and give the present active and passive infinitives.

1. *cōnspiciō, cōnspicere, cōnspexī, cōnspectum*

▶ EXERCISE 3

Conjugate the following verbs in the imperfect active voice.

1. *pugnō, pugnāre, pugnāvī, pugnātum*

2. *fugiō, fugere, fūgī, ——*

3. *veniō, venīre, vēnī, ventum*

Conjugate the following verbs in the imperfect passive voice.

4. *moveō, movēre, mōvī, mōtum*

5. *ostendō, ostendere, ostendī, ostentum*

▶ EXERCISE 4

Make the adjective in parentheses agree with the noun. For some, more than one answer is possible.

Example: mīlitis miserī (fortis)
mīlitis fortis

1. poētā iūstō (celeber)

2. puellārum multārum (fortis)

3. lupae malae (fortis)

4. praemia magna (celeber)

5. cōnsulēs bonī (ācer)

6. rēgum bonōrum (fēlīx)

7. viā longā (fēlīx)

▶ EXERCISE 5

Fill in the blanks with the correct form of the first or second person pronoun and translate the completed sentence. The verb in bold determines the person and number of the required personal pronoun.

Example: Nōmina hostium _____ dīcō. Itaque praemium mihi dare **dēbētis**.
Nōmina hostium vōbīs dīcō. Itaque praemium mihi dare dēbētis.
I am telling you (plural) the names of the enemies. Therefore you (plural) ought to give me a reward.

1. _____ esse sevērum dīcis. Sed animum **meum** tē nōn intellegere crēdō.

2. _____ vidēre possumus. Sed ā **vōbīs** nōn cōnspicimur.

3. Ā _____ valdē amāris. Sed **mē** nōn valdē amāre vidēris.

4. **Vidēris** mihi multōs habēre amīcōs. Itaque _____ esse fēlīcem putō.

5. Puella ā _____ amātur, sed _____ ūnīus assis aestimat. Itaque **doleō** et **sum** miser.

6. Intellegō, Mūcī, fortitūdinem **tuam** vincī nōn posse. Itaque _____ līberāre dēcernō.

▶ EXERCISE 6

Translate into Latin.

1. Must men fear the gods?

2. Do you say that these men are fortunate?

3. We must always love good and distinguished things (use –*que* for "and").

4. The cruel enemies were being killed.

5. We do not see that they are abandoning your camp.

6. Are the Greeks giving us gifts? I do not believe that they are good.

7. Bad things are not always observed by us.

8. We were fighting with all <our> might.

9. Were you leaving her behind?

▶ EXERCISE 7

Translate the following passage into English.

After Mucius Scaevola's exploits, the Etruscan king Porsenna decided to make peace with the Romans. It was stipulated as part of a peace agreement that the Romans would give hostages and the Etruscans would keep them. However, one of the hostages, a young woman named Cloelia, defiantly escaped from the prison camp with a group of young Roman women.

Cloelia et aliquot mulierēs ex castrīs Etrūscōrum fugiunt Rōmamque petunt. Tunc Porsenna magnā īrā capitur et lēgātōs ad Rōmānōs mittit: "Nēmō vestrum dēbet foedus nostrum ūnīus assis aestimāre. Itaque Cloelia dēbet ad castra Etrūscōrum revenīre. Sī Cloelia ad castra nostra revenit, eam līberābō." Cloelia id facit et rēx Etrūscōrum eam līberat. Is intellegit nōn sōlum virōs Rōmānōs, sed etiam mulierēs Rōmānās esse valdē fortēs.

aliquot – some, a certain number	**līberābō** – *future of* **līberō**, *first person singular*
Cloelia, Cloeliae, *f.* – Cloelia	**nēmō** – nobody, none
Etrūscus, Etrūscī, *m.* – Etruscan	**Porsenna, Porsennae,** *m.* – Porsenna
foedus, foederis, *n.* – treaty	**reveniō, revenīre, revēnī, reventum** – to return
lēgātus, lēgātī, *m.* – ambassador	**sī** (*conj.*) – if

The Romans set up a female equestrian statue in honor of Cloelia, which was unheard of at that time. Some believe that the statue, later destroyed, was to a goddess, and associated with Cloelia only because of the legend.

MERCURY

Mercury, known to the Greeks as Hermes, belonged to the younger generation of Olympian gods. Son of Zeus and the nymph Maia, he displayed signs of extreme intelligence and cunning from the day after his birth. He invented the lyre by carving the shell of a tortoise and stretching strings over it. He then stole the cattle of his older brother, the god Apollo, and quickly returned home. When Apollo finally found him there, he was innocently lying in his cradle and pretended to have nothing to do with the theft. Eventually Apollo and Hermes were reconciled when Hermes gave his brother the newly invented lyre.

Hermes gives Apollo the cithara in exchange for a herd of cattle. Francesco Albani (1578–1660).

After Hermes grew up, he became the official herald of the gods and was often represented with winged shoes, a traveler's hat, and a staff with two entwined snakes, called a caduceus. In addition to being the patron of merchants, thieves, and travelers, he was regarded as the trickster among the gods. He was also viewed as the god of boundaries, and the violation of boundaries, because he moved easily and often from one place to another; he even accompanied the souls of dead people to the underworld. Statues of the god Hermes, called herms, were placed on roads, in public locales, and on house doors in order to bring good luck.

A statue of Mercury with caduceus in hand stands atop Grand Central Station in New York City.

READ THE FOLLOWING PASSAGE

Mercurius erat deōrum nūntius. Ad hominēs saepe mittēbātur. Iuppiter Mercurium ad Aenēam mittit: nam Iuppiter nōn cupit Aenēam cum Dīdōne manēre. Itaque Aenēās Italiam petere ab eō iubētur, et eius iussa ē Mercuriō audit. Mercurius nōn sōlum deōrum iussa hominibus dīcēbat, sed etiam umbrās mortuōrum ad īnferōs dūcēbat. Itaque hominēs Mercurium nōn semper amābant: saepe eum timēbant!

Aenēās, Aenēae, *m.* – Aeneas
Dīdō, Dīdōnis, *f.* – Dido
dūcō, dūcere, dūxī, ductum – to lead
īnferī, īnferōrum, *m.* – the underworld, the inhabitants of the underworld
Italia, Italiae, *f.* – Italy

iussum, iussī, *n.* – command
Mercurius, Mercuriī, *m.* – Mercury
mortuī, mortuōrum, *m.* – the dead
nūntius, nūntiī, *m.* – messenger, message
umbra, umbrae, *f.* – shadow, ghost

ROMAN FOOD

In Chapter 10 you saw some Latin words relating to food and meals. The ancient Romans usually ate three meals a day: *ientāculum,* breakfast; *prandium,* lunch; *cēna,* dinner. They sometimes omitted the first two, however, or only ate very light fare, such as water in the morning, or a piece of bread with cheese. Lunch usually consisted of bread, cold meat, fruit, and vegetables, all washed down with a bottle of wine. The main meal for the Romans was dinner, which they ate after their bath, before nightfall.

Yet in imperial times, when excessive eating became more customary, dinner could begin as early as noon and last until midnight. It was served

Flagon with a straw covering and a glass goblet on a mosaic from a *trīclīnium.*

in a special room called the *trīclīnium,* which is also the name of the couch on which people reclined to eat. The *trīclīnium* consisted of three sections, arranged around three sides of the table. Reclining was not only more comfortable physically for those dining but was also considered a mark of elegance. Dinner guests washed their hands before dinner and frequently during dinner, since they used their fingers for handling their food, though knives with iron blades or handles of bone were used to cut up food, and spoons of bronze, silver, or bone were also available. Guests brought their own napkins.

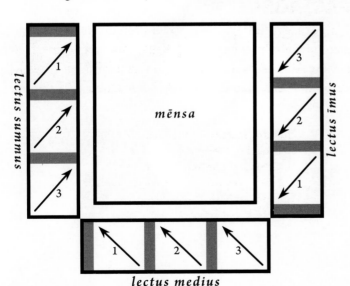

lectus medius

Diagram of a typical Roman dining room (*trīclīnium*) with a table (*mēnsa*) in the center surrounded on three sides by couches for the guests to recline upon while eating.

A Roman dinner could be comprised of as many as seven courses, and feature elaborate dishes of meat, fowl, and fish, artfully presented. The main meal consisted of three courses: the appetizer (*gustātiō*); the main course (*prīma mēnsa*); and the dessert course called the *mēnsa secunda*, "second table." Since eggs were eaten at the beginning of the meal and apples at the end, the expression *ab ōvō ūsque ad māla* (literally translated "from the egg to apples," our "from soup to nuts") characterizes the meal. During dinner itself, there were dances, recitations, and games, and, especially at relatively frugal meals, philosophical conversations. In the imperial period dining was sometimes marked by immoderation and excess: dinner guests might visit the so-called vomiting room after stuffing themselves with food so that they could continue their feasting.

From different periods of the Roman occupation near the Ljubljanica River in Slovenia come these artifacts: mortar, helmet, ladle, saucepan, oil lamps, and ax.

Wooden plates with spoons of bronze used by the Roman soldiers during the time of Caracalla.

Wine was also consumed, at times excessively, over the course of Roman banquets. The thickly textured wine from southern Italy was usually mixed with water, a custom the Romans shared with the Greeks. Romans also liked *mulsum*, a mixture of wine and honey. In his *Satyricon*, a novel in prose and verse, the first-century CE Roman author Petronius offers a picturesque description of a banquet hosted by a newly wealthy man of questionable taste named Trimalchio whose feast is characterized by both culinary and behavioral excesses.

EXPLORING THE MYTH OF THE TROJAN HORSE

NEVER LOOK A GIFT HORSE IN THE MOUTH

The story of the Trojan horse resonates throughout literature and art. It is first found in three separate accounts in Homer's *Odyssey* (4.266–89; 8.499–520; 11.523–38), written probably in the eighth century BCE. In Homer's account the crafty Odysseus conceived the idea of building a giant horse in which to conceal armed Greeks. Epeius was the craftsman of the horse. Homer does not tell us how many warriors the horse held, but he specifically mentions the heroes Odysseus, his usual companion Diomedes, the Spartan king Menelaus, the rather insignificant Antiklos, and Neoptolemus, Achilles's son. The Trojans debated what to do with the strange horse: to destroy it with axes, throw it over a cliff, or take it into their city. There is no mention in Homer of the Greek agent Sinon who, in later accounts such as Vergil's

Marble bust of Homer from the first or second century CE, discovered in Baiae, Italy.

(*Aeneid* 2.13–267), treacherously convinced the Trojans that the horse was a sort of symbolic offering to replace the Palladium, a sacred statue of Minerva (the Greek Athena) that had been stolen from her Trojan temple by Odysseus and Diomedes. Sinon pretended that the Greeks had returned home, since the gods were angry with them. In fact, they had concealed their fleet behind the island of Tenedos, just offshore from Troy. Sinon falsely claimed that, if the Trojans took the horse into the city, it would protect them. The opposite, of course, was true. The horse was so large that, in order to bring it into the city, the Trojans had to dismantle part of the walls and gates that had protected them so well for nearly ten years.

In Homer's account there is also no mention of the priest Laocoön who warned against bringing the horse into Troy. Laocoön first appears in a fragment of a Sophoclean play (fifth century BCE). His story is very familiar today primarily because of Vergil's vivid description but also because of a dramatic large sculpture of Laocoön and his sons being strangled by sea-serpents. This ancient sculpture was unearthed on the outskirts of Rome in 1506 CE and was assumed to be the statue that Pliny the Elder (first century CE) reports was in the palace of the emperor Vespasian (69–79 CE). The intriguing question is whether the sculpture predates Vergil's account (written prior to 19 BCE) or is a depiction of it. The sculpture is still a major attraction in the Vatican Museum in Rome.

As the story of the horse developed over time, new details were given. Vergil added the names of Thessandrus, Sthenelus, Thoas, Acamas, Machaon, and Epeius himself to those warriors hidden in the horse. He omitted Diomedes and Antiklos and, of course, called Odysseus by his Roman name, Ulysses. Quintus Smyrnaeus (fourth century CE) in his continuation of Homer's story, *The Fall of Troy* (Book 12.243ff.), names thirty warriors but adds that there were also many others. Smyrnaeus also depicts the prophetess Cassandra warning the Trojans about the danger hidden in the horse. In his version it is not Laocoön's gruesome death that undermines his warning but a madness sent by Athena.

Trojan horse used during the filming of the movie *Troy*.

One wonders about the origin of the story of the Trojan horse. Was it really an implement of war filled with armed men? Or was it symbolic? A wooden object would make sense as a replacement for the wooden Palladium. But why a horse? Horses, as the animals of the cavalry, are associated with war. The area of Troy itself was also famous for horses, such as the fabulous horses of the Trojan ally King Rhesus and the chariot-driving warriors of the Hyksos. Homer describes Ilium (Troy) as "rich in horses" and the Trojan hero Hektor as "breaker of horses." Neptune was the god who created horses and horses were sacrificed to him. He and Apollo were said to have built the great walls of Troy. It was because they were denied payment for their labor that Neptune then sided against the Trojans. Neptune was also called "earth-shaker" because of his association with earthquakes. Could the Trojan horse refer symbolically to the enmity of Neptune in causing an earthquake that destroyed Troy?

In later literature the story of the Trojan horse has come to epitomize treachery. In his *Inferno*, *Canto* 26.52–63, Dante (1265–1321) includes Odysseus and Diomedes in the Eighth Circle of hell that houses fraudulent counselors. They burn together wrapped in a shared flame. Sinon is also in the Eighth Circle housed with the falsifiers (*Canto* 30.91–129). He is unable to move for all eternity and a burning smoke rises from him as if from wet hands in wintertime. Chaucer (ca. 1343–1400) in his *Hous of Fame* follows Vergil's version and speaks of Sinon and his "false forswerynge [forswearing]" (153) as the cause of Troy's fall.

The first surviving artistic depiction of the Trojan horse is found on a Cycladic storage jar from about 670 BCE, not long after the apparent composition of the *Odyssey*. A wall painting from the Roman city of Pompeii (before 79 CE) shows several Trojans pulling the horse into the city with ropes. In a manuscript illustration, "The Trojan Horse Disgorges Its Burden," from a late fifteenth-century French version by LeFevre, three soldiers climb out of a hatch in the side of the horse. One of the more famous later depictions of the horse is a painting by Giovanni Tiepolo (1727–1804), *The Building of the Trojan Horse*.

In more recent times the story of the Trojan horse has been a popular theme in cartoons and movies. *The New Yorker* over the years has included numerous cartoons by artists such as Bender, Bliss, Larson, Fradon, Kliban, Ziegler, and others. They reinvent the theme by fashioning a Trojan cat, a Trojan dog, and many humorous variants. Other cartoonists have offered similarly witty takes on the theme. Hollywood has also embraced the image of the horse in a variety of films. One of the more extensive scenes in *Helen of Troy* (1956) reenacts the night that the festive Trojans brought the horse into the doomed city. The horse was enormous, but was made of balsa wood so that the actors could easily pull it! In *The Trojan Horse* (1961) a very large wooden horse is escorted into the city through elaborate gates. Wolfgang Petersen's recent film *Troy* (2004) includes the Trojan horse looming in the background as the Greeks run back to their ships.

A very different approach to the Trojan horse was taken by the comedy troupe Monty Python in *Monty Python and the Holy Grail* (1975). They parody the horse by creating a rabbit on wheels! King Arthur and his Knights of the Round Table have created it to fool the French, who indeed draw the animal into their castle. Unfortunately, the Knights had forgotten to climb inside! Much more recently the Trojan horse was featured in an episode of *The Simpsons* where Homer (Simpson) is Odysseus. Homer, Lenny, Carl, and Moe climb out of the horse and kill the Trojans who are "sleeping like babies."

The story of the Trojan horse has also entered the modern realm of computers and advertising. A particularly nasty computer virus that can cause a computer or whole system to crash is called a Trojan Horse. An advertising campaign for network security features a Trojan horse in the midst of a city. The horse is trapped in a cage fashioned from zeroes and ones.

Modern picture of a Trojan horse on the screen of a laptop computer.

At Troy today there is a large wooden horse with cut-out windows so that tourists can pretend to be invading Greeks. There is also a model (life-size or larger) in the Wisconsin Dells, Wisconsin, as part of a theme park named Mt. Olympus. The go-carts race on a pathway that goes underneath the wooden horse's belly.

The Trojan horse is a symbol that seems to thrive and gives testimony to the endurance of the classics in every age. It is intriguing to speculate how the symbol will continue to develop in the future.

Bonnie A. Catto
Professor of Classics
Assumption College
Worcester, Massachusetts

PHRASES AND QUOTATIONS RELATING TO WAR AND PEACE

PHRASES AND QUOTATIONS

- Arma cēdant togae. "The war should yield to peace," literally "Weapons should yield to the toga." Cicero (*On Duties* 1.77) quotes these words from his own lost poem about his consulship.

- Cāsus bellī. "A case for war." A modern Latin expression that applies to a situation provoking or justifying a war.

- Dīvide et imperā! "Divide and rule!" A motto of any imperialist policy. The source is unclear, though the phrase is repeated in many authors.

- Dulce et decōrum est prō patriā morī! "It is sweet and decorous to die for the fatherland." (Horace, *Odes* 3.2.13)

- Sī vīs pācem, parā bellum! "If you want peace, prepare for war!" A common Roman proverbial expression based on the Roman military historian Vegetius.

- Ubi sōlitūdinem faciunt, pācem appellant. "Where they make a desert, they call it peace." (Tacitus, *Agricola* 30.6) Words of a British leader about a Roman policy of expansion.

- Vae victīs! "Woe to the conquered!" (Based on Livy, *From the Founding of the City* 5) This phrase tells the story of the capture of Rome by the Gauls in the fourth century BCE, when it becomes clear that no rights existed for the defeated.

Sculpture of a Roman soldier. Villa Borghese.

CHAPTER 13

Present Tense Positive and Negative Imperatives; First and Second Person Personal Pronouns, Genitive Case; Third Person Possessive Pronoun and Adjective

A view of the Roman Forum showing the Via Sacra as well as the remains of the Temple of Vesta and the Temple of Antoninus and Faustina.

MEMORĀBILE DICTŪ

Carpe diem!

"Seize the day!" (Horace, *Odes* 1.11.8)

This phrase has become the byword for those who want to savor and treasure every moment in life, which is what Horace recommends in this poem, after stressing the uncertainty of the future.

READING

After the defeat of Antony and Cleopatra at Actium in 31 BCE, which brought an end to Rome's civil wars, Octavian assumed total control of the Roman state and adopted the name Augustus. Claiming, however, to be restoring the Roman Republic, he merely referred to himself as Rome's *prīnceps*, "first citizen." Historians thus refer to his reign, which lasted until his death in 14 CE, as the "Augustan principate." Although he continued to wage wars outside of Rome's boundaries during most of his principate, Augustus took credit for establishing an era of "Roman peace," the *pāx Rōmāna*.

Much of the literature produced during Augustus's principate, such as Vergil's *Aeneid*, treated topics of major political significance. Yet many of the authors who flourished during this period wrote of individual human concerns and emotions. Among them was Quīntus Horātius Flaccus (65–8 BCE), known to us as Horace, another poet who benefited from the patronage of Augustus's friend Maecenas.

Horace wrote poetry in various genres, most of Greek origin. His poems often voice a concern with the issue of human happiness, and assert that it can be achieved through the pursuit of equilibrium and moderation, as well as by fully appreciating every moment in life. Two phrases from his lyric verses called the *Odes* succinctly capture his philosophy of living, and abide with us today: *aurea mediocritās*, "the golden mean," and *carpe diem*, "seize the day."

The following passage is adapted from Horace, *Satire* 1.9, and describes an annoying encounter he experienced in the Roman Forum.

DĒ HOMINE IMPORTŪNŌ

1 Ambulābam in viā Sacrā et dē nūgīs meīs cōgitābam. Accurrit homō
   tantum nōmine mihi nōtus. Is bracchium meum capit atque dīcit:
   "Quid agis, dulcissime rērum?" "Bene," dīcō, "et cupiō omnia quae tū
   cupis." Tum discēdō. Is tamen mēcum ambulat. Eum rogō: "Quid prō
5 tē facere possum?" "Nōlī fugere," dīcit importūnus, "sed mēcum manē!"
   "Nōn mihi licet," respondeō, "dēbeō enim amīcum trāns Tiberim
   invīsere. Valē!" "Audī mē!" dīcit importūnus, "Nihil aliud facere dēbeō
   et nōn sum piger. Tē relinquere nōlō. Tēcum venīre possum." Miser
   ambulābam; nam eum ā mē discēdere cupiēbam. Importūnus
10 autem dē Maecēnāte eiusque amīcīs rogābat. "Ūnusquisque nostrum,"

respondēbam, "apud Maecēnātem locum suum habet: nōn tantum dīvitēs et doctī." Erāmus iam prope templum Vestae. Valdē cupiēbam ab importūnō relinquī, sed is mē nōn relinquēbat. Tunc homō ad nōs subitō venit et importūnum vocat: "Quō ambulās? Mēcum ad iūdicem venīre dēbēs." Deinde importūnum ad iūdicem dūcit et mē servat.

READING VOCABULARY

accurrō, accurrere, accurrī, accursum – to run up

***alius, alia, aliud** – another, other

***apud** + *accusative* – at the house of

***atque** (*conj.*) – and

audī! (*second person singular*) – hear!

bracchium, bracchiī, *n.* – arm

***discēdō, discēdere, discessī, discessum** – to leave, withdraw, go away

***dīves, dīvitis** – rich

***doctus, docta, doctum** – learned

***dūcō, dūcere, dūxī, ductum** – to lead

dulcissime rērum – dear fellow, *literally "the sweetest of all things"*

eius – his

***enim** (*adv.*) – for, in fact

importūnus, importūna, importūnum – boorish

invīsō, invīsere, invīsī, invīsum – to visit

***iūdex, iūdicis,** *m.* – judge

***licet** + *dative* + *infinitive* – it is allowed, it is permitted (for someone) (to do something)

locus, locī, *m.* – place

Maecēnās, Maecēnātis, *m.* – Maecenas

***mēcum** = **cum mē**

***nihil** – nothing

nōlī fugere! (*second person singular*) – do not run!

***nōlō** (*irregular verb*) – not to want, to be unwilling

nōtus, nōta, nōtum – known

nūgae, nūgārum, *f. pl.* – trifles

***omnis, omne** – each, every, all

piger, pigra, pigrum – lazy

***prō** + *ablative* – for, on behalf of

quae (*neuter plural accusative*) – what, which

***quid?** – what?

quid agis? – how are you?

quō? – to what place?

***respondeō, respondēre, respondī, respōnsum** – to answer

***rogō, rogāre, rogāvī, rogātum** – to ask

sacer, sacra, sacrum – holy, sacred

***suus, sua, suum** – his, her, its, their

***tantum** (*adv.*) – only

***tēcum** = **cum tē**

trāns Tiberim – on the other side of the Tiber River

***tum** (*adv.*) – then

ūnusquisque nostrum – each one of us

***valē!** (*second person singular*) – goodbye! (*literally "be well!"*)

Vesta, Vestae, *f.* – Vesta

Via Sacra – a street in the Roman Forum

* The words with an asterisk will need to be memorized.

COMPREHENSION QUESTIONS

1. Where was Horace when the described events happened?

2. What happened to Horace? What is he complaining about?

3. What did Horace say about Maecenas and his circle?

4. How did Horace get rid of his troubles?

LANGUAGE FACT I

PRESENT TENSE POSITIVE AND NEGATIVE IMPERATIVES

In the chapter reading passage you have noticed some new verb forms: *manē, valē, audī*. These are commands.

The command is a mood of the verb called the **imperative**. The mood you have been concerned with so far has been the **indicative**—it states the simple fact of an action.

The indicative mood represents the action as actually happening: *manēs,* "you remain."

The imperative mood represents the action as commanded to happen: *manē!* "remain!"

There are only two forms for the present active imperative: the second person singular (for commanding one person) and the second person plural (for commanding more than one person).

Here is how you form the present active imperative:

> **Singular active command**
> For verbs of all four conjugations, the singular form is identical to the stem (ending *–ā, –ē, –e,* and *–ī,* respectively). The imperative of the *–iō* verbs looks like that of third conjugation verbs.

> **Plural active command**
> The plural imperative form of all conjugations ends in *–te*.

For verbs of the first, second, and fourth conjugations, *–te* is added directly to the stem. In the third conjugation (including *–iō* verbs), *–e–* changes to *–i–* before *–te*.

For a **negative** command, use *nōlī* (singular) and *nōlīte* (plural) followed by an infinitive. Do not use *nōn*.

> *Nōlī discēdere!* "Do not go away!"
> *Nōlīte discēdere!* "Do not go away (plural)!"

BY THE WAY
The forms *nōlī* and *nōlīte* are present active imperatives of the irregular verb *nōlō*, "not to want."

Present Tense Positive and Negative Imperatives					
	First Conjugation	**Second Conjugation**	**Third Conjugation**	**Fourth Conjugation**	**Third Conjugation *–iō* Verbs**
Singular Positive	parā! (prepare!)	tenē! (hold!)	pete! (seek!)	audī! (hear!)	cape! (seize!)
Plural Positive	parāte! (prepare!)	tenēte! (hold!)	petite! (seek!)	audīte (hear!)	capite! (seize!)
Singular Negative	nōlī parāre! (do not prepare!)	nōlī tenēre! (do not hold!)	nōlī petere! (do not seek!)	nōlī audīre! (do not hear!)	nōlī capere! (do not seize!)
Plural Negative	nōlīte parāre! (do not prepare!)	nōlīte tenēre! (do not hold!)	nōlīte petere! (do not seek!)	nōlīte audīre! (do not hear!)	nōlīte capere! (do not seize!)

BY THE WAY

In an English translation, there is no difference between the singular and the plural commands.

STUDY TIP

Remember the Latin greetings *salvē* and *salvēte* from Chapter 1; these are second conjugation active imperative forms. Use **salvē** when greeting one person, and **salvēte** for two or more people. When bidding goodbye, use **valē** and **valēte**. Both *salvēre* and *valēre* mean "to be well."

▶ EXERCISE 1

Change the following present active infinitives into the positive imperative form indicated in parentheses. Translate each form.

Example: cōnspicere (plural)
cōnspicite!   observe (plural)!

1. pugnāre (plural)
2. ostendere (singular)
3. mittere (plural)
4. sentīre (singular)
5. invidēre (singular)
6. timēre (singular)
7. aestimāre (singular)
8. fugere (singular)

VOCABULARY TO LEARN

NOUN

iūdex, iūdicis, *m.* – judge

PRONOUNS

mēcum = cum mē – with me

nihil – nothing

quid? – what?

tēcum = cum tē – with you

ADJECTIVES

alius, alia, aliud – another, other

dīves, dīvitis – rich

doctus, docta, doctum – learned

omnis, omne – each, every, all

suus, sua, suum – his, her, its, their

VERBS

discēdō, discēdere, discessī, discessum – to leave, go away

dūcō, dūcere, dūxī, ductum – to lead

licet + *dative* + *infinitive* – it is allowed, it is permitted (for someone) (to do something)

nōlō (*irregular verb*) – not to want, to be unwilling

respondeō, respondēre, respondī, respōnsum – to answer

rogō, rogāre, rogāvī, rogātum – to ask

valē! – goodbye!

ADVERBS

tantum – only

tum – then

PREPOSITIONS

apud + *accusative* – at the house of

prō + *ablative* – for, on behalf of

CONJUNCTIONS

atque – and

enim – for, in fact

▶ EXERCISE 2

Find the English derivatives based on the Vocabulary to Learn in the following sentences. Write the corresponding Latin word.

1. The judicial power is separated from the executive one.
2. Nihilism is a frequently encountered attitude among young people.
3. There is alienation in big cities.
4. He was awarded a doctorate in law.
5. What would be your response to this accusation?
6. I gave a valedictory speech in my high school.
7. Do you have a driver's license?
8. The interrogation did not provide a lot of answers.
9. Who is omnipotent and omniscient?
10. An aqueduct is a structure through which water is transported.

The remains of the Temple
of Vesta, once a round structure.

▶ EXERCISE 3

Change the following positive imperatives into the negative and translate each negative form.

Example: respondē!
nōlī respondēre!   do not answer!

1. pugnāte!
2. discēde!
3. dolēte!
4. mittite!
5. vince!

6. putāte!
7. pete!
8. cape!
9. venīte!

▶ EXERCISE 4

Translate the following imperatives that Horace might have said to the boor and the boor to Horace.

Horace:
1. Free me!
2. Leave!
3. Flee!
4. Do not tell!
5. Leave me!

Boor:
1. Hear!
2. Believe me!
3. Wait!
4. Stay!
5. Answer!

LANGUAGE FACT II

FIRST AND SECOND PERSON PERSONAL PRONOUNS, GENITIVE CASE

When the personal pronouns *ego, tū, nōs,* and *vōs* were introduced in Chapter 12, you noticed that more was to be said about the genitives of these words. This is because the genitive of these pronouns is used quite differently from all the other declined forms.

Genitive of the First and Second Person Personal Pronouns			
First Person Singular	**Second Person Singular**	**First Person Plural**	**Second Person Plural**
meī	tuī	nostrī/nostrum	vestrī/vestrum

STUDY TIP

The genitive personal pronouns *meī, tuī, nostrī,* and *vestrī* are identical to the genitive singular masculine/neuter forms of the possessive adjectives, *meus, tuus, noster, vester.*

It may seem surprising, but in classical Latin these genitives are **not** used to indicate possession. Possession is indicated by possessive adjectives: *liber vester,* "your book," *amor meus,* "my love," etc.

The genitives of the personal pronouns are used in two situations:

- When the genitive of the personal pronoun is **partitive**.

Horace says to the boor in the chapter reading:

> *Ūnusquisque **nostrum** locum suum habet.* "Each one of us has his place."

The genitive *nostrum* expresses the totality, a part of which is indicated (*ūnusquisque*).

- When the genitive of the personal pronoun is joined to a noun that is closely related to a verb. This genitive is called **objective**.

Look at the following example:

> *Tē amō.* "I love you."

> *Meus amor tuī est magnus.* "My love for (of) you is great."

Tuī in the second sentence is an objective genitive. *Tuī* provides an object for the noun *amor* much in the same way as *tē* provides an object for the verb *amō*.

A verb simply has its accusative direct object. A noun, however, cannot take a direct object, and instead takes an objective genitive.

BY THE WAY

The forms *nostrum* and *vestrum* are used only when the genitive is partitive, and the forms *nostrī* and *vestrī* are used when the genitive is objective.

Examples:

> *multī vestrum,* "many of you (plural)" – **partitive**

> *amor vestrī,* "love of you (plural)" – **objective**

▶ EXERCISE 5

Translate into English. Identify the type of genitive (modifying/partitive/objective) in each sentence. The Reading Vocabulary may be consulted.

1. Paucī nostrum verba hominis importūnī audīre cupiunt.

2. Omnēs vestrum hominēs importūnōs fugere vidēminī.

3. Importūnus timōre meī nōn capiēbātur, sed mēcum ambulābat.

4. Da mihi auxilium propter tuum meī amōrem!

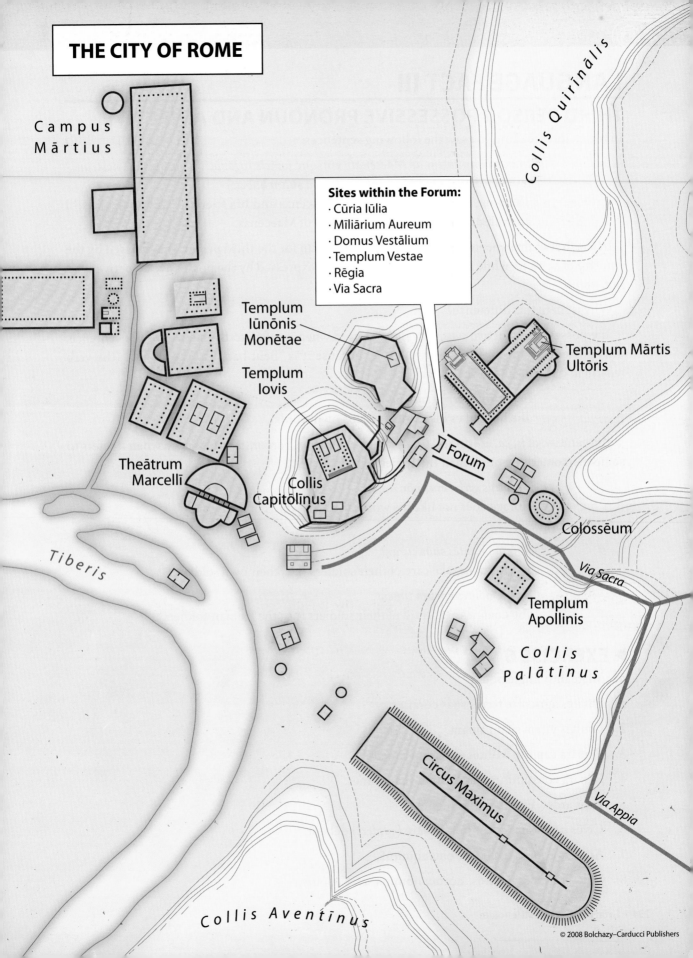

THE CITY OF ROME

Campus
Mārtius

Collis Quirīnālis

Sites within the Forum:
· Cūria Iūlia
· Mīliārium Aureum
· Domus Vestālium
· Templum Vestae
· Rēgia
· Via Sacra

Templum Iūnōnis
Monētae

Templum
Iovis

Templum Mārtis
Ultōris

Forum

Theātrum
Marcellī

Collis
Capitolīnus

Colossēum

Via Sacra

Tiberis

Templum
Apollinis

Collis
Palātīnus

Via Appia

Circus Maximus

Collis Aventīnus

LANGUAGE FACT III

THIRD PERSON POSSESSIVE PRONOUN AND ADJECTIVE

In the chapter reading you saw the following sentences:

> *Importūnus autem dē Maecēnāte **eiusque** amīcīs rogābat. "Ūnusquisque nostrum,"*
> *respondēbam, "apud Maecēnātem locum **suum** habet."*
>
> The boor, however, asked about Maecenas and **his** friends. "Each one of us," I
> answered, "has **his** place at the house of Maecenas."

In the first of these sentences the possessive pronoun for the third person is expressed by the genitive of *is, ea, id*, while in the second sentence it is expressed by the possessive adjective *suus, sua, suum*.

Why is there this difference?

The possessive adjective *suus, sua, suum* is used when it refers to the subject of the sentence. This possessive adjective is called reflexive, because it is "bent back" to the subject (the verb *reflectō* in Latin means to "bend back").

> *Importūnus verba **sua** amat.*
> The boor likes his words (i.e., his own words).

The genitive of *is, ea, id* (singular *eius*, and plural *eōrum, eārum, eōrum*) is used when it refers to someone/something other than the subject.

> *Horātius verba **eius** nōn amat.*
> Horace does not like his words (i.e., the words of the boor).

More examples:

> *Rōmānī mīlitēs **suōs** cūrant.*
> The Romans take care of their soldiers (i.e., their own soldiers).
>
> *Hostēs mīlitēs **eōrum** timent.*
> The enemies are afraid of their soldiers (i.e., the Roman soldiers).

▶ EXERCISE 6

Translate into English.

1. Dīvitēs agricolae terrās suās cūrant.

2. Omnēs vītam suam amant.

3. Dux īrā capitur. Mīlitēs eius īram timent.

4. Rēx īrā cōnsūmitur. Itaque īram suam timet.

5. Urbs ārdet. Eius flammās fugite!

6. Cīvēs casās suās ā flammīs servāre (*protect*) dēbent.

7. Amīcus equum dat. Cape eius equum!

8. Vidētis amīcōs nostrōs. Eōrum nōmina scīre cupitis.

▶ EXERCISE 7

Fill in the blanks with the correct third person possessive pronoun (her, his, its, their) and translate each sentence.

Example: Audiō puellam et _____ verba amō.
Audiō puellam et eius verba amō.   I hear the girl and I love her words.

1. Iūdicem timeō atque ___*eius*___ verba exspectō.
2. Rōma est mīlitum patria. Mīlitēs prō patriā ___*sua*___ pugnant.
3. Poētārum verba audīre cupimus. Verba enim _____ amāmus.
4. Puella passerem amat atque passerem in gremiō _____ tenet.

▶ EXERCISE 8

Translate into Latin. The Reading Vocabulary may be consulted.

1. Come with me!
2. Should I come with you?
3. Come with me (plural)!
4. Should we come with you?
5. Do not go away!
6. Do not go away (plural)!
7. Do not lead (plural) us to the judge!
8. The athlete was taking care of his body.
9. The boorish man was asking and the poet was answering nothing. The poet was not listening to his words.
10. All of us were asking you (plural). All of you (plural) had to answer.
11. The poet was saying to the boorish man: "Leave me because of love for me!"

TALKING

Quota hōra est? "What time is it?"

Est hōra prīma. "It's one o'clock."

. . . secunda. "It's two o'clock."

. . . tertia. "It's three o'clock."

. . . quārta. "It's four o'clock."

. . . quīnta. "It's five o'clock."

. . . sexta. "It's six o'clock."

. . . septima. "It's seven o'clock."

. . . octāva. "It's eight o'clock."

. . . nōna. "It's nine o'clock."

. . . decima. "It's ten o'clock."

. . . ūndecima. "It's eleven o'clock."

. . . duodecima. "It's twelve o'clock."

Est hōra prīma (secunda etc.) et quādrāns. "It's a quarter past one (two etc.)."

Est hōra prīma (secunda etc.) et dīmidia. "It's half past one (two etc.)."

Est hōra prīma (secunda etc.) et dōdrāns. "It's three quarters past one (two etc.)."

Est merīdiēs. "It's midday."

Est media nox. "It's midnight."

The Romans used sundials to determine the hour of the day.

Here is a table of the first ten cardinal and ordinal numerals in Latin.

	Cardinal numerals	**Ordinal numerals**
1-I	ūnus, ūna, ūnum	prīmus, prīma, prīmum
2-II	duo, duae, duo	secundus, secunda, secundum
3-III	trēs (m./f.), tria (n.)	tertius, tertia, tertium
4-IV	quattuor	quārtus, quārta, quārtum
5-V	quīnque	quīntus, quīnta, quīntum
6-VI	sex	sextus, sexta, sextum
7-VII	septem	septimus, septima, septimum
8-VIII	octō	octāvus, octāva, octāvum
9-IX	novem	nōnus, nōna, nōnum
10-X	decem	decimus, decima, decimum

Roman numerals are still used today, as seen engraved on this set of books.

BY THE WAY

The Romans used to count the daytime hours from the first hour, *hōra prīma* (about 6 AM), to the twelfth hour, *hōra duodecima* (about 6 PM). For example, our 11 AM is, according to the Romans, the fifth hour, *hōra quīnta*. The length of the Roman hour varied according to the time of year, since they told time by the sun.

They divided the night into watches: first watch, *vigilia prīma* (about 6 PM–9 PM), second watch, *vigilia secunda* (about 9 PM–midnight), third watch, *vigilia tertia* (about midnight–3 AM), fourth watch, *vigilia quārta* (about 3 AM–6 AM).

LATE FOR SCHOOL

Helena: Properā (*hurry*), Mārce! Sumus in morā (*delay*).

Mārcus: Dēbēmusne properāre?

Helena: Ita (*yes*), properāre dēbēmus.

Mārcus: Quota hōra est?

Helena: Est hōra octāva et quādrāns.

Mārcus: Tum properāre nōn dēbēmus. Nam schola (*school*) incipit (*starts*) horā octāvā et dīmidiā (*at 8:30*).

Helena: In scholam tamen hōrā octāvā et quādrante (*at 8:15*) intrāre dēbēmus. Nam librōs parāre dēbēmus.

Mārcus: Ego autem hōram prīmam exspectō.

Helena: Cūr? (*Why?*)

Mārcus: Nam hōrā prīmā est fīnis (*end*) scholārum.

Helena: Nōlī dē fīne scholārum nunc cōgitāre, sed mēcum venī!

DERIVATIVES

iūdex – injudicious, misjudge

nihil – annihilate, annihilation, nil

quid – quiddity, quip

alius – alien, alienate, inalienable

omnis – omnipotence, omnipresent, omniscient, omnivorous

dūcō – abduct, aqueduct, conduct, conduit, deduct, induce, induction, introduce, produce, redoubt, reduction, reproduction, seduce, subdue, viaduct

licet – illicit, leisure, license, licentious

respondeō – irresponsible, respond, response, responsive, responsibility

rogō – abrogate, arrogance, derogatory, interrogate, prerogative, surrogate

valē – avail, convalescent, equivalent, invalid, invaluable, prevail, valence, valiant, valid, valorous, value

prō – protect, protest, proponent, proposal, progress, projection, prominence, prologue, procrastinate, proclaim, proceed, profuse, provide, pronoun

First and Second Conjugation Verbs: Future Tense Active and Passive; Future Tense of *Sum* and *Possum*; Relative Pronouns; Relative Clauses

Pyramus and Thisbe. Lucas Cranach, the Elder (1472–1553).

MEMORĀBILE DICTŪ

Omnia vincit amor.

"Love conquers all things." (Vergil, *Eclogue* 10.69)

This sentence became proverbial for the power of love.

READING

One of the most brilliant and productive poets who lived during the reign of Augustus was Publius Ovidius Nāso (43 BCE–17 CE), whom English speakers call Ovid. He began his career as a writer of love poems, but expanded his literary repertoire to include more ambitious forms of poetry, most notably the mythological epic *Metamorphōsēs*, "Transformations." After his exile to the shores of Pontus on the Black Sea in 8 CE, to a place in what is now Romania, he turned his pen to a series of sorrowful reflections and laments, poems he called *Trīstia* ("Sad Songs") and "Letters from Pontus" (*Epistulae ex Pontō*). He was exiled by order of Augustus, but the reasons for his banishment remain unclear.

Below is an excerpt from the *Metamorphōsēs*: perhaps his most widely read work, it is a broadly ranging collection of mythological tales, and one of our best sources for earlier Greek mythology. Its title relates to the fact that every myth depicts the transformation of a human into an animal, vegetable, or mineral. In the text that follows, adapted from Book 4.55–166, you will be transported to the exotic oriental atmosphere of ancient Babylon.

The story explains why the mulberry tree produces dark-colored berries.

DĒ PȲRAMŌ ET THISBĒ

1   Pȳramus prope Thisbēn habitābat. Is eam amābat et ab eā amābātur.
    Propter odium tamen, quod erat inter eōrum parentēs, Pȳramus et
    Thisbē ūnā esse nōn poterant. Parietī, quī eōs sēparābat, verba saepe
    dīcēbant. "Semper, male pariēs, amantēs sēparās!" Sed quoque
5   parietem rogābant: "Licetne, bone pariēs, per tē verba mittere?"

    Pȳramus et Thisbē tandem clam convenīre dēcernunt. "Tē in agrīs
    prope arborem, in quā sunt pōma alba, hāc nocte vidēbō," inquit
    Pȳramus. Thisbē prīma venit et exspectat. Leaena subitō ad Thisbēn
    appropinquat. Leaena sanguinem in ōre habet. Nam leaena animal
10 comēdēbat. Thisbē timet et in spēluncam fugit, sed vēlāmen puellae
    in terram cadit. Leaena vēlāmen ōre suō tangit et sanguis in vēlāmine
    manet.

    Pȳramus venit et videt vēlāmen, in quō sanguis cōnspicitur. Thisbē
    iam nōn vīvere vidētur. Pȳramus valdē dolet et sē gladiō occīdit. Intereā
15 Thisbē ex spēluncā ambulat et videt Pȳramum in terrā mortuum iacēre.
    Thisbē gladium ex pectore Pȳramī eximit et sē quoque occīdit. Pȳramī
    et Thisbēs sanguis in terram fluit. Pōma arboris mox erunt rubra.

READING VOCABULARY

albus, alba, album – white

amāns, amantis, *m./f.* – lover

appropinquō, appropinquāre, appropinquāvī, appropinquātum + ad + *accusative* – to approach

arbor, arboris, *f.* – tree

cadō, cadere, cecidī, cāsum – to fall

clam (*adv.*) – secretly

comedō, comedere, comēdī, comēsum – to eat

conveniō, convenīre, convēnī, conventum – to meet

erunt – will be

eximō, eximere, exēmī, exēmptum – to take out

fluō, fluere, flūxī, fluxum – to flow

gladius, gladiī, *m.* – sword

hāc nocte – tonight

iam (*adv.*) – already, now

in quā (*feminine*) – on which

in quō (*neuter*) – in which

inter + *accusative* – between

intereā (*adv.*) – meanwhile

leaena, leaenae, *f.* – lioness

mortuus, mortua, mortuum – dead

mox (*adv.*) – soon

odium, odiī, *n.* – hatred

ōs, ōris, *n.* – mouth

parēns, parentis, *m./f.* – parent

pariēs, parietis, *m.* – wall

pectus, pectoris, *n.* – chest

per + *accusative* – through

pōmum, pōmī, *n.* – fruit, berry

prīmus, prīma, prīmum – first

Pȳramus, Pȳramī, *m.* – Pyramus

quī – which

quod – which

ruber, rubra, rubrum – red

sanguis, sanguinis, *m.* – blood

sēparō, sēparāre, sēparāvī, sēparātum – to separate, divide

tangō, tangere, tetigī, tāctum – to touch

Thisbē, Thisbēs (*gen.*), **Thisbē** (*dat.*), **Thisbēn** (*acc.*), **Thisbē** (*voc.*), *f.* – Thisbe

vēlāmen, vēlāminis, *n.* – veil

vidēbō – I will see

*Words with an asterisk will need to be memorized later in the chapter.

COMPREHENSION QUESTIONS

1. What was Pyramus and Thisbe's problem?

2. What resolution did they come to at last?

3. Why did Pyramus kill himself upon his arrival?

4. What happened to Thisbe at the end of the story?

LANGUAGE FACT I

FIRST AND SECOND CONJUGATION VERBS: FUTURE TENSE ACTIVE AND PASSIVE

In the Latin reading passage, Pyramus, when talking to Thisbe about the time they have arranged for a meeting, says: *Tē . . . hāc nocte vidēbō*, "I will see you tonight." The form *vidēbō* belongs to the future tense of the verb *videō*.

First and second conjugation verbs have similar future forms: add to the stem of the verb *–bō, –bis, –bit, –bimus, –bitis, –bunt* (active voice) and *–bor, –beris, –bitur, –bimur, –biminī, –buntur* (passive voice).

First Conjugation: Future Active

		Singular		Plural
First person	pará**bō**	I will/shall prepare	pará**bimus**	we will/shall prepare
Second person	pará**bis**	you will prepare	pará**bitis**	you will prepare
Third person	pará**bit**	s/he/it will prepare	pará**bunt**	they will prepare

First Conjugation: Future Passive

		Singular		Plural
First person	pará**bor**	I will/shall be prepared	pará**bimur**	we will/shall be prepared
Second person	pará**beris**	you will be prepared	pará**biminī**	you will be prepared
Third person	pará**bitur**	s/he/it will be prepared	pará**buntur**	they will be prepared

Second Conjugation: Future Active

		Singular		Plural
First person	tenē**bō**	I will/shall hold	tenē**bimus**	we will/shall hold
Second person	tenē**bis**	you will hold	tenē**bitis**	you will hold
Third person	tenē**bit**	s/he/it will hold	tenē**bunt**	they will hold

Second Conjugation: Future Passive

		Singular		Plural
First person	tenē**bor**	I will/shall be held	tenē**bimur**	we will/shall be held
Second person	tenē**beris**	you will be held	tenē**biminī**	you will be held
Third person	tenē**bitur**	s/he/it will be held	tenē**buntur**	they will be held

STUDY TIP

In an old fairy tale two princes had changed themselves into storks so that they could hear what people thought about them. One of them explained to the other how they could get back to their human form. "You have to remember and say a very difficult ancient word," said the prince, "MUTABOR."

For you, however, who have just learned the future tense, there will be no difficulty in the form *mūtābor*. It is simply the future passive indicative first person singular of the verb *mūtō*: "I will be transformed." Remember the form *mūtābor*, if you do not want to remain a stork!

BY THE WAY

The future tense of *amō* is *amābō*. It means not only "I will love," but also "please." For example: *Amābō tē, da mihi librum.* "Please, give me the book."

The logic is as follows: "I will love you, and I will be pleased with you, if you do such and such."

▶ EXERCISE 1

Change the following verbs into future active, in the person and number indicated. Translate the new form.

Example: sēparō (first person singular)
sēparābō   I will separate

1. iūdicō (first person singular)
2. aedificō (third person plural)
3. doceō (second person singular)
4. doleō (first person plural)
5. servō (third person singular)
6. iubeō (second person plural)
7. parō (third person plural)
8. iaceō (first person singular)
9. soleō (second person plural)
10. pugnō (third person singular)

VOCABULARY TO LEARN

NOUNS

arbor, arboris, *f.* – tree
gladius, gladiī, *m.* – sword
odium, odiī, *n.* – hatred
ōs, ōris, *n.* – mouth
parēns, parentis, *m./f.* – parent
pectus, pectoris, *n.* – chest
sanguis, sanguinis, *m.* – blood

PRONOUN

quī, quae, quod – which, who, that

ADJECTIVES

albus, alba, album – white
prīmus, prīma, prīmum – first
ruber, rubra, rubrum – red

VERBS

cadō, cadere, cecidī, cāsum – to fall
comedō, comedere, comēdī, comēsum – to eat
conveniō, convenīre, convēnī, conventum – to meet
fluō, fluere, flūxī, fluxum – to flow
sēparō, sēparāre, sēparāvī, sēparātum – to separate
tangō, tangere, tetigī, tāctum – to touch

ADVERBS

iam – already, now
mox – soon

PREPOSITION

per + *accusative* – through

▶ EXERCISE 2

Find the English derivatives based on the Vocabulary to Learn in the following sentences. Write the corresponding Latin word.

1. I will need to buy an expectorant for my cough.

2. Children need attentive parental care.

3. Please, approach this delicate problem with a lot of tact.

4. I am fluent in Spanish.

5. In our country there is separation of state and church.

6. Representatives from all over the world came to this convention.

7. Because of her sanguine character she bore the difficulties cheerfully.

8. Please, show me the album with the wedding pictures!

9. Under this rubric the issue of property is dealt with.

10. For this class you will need to prepare several oral presentations.

11. The gladiators came into the arena.

12. Doing so much homework is odious to me.

13. He was elected the prime minister of England.

14. Do you want to come for a walk in the arboretum?

15. As she spoke, there was a lovely cadence in her voice.

▶ EXERCISE 3

Change the present or imperfect tense verbs into the future, keeping the same person, number, and voice. Translate both forms.

Example: amābām   I loved/used to love/was loving
amābō   I will love

1. respondēbās
2. līberātur
3. sēparāris
4. nāvigat
5. cōgitābāmus
6. dēleō
7. dēbēbātis
8. docēbant
9. firmāminī
10. invidēmur
11. iūdicābantur
12. moveor

▶ EXERCISE 4

Change the verbs in the following passage into the future tense, keeping the same person, number, and voice. Then translate the passage.

Example: Amīcō fābulam nārrō.
Amīcō fābulam nārrābō.   I will tell story to (my) friend.

Puer puellam amat. Puer ā puellā amātur. Puer et puella ad arborem in agrīs ambulāre dēbent. Puella ibi exspectat et leaenam (*lioness*) videt. Puella cum leaenā nōn pugnat, sed timet et in spēluncā manet. Tum puer ad arborem ambulat. Puella apud arborem nōn vidētur. Puer rogat: "Ubi (*where*) es, amīca (*feminine of* amīcus)?" Puer et puella in morte nōn sēparantur. Semper potestis vōs amāre, puer et puella!

LANGUAGE FACT II

FUTURE TENSE OF *SUM* AND *POSSUM*

You have already learned the present and the imperfect tense of the irregular verbs *sum* and *possum*. In the story about Pyramus and Thisbe you read the following: *Pōma arboris mox erunt rubra*, "The berries of the tree will soon be red." In this sentence you see the future tense form of the verb *sum*.

Note the red color of the mulberry resulting from the spilling of blood according to myth.

Here is the future indicative of *sum* and *possum*.

Future Tense of *sum*					
	Singular			**Plural**	
First person	erō	I will/shall be	erimus	we will/shall be
Second person	eris	you will be	eritis	you will be
Third person	erit	s/he/it will be	erunt	they will be

Future Tense of *possum*					
	Singular			**Plural**	
First person	poterō	I will/shall be able	poterimus	we will/shall be able
Second person	poteris	you will be able	poteritis	you will be able
Third person	poterit	s/he/it will be able	poterunt	they will be able

BY THE WAY

In the same way as in the imperfect tense, also the future forms of *possum* are almost identical with those of *sum*, the prefix *pot-* being added in front of the forms of *sum*.

▶ EXERCISE 5

Change the present or imperfect tense verbs into the future, keeping the same person and number. Translate both forms.

Example: es

eris   you are   you will be

1. poterātis
2. erant
3. potest
4. sumus
5. possunt
6. erās
7. erātis
8. poterat
9. poteram
10. erat

▶ EXERCISE 6

Translate into Latin. The Reading Vocabulary may be consulted for names.

1. I am able to hear a story. I was able to hear a story. I will be able to hear a story.

2. Pyramus is not happy. He was not happy. He will not be happy.

3. You, Pyramus, are not happy. You, Pyramus, were not happy. You, Pyramus, will not be happy.

4. Are they able to meet? They were not able to meet. They will be able to meet.

5. You, Pyramus and Thisbe, are not able to be together. You, Pyramus and Thisbe, were able to be together, but will not be able to be together.

6. We were able to tell about love, we are able and we will be able.

LANGUAGE FACT III

RELATIVE PRONOUNS; RELATIVE CLAUSES

In the story at the beginning of the chapter Pyramus says:

> *Tē in agrīs prope arborem, in* **quā** *sunt pōma alba, hāc nocte vidēbō.*
> Tonight I will see you in the fields near the tree in **which** there are white berries.

This sentence contains a relative clause. A relative clause begins with a **relative pronoun** (in English "that," "who/whose/whom," or "which"). The relative pronoun stands in for a word in the main clause; this word is called the relative pronoun's **antecedent**, because it usually precedes the relative clause.

A relative pronoun has the same number and gender as its antecedent. In the example given above, the relative pronoun *quā* has the same number and gender as its antecedent *arborem*, i.e., singular and feminine.

A relative pronoun has its own case, independent of its antecedent. This is because a relative pronoun belongs to a separate part of a sentence, the relative clause. A relative clause has its own grammatical structure. In the example above, *quā* is ablative because it follows the preposition *in*. The relative pronoun may perform any case function.

Here is the declension of the relative pronoun.

Relative Pronoun							
			Singular				
	Masculine		**Feminine**			**Neuter**	
Nominative	quī	who, which, that	quae	who, which, that		quod	which, that
Genitive	cūius	whose, of whom, of which	cūius	whose, of whom, of which		cūius	of which
Dative	cui	to/for whom, to/for which	cui	to/for whom, to/for which		cui	to/for which
Accusative	quem	whom, which, that	quam	whom, which, that		quod	which, that
Ablative	quō	by/with whom, by/with which	quā	by/with whom, by/with which		quō	by/with which
			Plural				
	Masculine		**Feminine**			**Neuter**	
Nominative	quī	who, which, that	quae	who, which, that		quae	which, that
Genitive	quōrum	whose, of whom, of which	quārum	whose, of whom, of which		quōrum	of which
Dative	quibus	to/for whom, to/for which	quibus	to/for whom, to/for which		quibus	to/for which
Accusative	quōs	whom, which, that	quās	whom, which, that		quae	which, that
Ablative	quibus	by/with whom, by/with which	quibus	by/with whom, by/with which		quibus	by/with which

BY THE WAY

Some of the endings of the relative pronoun are similar to those of the first and second declension, while others resemble endings of the third declension. Some, e.g., genitive singular, resemble no noun declension.

Here are more examples of relative clauses. Note that a relative clause conveys information about a noun in the clause on which it depends, and in this way the whole relative clause functions like an adjective.

> *Puella quam Pȳramus amat est bona.*
> The girl that (whom) Pyramus loves is good.

Quam is feminine singular, since it refers to a feminine singular antecedent, *puella*; *quam* is accusative, since it is a direct object of *amat*.

> *Pariēs cui Pȳramus verba dīcit respondēre nōn potest.*
> The wall to which Pyramus says words cannot answer.

Cui is masculine singular, since it refers to *pariēs*; it is dative, since it is an indirect object of *verba dīcit*.

▶ EXERCISE 7

Find three more relative clauses in the Latin reading passage and translate. Give the reason for the case, number, and gender of the relative pronoun. The Reading Vocabulary may be consulted.

▶ EXERCISE 8

Translate the following Latin sentences into English, and English sentences into Latin.

1. My parents, whom I am asking about many things, know many things.
2. Pugnābitis cum mīlitibus quī timōrem in pectoribus suīs nōn habēbunt.
3. The citizens to whom swords are being given are strong.
4. Poēta, ex cūius ōre verba nunc audīmus, est celeber.
5. The sparrow seeks the finger of the mistress who is holding him.
6. The animal that she fears leaves.
7. Lacrimae fluēbant ex oculīs hominis cui fābula nārrābātur.
8. You ought not to have the hatred that is in your heart.
9. Puella dē cūius vītā is dolēbat vīvēbat.

A lion such as the one in this mosaic scared Thisbe.

TALKING

(*īnstrūmentum, īnstrūmentī,* n.) *computātōrium* – computer

computātōrium gestābile – laptop

interrēte, interrētis, n. – internet

īnscrīptiō (īnscrīptiōnis, f.) *ēlectronica* – e-mail address

epistula ēlectronica – e-mail

nūntiī subitāneī – instant messaging

Nāvigō in interrētī. "I surf the internet."

Per interrēte garriō. "I have an internet chat."

Quae est tua īnscrīptiō ēlectronica? "What is your e-mail address?"

Mitte ad mē epistulam ēlectronicam! "Send me an e-mail!"

Quaeram in interrētī. "I will check on the internet."

CHATTING ON THE INTERNET

Helena: Poterāsne, Mārce, herī (*yesterday*) pēnsum (*homework*) tuum facere?

Mārcus: Nōn poteram. Nam multa alia facere dēbēbam.

Helena: Nāvigābāsne in interrētī?

Mārcus: Aaa . . .

Marīa: (*INTRAT*) Salvēte, Mārce et Helena! Pulchrōs nūntiōs subitāneōs ad mē, Mārce, herī mittēbās.

Helena: Nūntiōs subitāneōs?!

Marīa: Ego et Mārcus herī diū in interrētī nāvigābāmus, et per interrēte garriēbāmus. Hodiē quoque nāvigābimus. Nōnne (*won't we*), Mārce?

Helena: Itaque nōn poterās, Mārce, pēnsum parāre propter nūntiōs quōs ad Marīam mittēbās. (*DISCĒDIT*) Valēte!

Mārcus: Manē, Helena! Nōlī mihi īrāscī (*get angry*)! Hodiē (*Today*) in interrētī nōn nāvigābō. Pēnsum meum parābō. Poterimus quoque ūnā ambulāre. Ambulābimusne hodiē ūnā?

Helena: Vidēbimus . . . Tē cōmpellābō (*will call*).

DERIVATIVES

arbor – arboreal

gladius – gladiolus, gladiator

odium – annoy, ennui, noisome, odious

ōs – oral, orifice, usher

parēns – parental, grandparent, repertoire, repertory

pectus – expectorate, parapet, pectoral

sanguis – consanguinity, sanguinary, sanguine

albus – albino, albumen, auburn, daub, dauber

prīmus – primary, primal, primacy, primate, primer, primeval, primitive, primogeniture, primrose, prince, princess, principal, principle

ruber – rouge, rubric, ruby

cadō – accident, cadence, cascade, casual, casualty, chance, cheat, chute, coincide, decadence, decay, deciduous, incident, occasion, occident, parachute

comedō – comestible

fluō – affluence, confluence, effluent, fluctuate, fluency, fluid, flume, flux, influence, influenza, mellifluous, reflux, superfluous

sēparō – separate, sever, several

tangō – attain, contact, contagious, contaminate, contiguous, contingent, disintegrate, distaste, entire, intact, intangible, integer, integral, intangible, integration, tact, tangent, tangible, taste

Third and Fourth Conjugation Verbs: Future Tense Active and Passive; Interrogative Pronouns and Adjectives

The death of Seneca, who was ordered to commit suicide by the emperor Nero. Luca Giordano (1634–1705).

MEMORĀBILE DICTŪ

Dūcunt volentem fāta, nōlentem trahunt.

"Destiny guides the individual who is willing, drags the unwilling." (Seneca, *Moral Letters* 107.11)

Originally written by the Greek philosopher Cleanthes, and translated into Latin by Seneca, this motto encapsulates the willingness of the Stoics to comply with destiny.

READING

Lūcius Annaeus Seneca (ca. 4 BCE–65 CE) is known as Seneca the Younger to distinguish him from his father, Seneca the Elder, an acclaimed teacher of Roman oratory. Born in Spain, he came to Rome as a child, and was attracted in his early years by philosophy, particularly Stoicism. A skilled orator who attained the political office of *quaestor*, he was exiled to Corsica in 41 CE by the emperor Claudius, but recalled in 49 CE through the influence of Claudius's wife Agrippina, and named tutor to her son, the future emperor Nero. Upon Nero's accession in 54 CE, Seneca became his political advisor and minister. Yet his authority with his former student waned, and he was forced to commit suicide—which he did with memorable Stoic fortitude—in 65 CE.

Seneca wrote dramas, which survive as the major ancient examples of tragedy in Latin, as well as philosophical essays and treatises, a work on natural phenomena, and a satire on Claudius's death. However, he is best known for his collection of writings addressed to his friend Lucilius. Called *Epistulae Mōrālēs*, "Moral Letters," they take the form of letters, but are better described as short essays addressing various philosophical issues from a personal perspective and in a conversational tone. In the letter below, an adapted version of *Epistulae Mōrālēs* 12, Seneca discusses old age, presenting it as a personal encounter.

SENECA SENECTŪTEM SUAM CONVENIT

1   Seneca Lūcīliō salūtem dīcit.

Ubīque argūmenta senectūtis meae videō. Est mihi vīlla rūstica. Veniō in vīllam meam et vīlicus mihi dīcit sē dēbēre multa in vīllā reparāre. Dīcit sē omnia facere, sē nihil neglegere, sed vīllam esse

5   vetustam. Sed ego vīllam aedificāveram! Quid mihi erit? Corpusne meum cadet sīcut vīllae meae saxa?

"Tū," inquam, "arborēs neglegis: nōn habent folia. Tūne aquam arboribus dās?"

"Arborēs," inquit, "semper cūrābam et cūrābō nec umquam ā mē

10   neglegentur. Sed sunt vetustae."

Id tibi dīcam, Lūcīlī, quod fortasse nōn crēdēs esse vērum: mē arborēs posuisse!

Tunc iānuam cōnspiciō. Ibi stat senex, quī mē spectat.

"Quis est senex?" inquam. "Cūr mē spectat?"

15   "Nōnne cognōscis mē?" inquit senex. "Ego sum Fēlīciō, quōcum solēbās puer lūdere. Eram quondam parvus amīcus tuus."

Difficile mihi est cognōscere amīcum meum! Nam senex, quī ante mē stat, quī dentēs nōn habet, nōn vidētur similis puerī parvī, quōcum lūdere solēbam!

20   Vīlla mea mihi vidēbātur dīcere: "Ecce senectūs tua!" Senectūs ad nōs omnēs veniet etiam imparātōs. Itaque eam exspectāre dēbēmus. Parātī esse dēbēmus.

READING VOCABULARY

aedificāveram – had built

*ante + *accusative* – in front of

*argūmentum, argūmentī, *n.* – proof, indication, argument

cadet – will fall

cognōscō, cognōscere, cognōvī, cognitum – to recognize, get to know

crēdēs – you will believe

*cūr? (*adv.*) – why?

dēns, dentis, *m.* – tooth

dīcam – I will say

*difficilis, difficile – difficult

*ecce (*interjection*) – look here!

*etiam (*adv.*) – even, also

Fēlīciō, ——, *m.* – Felicio, *a servant's name*

folium, foliī, *n.* – leaf

*fortasse (*adv.*) – perhaps

iānua, iānuae, *f.* – door

imparātus, imparāta, imparātum – unprepared

*inquam – I say/I said (*only introducing direct speech*)

Lūcīlius, Lūcīliī, *m.* – Lucilius *was a friend of Seneca's to whom he addressed his philosophical essays in the form of letters*

lūdō, lūdere, lūsī, lūsum – to play

neglegentur – they will be neglected

*neglegō, neglegere, neglēxī, neglēctum – to neglect

nōnne? – don't you?

parātus, parāta, parātum – prepared

*parvus, parva, parvum – small

posuisse – have placed, have planted

*quis? – who?

quōcum = **cum quō** – with whom (*the preposition* cum *is attached to the end of the relative pronoun*)

quondam (*adv.*) – once

reparō, reparāre, reparāvī, reparātum – to repair

*rūsticus, rūstica, rūsticum – rural, rustic

salūtem – health, greeting: *this is the accusative singular of the noun* salūs, salūtis, *f.; it appears at the beginning of a letter with the name of the sender in the nominative, the addressee in the dative, and the verb* dīcit.   *"dear... person"*

*saxum, saxī, *n.* – stone, rock

Seneca, Senecae, *m.* – Seneca

*senectūs, senectūtis, *f.* – old age

*sīcut (*adv.*) – just as

spectō, spectāre, spectāvī, spectātum – to gaze, stare at

*stō, stāre, stetī, statum – to stand

*ubīque (*adv.*) – everywhere

*umquam (*adv.*) – ever

veniet – will come

*vērus, vēra, vērum – true

*vetustus, vetusta, vetustum – old

vīlicus, vīlicī, *m.* – bailiff, steward

*vīlla, vīllae, *f.* – country house, villa

*Words marked with an asterisk will need to be memorized later in the chapter.

COMPREHENSION QUESTIONS

1. What were Seneca's first impressions when he visited his country house?

2. Who was Felicio and why did Seneca not recognize him?

3. What did Seneca learn from his visit to the country house?

LANGUAGE FACT I

THIRD AND FOURTH CONJUGATION VERBS: FUTURE TENSE ACTIVE AND PASSIVE

In the previous chapter you met the future tense of first and second conjugation verbs. In this chapter you meet the future tense of the third and fourth conjugations. Notice the verb forms in these sentences from the chapter reading passage.

> *Corpusne meum **cadet** sīcut vīllae meae saxa?*
> Will my body collapse, just like the stones of my villa?

> *"Arborēs," inquit, "semper cūrābam et cūrābō nec umquam ā mē **neglegentur**..."*
> "I always took care of the trees," he said, "and will take care of them and they will never be neglected by me..."

> *Id tibi **dīcam**, Lucīlī, quod fortasse nōn **crēdēs** esse vērum...*
> I shall tell you something, Lucilius, which you will perhaps not believe is true...

> *Senectūs ad nōs omnēs **veniet** etiam imparātōs.*
> Old age will come to all of us even <when we are> unprepared.

Boldface letters indicate the future forms belonging to the third and the fourth conjugations.

Instead of the consonant –*b*– that is characteristic of the future of the first and second conjugations, you see the vowels –*a*– and –*e*– in the future forms of the third and fourth conjugations.

STUDY TIP
In the future,
First and second conjugation,
You will see a "b,"
But in the third and fourth
It's an "a" or an "e."

Third conjugation verbs form their future by adding to the stem the personal endings: –*m*, –*s*, –*t*, –*mus*, –*tis*, –*nt* (active), and –*r*, –*ris*, –*tur*, –*mur*, –*minī*, –*ntur* (passive). The –*e*– of the stem changes to –*a*– in the first person singular active and passive.

Fourth conjugation verbs form their future by adding –*a*– to the stem in the first person singular active and passive, and –*e*– in the second and third persons, followed by the personal endings.

The future of third conjugation –*iō* verbs is identical to the future of fourth conjugation verbs.

Third Conjugation: Future Active

	Singular			Plural	
First person	pet**am**	I will/shall seek	pet**ēmus**	we will/shall seek
Second person	pet**ēs**	you will seek	pet**ētis**	you will seek
Third person	pet**et**	s/he/it will seek	pet**ent**	they will seek

Third Conjugation: Future Passive

	Singular			Plural	
First person	pet**ar**	I will/shall be sought	pet**ēmur**	we will/shall be sought
Second person	pet**ēris**	you will be sought	pet**ēminī**	you will be sought
Third person	pet**ētur**	s/he/it will be sought	pet**entur**	they will be sought

Fourth Conjugation: Future Active

	Singular			Plural	
First person	audi**am**	I will/shall hear	audi**ēmus**	we will/shall hear
Second person	audi**ēs**	you will hear	audi**ētis**	you will hear
Third person	audi**et**	s/he/it will hear	audi**ent**	they will hear

Fourth Conjugation: Future Passive

	Singular			Plural	
First person	audi**ar**	I will/shall be heard	audi**ēmur**	we will/shall be heard
Second person	audi**ēris**	you will be heard	audi**ēminī**	you will be heard
Third person	audi**ētur**	s/he/it will be heard	audi**entur**	they will be heard

Third Conjugation –*iō* verbs: Future Active

	Singular			Plural	
First person	capi**am**	I will/shall take	capi**ēmus**	we will/shall take
Second person	capi**ēs**	you will take	capi**ētis**	you will take
Third person	capi**et**	s/he/it will take	capi**ent**	they will take

Third Conjugation –*iō* verbs: Future Passive

	Singular			Plural	
First person	capi**ar**	I will/shall be taken	capi**ēmur**	we will/shall be taken
Second person	capi**ēris**	you will be taken	capi**ēminī**	you will be taken
Third person	capi**ētur**	s/he/it will be taken	capi**entur**	they will be taken

STUDY TIP

Note that in the third conjugation the future and present passive indicative second person singular are identical, aside from the length of the vowel *–e–*:

relinqueris – you are being abandoned

relinquēris – you will be abandoned

▶ EXERCISE 1

Change the present or imperfect tense verbs into the future, keeping the same person, number, and voice. Translate both forms.

Example: cadēbās   you were falling

cadēs   you will fall

1. mittitur
2. sciunt
3. comedēbāmus
4. dūcēbāminī
5. relinquitis
6. ostendēbar
7. occīdēbāmur
8. faciēbat

VOCABULARY TO LEARN

NOUNS

argūmentum, argūmentī, *n.* – proof, indication, argument

saxum, saxī, *n.* – stone, rock

senectūs, senectūtis, *f.* – old age

vīlla, vīllae, *f.* – country house, villa

PRONOUN

quis, quid? – who? what? (*interrogative pronoun*)

ADJECTIVES

difficilis, difficile – difficult

parvus, parva, parvum – small

quī, quae, quod? – what? which? (*interrogative adjective*)

rūsticus, rūstica, rūsticum – rural, rustic

vērus, vēra, vērum – true

vetustus, vetusta, vetustum – old

VERBS

inquam – I say/I said (*only introducing direct speech*)

neglegō, neglegere, neglēxī, neglēctum – to neglect

stō, stāre, stetī, statum – to stand

ADVERBS

cūr? – why?

etiam – even, also

fortasse – perhaps

sīcut – just as

ubīque – everywhere

umquam – ever

PREPOSITION

ante + *accusative* – in front of

INTERJECTION

ecce – look here!

▶ EXERCISE 2

Find the English derivatives based on the Vocabulary to Learn in the following sentences. Write the corresponding Latin word.

1. Where is the source of the difficulty?
2. Do not neglect your duties!
3. I usually get up at 6 AM.
4. This is a rather unrefined, rustic recipe.
5. Senile debility may come with old age.
6. Nothing moves here; everything is static.
7. These documents need to be verified.
8. The argumentation needs to be internally coherent and valid.
9. You can see advertisements everywhere: they are ubiquitous.
10. We may buy a house in a small village.

LANGUAGE FACT II

INTERROGATIVE PRONOUNS AND ADJECTIVES

In the reading passage adapted from Seneca at the beginning of this chapter you meet two new interrogative words. These are the equivalents of the English interrogative pronouns "who?" and "what?"

> ***Quid** mihi erit?*
> What will be <in store> for me?

> ***Quis** est senex?*
> Who is the old man?

In Latin there is an interrogative pronoun and an interrogative adjective. The interrogative pronoun stands alone, without modifying another noun. The interrogative adjective modifies a noun, and agrees with it in case, number, and gender (like any adjective).

The nominative singular interrogative pronoun is *quis* (masculine and feminine) and *quid* (neuter); it is *quī, quae, quae* in the plural. **Note that in the plural all forms of the interrogative pronoun are identical to those of the relative pronoun.**

A terra-cotta bust was found in Herculaneum and closely resembles the actual bust of Seneca now in the Archaeological Museum in Naples.

BY THE WAY

The reason for the lack of separate feminine forms in the singular is that an unspecified question beginning with *quis* is actually asking about a human person in general without reference to its gender.

Study these uses of the interrogative pronoun:

> *Quis veniet?* – "Who (m./f.) will come?"
>
> *Quem amās?* – "Whom (m./f.) do you love?"
>
> *Cūius est liber?* – "Whose (m./f.) book is it?"
>
> *Quī vōbīs auxilium dabunt?* – "Who will give you help?"

Sometimes a question is asked using an interrogative adjective. **The interrogative adjective is identical to the relative pronoun in all its forms.**

Study these uses of the interrogative adjective:

> *Quī ager est tuus?* – "Which field is yours?"
>
> *Quam fēminam amās?* – "Which woman do you love?"
>
> *Cūius magistrī verba audīs?* – "Which teacher's words do you hear?"
>
> *Quās terrās capiunt Rōmānī?* – "Which lands do the Romans seize?"

Here are the declensions of the interrogative pronoun and the interrogative adjective.

Interrogative Pronoun

Singular

	Masculine and Feminine		**Neuter**	
Nominative	quis	who	quid	what
Genitive	cūius	whose	cūius	of what
Dative	cui	to/for whom	cui	to/for what
Accusative	quem	whom	quid	what
Ablative	quō	by/with whom	quō	by/with what

Plural

	Masculine		**Feminine**		**Neuter**	
Nominative	quī	who	quae	who	quae	what
Genitive	quōrum	whose	quārum	whose	quōrum	of which
Dative	quibus	to/for whom	quibus	to/for whom	quibus	to/for which
Accusative	quōs	whom	quās	whom	quae	which
Ablative	quibus	by/with whom	quibus	by/with whom	quibus	by/with which

Interrogative Adjective

Singular

	Masculine		**Feminine**		**Neuter**	
Nominative	quī	which	quae	which	quod	which
Genitive	cūius	of which	cūius	of which	cūius	of which
Dative	cui	to/for which	cui	to/for which	cui	to/for which
Accusative	quem	which	quam	which	quod	which
Ablative	quō	by/with which	quā	by/with which	quō	by/with which

Plural

	Masculine		**Feminine**		**Neuter**	
Nominative	quī	which	quae	which	quae	which
Genitive	quōrum	of which	quārum	of which	quōrum	of which
Dative	quibus	to/for which	quibus	to/for which	quibus	to/for which
Accusative	quōs	which	quās	which	quae	which
Ablative	quibus	by/with which	quibus	by/with which	quibus	by/with which

STUDY TIP

The interrogative adjective is identical to the relative pronoun *quī, quae, quod* in all its forms. So, the interrogative adjective does not require knowing any new forms—you learned them when you learned the relative pronoun in Chapter 14.

The interrogative pronoun is identical in form to the relative pronoun only in the plural.

BY THE WAY

When the preposition *cum* ("with") is used with a relative or an interrogative pronoun or interrogative adjective, it is attached to the end of the word: *quōcum, quācum, quibuscum*. Compare *mēcum* and *tēcum*.

Ancient Roman villas, also known as country houses, were large and often elaborately decorated as the frescoes on the walls of the Villa of the Mysteries in Pompeii show.

▶ EXERCISE 3

Translate into Latin.

1. Whose villa is old?

2. Whose (plural) villas are old?

3. What villa is old?

4. Which villas are old?

5. Whom is the old man observing?

6. Which friends is the old man observing?

7. Which old man is observing me?

8. To which farmer will you give the field?

9. To which farmers will you give the fields?

10. Which farmers will give me the fields?

11. With whom will you walk to the villa?

12. With whom (plural) will you stay in the villa?

▶ EXERCISE 4

Translate the following questions. Then choose the best answer for each and translate. The Reading Vocabulary may be consulted.

1. Cui vīlicus dīcit sē dēbēre multa in vīllā reparāre?

     Vīlicus puerō dīcit sē omnia facere.

     Senecae vīlicus dīcit sē dēbēre multa in vīllā reparāre.

     Vīlicus dīcit vīllam Senecae esse vetustam.

2. Quid vīlicus sē neglegere dīcit?

     Vīlicus dīcit sē arborēs neglegere.

     Vīlicus dīcit Senecam nihil neglegere.

     Vīlicus dīcit sē nihil neglegere.

3. Quid dē sē cōgitat Seneca?

     Seneca cōgitat sē esse vetustum sīcut vīllam.

     Seneca cōgitat vīlicum dēbēre multa in vīllā reparāre.

     Seneca cōgitat vīllam ā vīlicō nōn cūrārī.

A Roman coin with a portrait of Nero's head.

4. Quae folia sunt in arboribus?

   Folia ā vīlicō negleguntur.

   Arborēs nōn habent folia.

   Folia pulchra in arboribus cōnspiciuntur.

5. Ā quō arborēs semper cūrābantur nec umquam neglegentur?

   Vīlicus arborēs semper cūrābat nec eās negleget.

   Arborēs negleguntur: itaque nōn habent folia.

   Ā Senecā arborēs semper cūrābantur nec umquam neglegentur.

6. Quae arborēs vetustae esse dīcuntur?

   Arborēs nōn sunt vetustae.

   Fēlīciō arborēs vetustās habet.

   Arborēs Senecae dīcuntur esse vetustae.

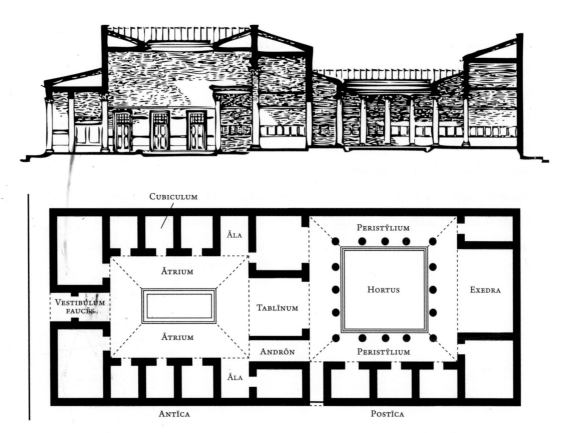

While ancient Roman villas were complex structures, a Roman city house (*domus*),
as the diagram shows, was much more compact.

7. Quem cōnspicit senex, quī in iānuā stat?

   Senex, quī in iānuā stat, dentēs nōn habet.

   Senecam cōnspicit senex, quī in iānuā stat.

   Ā Senecā cōnspicitur senex, quī in iānuā stat.

8. Ad quōs hominēs veniet senectūs?

   Ad imparātōs hominēs veniet senectūs.

   Ad Senecam veniet senectūs.

   Ad omnēs hominēs veniet senectūs.

▶ EXERCISE 5

Read the following dialogue, which is written partly in English and partly in Latin. Translate the English parts into Latin, and the Latin parts into English. The Reading Vocabulary may be consulted.

Fēlīciō: Who is coming to the villa now? Whom do I observe?

Seneca: Seneca sum. Vīlla est mea.

Fēlīciō: What are you saying? You can't be Seneca!

Seneca: Senecane esse nōn possum? Seneca sum!

Fēlīciō: You don't seem to me to be Seneca: You seem to me to be an old man!

Seneca: Senex sum et Seneca.

Fēlīciō: What man do you think I am?

Seneca: Putō tē esse senem, quī dentēs nōn habet.

Fēlīciō: What boy was accustomed to play with you as a boy?

Seneca: Fēlīciō, amīcus parvus, mēcum puerō lūdere solēbat.

Fēlīciō: Who do I seem to be to you? I was Fēlīciō. I am Fēlīciō. I will be Fēlīciō.

Seneca: Tū es Fēlīciō! Ego sum fēlīx! Difficile mihi erat, Fēlīciō, tē cognōscere. Nam, sīcut Seneca, tū quoque es senex. Sed amīcum meum tandem videō!

TALKING

rūrī – in the country

rūre – from the country

rūs – to the country

sēmita, sēmitae, f. – path

birota, birotae, f. – bicycle

birotā vehor, veheris, vehitur, vehimur, vehiminī, vehuntur – I, you, s/he, etc. ride a bicycle(s) (literally "I, you, s/he, etc. am, are, is carried on a bicycle")

deambulō, deambulāre – to take a walk (for sightseeing or pleasure)

mantica (f.) dorsuālis – backpack

sub dīvō – in the open, under the sky

tentōrium (n.) plicātile – foldable or roll-up tent

A TRIP TO THE COUNTRY

Marīa: Crās (*tomorrow*) ūnā cum parentibus rūs ībō (*I will go*).

Helena: Amāsne terram rūsticam?

Marīa: Terram rūsticam valdē amō. Parentēs quoque eam amant. Sī (*if*) ōtium (*leisure*) habēmus, terram rūsticam petimus.

Mārcus: Quid, Marīa, rūrī faciēs?

Marīa: Agrī sunt pulchrī, arborēs sunt pulchrae. In silvīs et ego et parentēs sēmitās petimus. Placet (*it pleases*) parentibus ibi deambulāre.

Christīna: Tibine, Marīa, in silvīs deambulāre placet?

Marīa: Ita vērō. (*Yes indeed.*) Sed parentēs nōn diū in silvīs manent. Post aliquot hōrās (*after a few hours*) fatīgantur (*they get tired*) et vīllam petere cupiunt. Sunt seniōrēs (*older*).

Christīna: Quid tunc facis? Tūne cum eīs vīllam petis?

Marīa: Interdum (*sometimes*). Sed interdum sōla (*alone*) agrōs et silvās petō. Ibi diū birotā vehor. Interdum mēcum manticam dorsuālem et tentōrium plicātile habeō. Tunc vīllam nōn petō, sed sub dīvō dormiō (*I sleep*).

DERIVATIVES

argūmentum – argument, argumentative

saxum – saxifrage, saxatile

vīlla – village, villain, villainous, villain

parvus – paraffin

rūsticus – rustic, rustication, rusticity

vērus – aver, veracity, verdict, verify, veritable, verity, very, verisimilitude

neglegō – neglect, negligee, negligence, neglectful, negligible

stō – armistice, arrest, assist, circumstance, circumstantial, consistent, constable, constant, constituency, constitute, constitution, contrast, cost, desist, destination, destiny, destitute, distance, establish, estate, exist, extant, insist, instant, institute, inconsistent, interstate, interstice, irresistible, obstacle, obstetrics, obstinate, persist, predestine, prostitute, reconstitute, resist, rest, restive, solstice, stability, stable, stage, stance, stanza, state, stately, statement, station, stationary, stationery, statistics, statue, stature, statute, stay, subsist, substantial, substitute, superstition

ubīque – ubiquitous, ubiquitousness

ante – advance, advantageous, antediluvian, ancient, antler, anterior, antics, antique, antiquity, disadvantageous, vanguard, vantage, *ante meridiem*

REVIEW 5: CHAPTERS 13–15

VOCABULARY TO KNOW

NOUNS

arbor, arboris, *f.* – tree

argūmentum, argūmentī, *n.* – proof, indication, argument

gladius, gladiī, *m.* – sword

iūdex, iūdicis, *m.* – judge

odium, odiī, *n.* – hatred

ōs, ōris, *n.* – mouth

parēns, parentis, *m./f.* – parent

pectus, pectoris, *n.* – chest

sanguis, sanguinis, *m.* – blood

saxum, saxī, *n.* – stone, rock

senectūs, senectūtis, *f.* – old age

vīlla, vīllae, *f.* – country house, villa

PRONOUNS

mēcum = cum mē – with me

nihil – nothing

quī, quae, quod – who, which, that (*relative pronoun*)

quis, quid? – who? what? (*interrogative pronoun*)

tēcum = cum tē – with you

ADJECTIVES

albus, alba, album – white

alius, alia, aliud – another, other

difficilis, difficile – difficult

dīves, dīvitis – rich

doctus, docta, doctum – learned

omnis, omne – each, every, all

parvus, parva, parvum – small

prīmus, prīma, prīmum – first

quī, quae, quod? – what? which? (*interrogative adjective*)

ruber, rubra, rubrum – red

rūsticus, rūstica, rūsticum – rural, rustic

suus, sua, suum – his, her, its, their

vērus, vēra, vērum – true

vetustus, vetusta, vetustum – old

VERBS

cadō, cadere, cecidī, cāsum – to fall

comedō, comedere, comēdī, comēsum – to eat

conveniō, convenīre, convēnī, conventum – to meet

discēdō, discēdere, discessī, discessum – to leave, go away

dūcō, dūcere, dūxī, ductum – to lead

fluō, fluere, flūxī, fluxum – to flow

inquam – I say/I said (*only introducing direct speech*)

licet + *dative* + *infinitive* – it is allowed, it is permitted for someone to do something

neglegō, neglegere, neglēxī, neglēctum – to neglect

nōlō (*irregular verb*) – not to want, to be unwilling

respondeō, respondēre, respondī, respōnsum – to answer

rogō, rogāre, rogāvī, rogātum – to ask

sēparō, sēparāre, sēparāvī, sēparātum – to separate

stō, stāre, stetī, statum – to stand

tangō, tangere, tetigī, tāctum – to touch

valē! – goodbye!

ADVERBS

cūr? – why?

etiam – even, also

fortasse – perhaps

iam – already, now

mox – soon

sīcut – just as

tantum – only

tum – then

ubīque – everywhere

umquam – ever

PREPOSITIONS

ante + *accusative* – in front of

apud + *accusative* – at the house of

per + *accusative* – through

prō + *ablative* – for, on behalf of

CONJUNCTIONS

atque – and

enim – for, in fact

INTERJECTION

ecce – look here!

▶ EXERCISE 1

Conjugate the following verbs in the future active voice.

1. *respondeō, respondēre, respondī, respōnsum*

2. *cadō, cadere, cecidī, cāsum*

3. *conveniō, convenīre, convēnī, conventum*

Conjugate the following verbs in the future passive voice.

1. *rogō, rogāre, rogāvī, rogātum*

2. *cōnspiciō, cōnspicere, cōnspexī, cōnspectum*

▶ EXERCISE 2

Give the imperative singular and plural of the following verbs and then change these forms into negative imperatives.

Example: cadō

cade   cadite   nōlī cadere   nōlīte cadere

1. comedō
2. discēdō
3. conveniō
4. neglegō
5. respondeō
6. rogō
7. sēparō
8. tangō
9. fugiō

▶ EXERCISE 3

Fill in the blanks with the missing relative pronoun, interrogative pronoun, or interrogative adjective. Translate the sentences.

Example: _____ vestrum respondēbit?
Quis vestrum respondēbit?   Which of you will answer?

1. Prope _____ arborem tē vidēbō?
2. Senectūs, _____ multī timent, nōn semper est mala.
3. Respondē hominī _____ tē rogat!
4. Vīlla rūstica, in _____ diū nōn vīvēbam, vetusta mihi vidēbātur.
5. _____ argumentīs ostendēs senectūtem esse bonam?

▶ EXERCISE 4

Fill in the blanks with the correct third person possessive form of *suus, sua, suum* or *eius, eōrum, eārum*. Translate the sentences.

Example: Vir ā poētā nōn discēdēbat, sed poēta nōn cupiēbat _____ verba audīre.
Vir ā poētā nōn discēdēbat, sed poēta nōn cupiēbat eius verba audīre.
The man was not leaving the poet, but the poet did not want to hear his words.

1. Hominēs saepe verba _____ amant, verba tamen aliōrum nōn amant.
2. Puer et puella amōrem _____ servāre cupiēbant, sed propter odium parentum difficile erat id facere.
3. Puer putābat puellam iam nōn vīvere et dē _____ morte dolēbat.
4. Omnēs senectūtem _____ timent.
5. Doctī _____ que verba multa dē senectūte docent.

▶ EXERCISE 5

Fill in the blanks with the correct genitive form of the first or second person, singular or plural pronoun. Identify the type of genitive. Translate the sentences.

Example: Vōs potestis mihi auxilium dare. Quis _____ mihi auxilium dabit?
Vōs potestis mihi auxilium dare. Quis vestrum mihi auxilium dabit?
You can give me help. Which of you will give me help?   Partitive genitive.

1. Propter amōrem _____ tēcum semper manēbō.

2. Hostēs gladium meum cōnspiciunt et propter timōrem _____ stant nec moventur.

3. Vōs estis mīlitēs crūdēlēs. Timor _____ nōs movet.

4. Nōs difficilia nōn timēmus. Multī enim _____ difficilia petunt.

5. Multīs hominibus licet in vīllam nostram convenīre, sed propter odium _____ nōn veniunt.

Statue of the Roman emperor
Augustus, who asked Vergil to write the *Aeneid*.

▶ EXERCISE 6

Translate into English.

The following text is adapted from Vergil's *Aeneid*, excerpts of which you read in Chapters 10 and 11. You remember how Aeneas abandoned Queen Dido, and how Dido, overwhelmed with grief, committed suicide. Later Aeneas met Dido's ghost in the underworld, but she turned her face away from her former lover, and refused to talk to him. The main reason for Aeneas's descent to the world of the dead, however, was to meet his father Anchises and to learn from him both his own fate and that of his people. Here Aeneas and Anchises converse in the land of the shadows.

"Nunc tē tua fāta docēbō. Diū nāvigābis, diū pugnābis et tandem domum veniēs. Nam novam urbem condēs. Nōmen urbis erit Rōma. Hominibus subiectīs Rōmānī parcent et hominēs superbōs vincent. Tandem imperātor omnibus populīs pācem dabit," inquit Anchīsēs.

"Quī imperātor pācem dabit, pater?" rogat Aenēās.

"Pāx omnibus populīs ab imperātōre Augustō dabitur, cūius nōmen ubīque audiētur," respondet Anchīsēs.

Aenēās, *m.* – Aeneas	**imperātor, imperātōris,** *m.* – emperor
Anchīsēs, *m.* – Anchises	**parcō, parcere, pepercī, parsum** + *dative* – to spare
condō, condere, condidī, conditum – to found	**populus, populī,** *m.* – people
domum – homeward, home	**subiectus, subiecta, subiectum** – subdued
fātum, fātī, *n.* – fate, destiny	**superbus, superba, superbum** – proud

CONSIDERING THE CLASSICAL GODS

Statue of Minerva wearing her helmet, from Austria.

MINERVA

Three more female goddesses belong to the family of the Olympians. Athene, or Athena, whose Latin name is Minerva, is a daughter of Jupiter and Metis, the goddess of wisdom. Because Jupiter feared that the offspring of Metis would overthrow him, he swallowed the pregnant Metis and delivered the baby Minerva from his own body: his concerns were confirmed when she emerged from her father's head already helmeted and shining in her armor. Minerva is the goddess not only of war but also of wisdom and practical intelligence. Skillful in weaving as well, she serves as a protectress of Athens, the city whose own name is related to her Greek name. According to Greek myth, however, the god Neptune at one time challenged Minerva's position, and the Athenians characteristically decided to choose their patron divinity by democratic election. In return for the people's support, Neptune offered a spring of salt water, Minerva an olive tree. She was victorious, and her gift of major importance—the olive oil produced by the tree—is of great significance in the Mediterranean world.

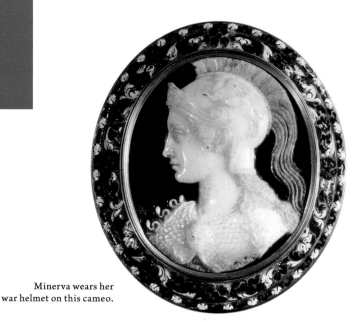

Minerva wears her war helmet on this cameo.

DIANA

We have already encountered Artemis, Apollo's twin sister, and the daughter of Zeus and Leto: known in Latin as Diana. She dwells in the woods, where a retinue of nymphs follows her. She is associated with virginity and hunting, and with the moon and magic. There are self-contradictory elements to the image of this goddess. Mistress of animals, she is also a huntress; a virgin, she also protects childbirth; although the possessor of youthful beauty and charm, she has a cold heart. When the hunter Actaeon saw her bathing, she turned him into a stag as punishment for having gazed at her naked body, and his own dogs devoured him. When Niobe, mother of seven sons and seven daughters, boasted that her children were greater than those of Leto, the goddess's own offspring Diana and Apollo took offense, and cruelly slaughtered all fourteen of her sons and daughters. Unable to endure her grief, Niobe turned into a stone.

Statue of Diana, the huntress.

VENUS

Aphrodite, called Venus in Latin, is the most beautiful goddess. Often referred to by the adjective "golden," she is said to possess a magic girdle that excites the power of love. Among her other symbols are the apple and pomegranate (since its seeds symbolize fertility), the goat (since it is associated with lust), the swan, the dove, and the sparrow (the love object in Catullus's Poem 2).

A Roman fountain presents a modest Venus flanked by tritons with their conch shell horns. The scallop shell represents Venus's birth from the foam of the sea.

Paradoxically, Venus is married to Vulcan, the crippled blacksmith of the Olympians. She often has other lovers, most notably Mars, the god of war. A skillful metal worker and craftsman, Vulcan is portrayed as having prepared a trap of chains for Venus and Mars, which caught them in the midst of their embraces. The boy Cupid, called Eros in Greek, who pierces human hearts with love arrows, is Venus's son. So is Aeneas, the result of her union with a mortal, the Trojan shepherd Anchises.

READ AND TRANSLATE THE FOLLOWING PASSAGES

Arachnē valdē bene texere poterat. Putābat sē posse Minervam vincere. Arachnē dīcēbat: "Minerva est dea, sed cum eā certābō eamque vincam. Eius ars nōn est valdē magna." Minerva verba Arachnēs audiēbat et magnā īrā movēbātur. "Nunc in arāneam mūtāberis," inquit Minerva, "semper texēs, sed verba dīcere nōn poteris." Propter īram deae misera Arachnē corpus arāneae iam habēbit.

Arachnē (*nom.*), **Arachnēs** (*gen.*) – Arachne (*this name means "spider" in Greek*)
arānea, arāneae, *f.* – spider
ars, artis, *f.* – art, skill
certō, certāre, certāvī, certātum – to compete

dea, deae, *f.* – goddess
Minerva, Minervae, *f.* – Minerva
mūtō, mūtāre, mūtāvī, mūtātum – to change
texō, texere, texuī, textum – to weave

Venus amōre Adōnidis ārdēbat. Nam Adōnis erat valdē pulcher. Mārs odiō movēbātur. "Quis est Adōnis?" inquit Mārs, "Homō quī ā deā amātur." Mārs aprum ad Adōnidem mittit, quī eum occīdit. Sanguis ex pectore Adōnidis fluit. Venus sanguinem videt et Adōnidem vocat: "Nōlī ā mē sēparārī! Amōre tuī teneor." Adōnis tamen iam nōn vīvere vidētur. Tum Venus Adōnidem in flōrem rubrum mūtat.

Adōnis, Adōnidis, *m.* – Adonis
aper, aprī, *m.* – boar
flōs, flōris, *m.* – flower

Mārs, Mārtis, *m.* – Mars
mūtō, mūtāre, mūtāvī, mūtātum – to change
Venus, Veneris, *f.* – Venus

CONNECTING WITH THE ANCIENT WORLD

ROMAN CITIES AND ROADS

CITIES IN THE ROMAN EMPIRE

In the reading for Chapter 13 we saw the poet Horace strolling in the Roman Forum. During the first two centuries CE, many new cities were founded in the Roman Empire, and other, older settlements were totally rebuilt. These Roman cities were ordinarily planned as a unit, usually on a grid pattern. In this respect they differed from Rome itself, which had grown up slowly and in a haphazard fashion. Except for a few isolated areas, such as the great *fora* designed and built by various emperors, Rome was a maze of poorly lit and badly drained alleys surrounded by wooden tenements (*insulae*).

By way of contrast, the newer provincial cities had excellent and well-drained roads, public latrines at carefully placed intervals, a good supply of water, public baths, mosaics and other artistic adornments, council buildings, and *basilicae*, buildings used for judicial proceedings or commercial exchanges. In some provincial cities one might find public libraries, and the market-places were decorated with inscriptions, in Greek or Latin, recording honors to citizens, decrees of emperors pertaining to the city, and other public and religious events.

The ruins of these provincial cities are still visible, especially in places such as Ephesus in Turkey and Djemila in North Africa. Wealthy local aristocrats often assumed the costs of the adornment and amenities for these cities, in accordance with a civic tradition started in classical Greece, which obligated those with substantial financial resources to sustain a greater share of enhancing the *polis*, or city-state.

Ruins of the ancient Roman city of Sabratha in Libya.

In the largest of the Roman provincial cities, there might be public distributions of grain, which allowed the very poorest inhabitants to obtain a certain basic subsistence, at little or no cost. Likewise in the cities with more substantial populations, the inhabitants might be entertained by gruesome gladiatorial contests—even in the Greek world under the Roman Empire—and chariot races. Nevertheless, most people in urban areas lived in cramped squalor, and the concept of privacy as we know it hardly existed.

A stretch of the old Appian Way, known as the *Via Appia*.

ROADS IN THE ROMAN EMPIRE

Roman cities were connected by an extensive road-system with excellent paved roads. The Romans were determined to be masters of the landscape. Furthermore, the roads were indispensable for their military operations, but they also facilitated commerce and travel to all parts of the empire. One of the most famous roads is the *Via Appia* (312 BCE), which connected Rome with southern Italy, called the "queen" of the roads, many parts of which still survive. This road was named after Appius Claudius, the magistrate responsible for its construction. The *Via Flaminia,* which went northward from Rome, and the *Via Aemilia,* an extension of this road later paved by Augustus, were likewise named after the magistrates who built them.

Milestones gave the name of the builder and the date of construction, and also indicated which emperors had a part in road-building. The actual work was done by soldiers between campaigns under the supervision of Roman field engineers. Construction depended on what material was available locally and the nature of the terrain. Thus, the surfacing material varied. Vitruvius, who worked for both Julius Caesar and Augustus as an architect, discusses the process of road construction. The field engineer mapped out as straight a line as possible. Trenches (*fossae*) were dug to the bedrock and dirt carried away in baskets. A foundation of lime mortar or sand was laid to form the level base (*pavīmentum*). The next layer consisted of more concrete mixed with stones, gravel, or sand and lime poured in layers. The top surface (*summum dorsum*) consisted of polygonal blocks of stone (which you see in pictures) that were six inches or more thick and carefully fitted on top of the still moist cement. When worn out and in need of repair, the stones were turned over and replaced in the top layer. Roads were higher in the middle than on the sides and had side gutters or ditches to help with drainage. For pedestrians a foot-path was available on either side, sometimes paved. The width of the road was supposed to allow two vehicles to meet and pass each other. Not all roads met this criterion, depending on their importance.

Since "all roads lead to Rome," Augustus in 20 BCE erected near the center of the Roman Forum the Golden Milestone (*Mīliārium Aureum*), a bronze monument that listed the distances to various cities in the empire via the large system of roads that the Romans had constructed. This inspired the Zero Milestone (1929) in Washington, DC, which is meant to be the point from which road distances in the United States can be calculated.

This fragment of a Roman milestone shows the distance to the next Roman town along the road, *Colonia Agrippina*, known today as Cologne, Germany.

EXPLORING ROMAN LAW

THE JUSTICE SYSTEM IN ANCIENT ROME

Horace is out for a relaxing, solitary stroll in downtown Rome when someone rushes up to him and insists on joining in—the Bore, the Boor, the Pest. Midway through the original text of this poem (words from which are quoted below), when the two have reached the Temple of Vesta at the Forum's east end, the reader learns that the Bore is a defendant in a lawsuit and that he has given guarantees to meet the plaintiff for their date in court. If he doesn't, he'll lose the case (*perdere lītem*). He asks Horace for legal counsel, but Horace begs off, claiming he knows nothing about Roman civil law (*cīvīlia iūra*). He nevertheless follows the Bore, apparently into the Forum proper where, as described at the end of the poem, the Bore's legal opponent (*adversārius*), the plaintiff, suddenly comes upon them. He asks Horace to witness, or testify to (*antestārī*), what he is going to do. Horace agrees. The plaintiff then seizes the Bore and hauls him off to court (*rapit in iūs*), both of them shouting. A crowd gathers to see what's going on. The long-suffering poet escapes—or does he? Despite the usual view (Horace flees the scene), it has been suggested that the satire's closing words are ironic: Horace has evaded further direct communication with the Bore, but now finds himself embroiled as witness in an obviously contentious lawsuit (T. Mazurek, *Classical Journal* 93 [1997–98] 1–17).

Statue of Justice holding the scales.

The two parts of *Satire* 1.9 just summarized are very interesting for Roman legal procedure and its social environment. We don't know the exact nature of the case against the Bore, but he was certainly a defendant in what we would call a "civil suit"; this was not a criminal case. The satire's technical language indicates that the procedures being followed dated back at least to the codification of Roman law known as the Twelve Tables (451–450 BCE). The original bronze tablets of this code have not survived—it's a hypothesis that they were destroyed during the Gallic invasion of the 390s BCE—but there are enough quotations from the Tables in later Roman authors to illustrate the local, the agrarian, and—most strikingly—the archaic nature of the code's provisions. Take for example Table 8.1: "If a person has sung against another person or composed a song (*carmen*) so as to cause loss of reputation (*infāmia*) or insult (*flāgitium*), let him be clubbed to death"; or the more sophisticated Table 8.2: "If a person has maimed another's limb, unless he makes an informal agreement to settle with him, let there be retaliation in kind (*tāliō*)."

Despite their antiquity, most of the Twelve Tables' provisions remained "the law of the land" four centuries later in Horace's lifetime (65–8 BCE). They would not be formally supplanted until the emperor Justinian's great codification (*Code, Digest, Institutes*) of the sixth century CE. It was this later codification, an extensive compilation of Roman laws and legal writings, that would have such a profound impact on later European law, perhaps most famously in France's Napoleonic Civil Code of 1804. England, on the contrary, had in the Middle Ages developed its own native Common Law system, largely resistant to outside influences. English Common Law in turn provided the basis for the American legal system. The lone exception is the state of Louisiana, a Spanish, then a French possession, which even today operates under a Civil Code dating to 1870 (earlier Louisiana codes date to 1808 and 1825).

Noteworthy for Horace's satire is that from the time of the Twelve Tables, and no doubt even earlier, it was the plaintiff's responsibility to see to the defendant's appearance in court: he had to do it himself. If the defendant did not cooperate, the plaintiff could seize the defendant by force (*per manum*), but for this to be legal he had to have a competent witness. Horace evidently felt it his duty as a Roman citizen to comply with the plaintiff's request. A less compliant person could have refused, since neither plaintiff nor defendant had any power to "subpoena" witnesses.

Note also that earlier the Bore had asked Horace for legal assistance. Horace was not a lawyer, but like many elite Romans, and despite his denial, he is known to have had an extensive grasp of the law. In the late Republic and early empire, the practice of Roman law was becoming more professionalized, but lawyers (even Cicero) and judges were not specifically trained; they had no degrees, there were no bar exams. Lawyers or advocates were therefore mostly educated amateurs. Romans eligible on the basis of their social status to serve as judges (*iūdicēs*) had their names listed in an album. Their names would be selected for individual cases in a preliminary hearing before the *praetor* (the chief judicial magistrate in Rome, elected annually) with the cooperation of the parties concerned. Some Romans did come to be recognized for their expertise in law, as evidenced in their legal opinions and extensive writings (later excerpted in Justinian's *Digest*). These specialists are usually referred to not as lawyers but as jurists.

Romans giving legal advice or acting as advocates, unlike American lawyers today (unless these are offering their services "prō bonō"), did not charge fees—this was thought to be unworthy of their elite social status—though they could accept honoraria. They were expected to provide assistance from a sense of social obligation or friendship. Notice therefore the audacity of the Bore in assuming Horace's friendship (Horace claimed he just knew the Bore's name, nothing more). Notice also the Bore's shamelessness, especially in the final scene as described above. No self-respecting Roman would want to have been at the center of such a public ruckus, thereby suffering loss of that essential Roman quality known as *dignitās*!

JAMES G. KEENAN
Professor of Classics
Loyola University Chicago
Chicago, Illinois

MĪRĀBILE AUDĪTŪ

PHRASES AND QUOTATIONS RELATING TO LEGAL MATTERS

PHRASES AND QUOTATIONS

- Alibi. Literally, "elsewhere." It is formed from the same verbal elements found in *alius*, "another," and *ibi*, "there." If individuals have an alibi, it means that they can show that they were somewhere else at the time when a crime took place.

- Cui prōdest? "Whom does <the crime> benefit?" A question posed when determining who has committed a crime by considering the motive.

- Dē iūre. "According to the law."

- Flagrante dēlictō. "While the crime is blazing," "red-handed." A legal term indicating that a criminal has been caught in the very act of committing an offense.

- Habeās corpus. "You should have the body!" A legal principle, which originated in ancient times, and according to which a person cannot be unlawfully detained.

- Prō bonō. "For the public good." An expression used for legal work undertaken voluntarily and without payment as a public service.

- Sub poenā. "Under <the threat of> penalty." Witnesses are summoned by a judicial authority to appear in court, and give or produce evidence, under the threat of punishment or penalty, an English word that is derived from Latin *poena*, punishment.

CHAPTER 16

Perfect Tense Verbs; Perfect Stem, Perfect Tense Active of All Conjugations; Perfect Tense of *Sum* and *Possum*; Dative of Possession

Oil painting of the eruption of Mt. Vesuvius. Jean Baptiste Genillon (1750–1829).

MEMORĀBILE DICTŪ

Quid sī nunc caelum ruat?

"What if the sky should fall now?" (Terence, *The Self-Tormentor* 719)

A proverbial saying for anything regarded as improbable and beyond our power.

READING

Born into a wealthy northern Italian family in about 61 CE, Gāius Plīnius Caecilius Secundus is known to us as Pliny, and specifically as Pliny the Younger, to distinguish him from his uncle and adopted father Pliny the Elder (ca. 23/24–79 CE). His career in public administration culminated in his governorship of Bithynia, a province in what is today Turkey. He appears to have died in around 112–113 CE.

An individual of immense learning and oratorical talent, Pliny has left us ten books of letters that offer a vivid picture of upper-class life during the Roman Empire at the height of its prosperity and power.

The following passage is an adapted and abbreviated version of the sixteenth letter in his sixth book of letters. Here he describes the eruption of Mt. Vesuvius, which destroyed the towns of Pompeii, Herculaneum, and Stabiae on the Bay of Naples in 79 CE. In this letter he also relates the death of his uncle, author of the *Historia Natūrālis*, "Natural History," a multi-volume encyclopedia of lore about the human as well as natural world.

DĒ MONTIS VESUVIĪ INCENDIŌ

1   Avunculus meus Mīsēnī erat classis praefectus. Eō diē, quō tantae
    clādis initium fuit, avunculus forīs iacēbat librīsque studēbat. Māter
    mea eī nūbem subitō ostendit novam et inūsitātam, quae in caelō prope
    montem Vesuvium vidēbātur esse. Nūbēs fōrmam habuit similem
5   fōrmae, quam in arboribus saepe vidēmus. Nam summa nūbēs in
    multās partēs sīcut in rāmōs sēparābātur. Avunculus, homō rērum
    nātūrae valdē studiōsus, causam nūbis intellegere cupīvit. Iussit igitur
    nāvēs parārī: nam ad lītus nāvigāre cupīvit, quod est prope montem
    Vesuvium. Deinde nauta epistulam avunculō dedit. "Fēmina," inquit
10 nauta, "quae prope montem Vesuvium habitat, epistulam ad tē mīsit."
    Avunculus epistulam lēgit et statim intellēxit in monte Vesuviō esse
    incendium magnum: fēminam perīculum timēre nāvibusque fugere
    cupere. Animus fortis avunculō erat. Cōnsilium igitur novum cēpit. Ad
    hominēs nāvigāre dēcrēvit, quī prope montem Vesuvium habitābant, et
15 eōs perīculō magnō līberāre. Nam saxa et cinerēs calidī ē caelō in eōs
    cadēbant. Illūc igitur nāvigāvit, sed numquam revēnit. Ibi enim fūmus
    fūnestus et cinerēs eum cum multīs aliīs oppressērunt.

READING VOCABULARY

*avunculus, avunculī, *m.* – uncle

*caelum, caelī, *n.* – sky, heaven, weather

calidus, calida, calidum – hot

*causa, causae, *f.* – cause, reason

cēpit cōnsilium – he made a plan

*cinis, cineris, *m.* – ash

*clādēs, clādis, *f.* – disaster

*classis, classis, f. – fleet

cupīvit – wanted, desired

dēcrēvit – he decided

dedit – gave

eō diē – on that day

*fēmina, fēminae, *f.* – woman

forīs (*adv.*) – outside

fuit – was

*fūmus, fūmī, *m.* – smoke

*fūnestus, fūnesta, fūnestum – deadly

habuit – had

*igitur (*conj.*) – therefore (*usually the second word in its clause*)

illūc (*adv.*) – to that place, thither

*incendium, incendiī, *n.* – conflagration, eruption

initium, initiī, *n.* – beginning

intellēxit – understood

inūsitātus, inūsitāta, inūsitātum – strange, unusual

iussit – he ordered

*lēgit – read

*lītus, lītoris, *n.* – shore

*māter, mātris, *f.* – mother

Mīsēnum, Mīsēnī, *n.* – Misenum, *a base for the imperial Roman navy in the Bay of Naples*; Mīsēnī – at Misenum

mīsit – sent

*mōns, montis, *m.* – mountain

nāvigāvit – he sailed

*nāvis, nāvis, f. – ship

*nūbēs, nūbis, f. – cloud

*numquam (*adv.*) – never

*oppressērunt – overwhelmed, suppressed

ostendit – pointed out

*pars, partis, f. – part

praefectus, praefectī, *m.* – prefect, commander, chief

rāmus, rāmī, *m.* – branch

rērum nātūra, nātūrae, f. – nature

revēnit – he returned

*studeō, studēre, studuī, —— + *dative* – to study, be eager for, be interested in

studiōsus, studiōsa, studiōsum + *genitive* – interested in, a student of

summus, summa, summum – the top of

Vesuvius, Vesuviī, *m.* – (Mt.) Vesuvius

*Words marked with an asterisk will need to be memorized later in the chapter.

COMPREHENSION QUESTIONS

1. What event interrupted the studies of Pliny's uncle?

2. What did Pliny's uncle decide to do?

3. What changed his mind?

4. What happened to Pliny's uncle at the end of the story?

LANGUAGE FACT I

PERFECT TENSE VERBS

In the Latin reading passage there are some new forms of verbs already treated in earlier chapters. These are forms of the perfect tense, a tense that refers primarily to past time:

> *cēpit* "s/he/it took" (perfect tense of *capiō*)
>
> *dedit* "s/he/it gave" (perfect tense of *dō*)
>
> *fuit* "s/he/it was" (perfect tense of *sum*)
>
> *habuit* "s/he/it had" (perfect tense of *habeō*)

In the same passage there are also perfect tense forms of verbs that have not appeared in previous chapters.

> *lēgit* "s/he read" (perfect tense of *legō*)

The meaning of the perfect differs in subtle ways from the imperfect—the past tense introduced in Chapter 11. While the imperfect tense refers to a **continuing** action or state in the past, the perfect indicates either a single act in the past or a **completed** action.

For example, *dīcēbat* means "s/he was saying" (i.e., a continuing action), but *dīxit* (the same verb in the perfect tense) usually means "s/he said" or "s/he did say" (once and for all).

But the perfect has yet another distinctive meaning. It can refer to an action completed just before the present time. In English the auxiliary verb "have" or "has" indicates this distinction. In Latin this nuance is clear from the context (e.g., adverbs may indicate that an action has just been completed). In the following sentences the verb *legere* ("to read") is used in the imperfect tense and in both meanings of the perfect tense.

> *Librum legēbat.* "S/he was reading the book."
>
> *Librum legēbat. Deinde dīxit: "Librum tandem lēgī."* "S/he was reading the book. Then s/he said: 'At last I have read the book.'"
>
> *Librum lēgit.* "S/he read the book."

When the past action is negative, or is to be emphasized, "did" is used in the translation.

> *Librum nōn lēgī.* "I did not read the book."
>
> *Librum lēgī.* "I did read the book."

▶ EXERCISE 1

Find and translate nine more perfect tense forms from the Latin reading passage.

VOCABULARY TO LEARN

NOUNS

avunculus, avunculī, *m.* – uncle

caelum, caelī, *n.* – sky, heaven, weather

causa, causae, *f.* – cause, reason

cinis, cineris, *m.* – ash

clādēs, clādis, *f.* – disaster

classis, classis, *f.* – fleet, class (of people)

fēmina, fēminae, *f.* – woman

fūmus, fūmī, *m.* – smoke

incendium, incendiī, *n.* – conflagration, eruption

lītus, lītoris, *n.* – shore

māter, mātris, *f.* – mother

mōns, montis, *m.* – mountain

nāvis, nāvis, *f.* – ship

nūbēs, nūbis, *f.* – cloud

pars, partis, *f.* – part

ADJECTIVE

fūnestus, fūnesta, fūnestum – deadly

VERBS

legō, legere, lēgī, lēctum – to read, choose

opprimō, opprimere, oppressī, oppressum – to overwhelm, suppress

studeō, studēre, studuī, —— + *dative* – to study, be eager for, be interested in

ADVERB

numquam – never

CONJUNCTION

igitur – therefore (*usually the second word in its clause*)

▶ **EXERCISE 2**

Find the English derivatives based on the Vocabulary to Learn in the following sentences. Write the corresponding Latin word.

1. Celestial phenomena greatly interest me.

2. Archaeologists found several cinerary urns at that site.

3. These people are introducing a totally subjective mode of thinking in which causality plays no role.

4. Terrible destruction was caused in the city by incendiary bombs.

5. Naval architecture is a very exacting science.

6. Karl Marx advocated an entire philosophy of history based on class conflict.

7. Your teacher has a very avuncular manner.

8. The littoral region here sustains a wide variety of plant and animal life.

9. This part of the hospital is the maternity ward.

10. Underprivileged people in the Roman world were cruelly oppressed.

11. The gender of this noun is feminine.

12. The carpet in the apartment was so dirty it had to be fumigated.

13. Why were you not present at the lecture?

14. I agree with you only partially.

15. I will be a lifelong student.

▶ EXERCISE 3

Translate each sentence with special attention to the previously discussed meanings of the perfect tense verb in parentheses.

Example: "Perīculum nōn intellēxī (first person singular), sed nunc intellegō," inquit avunculus. "Iam igitur dēcrēvī (first person singular) ad hominēs, quī prope montem habitant, nāvigāre."
"I did not understand the danger, but now I understand <it>," said uncle. "Therefore I have already decided to sail to the people who live near the mountain."

1. Nautae prope lītus manēbant. Caelum semper cōnspiciēbant. Deinde cōnsilium cēpērunt (third person plural). Nāvem parāre dēcrēvērunt (third person plural).

2. Epistulam ad hominēs, quī in viā exspectābant, statim mīsimus (first person plural), et eōs ad nōs venīre iussimus (first person plural).

3. Nautās exspectābāmus. Nunc eōrum nāvēs vidēre possumus. "Nautae," inquit amīcus meus, "vēnērunt (third person plural)!"

LANGUAGE FACT II

PERFECT STEM, PERFECT TENSE ACTIVE OF ALL CONJUGATIONS

The perfect is not only distinctive in its meaning; it has a series of forms that are very distinctive too.

You have already learned that **the principal parts** of a verb are used to make different verb forms. Most verbs have four principal parts. The first and second principal parts are important for the present, imperfect, and future tenses discussed in previous chapters. But the forms of the perfect active tense are derived from the **third** principal part of any verb.

Below are the principal parts of a verb from each conjugation. Note carefully the third principal part: this principal part is the form of the first person singular of the perfect active indicative.

First conjugation:	parō, parāre, **parāvī**, parātum – I prepare
Second conjugation:	teneō, tenēre, **tenuī**, tentum – I hold
Third conjugation:	dīcō, dīcere, **dīxī**, dictum – I say
Fourth conjugation:	audiō, audīre, **audīvī**, audītum – I hear
Third conjugation (–iō):	capiō, capere, **cēpī**, captum – I take

Learning the perfect forms is much easier than it might at first appear, because the perfect active endings are the same for **all** four conjugations. These endings are added to the perfect stem, which is found by dropping the –ī found in the third principal part.

Here are some general patterns for forming the perfect stem:

- Many first conjugation verbs form their perfect stem by adding –*v*– after the –*ā*– in the present stem (*parāvī*).
- Many fourth conjugation verbs form their perfect stem by adding –*v*– to the –*ī*– in the present stem (*audīvī*).
- Many second conjugation verbs have a perfect stem that ends in –*u*– before the –*ī* of the perfect ending (as in *tenuī* above).

None of these patterns is absolutely consistent.

Remember: add the same endings to the perfect stem of any verb, regardless of conjugation. Here is the perfect active of *parō* and *capiō*. Since the endings are the same, you do not need to learn different paradigms for all conjugations.

Perfect Active: *parō*			
Singular			
First person	parāv-ī	parāvī	I prepared, did prepare (or) I have prepared
Second person	parāv-istī	parāvistī	you prepared, did prepare (or) you have prepared
Third person	parāv-it	parāvit	s/he/it prepared, did prepare (or) s/he/it has prepared
Plural			
First person	parāv-imus	parāvimus	we prepared, did prepare (or) we have prepared
Second person	parāv-istis	parāvistis	you prepared, did prepare (or) you have prepared
Third person	parāv-ērunt	parāvērunt	they prepared, did prepare (or) they have prepared

Perfect Active: *capiō*			
Singular			
First person	cēp-ī	cēpī	I took, did take (or) I have taken
Second person	cēp-istī	cēpistī	you took, did take (or) you have taken
Third person	cēp-it	cēpit	s/he/it took, did take (or) s/he/it has taken
Plural			
First person	cēp-imus	cēpimus	we took, did take (or) we have taken
Second person	cēp-istis	cēpistis	you took, did take (or) you have taken
Third person	cēp-ērunt	cēpērunt	they took, did take (or) they have taken

STUDY TIP

When you learn a new verb, learn all four principal parts. The endings of the perfect active are themselves very simple, and the same for all the conjugations.

▶ EXERCISE 4

Change each infinitive into the perfect active form indicated in parentheses. Translate the changed form.

Example: iubēre (perfect active second person singular)
iussistī   you ordered/did order/have ordered

1. sēparāre (perfect active third person plural)

2. legere (perfect active first person plural)

3. discēdere (perfect active third person singular)

4. tangere (perfect active second person singular)

5. ārdēre (perfect active third person plural)

6. respondēre (perfect active second person plural)

7. cadere (perfect active second person singular)

8. dēlēre (perfect active third person plural)

9. opprimere (perfect active third person singular)

10. neglegere (perfect active first person plural)

11. stāre (perfect active third person plural)

Daylight view of Pompeii's forum, with its Capitoline Temple flanked by triumphal arches, with Mt. Vesuvius in the background.

► **EXERCISE 5**

Change the following present tense verbs into the perfect, keeping the same person and number. Translate the changed sentence. The Reading Vocabulary may be consulted.

Example: Ad hominēs nāvigāre dēcernō.
Ad hominēs nāvigāre dēcrēvī.   I decided to sail to the people.

1. Ego et avunculus librōs legimus.

2. Nūbem novam in caelō cōnspicimus.

3. Hominēs rērum nātūrae studiōsī causam nūbis novae intellegunt.

4. Dīcit nauta: "Mē iubēs nāvēs statim parāre."

5. Perīculum valdē timētis. Novum igitur cōnsilium capere dēbētis.

6. Saxa et cinerēs calidī ē caelō subitō cadunt.

7. Eōrum epistulam iam legō.

LANGUAGE FACT III

PERFECT TENSE OF *SUM* AND *POSSUM*

You have already learned the principal parts of the irregular verbs *sum* and *possum*. You will remember that they lack a fourth principal part, but each has a third principal part, which is the first person singular of the perfect tense.

> sum, esse, fuī, —— – to be
>
> possum, posse, potuī, —— – to be able

BY THE WAY

Sum and *possum* have no passive forms.

Now it is easy to supply all the forms of the perfect active for each verb.

Perfect Tense of *sum*

Singular

First person	fu-ī	fu**ī**	I was (or) I have been
Second person	fu-istī	fu**istī**	you were (or) you have been
Third person	fu-it	fu**it**	s/he/it was (or) s/he/it has been

Plural

First person	fu-imus	fu**imus**	we were (or) we have been
Second person	fu-istis	fu**istis**	you were (or) you have been
Third person	fu-ērunt	fu**ērunt**	they were (or) they have been

Perfect Tense of *possum*

Singular

First person	potu-ī	potu**ī**	I was able, could (or) I have been able
Second person	potu-istī	potu**istī**	you were able, could (or) you have been able
Third person	potu-it	potu**it**	s/he/it was able, could (or) s/he/it has been able

Plural

First person	potu-imus	potu**imus**	we were able, could (or) we have been able
Second person	potu-istis	potu**istis**	you were able, could (or) you have been able
Third person	potu-ērunt	potu**ērunt**	they were able, could (or) they have been able

Statue of a dancing faun in the *impluvium*
of the atrium in the House of the Faun in Pompeii.

▶ EXERCISE 6

Translate into Latin. The Reading Vocabulary may be consulted.

1. Were you (plural) able to see the stones and hot ashes in the sky?

2. At that time you were able to send a man to the people who lived near Mt. Vesuvius.

3. We were not able to read the woman's words.

4. Then there was suddenly a conflagration in the mountain.

5. I have already been able to read the letter of the woman. Now I am preparing the ships.

6. You were able to free the people from great danger.

LANGUAGE FACT IV

DATIVE OF POSSESSION

In the passage at the beginning of this chapter you might have thought the following sentence was distinctive. Here you see a usage of the dative case that has not been discussed so far.

> *Animus fortis avunculō erat.*
> My uncle had a brave spirit.

This sentence has been translated with the verb "have," even though the Latin verb "to have" is not present. The person who owns or has something may be expressed in the dative case with some form of the verb *esse* ("to be"). Here the Latin literally says "For/to my uncle there was a brave spirit." The dative of possession emphasizes the fact of possession.

Another example:

> *Mihi sunt multī librī.*
> I have many books.

BY THE WAY

You can, of course, express possession using the verb *habeō*. In this case, the dative of possession is not used:

> *Multōs librōs habeō.*

▶ EXERCISE 7

Translate into English.

1. Avunculō multī librī fuērunt, quibus per vītam suam studuit.

2. Puer verba avunculī audīvit et multōs librōs lēgit.

3. Avunculus dē clāde audīvit et cōnsilia cēpit. Nam auxilium aliīs dare dēbēbat.

4. Incendium, fūmus, cinis montem et lītus oppressērunt. Avunculō tamen animus semper fuit fortis.

5. Avunculus nautīs dīxit: "Nāvem parāvistis. Nunc classem parāte!" Nautae verba avunculī audīverunt.

6. "Nōlīte timēre!" omnibus dīxit avunculus. Sed timor multōs tenuit.

▶ EXERCISE 8

Translate into Latin in two ways, using both the verb *habeō* and the dative of possession.

Example: I have many friends.
Multōs amīcōs habeō.   Mihi sunt multī amīcī.

1. Do you have an uncle?

2. He has a small mouth.

3. We have cruel enemies.

4. What names do you (plural) have?

5. They have rustic villas.

A street in excavated Pompeii. Note the narrow road, the sidewalk, and in the middle of the street the raised stones that allowed people to cross the road, which might be filled with water or garbage.

▶ EXERCISE 9

Translate the following passage into English. Refer to both the Reading Vocabulary and the words explained below.

Plīnius: Nūbem magnam, quae est in caelō prope montem Vesuvium, iam cōnspexit māter. Nūbemne, avuncule, vidēre potes?

Avunculus: Nūbem vidēre possum. Sum senex, sed mihi sunt oculī bonī atque validī.

Plīnius: Quae est haec nūbēs? Eius fōrma mihi vidētur esse nova. Tālis forma arboribus, nōn nūbibus esse solet.

Avunculus: Ubi prīmum māter tua nūbem mihi ostendit, eam esse inūsitātam intellēxī. Ad montem igitur nāvigāre causamque nūbis investīgāre cupīvī. Sed cōnsilium mūtāvī.

Plīnius: Cūr cōnsilium mūtāvistī?

Avunculus: Fēmina, cūius vīlla ā monte Vesuviō nōn longē est, epistulam ad mē mīsit, in quā dīxit flammās ē monte venīre: saxa cinerēsque calidōs in hominēs cadere: ibi esse perīculum magnum.

Plīnius: Tūne igitur dē hominibus, quī ibi habitant, cōgitāvistī?

Avunculus: Ita vērō.

Plīnius: Quid faciēs?

Avunculus: Illūc nāvigābō hominēsque perīculō magnō līberābō.

Plīnius: Animus tibi est fortis!

haec (*feminine demonstrative*) – this
investīgō, investīgāre, investīgāvī, investīgātum – to trace out, investigate
ita vērō – yes indeed

mūtō, mūtāre, mūtāvī, mūtātum – to change
tālis, tāle – such a
ubi prīmum – as soon as
validus, valida, validum – healthy, strong

TALKING

fēriae, fēriārum, f. pl. – vacation

fēriās agere – have a holiday

acta, actae, f. – the (sandy) seashore

aprīcor, aprīcārī – to sunbathe

assāre in crāticulā (assō, assāre, assāvī) – to barbecue

folle volātilī lūdō (lūdere, lūsī, lūsum) – to play volleyball

harēna, harēnae, f. – sand

natō, natāre, natāvī, —— – to swim

sōl, sōlis, m. – the sun

sōle adustus, adusta, adustum – suntanned

sub dīvō – in the open, under the sky

umbella, umbellae, f. – sunshade, umbrella

unguentum, unguentī, n. – sunscreen

natātōrium, natātōriī, n. – swimming pool

RELAXING AT THE BEACH

Helena: Quandō (*when*), Christīna, ē lītore in urbem revēnistī (*returned*)?

Christīna: Et ego et parentēs herī (*yesterday*) revēnimus. Fēriās (*holidays*) bonās ēgimus. Lītus enim valdē amāmus.

Marīa: Adusta sōle mihi nōn vidēris. Nōnne (*surely*) tū et parentēs in actā aprīcārī solētis?

Christīna: Numquam forīs (*outside*) iacuimus, nisi (*unless*) unguentō oblitī (*smeared*). Medicī dīcunt hominēs nōn dēbēre diū in sōle manēre nisi unguentīs oblitōs.

Helena: Quid aliud cum parentibus in lītore fēcistī?

Christīna: Parva castella (*castles*) ex harēnā aedificāvimus. Folle volātilī lūsimus. Vespere (*in the evening*) cibum (*food*) in crāticulā assāre sub dīvō semper solēbāmus.

Mārcus: Ea omnia in terrā fēcistī. Aquamne timuistī? Nōnne natāre solēbātis?

Christīna: Māne (*in the morning*) in natātōriō natāre solēbam. Hōrīs postmerīdiānīs (*in the afternoon hours*) autem saepe in actā sub (*under*) umbellā iacēbam prope mare librīsque studēbam.

Mārcus: Etiam in lītore, etiam in fēriīs librōs cūrābās! Quī homō sīc (*so*) umquam fuit dīligēns (*diligent*) ut (*as*) tū?!

Christīna: In scholā Latīnā (*in the Latin class*) ante fēriās dē montis Vesuviī incendiō lēgimus. Eō tempore, quō incendium in monte fuit, Plīnius et eius avunculus forīs iacēbant librīsque studēbant!

DERIVATIVES

avunculus – avuncular

caelum – ceiling, celestial, cerulean

causa – accuse, accusative, because, excuse, inexcusable

cinis – incinerate, incinerator

classis – class, classic, classical, classification, classmate

fēmina – effeminate, female, feminine

fūmus – fume, fumigation, perfume, fumarole

incendium – censer, frankincense, incendiary, incense

lītus – littoral

māter – maternal, matrimonial, matrix, matron, matriculate, matricide, matrilineal, matriarchal

mōns – mount, mountain, surmount

nāvis – naval, nave, navy, circumnavigate

pars – apart, apartment, depart, department, forepart, impart, impartial, jeopardize, jeopardy, parcel, partiality, participation, participle, particle, particular, partisan, partner, party, repartee, tripartite

legō – coil, collect, cull, diligent, election, eligibility, intellect, intelligence, lecture, legend, legible, legion, lesson, predilection, recollect, sacrilege, select

opprimō – oppress, oppressive

studeō – etude, student, studio, studious, study

P luperfect Tense Active of All Conjugations; Pluperfect Tense of *Sum* and *Possum*; Fourth Declension Masculine, Feminine, and Neuter Nouns

The 64 CE fire in Rome as painted by Henryk Siemiradzki (1843–1902).

MEMORĀBILE DICTŪ

Sine īrā et studiō.

"Without anger and partisanship." (Tacitus, *Annals* 1.1)

This is the promise made by the Roman historian Tacitus in the beginning of his *Annals*. The phrase has become proverbial for claims of impartiality in historical writing.

READING

Pliny the Younger addresses the letter about the death of his uncle to his good friend, the historian Cornēlius Tacitus (ca. 56–116/120 CE). Tacitus's major writings include the *Historiae*, "Histories," covering the period between 69 and 96 CE, and the *Annālēs*, covering from 14 to 68 CE; in both works he exposes abuses of power by the Roman imperial government in those years. He also wrote three briefer works: the *Germānia*, the only surviving ethnographical and geographic treatise in Latin; the *Agricola*, a biography of his wife's father of that name, a one-time governor of Britain; and the *Dialogus dē Ōrātōribus*, "Dialogue about Orators," which seeks to explain the decline of political eloquence characteristic of the Roman Republic in his own time.

The following text, Chapters 38–39 of *Annālēs*, Book 15, tells about the fire that destroyed Rome in 64 CE. It does not omit the persistent rumor that the emperor Nero himself had started the conflagration, supposedly in pursuit of inspiration for his own artistic efforts about the fall of Troy! After having failed to dissipate the rumor despite offers of financial compensation to the fire's victims, Nero found a scapegoat, by accusing the Christians, a fairly new religious sect then making its presence visible in Rome, of having started the fire.

DĒ INCENDIŌ RŌMĀNŌ

1   Initium magnī incendiī Rōmānī fuit in tabernīs, in quibus flammae
     mercimōniīs facile alēbantur. Quae fuit eius incendiī causa? Fortasse
     Nerō imperātor dolō id fēcit; fortasse alia erat causa. Maiōrem tamen
     clādem Rōmānī numquam vīderant. Ignis impetū ventōrum vectus
5   circum corripuit nec eius vīs opprimī potuit. Domibus nōn erant
     mūnīmenta, templīs nōn erant mūrī. Viae erant angustae et flexae.
     Itaque sine impedīmentīs flammae omnia dēvastābant. Flammae iam
     ubīque ārdēbant antequam hominēs eās exstinguere temptāvērunt.
     Propter lacrimās et timōrēs fēminārum et propter eōs quī hūc atque
10   illūc currēbant omnia erant in tumultū. Omnia loca ex omnibus
     partibus ignī corripiēbantur. Virī mulierēsque in viīs et agrīs fugiēbant
     et multī eōrum in terram cadēbant. Nam eīs, quī omnia sua omnēsque
     suōs āmīserant, propter dolōrem iam nōn erant vīrēs. Itaque eōs ignis
     cōnsūmpsit. Aliī autem hominēs facēs in ignem iaciēbant, quod fortasse
15   iussū imperātōris faciēbant.

READING VOCABULARY

*alō, alere, aluī, altum/alitum – to feed, nourish

*āmīserant – had lost

angustus, angusta, angustum – narrow

antequam (*conj.*) – before

circus, circī, *m.* – circus, Circus Maximus

*corripiō, corripere, corripuī, correptum – to seize, occupy, engulf

*currō, currere, cucurrī, cursum – to run

*dēvastō, dēvastāre, dēvastāvī, dēvastātum – to devastate

*domibus – to the houses

*exstinguō, exstinguere, exstīnxī, exstīnctum – to extinguish

*facile (*adv.*) – easily

fax, fācis, *f.* – torch

flexus, flexa, flexum – curved

hūc atque illūc – hither and thither, to and fro

*iaciō, iacere, iēcī, iactum – to throw

impedīmentum, impedīmentī, *n.* – impediment

*imperātor, imperātōris, *m.* – general, emperor

*impetū – by force of

*initium, initiī, *n.* – beginning

*in tumultū – in uproar, in confusion

*iussū – by the order

*locus, locī, *m.* – place; **locī, locōrum,** *m. pl.* – passages of a book; **loca, locōrum,** *n. pl.* – geographical places

maiōrem (*accusative singular feminine*) – bigger, greater

mercimōnium, mercimōniī, *n.* – merchandise

mūnīmentum, mūnīmentī, *n.* – protection, fortification

*mūrus, mūrī, *m.* – wall

Nerō, Nerōnis, *m.* – Nero

*sine + *ablative* – without

taberna, tabernae, *f.* – shop

*temptō, temptāre, temptāvī, temptātum – to try

vectus, vecta, vectum – carried, driven

*ventus, ventī, *m.* – wind

vīderant – had seen

*Words marked with an asterisk will need to be memorized later in the chapter.

STUDY TIP

Remember to distinguish among:

    ignis – a general word for fire; fire as an element;

    flamma – a flame, a part of *ignis*;

    incendium – a conflagration, fire as a disastrous event.

COMPREHENSION QUESTIONS

1. How did the fire at Rome start?

2. Why did the fire spread so quickly?

3. Why did some people have no strength to flee?

4. Why were some people throwing torches into the fire?

LANGUAGE FACT I

PLUPERFECT TENSE ACTIVE OF ALL CONJUGATIONS

In the chapter reading about the fire of Rome, you meet several new verb forms:

> *vīderant,* "they had seen"

> *āmīserant,* "they had lost."

These are forms of the pluperfect active tense.

The pluperfect (literally "more than perfect") indicates an action already completed prior to another action in the past. In English the pluperfect is typically indicated by the auxiliary verb "had."

In the text above:

> *Maiōrem tamen clādem Rōmānī numquam vīderant.*
> However, the Romans had never seen a greater disaster.

The Romans had not seen a greater disaster *before* the great fire: this action of not seeing had **already** taken place before the great fire.

> *Nam eīs, quī omnia sua omnēsque suōs āmīserant, propter dolōrem iam nōn erant vīrēs.*
> In fact, those who had lost all their things and all their people did not have strength any more because of pain.

Some had lost all their things and all their people *before* they did not have any strength: this action of having lost everything had **already** taken place before their loss of strength.

The formation of the pluperfect active is simple, and is the same for all conjugations. Use the perfect tense stem, i.e., a verb's third principal part minus the ending *–ī*. To this stem add the pluperfect endings:

Pluperfect Active: *parō*				
	Singular		**Plural**	
First person	parā**veram**	I had prepared	parā**verāmus**	we had prepared
Second person	parā**verās**	you had prepared	parā**verātis**	you had prepared
Third person	parā**verat**	s/he/it had prepared	parā**verant**	they had prepared

Pluperfect Active: *capiō*				
	Singular		**Plural**	
First person	cēp**eram**	I had taken	cēp**erāmus**	we had taken
Second person	cēp**erās**	you had taken	cēp**erātis**	you had taken
Third person	cēp**erat**	s/he/it had taken	cēp**erant**	they had taken

▶ EXERCISE 1

Change the perfect tense verbs into the pluperfect, keeping the same person and number. Translate the changed form.

Example: aluī
alueram   I had nourished

1. corripuī
2. temptāvī
3. exstīnxī
4. āmīsī
5. cucurrī
6. lēgī

VOCABULARY TO LEARN

NOUNS

cornū, cornūs, *n.* – horn

domus, domūs, *f.* – house, home

imperātor, imperātōris, *m.* – general, emperor

impetus, impetūs, *m.* – impetus, force, attack

initium, initiī, *n.* – beginning

iussus, iussūs, *m.* – order (*this word typically occurs only in the ablative singular*)

locus, locī, *m.* – place; **locī, locōrum,** *m. pl.* – passages of a book; **loca, locōrum,** *n. pl.* – geographical places

manus, manūs, *f.* – hand

mūrus, mūrī, *m.* – wall

tumultus, tumultūs, *m.* – uproar, confusion

ventus, ventī, *m.* – wind

VERBS

alō, alere, aluī, altum/alitum – to feed, nourish

āmittō, āmittere, āmīsī, āmissum – to lose

corripiō, corripere, corripuī, correptum – to seize, engulf

currō, currere, cucurrī, cursum – to run

dēvastō, dēvastāre, dēvastāvī, dēvastātum – to devastate

exstinguō, exstinguere, exstīnxī, exstīnctum – to extinguish

iaciō, iacere, iēcī, iactum – to throw

temptō, temptāre, temptāvī, temptātum – to try

ADVERB

facile – easily

PREPOSITION

sine + *ablative* – without

The Latin words *cornū* (horn) and *cōpia* (supply) are the two roots of the English word cornucopia, known as a horn of plenty.

▶ EXERCISE 2

Find the English derivatives based on the Vocabulary to Learn in the following sentences. Write the corresponding Latin word.

1. An attempt was made to rescue the lost mountaineers.
2. It is now time for your local weather forecast.
3. The dinosaurs are an extinct species.
4. The divorce decree determined which spouse had to pay alimony to the other.
5. I cannot breathe well; the ventilation in the building is not good.
6. Government officials assessed the areas devastated by the hurricane.
7. "Sit down!" is a jussive sentence.
8. After the initial shock, everyone is trying to cope with the bad news.
9. Could you describe to me the curriculum of your program?
10. In imperial times Rome expanded throughout the Mediterranean world.
11. We admired the murals in the old church.
12. These are problems of a domestic nature.
13. Would you agree to be a facilitator for our discussion?
14. I feel rejected by you.
15. Those were tumultuous times for the Roman Republic.
16. Nowadays fewer and fewer people do manual work.
17. Impetuous people often regret their actions when it is too late!

▶ EXERCISE 3

Change the present tense verbs into the pluperfect, keeping the same person and number. Translate the changed form.

Example: agimus
ēgerāmus   we had driven/behaved/done

1. rogātis
2. discēdunt
3. alitis
4. studet
5. fugis
6. stās
7. habēmus
8. legō
9. invidētis
10. tangis
11. sciō

LANGUAGE FACT II
PLUPERFECT TENSE OF *SUM* AND *POSSUM*

Once you know the perfect stem of *sum* and *possum*, you can easily supply the perfect and pluperfect forms, since the endings are identical to those of other verbs.

You have already met the perfect forms of *esse* and *posse* in the previous chapter. Here are their pluperfect forms.

Pluperfect Tense of *sum*				
	Singular		**Plural**	
First person	**fueram**	I had been	**fuerāmus**	we had been
Second person	**fuerās**	you had been	**fuerātis**	you had been
Third person	**fuerat**	s/he/it had been	**fuerant**	they had been

Pluperfect Tense of *possum*				
	Singular		**Plural**	
First person	**potueram**	I had been able	**potuerāmus**	we had been able
Second person	**potuerās**	you had been able	**potuerātis**	you had been able
Third person	**potuerat**	s/he/it had been able	**potuerant**	they had been able

▶ EXERCISE 4

Translate into Latin. Personal pronouns can be omitted.

1. We had not been able to run.
2. I had already been in the villa.
3. I had not been able to leave my mother.
4. Had you (plural) already been in a disaster?
5. Had you been able to walk to the shore?
6. Many women had already been in the ship.
7. Had you (plural) been able to flee?
8. Men had not been able to extinguish the conflagration.
9. The judge had not been able to stand.
10. The smoke had already been everywhere.
11. Had you often been there?
12. We had already been in a storm.

LANGUAGE FACT III

FOURTH DECLENSION MASCULINE, FEMININE, AND NEUTER NOUNS

In the chapter reading you saw some words with unfamiliar endings:

> *impetū ventōrum*
> by the force of the winds

> *Omnia erant in tumultū.*
> Everything was in confusion.

> *iussū imperātōris*
> by the order of the emperor

The forms *impetū, tumultū,* and *iussū* belong to the fourth declension. This declension has the characteristic vowel ***u***, which appears in almost all its cases.

A bust of a young Nero.

Nouns of this declension are mostly masculine, with a few feminines and neuters.

Feminine and masculine nouns of the fourth declension have identical endings.

Neuter nouns have the ending –*ū* in the nominative singular, and follow their own sub-type.

Here are the declensions of the two sub-types of the fourth declension: masculine/feminine nouns and neuter nouns.

Fourth Declension Masculine, Feminine, and Neuter Nouns

Singular

	Masculine		Feminine		Neuter	
Nominative	tumult**us**	the confusion	man**us**	the hand	corn**ū**	the horn
Genitive	tumult**ūs**	of the confusion	man**ūs**	of the hand	corn**ūs**	of the horn
Dative	tumult**uī**	to/for the confusion	man**uī**	to/for the hand	corn**ū**	to/for the horn
Accusative	tumult**um**	the confusion	man**um**	the hand	corn**ū**	the horn
Ablative	tumult**ū**	by/with the confusion	man**ū**	by/with the hand	corn**ū**	by/with the horn
Vocative	tumult**us**	o, confusion	man**us**	o, hand	corn**ū**	o, horn

Plural

	Masculine		Feminine		Neuter	
Nominative	tumult**ūs**	the confusions	man**ūs**	the hands	corn**ua**	the horns
Genitive	tumult**uum**	of the confusions	man**uum**	of the hands	corn**uum**	of the horns
Dative	tumult**ibus**	to/for the confusions	man**ibus**	to/for the hands	corn**ibus**	to/for the horns
Accusative	tumult**ūs**	the confusions	man**ūs**	the hands	corn**ua**	the horns
Ablative	tumult**ibus**	by/with the confusions	man**ibus**	by/with the hands	corn**ibus**	by/with the horns
Vocative	tumult**ūs**	o, confusions	man**ūs**	o, hands	corn**ua**	o, horns

BY THE WAY

Fourth declension masculine/feminine nouns look identical to second declension masculine nouns in their nominative singular forms. The genitive singular form of the noun will indicate whether it is from the fourth or second declension.

STUDY TIP

The neuter rule applies in the fourth declension: the neuter nominative, accusative, and vocative have identical forms.

Note also that the dative of *cornū* does not have the ending –*uī*: the dative ending –*uī* only occurs in masculine and feminine nouns.

There is one more fourth declension noun in the text at the beginning of the chapter: *domus*.

> *Domibus nōn erant mūnīmenta.*
> The houses did not have protections.

Domus has a few irregular forms (variable between the fourth and the second declensions), and it will be worthwhile to learn them, because this word is so common.

Declension of *domus*		
	Singular	**Plural**
Nominative	dom**us**	dom**ūs**
Genitive	dom**ūs**	dom**uum** (dom**ōrum**)
Dative	dom**uī** (dom**ō**)	dom**ibus**
Accusative	dom**um**	dom**ōs** (dom**ūs**)
Ablative	dom**ō** (dom**ū**)	dom**ibus**
Vocative	dom**us**	dom**ūs**

BY THE WAY

You already know a very important form of *domus* that does not appear on the list above, because it does not fit in the usual paradigm of cases. This form is *domī*, which is only used to mean "at home." *Domī* is called the locative, because it refers to a "location."

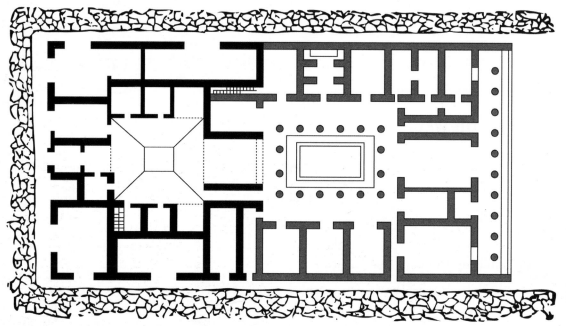

Compare this plan of the House of the Faun in Pompeii with the Roman *domus* on p. 263.

▶ EXERCISE 5

Decline the following nouns.

1. *impetus, impetūs,* m. – attack

2. *genū, genūs,* n. – knee

▶ EXERCISE 6

Make the adjective in parentheses agree with the noun. For some, more than one answer is possible.

Example: manuī (meus)
manuī meae

1. cornibus (longus)
2. tumultuum (magnus)
3. impetuī (fūnestus)
4. domūs (noster)
5. cornū (pulcher)

6. manum (armātus)
7. domibus (vester)
8. cornua (omnis)
9. manibus (multus)

The ruins of the Roman Forum may begin to give you an idea of
what this busy place looked like at the time of the fire in Rome in 64 CE.

▶ EXERCISE 7

The following imaginary dialogue is between two Romans in the Roman Forum during the fire of 64 CE. Translate the parts that are in English into Latin, and the parts that are in Latin into English. The Reading Vocabulary may be consulted.

Rōmānus 1: Fūmum et flammās cōnspiciō. Ex quā parte urbis vēnērunt? Quae est causa tumultūs?

Rōmānus 2: Therefore you do not know that Rome is on fire.

Rōmānus 1: Vērumne dīcis? Quod incendium? Quis id fēcit?

Rōmānus 2: The emperor ordered people to make the fire. For he had always desired to see the city in flames.

Rōmānus 1: Nōn possum id crēdere. Ārdetne Rōma iussū imperātōris?

Rōmānus 2: It is true, however. I saw people who had prepared torches and were throwing them with their hands in the houses and the temples.

Rōmānus 1: Nunc dē domō meā cōgitō. Familia enim mea domī est. Corripiturne domus mea quoque flammīs? Manetne familia domī?

Rōmānus 2: I do not know. I saw many men and women who were fleeing. They had abandoned their houses and all their things.

Rōmānus 1: Cōnspice! Perīculum iam est prope nōs. Quis hās flammās exstinguet?

Rōmānus 2: The force of the fire is too great and cannot be suppressed. The disaster will destroy Rome.

TALKING

valētūdō, valētūdinis, f. – health

Quālis est valētūdō tua? "How is your health?"

Quōmodo tē habēs? "How are you?"

Valētūdō mea est bona/prōspera. "My health is good."

Valētūdō mea est mala/adversa. "My health is bad."

Bene valeō. "I am feeling well."

Haud bene valeō. "I am not feeling well."

Aegrōtō. "I am ill."

Remedium quaerō. "I am looking for a remedy/cure."

Dēbēs adīre medicum. "You have to go to the doctor."

medicus, medicī, m.; *medica, medicae,* f. – doctor

nosocoma, nosocomae, f. – nurse

nosocomium, nosocomiī, n. – hospital

medicāmentum, medicāmentī, n. – medicine, drug

assicūrātiō, assicūrātiōnis, f. *medica* – insurance

febrīcitō, febrīcitāre, febrīcitāvī, —— – to have a fever

Gravēdine (gravēdō, gravēdinis, f.*) labōrō (labōrāre, labōrāvī, labōrātum).* "I have a cold."

Caput <mihi> dolet. "I have a headache."

Sūme aspirīnum. "Take aspirin."

RECOVERING FROM AN ACCIDENT

Magistra: (*teacher*) Salvēte, omnēs! Nōn videō Marīam. Vōsne Marīam vīdistis?

Christīna: Marīa mē herī (*yesterday*), magistra, telephonicē compellāvit (*called me on the phone*). Manum suam frēgerat (*had broken*). Vōs scītis Marīam amāre agrōs. Dum ambulat in agrīs, ceciderat.

Magistra: Ēheu (*alas*), dē eā clāde doleō. Quid nunc Marīa facit?

Christīna: Herī, eō tempore quō mēcum verba faciēbat, iam petīverat nosocomium et vīderat medicum. Medicus in manū gypsum (*cast*) posuerat. Propter dolōrem Marīa medicāmenta capere dēbēbat. Fortasse nunc quoque valētūdinem cūrat.

Helena: (AD CHRISTĪNAM ET MĀRCUM) Poterimusne post scholam (*after school*) domum Marīae petere? Nam cupiō eam vidēre et cum eā manēre. Fortasse Marīa quoque cupit amīcōs vidēre.

Magistra: Bonum cōnsilium.

MARĪA INTRAT, QUAE GYPSUM IN MANŪ GERIT

Marīa: Salvēte, amīcī amīcaeque (*male and female friends*)!

Omnēs: Salvē, Marīa! Gaudēmus (*we are glad*) tē esse in scholā! Quōmodo sē habet manus tua?

Marīa: Manus valdē dolet. Itaque scrībere (*to write*) nōn possum.

Magistra: Manus tua sinistra (*left*) aegrōtat nec eā manū scrībere potes. Sed dextra tua bene valēre vidētur. Itaque dextrā scrībere poteris.

DERIVATIVES

cornū – cornea, corner, cornet, cornucopia, unicorn

initium – initial, initiate, initiation, initiative

locus – couch, dislocate, lieu, lieutenant, local, locality, location, locomotive

manus – amanuensis, emancipation, maintain, manacle, manage, manatee, maneuver, manicure, manifest, manipulate, manner, manual, manufacture, manumission, manure, manuscript, mismanage

mūrus – mural, immure

tumultus – tumult, tumultuous

ventus – vent, ventilate, ventilator, hyperventilate

alō – adolescentia, alimony, adult, coalesce, coalition, alumnus (alumna, alumni)

currō – concourse, concur, corridor, corsair, courier, course, current, currency, discourse, cursor, excursion, incur, occur, precursor, recourse, recurrent, succor

dēvastō – devastate, devastation

exstinguō – extinct, extinguish, extinguisher

iaciō – abject, adjective, conjecture, dejected, eject, injection, jet, jetty, jut, object, objective, projectile, projector, reject, subject, trajectory

temptō – attempt, tempt, temptation, tentacle, tentative

sine – sinecure

Future Perfect Tense Active of All Conjugations; Future Perfect Tense of *Sum* and *Possum*; Fifth Declension Nouns

Detail from a second century CE statue of Cupid and Psyche from a home in Ostia.

MEMORĀBILE DICTŪ

Quod nēmō nōvit paene nōn fit.

"What no one knows almost does not happen." (Apuleius, *Transformations* 10.3)

This saying exemplifies the logic "Not known, not done" aimed at alleviating the remorse of the human conscience over bad deeds.

READING

In the middle of the second century CE, which coincided with a relatively stable period for Roman society under a series of "good" emperors—Hadrian, Antoninus Pius, and Marcus Aurelius (117–180 CE)—Latin literature developed an increasingly pronounced taste for "archaism": the use of rare or obsolete words and expressions from early Latin. A major work that represents this archaizing trend is the "Golden Ass," or *Metamorphōsēs*, "Transformations," by the North African writer Āpulēius. Along with the *Satyricon* of Petronius, which was likely written in the time of Nero, it is one of the two examples that have survived of the ancient novel in Latin.

In it, Apuleius relates the story of Lucius, a Greek whose excessive curiosity and interest in magic result in his transformation into a donkey. Apuleius's love of archaic and rare words adds to the color and vividness of his narration about the adventures and misfortunes experienced by Lucius, in the form of a beast of burden. The same stylistic traits figure in the excerpt from the novel that you will read here, the love story of Cupid and Psyche.

DĒ CUPĪDINE ET PSȲCHĒ

1   Rēx trēs fīliās habēbat. Duae eārum erant pulchrae, sed tertia
soror erat pulchritūdine praeclāra. Nōmen eī erat Psȳchē. Propter
pulchritūdinem Psȳchē ā multīs virīs colēbātur. Tandem Venus putāvit
Psȳchēn, quae nōn erat dea, nōn dēbēre ab aliīs tam multum colī.

5   Itaque Venus Cupīdinem, fīlium suum, vocāvit eīque dīxit: "Mitte, fīlī,
sagittam in cor Psȳchēs! Puella malī virī amōre corripī dēbēbit." Cupīdō
puellam petīvit, eam cōnspexit et ipse amōre statim ārsit. Puella
quoque iam nōn poterat alium virum amāre. Sorōrēs marītōs habēbant,
sed Psȳchē marītum nōn habēbat. Pater dē fīliae fātō valdē dolēbat

10 et cōnsilia deōrum dē eā rē petīvit. Deī rēgī ita respondērunt: "Sī
cōnsilium nostrum petis, audī! Dūc fīliam tuam in summum montem
et discēde! Cum discesseris, belua ad eam veniet." Rēx dolēbat, sed
fīliam ad montem dūxit. Ibi somnus Psȳchēn cēpit. Post somnum
Psȳchē vīdit sē esse in domō pulchrā et intellēxit sē iam habēre

15 marītum valdē bonum, quī eam amābat atque cūrābat. Is tamen faciem
suam uxōrī numquam ostendēbat. Psȳchē eius faciem vidēre cupīvit et,
dum marītus dormiēbat, lūmen ad faciem mōvit. Gutta oleī in faciem
marītī cecidit eumque ex somnō excitāvit. Marītus erat ipse Cupīdō!
"Cūr id fēcistī?!" exclāmāvit Cupīdō et statim ēvanuit. Psȳchē eum

20   per omnēs terrās diū quaesīvit. Nam Venus fīlium suum occultāverat. Cupīdō quoque cum Psȳchē esse cupiēbat. Tandem Venus auxilium iīs dare dēcrēvit. Itaque Cupīdō et Psȳchē semper ūnā manēre poterunt. Magna est vīs amōris.

READING VOCABULARY

belua, beluae, *f.* – beast

*__colō, colere, coluī, cultum__ – to worship, cultivate

cor, cordis, *n.* – heart

*__cum__ (*conj.*) – when, after

cum discesseris – when you leave

Cupīdō, Cupīdinis, *m.* – Cupid (*in Greek* Eros)

*__dea, deae,__ *f.* – goddess

*__dē rē__ – about the thing

*__dormiō, dormīre, dormīvī, dormītum__ – to sleep

duae (*feminine*) – two

dūc! – *present imperative of* dūcō, dūcere, dūxī, ductum, *to lead, take*

ēvānēscō, ēvānēscere, ēvānuī, —— – to disappear

*__excitō, excitāre, excitāvī, excitātum__ – to awaken, wake up, rouse, stir up

*__exclāmō, exclāmāre, exclāmāvī, exclāmātum__ – to exclaim

*__faciem__ – face

*__fātum, fātī,__ *n.* – fate, destiny

gutta, guttae, *f.* – drop

ipse (*masculine nominative singular*) – himself

*__ita__ (*adv.*) – so, in such a way

lūmen, lūminis, *n.* – light

*__marītus, marītī,__ *m.* – husband

*__multum__ (*adv.*) – much

*__occultō, occultāre, occultāvī, occultātum__ – to hide

oleum, oleī, *n.* – oil

*__pater, patris,__ *m.* – father

*__post__ + *accusative* – after

Psȳchē, Psȳchēs (*gen.*), **Psȳchē** (*dat.*), **Psȳchēn** (*acc.*), **Psȳchē** (*abl.*) – Psyche

pulchritūdō, pulchritūdinis, *f.* – beauty

*__quaerō, quaerere, quaesīvī, quaesītum__ – to look for, search

sagitta, sagittae, *f.* – arrow

*__sī__ (*conj.*) – if

*__somnus, somnī,__ *m.* – sleep

summus, summa, summum – the top of

*__tam__ (*adv.*) – so

tertius, tertia, tertium – third

trēs (*nominative and accusative*) – three

*__uxor, uxōris,__ *f.* – wife

Venus, Veneris, *f.* – Venus (*Greek* Aphrodite)

*Words marked with an asterisk will need to be memorized later in the chapter.

COMPREHENSION QUESTIONS

1. Why did Venus decide to punish Psyche?

2. What happened when Cupid was sent to Psyche?

3. Why did Psyche stay unmarried for a long time?

4. Who was the secret husband to whom Psyche was taken?

5. Why were Cupid and Psyche separated?

6. What happened at the end of the story?

LANGUAGE FACT I
FUTURE PERFECT TENSE ACTIVE OF ALL CONJUGATIONS

In the Latin reading passage you noticed a verb form whose tense you do not yet know: *discesseris*.

Discesseris is an active form of the **future perfect** tense.

The future perfect active is formed by adding the endings *–erō, –eris, –erit, –erimus, –eritis, –erint* to the perfect stem.

Once again (as in the perfect and pluperfect active) there is no difference in endings among the four conjugations: simply add the new endings to the perfect stem.

Future Perfect Active: *parō*		
	Singular	
First person	parā**verō**	I will/shall have prepared
Second person	parā**veris**	you will have prepared
Third person	parā**verit**	s/he/it will have prepared
	Plural	
First person	parā**verimus**	we will/shall have prepared
Second person	parā**veritis**	you will have prepared
Third person	parā**verint**	they will have prepared

Future Perfect Active: *capiō*		
	Singular	
First person	cē**perō**	I will/shall have seized
Second person	cē**peris**	you will have seized
Third person	cē**perit**	s/he/it will have seized
	Plural	
First person	cē**perimus**	we will/shall have seized
Second person	cē**peritis**	you will have seized
Third person	cē**perint**	they will have seized

STUDY TIP

The endings of the future perfect closely resemble the future forms of *sum: erō, eris, erit, erimus, eritis, erunt*. The only difference is in the third person plural ending, *–erint*.

STUDY TIP

Do not confuse the following third person plural forms!

erunt – they will be (future active)

amāv**ērunt** – they loved (perfect active)

amāv**erint** – they will have loved (future perfect active)

The future perfect tense indicates an action that will have been completed before a future action occurs. It is translated in English in the following way: "I will (shall) have done something (before something else happens)."

The future perfect tense is rarely used by itself in a sentence. It is commonly used in a subordinate clause to indicate an action prior to a simple future tense that appears in the main clause.

Cum **discesseris**, belua ad eam veniet.
When you will have left (you leave), a beast will come to her.

Sī **exspectāveris**, ad tē veniam.
If you will have waited (you wait), I will come to you.

STUDY TIP

Note that in "when" and "if" clauses English uses the simple present tense where Latin uses the future perfect tense, along with the simple future tense in the main clause (where Latin also uses the simple future). In fact, the Latin construction represents real time much more exactly than English, since the event in the "when" or "if" clause will have to happen before the conclusion. This will help you remember how these sentences are constructed in Latin.

Apuleius, author of *Metamorphōsēs*, lived during the reign of Marcus Aurelius, the emperor seated on this bronze equestrian statue. Michelangelo placed this statue on the Capitoline Hill but during the 1980s it was moved inside the Capitoline Museum to protect it from pollution. A replica stands in its place outside the museum today.

▶ EXERCISE 1

Change the future tense verbs into the future perfect, keeping the same person and number. Translate the changed form.

Example: ambulābis
ambulāveris   you will have walked

1. legēmus
2. studēbit
3. veniētis
4. quaerent
5. occultābunt
6. respondēbitis
7. excitābō
8. dūcēs
9. exstinguēmus
10. iaciam
11. corripient
12. exclāmābō
13. negleget
14. dēvastābitis

VOCABULARY TO LEARN

NOUNS

dea, deae, *f.* – goddess
diēs, diēī, *m./f.* – day
faciēs, faciēī, *f.* – face
fātum, fātī, *n.* – fate, destiny
marītus, marītī, *m.* – husband
merīdiēs, merīdiēī, *m.* – midday
pater, patris, *m.* – father
rēs, reī, *f.* – thing, matter
somnus, somnī, *m.* – sleep
uxor, uxōris, *f.* – wife

VERBS

colō, colere, coluī, cultum – to worship, cultivate
dormiō, dormīre, dormīvī, dormītum – to sleep
excitō, excitāre, excitāvī, excitātum – to awaken, wake up, rouse, stir up

exclāmō, exclāmāre, exclāmāvī, exclāmātum – to exclaim
occultō, occultāre, occultāvī, occultātum – to hide
quaerō, quaerere, quaesīvī, quaesītum – to look for, search

ADVERBS

ita – so, in such a way
multum – much
tam – so

PREPOSITION

post + *accusative* – after

CONJUNCTIONS

cum – when, after
sī – if

Find which of the words below are English derivatives based on the Vocabulary to Learn of Chapter 18 in the following list. Write the corresponding word. For some, more than one English word can be related to the same Latin word.

excitement	duchess
extinction	duke
extortion	facial
question	fatal
querulous	factitious
occultism	marital
occident	maroon
exclamation	dormitory
excavation	dormant
cumin	doorway
cult	paternal
culture	pottery
ductile	

► EXERCISE 3

Change the present tense verbs into the perfect, the imperfect tense verbs into the pluperfect, and the future tense verbs into the future perfect. Translate the changed form.

Example: amābās
amāverās   you had loved

1. cadunt
2. iaciētis
3. occultābās
4. temptābit
5. legēbāmus
6. quaeris
7. iubēbō
8. stābant
9. occīdēmus
10. respondēbunt
11. veniam

FUTURE PERFECT TENSE OF *SUM* AND *POSSUM*

The future perfect of *esse* and *posse* is not so irregular as one might expect. Once you know the perfect stems of these verbs (*fu–* and *potu–*), you simply add the future perfect active endings.

Future Perfect Tense of *sum*

Singular

First person	fuerō	I will/shall have been
Second person	fueris	you will have been
Third person	fuerit	s/he/it will have been

Plural

First person	fuerimus	we will/shall have been
Second person	fueritis	you will have been
Third person	fuerint	they will have been

Future Perfect Tense of *possum*

Singular

First person	potuerō	I will/shall have been able
Second person	potueris	you will have been able
Third person	potuerit	s/he/it will have been able

Plural

First person	potuerimus	we will/shall have been able
Second person	potueritis	you will have been able
Third person	potuerint	they will have been able

▶ EXERCISE 4

Change the following verbs to the future perfect tense, keeping the same person and number, and translate both forms.

Example: potuistis

potueritis you (plural) were able you (plural) will have been able

1. potuērunt
2. es
3. eram
4. eritis
5. poterāmus
6. potueram
7. fuit
8. poterās
9. fueram

LANGUAGE FACT III

FIFTH DECLENSION NOUNS

In the story about Cupid and Psyche, you encountered two nouns that belong to the fifth declension (the last declension in Latin!). You probably did not notice any peculiarity in these forms, since they resemble the third declension: *dē eā rē*, "about this thing"; *faciem*, "face," *ad faciem*, "to the face"; *in faciem*, "onto the face."

There are not many words in the fifth declension (just as there are not too many words belonging to the fourth declension). The characteristic vowel throughout the fifth declension is *–e–*.

Here are the paradigms of two words of the fifth declension. The first one is the very common Latin word *rēs, reī*, f., "thing," and the second one is *diēs, diēī*, m./f., "day."

Fifth Declension

Singular

Nominative	rēs	the thing	diēs	the day
Genitive	reī	of the thing	diēī	of the day
Dative	reī	to/for the thing	diēī	to/for the day
Accusative	rem	the thing	diem	the day
Ablative	rē	by/with the thing	diē	by/with the day
Vocative	rēs	o, thing	diēs	o, day

Plural

Nominative	rēs	the things	diēs	the days
Genitive	rērum	of the things	diērum	of the days
Dative	rēbus	to/for the things	diēbus	to/for the days
Accusative	rēs	the things	diēs	the days
Ablative	rēbus	by/with the things	diēbus	by/with the days
Vocative	rēs	o, things	diēs	o, days

STUDY TIP

Here is a tip to remember the dative and ablative plural of *rēs*. The word "rebus," with the meaning of "crosswords" or "puzzle," is derived from a medieval game monks played that involved the names of different things. Literally, it is the ablative plural of *rēs*, "<to play> with things."

BY THE WAY

Note that words like *diēs*, which have a vowel before the nominative singular ending *–ēs* (e.g., *diēs* and *faciēs*), have a long *–ē–* in the genitive and dative singular endings *–ēī*. This is an exception to the general rule that vowels in front of vowels are short—but there is no rule without exceptions.

Fifth declension nouns are mostly feminine, with a couple of masculine exceptions: *diēs, diēī* can be both masculine and feminine: it is masculine, unless it indicates a day decided upon (like a deadline or an appointment); and *merīdiēs, merīdiēī* (derived from *diēs*), which is masculine. The latter means literally "midday," and sometimes "south" (since the sun points south at midday).

BY THE WAY
The abbreviations AM and PM are from the Latin *ante merīdiem*, "before midday," and *post merīdiem*, "after midday."

STUDY TIP
This gender/declension bell curve illustrates the most frequent genders in each of the five declensions.

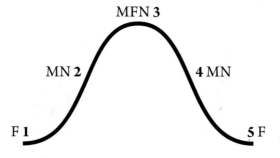

BY THE WAY
You have probably heard the Spanish greeting *Buenos días*. It means literally "Good day." *Buenos* comes from *bonus* and *días* from the fifth declension noun *diēs*.

▶ EXERCISE 5
Make the noun in parentheses agree with the adjective. Translate the phrase.

Example: bonīs (rēs)
rēbus   to/for good things *or* by/with good things

1. fēlīcī (diēs)
2. longārum (diēs)
3. miserō (merīdiēs)
4. pulchrae (faciēs)
5. omnibus (diēs)

6. multōrum (diēs)
7. vetustam (faciēs)
8. iūstās (rēs)
9. fūnestā (rēs)

The look of love on these sculptured faces is a reminder of Cupid and Psyche's feelings.

▶ EXERCISE 6

Translate into English.

1. Sī bene salūtāveris, bene salūtāberis.

2. Cum faciem marītī cōnspexerit, intelleget eum esse Cupīdinem.

3. Sī cupīveris mē amāre, tē quoque amābō.

4. Sī ante merīdiem mē excitāveris, multās rēs faciam.

5. Sī eius fāta occultāverimus, nōn timēbit.

6. Cum locum diū quaesīveritis, tandem eum cōnspiciētis.

▶ EXERCISE 7

Translate into Latin. Use a future perfect in the subordinate clause.

timerimus

1. If we do not fear the fates, we will win.

2. If the wife desires to look at the face of the husband, she will wake him up.

3. When a happy day comes, all things will be good.

4. When the father leads her to the mountain, he will have to leave her there.

5. When you sleep for a long time, it will already be midday.

6. If the goddess gives help, we will soon be husband and wife.

TALKING

dēns, dentis, m. – tooth

gingīva, gingīvae, f. – gum

gena, genae, f. – cheek

obtūrāmentum, obtūrāmentī, n. – filling

Dēns <mihi> dolet. "I have a toothache."

Not always represented as a chubby cherub, this statue shows a youthful Eros or Cupid.

Dēbeō īre ad medicum dentārium. "I have to go to the dentist."

Dentēs mundō (mundāre, mundāvī, mundātum). "I clean my teeth."

Medicus dentārius dentēs radiīs dēpinget (dēpingō, dēpingere, dēpīnxī, dēpictum). "The dentist will take X-rays of the teeth."

Medicus dentārius terebram adhibēbit (adhibeō, adhibēre, adhibuī, adhibitum). "The dentist will use the drill."

Dolōrem timeō. "I am afraid of the pain."

Medicus dentārius tibi medicāmen anaestheticum ministrābit (ministrō, ministrāre, ministrāvī, ministrātum). "The dentist will give you anesthesia."

Nihil in genā meā sentiō. "I have no feeling in my cheek."

Dentēs bis in annō mundārī dēbent. "<One's> teeth have to be cleaned twice a year."

GOING TO THE DENTIST

Christīna: Salvē, Marīa! Quōmodo nunc valēs? (*How are you now?*) Quōmodo manus tua valet?

Marīa: Iam manus mea bene valet. Quōmodo vōs valētis, Helena et Christīna?

Christīna: Ego bene valeō.

Helena: Ego autem male (*badly*) valeō.

Christīna et Marīa: Cūr?

Helena: Hodiē (*today*) ad medicum dentārium īre dēbeō. Medicum dentārium timeō.

Marīa: Omnēs ad medicum dentārium bis in annō īre dēbēmus. Nam dentēs mundārī debent. Nōlī timēre!

Helena: Sed dēns meus dolet. Propter eam causam medicum dentārium petō.

Christīna: Tū, Helena, nimis (*too*) multa crūstula (*cookies*) comedere solēs. Itaque medicus in dentem tuum obtūrāmentum pōnet. Prīmum (*first*) fortasse dentem radiīs dēpinget.

Helena: Dolōrem timeō.

Christīna: Medicus medicāmen anaestheticum tibi ministrābit. Cum medicāmen tibi ministrāverit, tunc terebram adhibēbit. Nōlī timēre! Quandō (*when*) īre dēbēbis?

Helena: Merīdiē. Prīmum prandium (*lunch*) comedam et crūstula.

DERIVATIVES

diēs – adjourn, dial, diary, dismal, diurnal, journal, journey, meridian, sojourn

fātum – fatal, fatality, fate

marītus – marital, marriage, marry

merīdiēs – meridian

pater – paternal, patrician, patrilineal, patriarchal, patrimony, Patrick, patron, patronage, patronize, patter

rēs – real, realist, reality, realize, really, realty, republic

somnus – somnambulist, somniferous, somnific, somniloquist, somnolent, Somnus

uxor – uxoricide, uxorious

colō – agriculture, colonial, colonize, cult, cultivate, cultivator, culture, horticulture

dormiō – dormant, dormer, dormitory

excitō – excite, excitement

exclāmō – exclaim, exclamation, exclamatory

occultō – occult, occultism, occultation

quaerō – acquire, acquisition, conquer, conquest, exquisite, inquest, inquire, perquisite, query, quest, question, require, request, prerequisite

VOCABULARY TO KNOW

NOUNS

avunculus, avunculī, *m.* – uncle

caelum, caelī, *n.* – sky, heaven, weather

causa, causae, *f.* – cause, reason

cinis, cineris, *m.* – ash

clādēs, clādis, *f.* – disaster

classis, classis, *f.* – fleet, class (of people)

cornū, cornūs, *n.* – horn

dea, deae, *f.* – goddess

diēs, diēī, *m./f.* – day

domus, domūs, *f.* – house, home

faciēs, faciēī, *f.* – face

fātum, fātī, *n.* – fate, destiny

fēmina, fēminae, *f.* – woman

fūmus, fūmī, *m.* – smoke

imperātor, imperātōris, *m.* – general, emperor

impetus, impetūs, *m.* – impetus, force, attack

incendium, incendiī, *n.* – conflagration, eruption

initium, initiī, *n.* – beginning

iussus, iussūs, *m.* – order (*this word typically occurs only in the ablative singular*)

lītus, lītoris, *n.* – shore

locus, locī, *m.* – place; **locī, locōrum,** *m. pl.* – passages of a book; **loca, locōrum,** *n. pl.* – geographical places

manus, manūs, *f.* – hand

marītus, marītī, *m.* – husband

māter, mātris, *f.* – mother

merīdiēs, merīdiēī, *m.* – midday

mōns, montis, *m.* – mountain

mūrus, mūrī, *m.* – wall

nāvis, nāvis, *f.* – ship

nūbēs, nūbis, *f.* – cloud

pars, partis, *f.* – part

pater, patris, *m.* – father

rēs, reī, *f.* – thing, matter

somnus, somnī, *m.* – sleep

tumultus, tumultūs, *m.* – uproar, confusion

uxor, uxōris, *f.* – wife

ventus, ventī, *m.* – wind

ADJECTIVE

fūnestus, fūnesta, fūnestum – deadly

VERBS

alō, alere, aluī, altum/alitum – to feed, nourish

āmittō, āmittere, āmīsī, āmissum – to lose

colō, colere, coluī, cultum – to worship, cultivate

corripiō, corripere, corripuī, correptum – to seize, engulf

currō, currere, cucurrī, cursum – to run

dēvastō, dēvastāre, dēvastāvī, dēvastātum – to devastate

dormiō, dormīre, dormīvī, dormītum – to sleep

dūcō, dūcere, dūxī, ductum – to lead, take

excitō, excitāre, excitāvī, excitātum – to awaken, wake up, rouse, stir up

exclāmō, exclāmāre, exclāmāvī, exclāmātum – to exclaim

exstinguō, exstinguere, exstīnxī, exstīnctum – to extinguish

iaciō, iacere, iēcī, iactum – to throw

legō, legere, lēgī, lēctum – to read, choose

occultō, occultāre, occultāvī, occultātum – to hide

opprimō, opprimere, oppressī, oppressum – to overwhelm, suppress

quaerō, quaerere, quaesīvī, quaesītum – to look for, search

studeō, studēre, studuī, —— + *dative* – to study, be eager for, be interested in

temptō, temptāre, temptāvī, temptātum – to try

ADVERBS

facile – easily

ita – so, in such a way

multum – much

numquam – never

tam – so

PREPOSITIONS

post + *accusative* – after

sine + *ablative* – without

CONJUNCTIONS

cum – when, after

igitur – therefore (*usually the second word in its clause*)

sī – if

▶ EXERCISE 1

Conjugate the following verbs in the perfect active and give the translation for each form.

1. *occultō, occultāre, occultāvī, occultātum*

2. *studeō, studēre, studuī, ——*

3. *opprimō, opprimere, oppressī, oppressum*

4. *dormiō, dormīre, dormīvī, dormītum*

5. *iaciō, iacere, iēcī, iactum*

▶ EXERCISE 2

Conjugate the following verb in the pluperfect active and give the translation of each form.

1. *temptō, temptāre, temptāvī, temptātum*

▶ EXERCISE 3

Conjugate the following verb in the future perfect active and give the translation of each form.

1. *alō, alere, aluī, altum*

Pliny's uncle, Pliny the Elder, sailed across the Bay of Naples (seen in this panoramic view) in an attempt to rescue people being threatened by the eruption of Mt. Vesuvius, looming in the background.

▶ EXERCISE 4

Give the perfect, pluperfect, and future perfect active first person singular for each of the following verbs.

Example: āmittō

āmīsī   āmīseram   āmīserō

1. corripiō
2. currō
3. dūcō
4. dēvastō
5. excitō
6. exclāmō
7. exstinguō
8. legō
9. quaerō

▶ EXERCISE 5

Decline the following phrases.

1. *manus longa*

2. *spēs fēlīx (spēs, speī,* f. – hope)

▶ EXERCISE 6

Translate into Latin.

1. If you see fire, flee! (use the future perfect tense in the subordinate clause)

2. The conflagration had seized all the houses.

3. If you are able to flee, you will be saved. (use the future perfect tense in the subordinate clause)

4. Do you have strength? Will you be able to run? (use the dative of possession in this sentence)

5. Fire, smoke, ashes came from the mountain and devastated the shore.

6. Many people did not have houses any more. They had lost everything. (use the dative of possession in this sentence)

7. "Fates are cruel!" exclaimed people.

▶ EXERCISE 7

For each question, choose the best answer and translate. The Reading Vocabulary for Chapters 16–18 may be consulted.

1. Cūr avunculus Plīniī, quī studēbat, librōs suōs relīquit?

   Avunculus ambulāre cupiēbat.

   Avunculus librōrum iam nōn erat studiōsus.

   Avunculus causam nūbis inūsitātae intellegere cupīvit.

2. Cūius epistulam tunc nauta avunculō dedit?

   Nauta epistulam mātris Plīniī avunculō dedit.

   Nauta epistulam suam avunculō dedit.

   Nauta epistulam fēminae, quae prope montem Vesuvium habitābat, avunculō dedit.

3. Cūr fēmina epistulam ad avunculum mīserat?

   Fēmina perīculum timēbat et auxilium petēbat.

   Fēmina cum avunculō nāvigāre cupiēbat.

   Fēmina cum avunculō librōs legere cupiēbat.

4. Potuitne avunculus fēminam servāre?

   Avunculus fēminam servāre nōn potuit; nam fūmus cinerēsque eam ūnā cum aliīs oppressērunt.

   Avunculus omnēs servāvit.

   Avunculus ūnā cum multīs aliīs revēnit.

5. Ex quō locō incendium Rōmānum initium cēpit?

   Incendium ex tabernīs, in quibus erant mercimōnia, initium cēpit.

   Incendium ex templīs et ex domibus initium cēpit.

   Incendium ex agrīs initium cēpit.

6. Fuitne Nerō causa incendiī?

   Omnēs putant Nerōnem esse causam incendiī.

   Nerō fortasse fuit causa incendiī.

   Omnēs dīcunt Nerōnem nōn esse causam incendiī.

7. Quid Cupīdō dē Psȳchē sentiēbat?

   Cupīdō amōre Psȳchēs ārsit.

   Cupīdō volēbat Psȳchēn beluae dare.

   Cupīdō Psȳchēn numquam vīdit.

8. Potuitne tandem Psȳchē esse uxor Cupīdinis?

   Psȳchē diū Cupīdinem quaesīvit, sed eum nōn vīdit.

   Venus Cupīdinem ā Psȳchē semper occultāvit.

   Tandem Cupīdō et Psȳchē ūnā fēlīcēs esse poterant.

BACCHUS

Bacchus, the ancient Greco-Roman god of wine, was also called Dionysus in Greek and Līber in Latin. He was a relatively late addition to the pantheon of the twelve Olympian gods. His father is Jupiter; his mother, Semele, a mortal woman. Consequently he is the only deity on Olympus of partially human descent. The circumstances of his birth are extraordinary. Ever-vengeful and eternally jealous, Juno paid a visit to the young princess Semele, who had been rejoicing in Jupiter's attentions, and convinced Semele to ask her divine lover to manifest himself to her with a display of his true divine power. Jupiter thus appeared with his thunderbolt

A floor mosaic from Corinth, Greece, showing the head of Bacchus.

and lightning, which no human was able to see at a close distance, and consumed Semele by fire. Since Semele had conceived a child by Jupiter, he removed the infant from her womb and implanted him in his thigh, delivering the baby several months later. This story of how Jupiter gave birth to Bacchus has much in common with the account, which you read in an earlier chapter, of how Jupiter swallowed Minerva's mother and delivered her daughter from his head.

A brooch portraying the head of a youthful Bacchus.

Bacchus is conceptualized as the complete opposite of Apollo. Whereas Apollo represents all that is rational, moderate, and harmonious, Bacchus is irrational, immoderate, and excessive. Not only is he god of wine and uncontrolled emotion, but also of vegetation and the uncontrolled power of nature. A diverse group of followers composes his retinue: female worshippers called bacchants, or maenads (a word literally meaning "crazy women") who run wild in the forest, dancing, singing, and producing wine by scratching the earth while in an inspired state; satyrs, little men with horns on their head and the tail of a horse or a goat, also representing the uncontrollable forces of nature; sileni, older satyrs; and finally Pan, god of the woods, shepherds, and fertility, represented as a man with the horns, hindquarters, and feet of a goat, who would surprise humans in the forests and inspire terror in them (our word "panic" is derived from his name).

The Spanish painter Diego Velásquez (1599–1660) in *The Feast of Bacchus* depicts the god of wine surrounded by peasants dressed in the garb of the seventeenth century.

Mosaic from Roman Britain showing Bacchus riding a tiger.

READ AND TRANSLATE THE FOLLOWING PASSAGE

This story tells about the origin of the flute.

Pān erat deus agrōrum et silvārum. Pān semper nympham Sȳringem quaerēbat. Nam ex tempore quō Sȳringem cōnspexerat, is amōre ārsit, sed Sȳrinx Pāna nōn amābat. Pān Sȳringī dīcēbat: "Sī mea fueris, dōna pulchra tibi dabō." Nympha tamen nōn cupiēbat dōna habēre et ā deō amārī, et fūgit. Pān post eam quoque cucurrit et eam capere temptāvit. Tandem nympha ad rīvum pervēnit et in rīvum intrāvit. Deī Sȳringem servāvērunt eamque in harundinem mūtāvērunt. Tum Pān ex harundine organum mūsicum parāvit, quō organō mūsicō posteā lūdēbat.

harundō, harundinis, *f.* – reed
lūdō, lūdere, lūsī, lūsum – to play
mūsicus, mūsica, mūsicum – musical
mūtō, mūtāre, mūtāvī, mūtātum – to transform
nympha, nymphae, *f.* – nymph
organum, organī, *n.* – instrument

Pān, Pānos (*gen.*), **Pāna** (*acc.*) – Pan
perveniō, pervenīre, pervēnī, perventum – to arrive
Sȳrinx, Sȳringis, *f.* – *a name of the nymph turned into a reed, which was used for the creation of the musical instrument syrinx or flute (compare "syringe," so called because of its shape)*

CONNECTING WITH THE ANCIENT WORLD

GLADIATORIAL GAMES

The Romans were said to desire only *pānem et circēnsēs* (Juvenal, *Satires* 10.81), "bread and entertainment." This statement may not apply to the Romans of the early Republic, who are said to have been industrious and self-disciplined. But by imperial times most of those who lived in the Roman world did not have much of a stake or share in Rome's wealth and power, and even the affluent and advantaged seem to have craved immediate pleasures that suggest an interior emptiness: such, at least, is the implication of the overeating and vomiting at banquets, and the bloody spectacles often seen in the amphitheatres.

The exterior of Rome's Colosseum shows three levels of decoration, Doric, Ionic, and Corinthian, in the respective levels of arches. Each arch on the lower level served as an entrance and bore a Roman numeral.

Rome's amphitheatre, the Colosseum, was the most famous of Roman amphitheatres but the first amphitheatres were built in Campania like the one at Pompeii depicted here. Note that spectators entered via staircases mounted on the outside wall of the amphitheatre.

The gladiatorial games rank among the most famous of these spectacles. They were staged in the great Roman amphitheatres; while the Greeks built semi-circular performance spaces accommodated to natural slopes, the Romans never complied with nature, preferring instead to erect fully circular amphitheatres regardless of the physical surroundings. The most celebrated amphitheatre was, of course, the Roman Colosseum, a multi-storied building with complicated layers of seats, reflecting the organization of Roman society as a whole. People from all classes attended the gladiatorial competitions, and the emperor played a leading role in the event as well.

Mosaic from the House of the Gladiator in Cyprus showing two gladiators and their Greek names, Margareites and Hellenikos.

The name gladiator comes from *gladius*, "sword," the weapon with which the gladiators fought. Gladiators were slaves, prisoners of war, convicted criminals, and occasionally people of free birth who chose this occupation for the lack of anything better. In fact, the gladiatorial profession had a certain appeal and prestige, although the owners or trainers of gladiatorial troops, called *lanistae*, ranked at the bottom of the social scale, despite the wealth that many acquired.

Combats between gladiators did not necessarily end with the death of the loser. After one of the combatants acknowledged that he had been defeated, it was possible for him to be spared; the public only needed to shout *mitte*, "set him free," and the emperor would signify with a gesture of his thumb whether the loser should live or die. A thumb directed upward seems to have meant "kill him," while a thumb pointed downward signaled "let him go." The pride and savage joy with which large audiences watched these spectacles probably is connected with the military enthusiasms of the ancient Romans, which had brought their city to world supremacy.

In addition to single combats with swords, there were fights between men and animals; this practice survives in the modern bullfights that still take place in Spain and Latin America. There were also fights between animals themselves. The exhibition of exotic animals from different parts of the Roman Empire had a political purpose, reminding the spectators how far the boundaries of the Roman world extended, and of all the living creatures that it had subdued and now contained. Other forms of entertainment included the ever-popular chariot races and a small-scale naval battle between gladiators called a *naumachia*, for which the emperors would flood an entire square with water from the Tiber River.

A poster showing the armor of gladiators and the Latin phrase *Avē Caesar, Imperātor, Moritūrī Tē Salūtant*. ("Hail Caesar, emperor, those about to die salute you.")

The seats, the arena, and the sub-structures under the arena are seen in this view of the interior of the Colosseum.

EXPLORING ROMAN DISASTERS

EARTH, AIR, FIRE, AND WATER

In modern times we witness untold suffering and loss of life from disasters such as floods, earthquakes, fire, violent winds, and volcanoes. The ancient Romans also suffered from the ravages of such occurrences.

For tens of thousands of years, a dozen volcanoes or more have menaced the Italian peninsula, from Lardarello (between Italy's western coast and Sienna) to Pantelleria (between Sicily and Tunisia). Lake Albano, just southeast of Rome, is located in the crater of a volcano. The Aeolian islands, just north of Sicily and off the toe of Italy, contain four volcanoes, one of which, Vulcano, contains the source for our word "volcano." Not surprisingly, popular legend in ancient times said that the fire-god Vulcan had his forges in this part of the world. Mt. Etna, near Sicily's eastern coast, is Europe's tallest active volcano: almost 3,000 feet taller than Washington State's Mt. St. Helens, whose eruption on May 18th, 1980, killed 57 people. At almost 11,000 feet tall, Etna is more than twice as tall as Vesuvius (ca. 4,200 feet), whose eruption caused the most famous natural disaster to strike the Roman world.

View of an active volcano.

Fresh lava from a volcano.

In 63/62 CE, Herculaneum and Pompeii had suffered damage from an earthquake, but on August 24th, 79 CE, the two-day long eruption of Mt. Vesuvius, which had been the site of the rebel slave Spartacus's camp in 71 BCE, devastated the western coast of Italy near the Bay of Naples, especially the towns of Herculaneum and Pompeii. Although we do not know how many people survived Vesuvius's eruption, the loss of life was 500 times greater than that of Mt. St. Helens and is probably equal to that caused by the eruptions of Mt. Pelée on the Caribbean island of Martinique from April to August 1902, in which approximately 30,000 people died. Whereas the Pompeians were buried beneath about thirteen feet of volcanic pumice and ash, flows of lava and mud over sixty feet deep covered Herculaneum. Thanks to the innovative techniques of Italian archaeology, Giuseppe Fiorelli (1823–1896) poured plaster into cavities made in the ash and when the plaster hardened he removed the surrounding ash. In a few cases, we are able to see the exact position in which both humans and animals died.

Letters (6.16 and 6.20) from Pliny the Younger, who was in the region during Vesuvius's eruption, describe in detail the appearance of the volcano's cloud (shaped like the umbrella pine trees that grow in Italy), and tell about the heroic efforts of his uncle, Pliny the Elder, who lost his life while investigating the eruption and trying to rescue people by ship from the affected area. Just

A plaster cast of one of many victims who died during the eruption of Mt. Vesuvius.

as in modern times we see political leaders touring disaster sites and attempting to offer some measure of support and comfort to the victims, Titus, the Roman emperor at the time of Vesuvius's eruption, is reported to have shown a fatherly care and concern with respect to relief efforts needed to help the people affected by the eruption (Suetonius, *Titus* 8.3). Archaeologists continue to excavate sites in the Naples region, which have provided a massive amount of information about life in these ancient Roman towns. Not only did the eruption of Vesuvius bury persons, their possessions, and homes, but now multi-spectral imaging with infrared and ultra-violet light is allowing scholars to begin to read some of the almost 1800 papyrus scrolls that were found charred in Herculaneum's so-called Villa of the Papyri.

In contrast to the disaster caused by Vesuvius in 79 CE, probably the second most famous disaster to strike the Romans was caused by fire. Unlike the horrific fire that ravaged Chicago in October of 1871, which was rumored to have started when a cow kicked over a lantern, Rome's worst fire was rumored to have been started upon the orders of its emperor, Nero (Suetonius, *Nero* 38.1; Dio Cassius 62.16.1–2). Nero is even reported to have sung a poem about the fiery destruction of Troy (Suetonius, *Nero* 38.1; Tacitus, *Annals* 15.39; Dio Cassius 62.18.1) while watching the blaze from the roof of his palace, and later to have built a new palace, the *Domus Aurea* ("Golden House"), on ground leveled by the fire.

Although we tend to think of Rome as being a city of fired brick, limestone, and marble, most of the city's inhabitants lived in cheaply constructed apartment buildings (*īnsulae*), whose wooden framing was highly susceptible to fires. Thus, it is not surprising that fire caused a disaster that Dio Cassius (62.17.3) would describe as the worst disaster to befall Rome since the Gauls had sacked the city around 386 BCE. As is the case in many fires, such as those that frequently ravage California, high winds contributed to the week-long fire that destroyed Rome. On July 19th, 64 CE, this fire started near the Circus Maximus, southwest of the Palatine Hill, and swept northward. It completely destroyed over twenty percent of the city and left only about a quarter of the city unscathed. Comparable to the situation after Hurricane Katrina in New Orleans, in which even some police officers were found looting, in Dio Cassius we read of Roman soldiers, with a view toward looting, helping to spread the fire. Despite rumors that Nero was responsible for the fire, Tacitus does report that the emperor did provide emergency housing (some space even in his own gardens) for those displaced by the blaze and made grain available at a reduced price. Still, Tacitus (*Annals* 15.44) also says that Nero tried to shift blame for the fire from himself to the city's Christians, whom Tacitus says were generally disliked. Nero had many Christians arrested and tortured, either by crucifixion, setting fire to them, or feeding them to dogs.

Although not as well-known as the eruption of Vesuvius or Nero's fire, the Romans, like the inhabitants of New Orleans during Hurricane Katrina in August 2005, were vexed by floods. As with the Hebrew story of Noah in Genesis, the Romans preserved in their mythical tradition the story of a great flood. A detailed account of this appears in Ovid's *Metamorphōsēs* (1.163–415). According to Ovid, Jove decided to destroy the human race by flood because of their wicked nature. Just as the Hebrew God did for Noah, Jove decided to save Deucalion and his wife Pyrrha because of their virtuous behavior. After nine days of rain (compare forty in Genesis), the boat carrying Deucalion and his wife came to rest on the slopes of Mt. Parnassus in central Greece.

In contrast, the second-century CE mythographer Hyginus (*Fables* 153) has their boat land on Italian soil, namely the slopes of Mt. Etna in Sicily. After landing on the mountain, Deucalion and Pyrrha created a new human race by throwing stones behind their backs. The stones Deucalion threw turned into men, while Pyrrha's stones became women. Pliny the Elder (*Natural Histories* 3.112), writing in the first century CE, relates that the Umbrians, the oldest of Italy's tribes (living in the region northeast of Rome), also survived the flood.

For Rome herself, the threat of flood was a frequent possibility because of the city's location on the Tiber River. Interestingly enough, the flooding of the Tiber traditionally contributed to the survival of Rome's founders, Romulus and Remus. When the evil king Amulius ordered his henchmen to drown these twin sons of his fraternal niece, the men were unable to approach the Tiber because it had flooded. Therefore, the men left the infants in a gentle pool of shallow water from which they were later rescued (see Livy, *Ab Urbe Conditā* 1.4.5–7). According to tradition, Romulus founded Rome on April 21st, 753 BCE. While one natural disaster helped save the infant Romulus, another natural phenomenon marked him as a divine. According to the Roman historian Livy (1.16.2), Romulus's mortal life on earth ended when a whirlwind (*procella*) swept him up into heaven.

Although the Tiber's flooding contributed to the salvation of Romulus, floods were more often regarded as a sign of the divine displeasure. During the middle of the fourth century BCE, a plague led the Romans to try to appease the wrath of the gods by holding Rome's first theatrical productions in the Circus Maximus. When, at this time, the Tiber flooded the Circus, the Romans were even more convinced that the gods were displeased with them. Four centuries later, the Tiber's floods were still wreaking havoc upon Rome and contributed to the city not appearing as majestic as might be expected for the capital of a vast empire. Whereas in modern times people put up sandbags to protect their homes from flooding, during Augustus's rule he had the Tiber cleared of trash and widened in an effort to diminish the threat of the flooding.

Although the forces of nature that affected the ancient Romans are removed from us by some two thousand years, the toll upon both people and property was as real then as it is today. With the eruption of Vesuvius, this disaster sealed a moment in time that allows us an astonishing glimpse into the lives of an ancient culture. Ancient reports of such disasters also reveal that government officials, both then and now, struggle to prevent or to cope with the suffering of their people; and, both in the past and present, government officials are sometimes blamed for contributing to or not alleviating suffering. Most ancient Romans, of course, would attribute such disasters to divine anger. Although most Americans would discount this cause for natural disasters, even in our own times we can find some well-known religious leaders who will attribute events such as Hurricane Katrina to God's wrath.

JOHN E. THORBURN
Associate Professor of Classics
Baylor University
Waco, Texas

QUOTATIONS RELATING TO ATTITUDES TOWARD AND COPING WITH MISFORTUNES

QUOTATIONS

- Animus meminisse horret. "My mind shudders to remember." (Vergil, *Aeneid* 2.12) The words of Aeneas when he starts telling the tragic story of the fall of Troy.

- Citō ārēscit lacrima, praesertim in aliēnīs malīs. "The tear dries out quickly, especially <shed> for the misfortunes of others." (Cicero, *The Divisions of Oratory* 57)

- Commūne naufragium omnibus est cōnsōlātiō. "A common shipwreck is a comfort to everyone." Anonymous saying about the paradoxical human way of accepting misfortune when someone else is involved.

- Nē cēde malīs. "Do not yield to misfortunes!" (Vergil, *Aeneid* 6.95) The Cumaean Sibyl, a prophetess, encourages Aeneas on the difficult path in front of him.

Pompeii was not the only city destroyed by the eruption of Mt. Vesuvius. This excavated street scene comes from the ruins of Herculaneum, also destroyed by the volcano's eruption in 79 CE. To the right behind the columns, one can see the petrified mud of the mudslide caused by Mt. Vesuvius's eruption.

CHAPTER 19

Perfect Passive Participle; Perfect Tense Passive of All Conjugations; Review of Principal Parts of Verbs; Demonstrative Pronoun and Adjective *Hic*

Anonymous depiction of Attila the Hun
called the "scourge of God."

MEMORĀBILE DICTŪ

Imperium sine fīne.

"Empire without end." (Vergil, *Aeneid* 1.279)

Jupiter promises Aeneas's mother Venus that he will bestow this gift upon the future Roman race. The idea of Rome as unending in time as well as space survives in the description of Rome as "the eternal city."

READING

A historian with a vivid and intense literary Latin style, Ammiānus Marcellīnus was born in the city of Antioch in Syria in around 330 CE, where he received a Greek literary education. His *Rēs gestae ā fīne Cornēlī Tacitī* ("Deeds accomplished from the end of Cornelius Tacitus's [history]") was designed as a continuation of Tacitus's *Annālēs* and *Historiae*. While the first thirteen books of his narrative have been lost, Books 14 through 31 survive. They contain a compelling account of events from 353 to 378 CE, some of which Ammianus—a Roman army officer stationed in both the western and eastern parts of the empire and a participant in the emperor Julian's campaigns against the Persians—witnessed at first hand. Of special interest are his digressions on noteworthy aspects of culture, society, and politics.

In this passage, adapted from Book 31.2.1–11, Ammianus describes the customs of the fearsome Huns, a nomadic people who originally came from central Asia. Their movements in the third and fourth centuries CE pushed other peoples westward into the Roman Empire, especially the Germanic Ostrogoths and Visigoths, well before the Huns themselves began invading the Roman Empire in the mid-fifth century CE.

DĒ HŪNĪS

1   Dē Hūnīs in librīs patrum nostrōrum nōn multa sunt dicta. Hī sunt
    ferī et ferōcēs. Terribilēs vidērī cupiunt timōremque in aliīs hominibus
    excitāre. Itaque faciēs eōrum cōnsultō vulnerantur. Postquam vulnera
    sānāta sunt, cicātrīcēs manent, propter quās barba crēscere nōn potest.

5   Hōrum fōrma nōn est pulchra, sed terribilis!

    Rādīcēs herbārum, quae correptae sunt ex agrīs, comedunt et
    animālium carnem, quae nōn cocta est sed paulisper trīta. Nam carō,
    antequam ab eīs comeditur, posita est inter equum et femora eius quī in
    equō sedet et ibi paulisper manet.

10 Casās nōn habent, sed forīs habitant et vīvunt. Vestīmenta gerunt ex
    animālium pellibus facta.

    Semper in equīs manent: in equīs comedunt, in equīs dormiunt, in
    equīs pugnant. In hostēs impetūs celeriter faciunt, quōs in proeliō saepe
    laqueīs capiunt et captōs gladiīs occīdunt.

READING VOCABULARY

antequam (*conj.*) – before

***barba, barbae,** f.* – beard

captōs – seized

***carō, carnis,** f.* – meat, flesh

***celeriter** (*adv.*) – swiftly

cicātrīx, cicātrīcis, f. – scar

cocta est – has been cooked

cōnsultō (*adv.*) – on purpose

correptae sunt – have been snatched

***crēscō, crēscere, crēvī, ——** – to grow

facta – made

femur, femoris, n. – the upper leg, the thigh

***ferōx, ferōcis** (*genitive*) – fierce, ferocious

ferus, fera, ferum – wild, savage

***forīs** (*adv.*) – outside, in the open

gerō – *with clothing or articles of clothing as its object, this verb means "to wear"*

***herba, herbae,** f. – plant, vegetation

***hī** – these <people>

hōrum – of these <people>

Hūnī, Hūnōrum, m. pl. – the Huns

***inter** + *accusative* – between, among

laqueus, laqueī, m. – noose, lasso

paulisper (*adv.*) – for a little while

***pellis, pellis,** f. – skin, hide

posita est – has been placed

***postquam** (*conj.*) – after

***proelium, proeliī,** n. – battle, combat

rādīx, rādīcis, f. – root

***sānāta sunt** – have been healed

***sedeō, sedēre, sēdī, sessum** – to sit

sunt dicta – have been said

***terribilis, terribile** – terrifying

***trīta <est>** – has been rubbed

***vestīmentum, vestīmentī,** n. – garment, *pl.* clothes

***vīvō, vīvere, vīxī, vīctum** – to live

***vulnerō, vulnerāre, vulnerāvī, vulnerātum** – to wound

***vulnus, vulneris,** n. – wound

*Words marked with an asterisk will need to be memorized later in the chapter.

COMPREHENSION QUESTIONS

1. Why did the Huns wound their own faces?

2. What was the Huns' diet?

3. Where did the Huns live?

4. What was used for the Huns' attire?

LANGUAGE FACT I
PERFECT PASSIVE PARTICIPLE

In the passage above there are some words that function like adjectives, yet they are related to verbs. In fact, their forms are familiar too, because you have already learned these forms as the **fourth** principal part of the verb.

> *Vestīmenta gerunt ex animālium pellibus **facta**.*
> They wear clothes <having been> **made** from the skins of animals.

Note that "having been" is inserted in angle brackets before the perfect passive participle, where English idiom does not usually express it.

> *Hostēs in proeliō saepe laqueīs capiunt et **captōs** gladiīs occīdunt.*
> They often catch enemies in battle with lassos, and with swords they slay the enemies <having been> caught.

These words are **participles,** which are verbal adjectives. Like verbs, participles have tense and voice. Like adjectives, participles modify and agree with a noun or pronoun in case, number, and gender.

In the sentences above, you see the **perfect passive participle**. This participle is perfect, since it refers to something that has already been done, and its voice is passive. Thus, in the first sentence *facta* (modifying *vestīmenta*) means "having been made" or, as commonly shortened in English, simply "made"; in the second sentence *captōs* (modifying *hostēs*) means "having been caught" or "caught."

For most Latin verbs there are three other participles: these will be introduced in later chapters.

Below are the principal parts of verbs from each conjugation. Note carefully the neuter **fourth** principal part, which reveals the form of the perfect passive participle of each verb.

First conjugation:	occultō, occultāre, occultāvī, **occultātum** ("concealed"/"having been concealed")
Second conjugation:	videō, vidēre, vīdī, **vīsum** ("seen"/"having been seen")
Third conjugation:	dīcō, dīcere, dīxī, **dictum** ("said"/"having been said")
Fourth conjugation:	audiō, audīre, audīvī, **audītum** ("heard"/"having been heard")
Third conjugation –iō:	capiō, capere, cēpī, **captum** ("caught"/"having been caught")

By taking the *–um* ending off the fourth principal part, you have found the stem of the perfect passive participle. This is one more reason why it is important to **learn all principal parts with each verb**.

The first and second declension adjective endings *–us, –a, –um* are added to the stem of the perfect passive participle. Participles, because they are adjectives, have case endings. Since the perfect passive participle is an adjective of the first and second declensions, you already know its endings. As a reminder, look at all the forms of *captus, capta, captum* ("caught").

Declension of the Perfect Passive Participle

Singular

	Masculine	Feminine	Neuter
Nominative	capt**us**	capt**a**	capt**um**
Genitive	capt**ī**	capt**ae**	capt**ī**
Dative	capt**ō**	capt**ae**	capt**ō**
Accusative	capt**um**	capt**am**	capt**um**
Ablative	capt**ō**	capt**ā**	capt**ō**
Vocative	capt**e**	capt**a**	capt**um**

Plural

	Masculine	Feminine	Neuter
Nominative	capt**ī**	capt**ae**	capt**a**
Genitive	capt**ōrum**	capt**ārum**	capt**ōrum**
Dative	capt**īs**	capt**īs**	capt**īs**
Accusative	capt**ōs**	capt**ās**	capt**a**
Ablative	capt**īs**	capt**īs**	capt**īs**
Vocative	capt**ī**	capt**ae**	capt**a**

The perfect passive participle can be represented in various ways in English. The most literal way to represent the meaning is to include "having been" before the English past participle. So, for example, *vīsus, vīsa, vīsum* is translated "having been seen" or simply "seen." It is also possible to represent the meaning of the perfect passive participle with a clause or a phrase. You will see how this can be done in future chapters.

Here are some perfect passive participles:

> *vocātus, vocāta, vocātum* – having been called, called
>
> *aedificātus, aedificāta, aedificātum* – having been built, built
>
> *quaesītus, quaesīta, quaesītum* – having been sought, sought
>
> *vīsus, vīsa, vīsum* – having been seen, seen
>
> *neglēctus, neglēcta, neglēctum* – having been neglected, neglected

Note that the perfect passive participle refers to a time before that of the main verb. This is always true no matter the tense of the main verb. The tense of the participle is relative to the tense of the main verb, **not** to the present tense of the person narrating. Notice the examples that follow.

Vocātus ab imperātōre vēnit.
Having been called by the general, he came. (or) Called by the general, he came.

Here the main verb is in the perfect tense. The participle *vocātus* ("having been called") refers to a time even before the action described by *vēnit*, i.e., first the man was called by the general, then (obeying the call) he came.

Mīlitibus vocātīs praemia magna imperātor dabit.
To the soldiers having been called/summoned the general will give large rewards.
(or) To the called/summoned soldiers the general will give large rewards.

Here the main verb *dabit* ("will give") is in the future. The perfect participle *vocātīs* ("having been called") refers to some time before the action of this future verb. First the soldiers will be called, then the general will give them the rewards.

STUDY TIP

There are also principal parts in English verbs: for example, "see," "saw," "seen." The past participle in English "seen" corresponds roughly to the fourth principal part, or perfect passive participle in Latin. Another way to find a past participle of any verb in English is to start a phrase with the words "having been . . ." and then think of the form that would appropriately follow these words. In the case of the verb "to see," for example, the correct form after "having been . . ." is "seen."

BY THE WAY

Note that, with the exception of some verbs that you will study later, there is no perfect participle in Latin with an active meaning. So while you have *vocātus* meaning "having been called," there is no Latin participle that means "having called." In Latin, however, the idea equivalent to the perfect active participle (i.e., a phrase like "having called") can easily be expressed in other ways: these various equivalents to the meaning of a perfect active participle will be studied later.

▶ EXERCISE 1

Translate into English.

1. Hūnōs ā nōbīs vīsōs timēbāmus.

2. Hūnī urbem ā cīvibus relictam dēvastāvērunt.

3. Animālia ad nōs ducta cūrāre dēbēmus.

4. Hostēs victōs capere potuimus.

5. Dē rēbus ā Rōmānīs gestīs multa nunc legimus.

6. Praemium tibi dēbitum habēs.

VOCABULARY TO LEARN

NOUNS

barba, barbae, *f.* – beard

carō, carnis, *f.* – meat, flesh

herba, herbae, *f.* – plant, vegetation

pellis, pellis, *f.* – skin, hide

proelium, proeliī, *n.* – battle, combat

vestīmentum, vestīmentī, *n.* – garment, *pl.* clothes

vulnus, vulneris, *n.* – wound

DEMONSTRATIVE PRONOUN/ ADJECTIVE

hic, haec, hoc – this

ADJECTIVES

ferōx, ferōcis – fierce, ferocious

terribilis, terribile – terrifying

VERBS

coquō, coquere, coxī, coctum – to cook

crēscō, crēscere, crēvī, —— – to grow

sānō, sānāre, sānāvī, sānātum – to heal

sedeō, sedēre, sēdī, sessum – to sit

terō, terere, trīvī, trītum – to wear out, rub

vīvō, vīvere, vīxī, vīctum – to live

vulnerō, vulnerāre, vulnerāvī, vulnerātum – to wound

ADVERBS

celeriter – swiftly

forīs – outside, in the open

PREPOSITION

inter + *accusative* – between, among

CONJUNCTION

postquam – after

▶ EXERCISE 2

Find the English derivatives based on the Vocabulary to Learn in the following sentences. Write the corresponding Latin word.

1. You should go to the barber and get a haircut!

2. The clergy were conspicuous in the ceremony with their splendid vestments.

3. A crescendo of sound came from the orchestra as the symphony began.

4. All restaurants and public eating places must be sanitary.

5. I like herbal dressing on my salad.

6. The warehouse was filled with victuals for the army.

7. The general decided to retreat, knowing his troops would be too vulnerable in such an exposed position.

8. The celerity of the cheetah, the fastest of all land animals, is amazing.

9. That old saying is too trite for me to use it again.

10. That is an interesting concoction you have prepared. Does it taste good?

LANGUAGE FACT II

PERFECT TENSE PASSIVE OF ALL CONJUGATIONS

In some sentences of the passage at the beginning of the chapter the perfect passive participle is used together with forms of the verb *sum* ("to be").

> *Dē Hūnīs in librīs patrum nostrōrum nōn multa **sunt dicta**.*
> Not many things **have been said** about the Huns in the books of our fathers.

> *Postquam vulnera **sānāta sunt**, cicātrīcēs manent . . .*
> After the wounds **have been healed**, scars remain . . .

> *Rādīcēs herbārum, quae **correptae sunt** ex agrīs, comedunt et animālium carnem, quae nōn **cocta est** sed paulisper **trīta <est>**.*
> They eat the roots of plants, which **have been snatched** from fields and the meat of animals, which **has not been cooked**, but **rubbed** for a little while.

> *Carō, antequam ab eīs comeditur, **posita est** inter equum et femora eius quī in equō sedet . . .*
> The meat, before it is eaten by them, **has been placed** between the horse and the thighs of the person who sits on the horse . . .

Sometimes the perfect passive participle means "was . . ." rather than "has/have been . . ." as in the following sentence.

> *Urbs ā Hūnīs **est dēvastāta**.*
> The city **was devastated** by the Huns.

In these sentences you see the **perfect passive indicative** whose forms are made up of the perfect passive participle in combination with the present indicative of the verb *sum*. This is true of all conjugations. So, once you know the perfect passive participle of a verb, it is easy to form the perfect passive indicative. For example, here are the forms of the perfect passive indicative of *exspectāre* and *audīre*.

Horses had various uses for both the Huns and the Romans not only in war but also in other aspects of their lives.

Perfect Passive: *exspectō*

Singular

First person	exspectātus, exspectāta, (exspectātum) sum	I was awaited, have been awaited
Second person	exspectātus, exspectāta, (exspectātum) es	you were awaited, have been awaited
Third person	exspectātus, exspectāta, exspectātum est	s/he/it was awaited, has been awaited

Plural

First person	exspectātī, exspectātae, (exspectāta) sumus	we were awaited, have been awaited
Second person	exspectātī, exspectātae, (exspectāta) estis	you were awaited, have been awaited
Third person	exspectātī, exspectātae, exspectāta sunt	they were awaited, have been awaited

Perfect Passive: *audiō*

Singular

First person	audītus, audīta, (audītum) sum	I was heard, have been heard
Second person	audītus, audīta, (audītum) es	you were heard, have been heard
Third person	audītus, audīta, audītum est	s/he/it was heard, has been heard

Plural

First person	audītī, audītae, (audīta) sumus	we were heard, have been heard
Second person	audītī, audītae, (audīta) estis	you were heard, have been heard
Third person	audītī, audītae, audīta sunt	they were heard, have been heard

Note that parentheses have been placed around some of the neuter forms of the participial elements in these verbs. This is because people, not things, are usually the subjects of first and second person passive verbs.

There are two important things to remember about the use of the perfect passive tense:

First, the participial element of the verb will agree in case, number, and gender with the subject of the verb. If the subject is singular, the participial element of the verb will be nominative singular agreeing with that subject. Its gender will, of course, be the same as the subject's, e.g., *Puella exspectāta est* ("The girl has been expected/awaited"). Similarly, if the verb is plural, the participial element of the verb will be in the nominative plural and agree with the subject in gender, e.g., *Nōs cīvēs nōn sumus audītī* ("We citizens have not been heard").

Second, the word order of the perfect passive verb is flexible. The auxiliary verb may either follow or precede the participial element, and it may even be separated from it by a few intervening words, especially adverbs, e.g., *Sum quoque in urbe relictus* ("I too have been left in the city").

BY THE WAY

The participial element of a perfect passive verb will always be nominative (singular or plural) in direct speech, since it will agree with the nominative subject.

> *Puella est exspectāta.*
> The girl has been awaited.

The perfect passive participle by itself can appear in any case, since it is simply an adjective agreeing with a noun.

> *Puellae exspectātae praemium dedimus.*
> We gave the reward to the girl having been awaited.

STUDY TIP

Be careful **never** to translate the perfect passive tense auxiliary verb (*sum, es, est*, etc.) as the equivalent of the present tense. *Puella est exspectāta* means "the girl **has been** awaited," **NOT** "the girl **is** awaited." The phrase "is awaited" is *exspectātur*, a present passive tense in Latin.

▶ EXERCISE 3

Fill in the blanks in the following sentences with the correct form of the perfect passive tense of the verb using the infinitive in parentheses. Then translate each sentence. The Reading Vocabulary may be consulted.

Example: Casae ā Hūnīs nōn _____. (aedificāre)
Casae ā Hūnīs nōn sunt aedificātae.   The dwellings were not/have not been built by the Huns.

1. Agrīne vestrī ā Hūnīs _____? (dēvastāre)

2. Timorne in Rōmānīs ā Hūnīs _____? (excitāre)

3. Faciēsne Hūnōrum cōnsultō _____? (vulnerāre)

4. Urbēs Rōmānōrum tandem _____. (līberāre)

5. Vestīmenta eōrum ex animālium pellibus _____. (facere)

6. Sumus fēlīcēs: nōs laqueīs Hūnōrum nōn _____. (capere)

7. Dīcō vōs esse fēlīcēs, quī ā Hūnīs nōn _____. (capere)

▶ EXERCISE 4

Translate into English. Some of these sentences contain a perfect passive verb, while others have a perfect passive participle. Identify which of the two is used in each sentence. The Reading Vocabulary may be consulted.

Example: Nōn multa dē Hūnīs sunt dicta.
Not many things have been/were said about the Huns.   perfect passive tense

1. Verba dicta audīvimus.

2. Faciēs Hūnōrum vulnerātās vidēmus.

3. Faciēs Hūnōrum cōnsultō sunt vulnerātae.

4. Rādīcēs herbārum ex agrīs correptae sunt.

5. Rādīcēs herbārum ex agrīs correptās comedere nōn possumus.

6. Carnem coctam comedere solēmus.

7. Carō nōn est cocta.

8. Hostēs in proeliō sunt captī.

9. Hostēs in proeliō captōs vidēre nōn potuimus.

LANGUAGE FACT III

REVIEW OF PRINCIPAL PARTS OF VERBS

This is a good time to review some basic points about the four principal parts of a typical verb of any conjugation.

In chart form:

First principal part	**Second principal part**
a. Supplies 1st person singular, present active tense.	a. Supplies present active infinitive.
b. Distinguishes –iō verbs from other third conjugation verbs.	b. Indicates verb's present stem, used in present, future, and imperfect tenses (active and passive).
c. Clarifies distinction between second conjugation verbs (–ēre) and third conjugation verbs (–ere).	c. Indicates verb's conjugation.
Third principal part	**Fourth principal part**
a. Supplies 1st person singular, perfect active tense.	a. Supplies supine (to be learned later).
b. Indicates verb's perfect active stem, used in perfect, pluperfect, and future perfect (active).	b. Indicates perfect passive participle stem.
	c. Indicates verb's perfect passive stem, used in perfect, pluperfect, and future perfect (passive).

In summary form:

1. From the **second principal part** (**present active infinitive**), you learn the present stem of the verb, and therefore the conjugation to which it belongs.

2. From the **first principal part** (**first person singular, present active indicative**), you can detect third conjugation –*iō* verbs and easily distinguish verbs belonging to the second conjugation (with a few exceptions).

3. From the **first and second principal parts** you can form the present, future, and imperfect tenses, active and passive.

4. From the **third principal part** (**first person singular perfect active indicative**) you can form the perfect, future perfect, and pluperfect tenses of the verb in the active voice.

5. From the **fourth principal part** (**nominative neuter singular perfect passive participle**—sometimes called the supine, about which you will learn later) you can form the perfect, future perfect, and pluperfect tenses of the verb in the passive voice.

▶ EXERCISE 5

Change the following verbs below into the form indicated in parentheses and translate the changed form.

Example: timeō (first person plural imperfect passive)
timēbāmur   we were being feared

1. sānō (third person plural perfect passive)
2. doceō (third person singular future passive)
3. vīvō (first person singular pluperfect active)
4. vulnerō (second person plural perfect passive)
5. iaciō (second person singular future passive)
6. āmittō (second person singular imperfect passive)
7. colō (first person plural perfect active)
8. crēscō (third person plural future active)
9. sedeō (second person singular future perfect active)
10. ārdeō (second person singular pluperfect active)
11. terō (third person singular pluperfect active)

LANGUAGE FACT IV

DEMONSTRATIVE PRONOUN AND ADJECTIVE *HIC*

You have already learned the first and second person personal pronouns, as well as the pronoun *is, ea, id*, which is both a third person personal pronoun, as well as a demonstrative adjective ("this," "that").

In the reading at the beginning of this chapter you have met another demonstrative word that means "this."

> *Hī sunt ferī et ferōcēs.*
> **These** \<people> are ferocious and wild.

> *Hōrum fōrma nōn est pulchra, sed terribilis!*
> The appearance of **these** \<people> is not handsome, but terrifying!

Here is the declension of *hic, haec, hoc.*

Demonstrative Pronoun/Adjective *hic*		
Singular		
	Masculine	**Feminine**	**Neuter**

	Masculine	Feminine	Neuter
Nominative	hic	haec	hoc
Genitive	huius	huius	huius
Dative	huic	huic	huic
Accusative	hunc	hanc	hoc
Ablative	hōc	hāc	hōc

Plural

	Masculine	Feminine	Neuter
Nominative	hī	hae	haec
Genitive	hōrum	hārum	hōrum
Dative	hīs	hīs	hīs
Accusative	hōs	hās	haec
Ablative	hīs	hīs	hīs

▶ EXERCISE 6

Translate into Latin.

1. They often remain on these horses.

2. This is the sword of this general.

3. They eat only these plants.

4. These are the names of brave men.

5. Wounds remain in/on the face of this soldier.

6. Many things have been said about the bravery of these women.

7. Do not (plural) give these great rewards to these ferocious people!

Horses played an important role in the lives of ancient people, whether Greeks, Romans, or Huns.

▶ EXERCISE 7

Translate the following dialogue into English. Refer both to the Reading Vocabulary and to the words explained below.

A Roman ambassador around the year 440 CE has come to the camp of the Huns to negotiate with Attila, their king, about the tribute that the Romans will pay the Huns to stop them from attacking Roman territory.

Rōmānus: Cūr Hūnī terribilēs vidērī cupiunt?

Attila: Nōn est nōbīs difficile hostēs vincere, quī nōs timent.

Rōmānus: Multī dīcunt propter hanc causam faciēs Hūnōrum cōnsultō vulnerārī. Estne hoc vērum?

Attila: Vērum est! Mīlitēsne meī tibi videntur esse ferōcēs?

Rōmānus: Ita! Hōs hominēs timeō.

Attila: Itaque nōn erit difficile Hūnīs Rōmānōs in proeliō vincere.

Rōmānus: Ita crēdimus. Iam ā Rōmānīs sum ad tē missus, quī cupiunt Hūnīs multa dōna dare. Sī Hūnī Rōmānōs in pāce relīquerint, Rōmānī Hūnīs dōna, praemia, multās rēs bonās dabunt.

Attila: Cōnsilium praeclārum! Amō hoc cōnsilium. Sed dē dōnīs et praemiīs, quae Rōmānī Hūnīs dabunt, posteā dīcēmus. Nunc cēnābimus.

Rōmānus: Cōnsilium praeclārum! Mēne ad casam tuam dūcēs? Ubi cēna habēbitur?

Attila: Nōs Hūnī sumus fortēs, ferī, ferōcēs, nōn miserī, sīcut vōs Rōmānī. Casās nōn habēmus, sed forīs habitāmus et vīvimus. Forīs igitur cēnābimus. Cibum bonum nōbīscum habēbis.

Rōmānus: Cēnāre sum parātus. Sed quid videō? Estne haec carō cocta? Et quae sunt hae herbae? Herbae nōn videntur esse, sed herbārum rādīcēs!

Attila: Hoc est vērum, quod dē herbīs dīxistī. Carō autem cocta nōn est, sed paulisper trīta. Carō enim, antequam ā nōbīs comeditur, posita est inter equum et femora eius quī in equō sedet et ibi paulisper manet. Carō igitur est ad cēnam bene parāta. Quid dīcis? Cēnābisne nōbīscum?

Rōmānus: Iūlius Caesar quondam dīxit: "Vēnī, vīdī, vīcī!" Hic Rōmānus, quī cum Hūnīs cēnāre dēbet, haec verba dīcit: "Vēnī, vīdī, victus sum."

cēna, cēnae, *f.* – dinner
cēnō, cēnāre, cēnāvī, —— – to dine
cibus, cibī, *m.* – food

nōbīscum = cum nōbīs
quondam (*adv.*) – once
ubi? – where?

TALKING

abstergeō, abstergēre, abstersī, abstersum – to wipe away

armārium, armāriī, n. – cupboard, closet

excutiō, excutere, excussī, excussum – to shake out

exsūgō, exsūgere, exsūxī, exsūctum – to suck out

<pulveris> haurītōrium, haurītōriī, n. – vacuum cleaner

lavō, lavāre, lāvī, lautum – to wash

lectum sternō, sternere, strāvī, strātum – to make a bed

lectus, lectī, m. – bed

lintea, linteōrum, n. pl. – linens

māchina (māchinae, f.) *lavātōria* – washing machine

mundus, munda, mundum – neat and clean

ōrdinō, ōrdināre, ōrdināvī, ōrdinātum – to arrange, put in order

pavīmentum, pavīmentī, n. – floor

pulvis, pulveris, m. – dust

(domum) pūrgō, pūrgāre, pūrgāvī, pūrgātum – to clean (the house)

scōpae, scōpārum, f. pl. – broom

tapēte, tapētis, n. – carpet

vēlum, vēlī, n. – curtain

verrō, verrere, verrī, versum – to sweep

CLEANING THE HOUSE

Christīna: Ubi (*where*) herī (*yesterday*) erās? Birotīs (*on bicycles*) vectī sumus (*we rode*). Pulchrum erat caelum!

Marīa: Auxilium mātrī dare dēbēbam. Māter enim domum pūrgāre herī dēcrēvit.

Mārcus: Quid fēcit pater tuus?

Marīa: Pater quoque auxilium mātrī dedit. Māter eum iussit pavīmentum scōpīs verrere.

Mārcus: Paterne hoc fēcit?

Marīa: Pater nōn solum hoc fēcit, sed etiam multās aliās rēs.

Mārcus: Quae aliae rēs ā patre sunt factae?

Marīa: Pater lintea lectōrum omniaque tapētia excutere dēbēbat.

Helena: Pater tuus dīligenter (*with care*) labōrāvit (*worked*). Quid tū, Marīa, faciēbās?

Marīa: Māter mē iussit rēs in armāriīs positās ōrdināre. Dēbēbam quoque pulverem abstergēre, quī in armāriīs anteā (*earlier*) crēverat. Etiam iussū mātris pulverem ē vēlīs et ē pavīmentō celeriter haurītōriō exsūxī.

Helena: Quam (*how*) dīligenter labōrāvistis! Sine dubiō (*doubt*) nihil aliud facere dēbēbātis!

Marīa: Etiam aliās rēs fēcimus. Et ego et pater omnēs lectōs strāvimus. Deinde multa lintea in māchinā lavātōriā lāvimus. Domus nostra nunc est munda!

Mārcus: Quid fēcit māter tua?

Marīa: Māter nōs haec omnia facere iussit.

DERIVATIVES

carō – carnage, carnal, carnation, carnival, carnivorous, carrion, charnel, incarnate, incarnation, reincarnation

herba – arbor, herb, herbicide, herbivorous

pellis – pelisse, surplice

vestīmentum – vestment

vulnus – invulnerable, vulnerable

ferōx – ferocious, ferocity, fierce

terribilis – terrible, terribly

coquō – apricot, biscuit, concoct, cook, cuisine, kitchen, precocious, terra-cotta (*adj.*)

crēscō – accrue, concrete, crescent, crew, decrease, excrescence, increase, increment, recruit, crescendo

sānō – insane, sanitarium, sanatorium, sanitary, sanitation

sedeō – assess, assiduous, assizes, besiege, insidious, obsession, possession, possessive, preside, president, reside, residence, residual, residue, sedate, sedative, sedentary, sediment, session, size, subside, subsidiary, subsidy, supersede, surcease

terō – contrite, detriment, trite

vīvō – convivial, revive, survive, viand, victuals, vital, vitally, vitamin, vivacious, vivacity, vivid, vivify, viviparous

celeriter – celerity

forīs – foreclose, foreign, forest, forfeit

inter – enter, entrails, entrance, entrée, intern, internal, intimacy, intimate, intrinsic

Pluperfect Tense Passive of All Conjugations; Perfect Active and Passive Infinitives; Demonstrative Pronoun and Adjective *Ille*

A young Augustine with his mother Monica. Ary Scheffer (1795–1858).

MEMORĀBILE DICTŪ

Cor ad cor loquitur.
"Heart to heart," literally "A heart speaks to a heart."

A Latin saying that originated in the autobiographical *Confessions* of the influential early Christian writer Augustine, and is echoed in our English expression "heart to heart talk." This phrase was also the motto of Cardinal J. H. Newman in the nineteenth century.

READING

Aurēlius Augustīnus (354–430 CE), perhaps the most important early Christian thinker, was born in Tagaste in northern Africa, a part of the Roman Empire that is today Algeria. Although his mother, Monica, was a devout Christian, he rejected her beliefs as a young man. He moved to Rome, where he taught rhetoric and benefited from the patronage of the pagan orator Symmachus. In 386, however, while serving as public orator of Milan, Augustine was converted to Christianity by Ambrose, bishop of Milan. He himself later became bishop of Hippo in North Africa.

Among his most famous works are the *Cōnfessiōnēs,* "Confessions," and the *Dē Cīvitāte Deī,* "About the City of God." The latter work, imbued with a Christian vision, represents human history as part of a divine plan.

In the following passage, *Cōnfessiōnēs* 2.4.9, Augustine recalls an episode of his youth.

DĒ FŪRTŌ PIRŌRUM

1   Cum lēgēs hūmānae tum dīvīnae fūrtum pūnīre solent. Etiam fūr alium fūrem aequō animō nōn tolerat. Nec fūr dīves fūrem pauperem tolerat. Ego quoque fūrtum facere cupīvī et fēcī. Hoc tamen nōn propter egestātem fēcī, sed propter amōrem inīquitātis. Petīvī enim

5   rēs quibus abundābam, nōn quibus egēbam. Nam ipsō fūrtō dēlectārī cupiēbam, nōn rēbus quās petēbam. Prope domum meam erat pirus pōmōrum plēna, quae valdē pulchra vidēbantur. Ego et paucī aliī adulēscentēs improbī domōs nostrās noctū (per tōtum enim diem lūserāmus) relīquimus et illam arborem petīvimus. Omnia pōma ex

10   eā excussimus et nōbīscum asportāvimus. Pauca eōrum comēdimus, paene omnia porcīs ēiēcimus. Nam nōn cupiēbāmus comedere pōma, quae ā nōbīs erant capta. Omnēs enim in domibus nostrīs bonīs cibīs abundābāmus. Cupiēbāmus contrā lēgēs rēs facere et inīquitāte dēlectārī. Huius malitiae causa erat ipsa malitia. Rēs malās, rēs inīquās

15   amāvī, amāvī rēs malās et inīquās facere.

      Nunc adolēvī et cor meum iam intellegit mē rēs malās amāvisse, iam intellegit rēs malās ā mē esse factās.

READING VOCABULARY

*abundō, abundāre, abundāvī, abundātum + *ablative* – to abound with

adolēscō, adolēscere, adolēvī, adultum – to grow up

*adulēscēns, adulēscentis, *m./f.* – young man, young lady

*aequus, aequa, aequum – even; **aequō animō** – indifferently (with an even spirit)

amāvisse – have loved

asportō, asportāre, asportāvī, asportātum – to carry away

cibus, cibī, *m.* – food

*cor, cordis, *n.* – heart

cum . . . tum . . . – both . . . and . . .

*dēlectō, dēlectāre, dēlectāvī, dēlectātum – to delight, please

*dīvīnus, dīvīna, dīvīnum – divine

*egeō, egēre, eguī, —— + *ablative* – to lack something

egestās, egestātis, *f.* – lack, poverty

ēiciō, ēicere, ēiēcī, ēiectum – to throw away

erant capta – had been taken

esse factās – have been done

excutiō, excutere, excussī, excussum – to shake off

*fūr, fūris, *m.* – thief

*fūrtum, fūrtī, *n.* – theft

*hūmānus, hūmāna, hūmānum – human

*illam – that

improbus, improba, improbum – bad, wicked

*inīquitās, inīquitātis, *f.* – injustice

inīquus, inīqua, inīquum – unjust

ipsa – itself

ipsō – by itself

*lēx, lēgis, *f.* – law

*lūdō, lūdere, lūsī, lūsum – to play

malitia, malitiae, *f.* – badness, wickedness

nōbīscum = cum nōbīs

*noctū (*adv.*) – during the night

*paene (*adv.*) – almost

*pauper, pauperis (*genitive*) – poor

pirum, pirī, *n.* – pear (fruit)

pirus, pirī, *f.* – pear tree

*plēnus, plēna, plēnum + *genitive* or + *ablative* – full of

*pōmum, pōmī, *n.* – fruit

porcus, porcī, *m.* – pig

*pūniō, pūnīre, pūnīvī, pūnītum – to punish

tolerō, tolerāre, tolerāvī, tolerātum – to tolerate, bear

tōtus, tōta, tōtum – whole

*Words marked with an asterisk will need to be memorized later in the chapter.

COMPREHENSION QUESTIONS

1. What did Augustine steal, and what did he do with the things he stole?

2. What was Augustine's motivation to steal?

3. When did the theft happen, and when does Augustine write about it?

LANGUAGE FACT I

PLUPERFECT TENSE PASSIVE OF ALL CONJUGATIONS

Take a close look at one of the sentences from Augustine's autobiography:

> *Nōn cupiēbāmus comedere pōma, quae ā nōbīs* **erant capta.**
> We did not want to eat the fruits that **had been taken** by us.

In Chapter 17 you learned the **pluperfect active** of verbs of all conjugations. Now you meet the **pluperfect passive**.

The pluperfect passive is formed much like the perfect passive you learned in the last chapter, using a nominative perfect passive participle with a form of *sum* as an auxiliary verb for all conjugations.

Yet, the pluperfect passive is easily distinguished from the perfect passive—while the perfect passive has as its auxiliary verb the **present** forms of *sum*, the pluperfect passive has as its auxiliary verb the **imperfect** forms of *sum*. The pluperfect passive of the verb *parō* will serve as an example for all conjugations.

Pluperfect Passive: *parō*		
Singular		
First person	parātus, parāta, (parātum) eram	I had been prepared
Second person	parātus, parāta, (parātum) erās	you had been prepared
Third person	parātus, parāta, parātum erat	s/he/it had been prepared
Plural		
First person	parātī, parātae, (parāta) erāmus	we had been prepared
Second person	parātī, parātae, (parāta) erātis	you had been prepared
Third person	parātī, parātae, parāta erant	they had been prepared

STUDY TIP

Note that in the plural not only the verb *sum*, but also the participle needs to be plural.

▶ EXERCISE 1

Change the pluperfect active verbs into the pluperfect passive, keeping the same person and number. Translate the passive form.

Example: nārrāverat

nārrātus, nārrāta, nārrātum erat   s/he/it had been told

1. dēlectāverāmus
2. lēgerant
3. oppresserātis
4. rogāverat
5. līberāverāmus

6. relīquerās
7. pūnīveram
8. quaesīverant
9. excitāverātis

VOCABULARY TO LEARN

NOUNS

adulēscēns, adulēscentis, *m./f.* – young man, young lady

cor, cordis, *n.* – heart

fūr, fūris, *m.* – thief

fūrtum, fūrtī, *n.* – theft

inīquitās, inīquitātis, *f.* – injustice, mischief

lēx, lēgis, *f.* – law

pōmum, pōmī, *n.* – fruit

DEMONSTRATIVE PRONOUN/ ADJECTIVE

ille, illa, illud – that

ADJECTIVES

aequus, aequa, aequum – even; **aequō animō** – indifferently

dīvīnus, dīvīna, dīvīnum – divine

hūmānus, hūmāna, hūmānum – human

pauper, pauperis – poor

plēnus, plēna, plēnum + *genitive* or + *ablative* – full of

VERBS

abundō, abundāre, abundāvī, abundātum + *ablative* – to abound with

dēlectō, dēlectāre, dēlectāvī, dēlectātum – to delight, please

egeō, egēre, eguī, —— + *ablative* – to lack something

lūdō, lūdere, lūsī, lūsum – to play

pūniō, pūnīre, pūnīvī, pūnītum – to punish

ADVERBS

noctū – during the night

paene – almost

▶ EXERCISE 2

Find the English derivatives based on the Vocabulary to Learn in the following sentences. Write the corresponding Latin word.

1. They were very cordial to me and welcomed me at their home.

2. That spy was making furtive telephone calls.

3. Do you need legal advice?

4. The dinner was delicious.

5. We need to take punitive action.

6. Why do you have this adolescent attitude?

7. All people must have equal rights.

8. I will be going to Divinity School next fall.

9. The whole summer we have been working in Habitat for Humanity.

10. His best trait is that he has patience in abundance.

LANGUAGE FACT II

PERFECT ACTIVE AND PASSIVE INFINITIVES

Now return to Augustine's autobiography and take a close look at this sentence.

> *Cor meum iam intellegit mē rēs malās **amāvisse**, iam intellegit rēs malās ā mē **esse factās**.*
> My heart already understands that I loved bad things; it already understands that bad things were done by me.

So far you have only learned the present active and passive infinitives. In the sentences above there are two new infinitives—the perfect active and perfect passive infinitives. *Amāvisse* is a perfect active infinitive, and *esse factās* is a perfect passive infinitive.

Unlike the present active and passive infinitives, the perfect active infinitive has the same endings for all conjugations, and the perfect passive infinitive is formed the same way for all conjugations.

Augustine as bishop of Hippo.

The perfect **active** infinitive is made up of the perfect active stem (from the verb's **third** principal part) with the ending *–isse*.

The perfect **passive** infinitive is made up of the perfect passive participle (the verb's **fourth** principal part), which must agree in case, number, and gender with the expressed or implied noun or pronoun that is its subject, along with *esse*, the infinitive of the verb "to be."

Perfect Active Infinitive	
parāv-isse	to have prepared

Perfect Passive Infinitive	
parātus, parāta, parātum esse	to have been prepared

BY THE WAY

The perfect infinitive of *sum* is *fuisse*, and of *possum* is *potuisse*. Both forms are formed regularly by adding the suffix *–isse* to the perfect stems *fu–* and *potu–*. Remember that *sum* and *possum* do not have passive forms and thus do not have perfect passive infinitives.

Present and Perfect Infinitives			
Present Active Infinitive	**Present Passive Infinitive**	**Perfect Active Infinitive**	**Perfect Passive Infinitive**
parāre to prepare	parārī to be prepared	parāvisse to have prepared	parātus, parāta, parātum esse to have been prepared

When are the perfect infinitives used?

Perfect infinitives are used in the accusative and infinitive construction (the indirect statement) in a way similiar to the present infinitives with one major difference—while the **present** infinitive indicates **the same time as** the main verb, the **perfect** infinitive always indicates **a time before** the main verb. The tense of the infinitive is relative to that of the main verb. By studying these two sentences, you will understand this concept better.

Perfect infinitive (time before the main verb).

> *Augustīnus intellēxit sē rēs malās iam fēcisse.*
> Augustine understood that he had already done bad things.

Present infinitive (same time as the main verb).

> *Augustīnus nōn intellegēbat sē rēs malās tunc facere.*
> Augustine did not understand that he was doing bad things at that time.

Note that in the accusative and infinitive construction the participle (which is a part of the perfect passive infinitive) is always in the accusative, and that it agrees in number and gender with the accusative subject of the indirect statement.

*Dīcō **virum** esse **cōnspectum.*** "I say that the man has been looked at."

*Dīcō **virōs** esse **cōnspectōs.*** "I say that the men have been looked at."

*Dīcō **fēminam** esse **cōnspectam.*** "I say that the woman has been looked at."

*Dīcō **fēminās** esse **cōnspectās.*** "I say that the women have been looked at."

BY THE WAY
The word "to," which usually translates the infinitive, is rarely used in the English translation of the accusative and infinitive construction.

▶ EXERCISE 3

Translate the following sentences and then change all the present infinitives into perfect infinitives. Translate the changed sentence. The Reading Vocabulary may be consulted.

Example: Dīcō mē librum legere.

I say that I am reading a book.   Dīcō mē librum lēgisse.   I say that I have read a book.

1. Augustīnus dīcit prope domum suam arborem esse et eam arborem multa pōma pulchra habēre.

2. Augustīnus nārrat sē rēs malās cupere et fūrtō dēlectārī.

3. Augustīnus dīcit omnia pōma ab adulēscentibus ex arbore excutī atque asportārī.

4. Augustīnus dīcit sē pauca pōma comedere et paene omnia ēicere.

Augustine must have stolen
a pear as tempting as this one.

▶ EXERCISE 4

Fill in the blanks with the correct form of the pluperfect passive indicative, or the perfect infinitive and translate the sentences. The Reading Vocabulary may be consulted.

Example: Dīxī mē haec omnia iam _____. (audiō)
Dīxī mē haec omnia iam audīvisse.   I said that I had already heard all these things.

1. Omnia pōma ab Augustīnō et ab eius amīcīs iam ex arbore _____. Tunc pauca pōma eī comēdērunt. (excutiō)

2. Adulēscentēs paucīs tantum pomīs _____. Alia pōma porcīs ēiēcērunt. (dēlectō)

3. Improbī adulēscentēs putābant fūrtum bene _____. (faciō)

4. Augustīnus tandem intellēxit sē nōn bene _____. (faciō)

LANGUAGE FACT III

DEMONSTRATIVE PRONOUN AND ADJECTIVE *ILLE*

In Chapter 19 you learned the demonstrative *hic, haec, hoc* ("this"). In this chapter reading you encountered another demonstrative word that means "that."

> **Illam** arborem petīvimus.
> We went to **that** tree.

Here is the declension of the demonstrative pronoun and adjective *ille*.

Demonstrative Pronoun/Adjective *ille*		
Singular		
	Masculine	**Feminine**	**Neuter**
Nominative	ille	illa	illud
Genitive	illīus	illīus	illīus
Dative	illī	illī	illī
Accusative	illum	illam	illud
Ablative	illō	illā	illō
Plural		
	Masculine	**Feminine**	**Neuter**
Nominative	illī	illae	illa
Genitive	illōrum	illārum	illōrum
Dative	illīs	illīs	illīs
Accusative	illōs	illās	illa
Ablative	illīs	illīs	illīs

STUDY TIP

Note that the declension of *ille, illa, illud* is quite similar to the declension of *is, ea, id* (which you learned in Chapter 12). The genitive and dative singulars are irregular, while the rest resemble first and second declension endings.

BY THE WAY

The demonstrative *hic, haec, hoc* means "this" and indicates a person or thing that is close; the demonstrative *ille, illa, illud* means "that" and indicates a person or thing that is far. When a series of things or persons has been mentioned, *hic* often refers to the last in the series and means "the latter," while *ille* refers to a previously mentioned person or thing and means "the former."

Just as is true with *is, ea, id*, both *hic, haec, hoc* and *ille, illa, illud* can be used either as demonstrative pronouns or as demonstrative adjectives.

Demonstrative Pronoun	*Hic mox respondēbit.* "He (this \<man\>) will reply soon."
Demonstrative Adjective	*Hic vir mox respondēbit.* "This man will reply soon."
Demonstrative Pronoun	*Illae dōna exspectant.* "They (those \<women\>) expect gifts."
Demonstrative Adjective	*Illae mulierēs dōna exspectant.* "Those women expect gifts."

▶ EXERCISE 5

Substitute *ille* for *hic* in the following phrases. Give the case and number of each phrase and translate.

Example: hoc fūrtum
illud fūrtum   nominative *or* accusative singular   that theft

1. hās inīquitātēs
2. hī fūrēs
3. huius cordis
4. hīs adulēscentibus
5. hārum lēgum
6. hōrum pōmōrum
7. hāc causā
8. hīs lītoribus
9. haec odia
10. hōc saxō
11. huic carnī

▶ EXERCISE 6

Fill in the blanks with the correct pluperfect passive form of the verb in the parentheses and translate both sentences.

Example: Domum vīdimus. Iam _____. (aedificō)
Domum vīdimus. Iam erat aedificāta.   We saw the house. It had already been built.

1. Hostēs fūgērunt. Iam ā nōbis _____. (vincō)

2. Flammās vīdimus. Incendium nōn _____. (exstinguō)

3. Diū tē quaesīvī. Nam bene _____. (occultō)

4. Puer nōn gaudēbat. Nam ā mātre _____. (pūniō)

5. Ad nōs vēnistis. Nam ā nōbīs _____. (vocō)

TALKING

argentāria, argentāriae, f. – bank

computus, computī, m. – account

fiscus, fiscī, m. – safe, account

nummī, nummōrum, m. pl. – coins

monēta (monētae, f.) *chartācea* – paper money

pecūlium, pecūliī, n. – savings

syngrapha, syngraphae, f. or *assignātiō (assignātiōnis,* f.) *argentāria* – a check

chartula (chartulae, f.) *creditōria* – credit card

talērus, talērī, m./*dollarium, dollariī,* n. – dollar

centēsima, centēsimae, f. – cent, penny

pecūnia numerāta – cash

emō, emere, ēmī, ēmptum – to buy

solvō, solvere, solvī, solūtum – to pay

Quantī cōnstat? "How much does it cost?"

Cōnstat decem talērīs (dollariīs). "It costs ten dollars."

The Romans minted various types of coins such as the *as, dēnārius,*
and *aureus.* This coin is a *dēnārius.* Coins in general were called *nummī,*
which word is related to the English word "numismatics," the study of coins.

Pecūniam dēpōnō (dēpōnere, dēposuī, dēpositum). "I deposit money."

Pecūniam collocō (collocāre, collocāvī, collocātum). "I invest money."

Pecūniam eximō (eximere, exēmī, exēmptum). "I take out money."

Commodō (commodāre, commodāvī, commodātum) pecūniam. "I lend money."

Mūtuor pecūniam. "I borrow money."

Pecūniae (dative) parcō. "I save money."

GOING SHOPPING

Marīa: Salvēte, amīcae! Vultisne (*do you all want*) mēcum venīre?

Helena: Quō (*where, to which place*) venīre dēbēmus?

Marīa: Ad vīcum tabernārum (*mall*). Vestīmentum enim ibi vīdī, quod emere (*buy*) cupiō.

Helena: Quāle (*what kind*) est illud vestīmentum?

Marīa: Est vestīmentum aestīvum (*summer*) valdē pulchrum. Vestīmentum aestīvum diū ā mē erat quaesītum et tandem praeteritā hebdomade (*last week*) rem pulchram cōnspexī.

Christīna: Cūr statim nōn ēmistī?

Marīa: Pecūniā egēbam.

Helena: Quid nunc? Estne tibi nunc pecūnia?

Marīa: Pater chartulam creditōriam mihi dedit.

Helena: Vērumne dīcis? Quantī cōnstat vestīmentum quod habēre cupis?

Marīa: Centum (*one hundred*) talērīs.

Christīna: Ego pecūniae parcō et pecūlium in argentāriā habeō. Sī vestīmentum emere cupiō, pecūniam ex fiscō eximō. Rēs chartulā creditōriā nōn emō et pecūniam nōn dēbeō.

Marīa: Tū es fēlīx. Ex manibus meīs pecūnia fluere vidētur.

DERIVATIVES

cor – concord, cordial, core, courage, courageous, discord, discourage, encourage, record

fūr – ferret, furtive

inīquitās – iniquitous, iniquity

lēx – allege, allegation, colleague, college, delegate, disloyal, illegal, illegitimate, legacy, legislation, legislator, privilege, loyal, relegate

pōmum – pomegranate, pommel, pummel

aequus – adequate, equable, equal, equanimity, equidistant, equilibrium, equinox, equipoise, equivalent, equivocate, unequal

dīvīnus – divine, diviner, divinity

pauper – impoverish, poor, poverty, pauper

plēnus – accomplish, complement, compliment, complete, compliance, depletion, expletive, implement, plenary, plenipotentiary, plenteous, plenty, replete, supplement, supply

abundō – abound, abundance

egeō – indigence, indigent

lūdō – allude, collusion, delude, disillusion, elude, elusive, illusion, interlude, ludicrous, prelude, postlude

pūniō – punishment, punish

paene – peninsula, penult, peneplain, antepenult

CHAPTER 21

Fourteenth-century illuminated manuscript of the writings of Boethius,
illustrating the wheel of fortune.

MEMORĀBILE DICTŪ

Tempora mūtantur et nōs mūtāmur in illīs.

"Times are changing and we are changing in them."

This well-known line of verse probably dates from some time in the Middle Ages, and concisely
expresses the recognition that human life and human beings change and are changeable.

READING

Anicius Manlius Severīnus Boēthius (ca. 480–ca. 524 CE) lived after the dissolution of the Roman Empire in the West, at a time when the Ostrogoths under Theodoric the Great had established a kingdom in Italy. Scion of a noble Roman family, Boethius served in the king's administration; eventually, for reasons that are unclear, the king turned against Boethius, accused him of sedition, and sentenced him to death.

Boethius knew Greek well, and translated Plato and Aristotle into Latin. He also wrote important treatises on music and Christian theology. But his literary masterpiece, written in prose alternating with verse, is the *Cōnsōlātiō Philosophiae*, the "Consolation of Philosophy." It takes the form of a dialogue between Philosophy, allegorically represented as a mystical female figure, and the imprisoned Boethius himself.

In the selection below, adapted from the second book of the *Cōnsōlātiō Philosophiae*, Fortune is personified, and speaks in her own defense against those who blame "bad fortune" for the loss of power and prosperity. Her nature, it seems, is "to come and go." Here the action of Fortune is compared to that of an endlessly turning wheel that raises people up for a time, but always sends them back down to a lowly condition. This image of the "wheel of fortune" was very popular during the Middle Ages and early modern era; it is frequently depicted in drawings or paintings in medieval manuscripts.

DĒ ROTĀ FORTŪNAE

1   Tū multās rēs ā mē accēpistī. Tē diū alēbam. Dīvitiās habēbās et
honōrēs. Errāvistī. Putābās tē illās rēs tibi ad tempus datās semper
habitūrum esse. Sed cōnstantia est ā mē aliēna. Semper discessūra nihil
tibi dedī. Tandem ā mē relictus es. Dīvitiae et honōrēs mēcum

5   discessērunt. Cūr mē reprehendis? Nihil, quod erat tuum, ex tē ēripuī.
Fūrtī mē accūsāre nōn poteris!

Hominēs multās rēs habent, sed nihil possident. Ego Fortūna omnia
possideō. Sī rēs hominibus ā mē datae erunt, illās rēs posteā recipiam.
Nam omnēs rēs illae sunt meae, nōn hominum. Sī homō ā mē relictus

10   erit, omnēs rēs eī datae mēcum discēdent. Omnium dīvitiārum
rērumque quās hominēs habent externās sum domina. Numquam cum
ūllō homine semper maneō, sed omnēs dīvitiae rēsque externae semper
mēcum manent.

Omnia in vītā hominum semper mūtantur. Hominēs vīvunt sīcut in
magnā rotā, quae circum axem semper versātur. Haec rota est mea!
Homō, quī in rotā meā sublātus erit, posteā prō certō dēscendet et
cadet. Homō igitur, quī dīvitiās et honōrēs habet, prō certō scīre dēbet
sē tandem illās rēs relictūrum esse.

READING VOCABULARY

*accipiō, accipere, accēpī, acceptum – to accept, receive

*accūsō, accūsāre, accūsāvī, accūsātum + *accusative* + *genitive* – to accuse someone of something

ad tempus – for the time being, for a while

*aliēnus, aliēna, aliēnum + ā/ab + *ablative* – foreign to, inconsistent with

*axis, axis, *m.* – axle, axis

*circum + *accusative* – around

*cōnstantia, cōnstantiae, *f.* – constancy

datae erunt – will have been given/are given

*dēscendō, dēscendere, dēscendī, dēscēnsum – to descend

discessūra – about to depart/go away

*dīvitiae, dīvitiārum, *f. pl.* – wealth, riches

*ēripiō, ēripere, ēripuī, ēreptum – to snatch away

*errō, errāre, errāvī, errātum – to wander, make a mistake

*externus, externa, externum – outward, external

*fortūna, fortūnae, *f.* – fortune, the goddess Fortune

habitūrum esse – going to have/would have

*honor, honōris, *m.* – honor, public office or distinction

*mūtō, mūtāre, mūtāvī, mūtātum – to change

*possideō, possidēre, possēdī, possessum – to possess

*prō certō – for certain, for sure

*recipiō, recipere, recēpī, receptum – to take back

relictūrum esse – will leave behind

relictus erit – will have been left/abandoned/is left/abandoned

*reprehendō, reprehendere, reprehendī, reprehēnsum – to blame, rebuke

*rota, rotae, *f.* – wheel

sublātus erit – will have been raised up/is raised up

*tollō, tollere, sustulī, sublātum – to lift up, raise; destroy

*ūllus, ūlla, ūllum – any

*versō, versāre, versāvī, versātum – to turn

*Words marked with an asterisk will need to be memorized later in the chapter.

COMPREHENSION QUESTIONS

1. Of what does Boethius accuse Fortune?

2. Why does Fortune reject Boethius's accusations?

3. What does Fortune say about her relationship with men?

4. What does Fortune want to say with the image of the wheel?

LANGUAGE FACT I

FUTURE PERFECT TENSE PASSIVE OF ALL CONJUGATIONS

In the chapter reading you see some verb forms that consist of the perfect passive participle together with the future forms of *sum*.

> *Sī rēs hominibus ā mē **datae erunt**, illās rēs posteā recipiam.*
> If things will have been given to people by me, I will take those things back afterward.
> Or, in more colloquial English: If things are given to people by me, I will take those things back afterward.

> *Sī homō ā mē **relictus erit**, omnēs rēs eī datae mēcum discēdent.*
> If a person will have been abandoned by me, all things given to him will go away <from him> with me.
> Or, in more colloquial English: If a person is abandoned by me, all things given to him will go away <from him> with me.

> *Homō, quī in rotā meā **sublātus erit**, posteā prō certō dēscendet et cadet.*
> A person who will have been lifted up in my wheel will afterward descend and fall for certain.
> Or, in more colloquial English: A person who is lifted up on my wheel will afterward descend and fall for certain.

These are forms of the future perfect tense passive; they are formed with the perfect passive participle along with forms of *erō*, the future tense of *sum*.

You now know all the tenses in the active and the passive voice.

BY THE WAY

When you studied the future perfect active in Chapter 18, it was used to indicate **a time before a future time**. This is equally true of the future perfect passive. So keep in mind what you already know about the meaning of the future perfect—where Latin (more accurately) uses the future perfect, English typically uses the simple present. Colloquial English (as the above sentences demonstrate) rarely or never says "will have."

As in the perfect and pluperfect passive, you do not need separate paradigms for the future perfect passive of all four conjugations. Once you know the perfect passive participle (from the fourth principal part of most verbs), simply combine it with the future tense of the verb *sum*.

STUDY TIP

Note that in the third person plural of the future perfect the active ending is *–erint* but the passive participle accompanies *erunt*, e.g., *audīverint*, but *audītī erunt*.

Future Perfect Passive: *exspectō*		
Singular		
First person	exspectātus, exspectāta, (exspectātum) erō	I will/shall have been awaited
Second person	exspectātus, exspectāta, (exspectātum) eris	you will have been awaited
Third person	exspectātus, exspectāta, exspectātum erit	s/he/it will have been awaited
Plural		
First person	exspectātī, exspectātae, (exspectāta) erimus	we will/shall have been awaited
Second person	exspectātī, exspectātae, (exspectāta) eritis	you will have been awaited
Third person	exspectātī, exspectātae, exspectāta erunt	they will have been awaited

Future Perfect Passive: *audiō*		
Singular		
First person	audītus, audīta, (audītum) erō	I will/shall have been heard
Second person	audītus, audīta, (audītum) eris	you will have been heard
Third person	audītus, audīta, audītum erit	s/he/it will have been heard
Plural		
First person	audītī, audītae, (audīta) erimus	we will/shall have been heard
Second person	audītī, audītae, (audīta) eritis	you will have been heard
Third person	audītī, audītae, audīta erunt	they will have been heard

Note that parentheses have been placed around some of the neuter forms of the participial elements in these verbs. This is because people, not things, are usually the subjects of first and second person passive verbs.

STUDY TIP

Keep in mind that the entire perfect system in the passive voice (i.e., the perfect, pluperfect, and future perfect passive) is formed by combining the perfect passive participle with the appropriate tense of *sum*:

- the perfect passive is formed with the perfect passive participle and with the present tense of *sum*;
- the pluperfect passive is formed with the perfect passive participle and with the imperfect tense of *sum*;
- the future perfect passive is formed with the perfect passive participle and with the future tense of *sum*.

▶ EXERCISE 1

Translate the following perfect or pluperfect passive forms and then change them into the future perfect passive, keeping the same person and number. Translate the changed form.

Example: dictum est

it was/has been said   dictum erit   it will have been said

1. mūtāta sum
2. acceptus erās
3. reprehēnsae estis
4. accūsātī sunt

5. versātī sumus
6. neglēctus eram
7. sublātum est

VOCABULARY TO LEARN

NOUNS

axis, axis, *m.* – axle, axis

cōnstantia, cōnstantiae, *f.* – constancy

dīvitiae, dīvitiārum, *f. pl.* – wealth, riches

fortūna, fortūnae, *f.* – fortune, the goddess Fortune

honor, honōris, *m.* – honor, public office or distinction

rota, rotae, *f.* – wheel

ADJECTIVES

aliēnus, aliēna, aliēnum + ā/ab + *ablative* – foreign to, inconsistent with

externus, externa, externum – outward, external

futūrus, futūra, futūrum – about to be (*the future active participle of* sum, esse, fuī)

ūllus, ūlla, ūllum – any

VERBS

accipiō, accipere, accēpī, acceptum – to accept, receive

accūsō, accūsāre, accūsāvī, accūsātum + *accusative* + *genitive* – to accuse someone of something

dēscendō, dēscendere, dēscendī, dēscēnsum – to descend

ēripiō, ēripere, ēripuī, ēreptum – to snatch away

errō, errāre, errāvī, errātum – to wander, make a mistake

mūtō, mūtāre, mūtāvī, mūtātum – to change

possideō, possidēre, possēdī, possessum – to possess

recipiō, recipere, recēpī, receptum – to take back

reprehendō, reprehendere, reprehendī, reprehēnsum – to blame, rebuke

tollō, tollere, sustulī, sublātum – to lift up, raise; destroy

versō, versāre, versāvī, versātum – to turn

PREPOSITION

circum + *accusative* – around

PREPOSITIONAL PHRASE USED ADVERBIALLY

prō certō – for certain, for sure

▶ EXERCISE 2

Find the English derivatives based on the Vocabulary to Learn in the following sentences. Write the corresponding Latin word.

1. The rotary motion of a cyclone is said to add force to its violent winds.

2. We should not reject things simply because they seem alien to us.

3. Our descendants must inherit a safer and cleaner world.

4. You do not need to speak in such an accusatory tone.

5. The motion of the hummingbird often appears to be quite erratic.

6. Sometimes distinguished citizens are given honorary degrees, even when they have never completed the academic curriculum leading to the degree.

7. When you buy dinner for these visitors, please be sure to ask the waiter to give you a receipt.

8. Scientists are steadily learning more about genetic mutations.

9. I often think my parents are too possessive.

10. Unethical behavior in anyone, but especially in a public official, is reprehensible.

LANGUAGE FACT II

FUTURE ACTIVE PARTICIPLE

In the passage at the beginning of the chapter, you saw a new form of participle. This is the future active participle. It occurs in this sentence:

> *Semper **discessūra** nihil tibi dedī.*
> Always **about to go away** I gave you nothing.

The future active participle has the meaning "(being) about to . . . ," or "(being) ready to . . . ," or "(being) on the point of . . . ," or "going to . . . ." The future active participle, especially in the works of writers who lived after Cicero, also may indicate the intention or purpose of the subject.

The stem of the future participle is the same as that of the perfect passive participle, so it is found in a verb's fourth principal part. The endings of the future participle are the same for all conjugations. The future participle of any verb is formed by taking away the *–um* of the fourth principal part and substituting in its place the endings *–ūrus, –ūra, –ūrum*. Here are the future participles of a few verbs already familiar to you.

> *audītūrus, audītūra, audītūrum* – about to hear/going to hear
>
> *cōnspectūrus, cōnspectūra, cōnspectūrum* – about to observe/going to observe
>
> *cūrātūrus, cūrātūra, cūrātūrum* – about to care for/going to care for
>
> *missūrus, missūra, missūrum* – about to send/going to send
>
> *receptūrus, receptūra, receptūrum* – about to take back/going to take back

Remember that the English word "future" is derived from the future active participle of *sum*: *futūrus, futūra, futūrum*. In fact the verb *sum, esse, fuī, ——* has no perfect passive participle, so you can consider *futūrus, futūra, futūrum* as the fourth principal part of this verb.

▶ EXERCISE 3

Write the three nominative singular forms of the future active participle for each of the following verbs. Translate each participle.

Example: curō

curātūrus, -a, -um   about to care *or* going to care

1. legō
2. mūtō
3. respondeō
4. temptō
5. currō

6. cadō
7. dormiō
8. pugnō
9. cupiō
10. gerō

11. stō
12. possideō
13. agō
14. dēleō

LANGUAGE FACT III

FUTURE ACTIVE INFINITIVE

Now that you know how to form the future active participle, you also know how to form the future active infinitive. There are a few examples of the future active infinitive in the passage at the beginning of this chapter.

Putābās tē illās rēs tibi ad tempus datās semper **habitūrum esse**.
You thought you would always have those things given to you for the time being.

Homō igitur, quī dīvitiās et honōrēs habet, prō certō scīre dēbet sē tandem illās rēs **relictūrum esse**.
Therefore a person who has wealth and honors ought to know for certain that he will finally leave those things behind.

The future active infinitive consists of the future active participle and *esse* (the infinitive of *sum*). The participle, of course, agrees in case, number, and gender with its subject. In the accusative and infinitive construction after a verb of speaking or thinking, the participle will agree with the accusative subject. If the future active infinitive is used after the verb *videor*, "I seem," the participle is in the nominative.

Hic homō **errātūrus esse** *vidētur*.
This man seems to be going to/about to make a mistake.

You can now make indirect statements (after a verb of saying or thinking) expressing different time relations to the main verb: before, same time, and after. To illustrate this, consider these sentences.

(1) *Putās tē verba Fortūnae audīre.* **(same time in the present)**
You think you are hearing the words of Fortune.

Putābās tē verba Fortūnae audīre. **(same time in the past)**
You thought you were hearing the words of Fortune.

(2) *Putās tē verba Fortūnae audīvisse.* **(time before present time)**
You think you have heard the words of Fortune.

Putābās tē verba Fortūnae audīvisse. **(time before past time)**
You thought you had heard the words of Fortune.

(3) *Putās tē verba Fortūnae audītūrum esse.* (Note that if *tē* referred to a female person, then the infinitive would be *audītūram esse.*) **(time after present time)**
You think you are going to hear/will hear the words of Fortune.

Putābās tē verba Fortūnae audītūrum esse. **(time after past time)**
You thought you were going to hear/would hear the words of Fortune.

These sentences clearly illustrate the following principles:

(1) In an indirect statement, the present infinitive refers to time contemporary with the main verb (regardless of the tense of the main verb).

Natural Science and Philosophy are personified in this reproduction of a woodcut from a German edition of Boethius.

(2) In an indirect statement, the future infinitive refers to time after that of the main verb (regardless of the tense of the main verb).

(3) In an indirect statement, the perfect infinitive refers to time prior to that of the main verb (regardless of the tense of the main verb).

In general, the tense of the infinitive in the indirect discourse does not indicate time on its own, but a time relation to the verb of the main clause.

BY THE WAY

Latin has no future passive infinitive that is commonly used. The ideas and relationships that would be expressed by a future passive infinitive can be expressed in Latin, but by other constructions that you will learn later.

▶ EXERCISE 4

Identify whether a future active participle or a future active infinitive is used in the following sentences and then translate each sentence.

Example: Fortūna dīvitiās et honōrēs semper ēreptūra timētur ā mē.
(future active participle)   Fortune, always about to snatch away riches and honors, is feared by me.

1.   Fortūnam dīvitiās et honōrēs ēreptūram esse crēdō.

2.   Fortūna dīvitiās et honōrēs ēreptūra esse vidētur.

3.   Dōna et praemia datūra Fortūna ab hominibus amātur.

4.   Fortūna dōna et praemia datūra esse vidētur.

5.   Fortūnam dōna et praemia datūram esse nōn crēdimus.

▶ EXERCISE 5

Translate into Latin.

1.   Fortune seems to be about to give me nothing.

2.   We believe that Fortune will never leave.

3.   I am going to abandon my riches.

4.   You (plural) believe that Fortune will always possess all external things.

5.   Do I seem to you to be going to descend soon on Fortune's wheel?

► EXERCISE 6

Translate the following questions. Then choose the best answer for each and translate. The Reading Vocabulary may be consulted.

1. Cūr Boēthius sē errāvisse dīcit?

    Tandem ā Fortūnā relictus est.

    Fortūna omnia possidēbat.

    Putābat sē dīvitiās et honōrēs semper habitūrum esse.

2. Cūr dīcit Fortūna sē fūrtī accūsārī nōn posse?

    Dīvitiae et honōrēs cum Fortūnā discessērunt.

    Fortūna nihil, quod erat Boēthiī, ex eō ēripuit.

    Fortūna erat semper discessūra et tandem Boēthium relīquit.

3. Cūr cōnstantia ā Fortūnā aliēna esse dīcitur?

    Fortūna numquam cum ūllō homine semper manet.

    Sī rēs hominibus ā Fortūnā datae erunt, Fortūna illās rēs posteā recipiet.

    Fortūna omnia possidet.

4. Cūr omnēs dīvitiae rēsque externae dīcuntur esse Fortūnae, nōn hominum?

    Hominēs multās rēs habent, sed nihil possident.

    Hominēs putant sē rēs sibi ad tempus datās semper habitūrōs esse.

    Dīvitiae rēsque externae cum homine manent dum Fortūna cum eō manet, sed semper cum Fortūnā manent.

5. Cūr hominēs dīcuntur vīvere sīcut in magnā rotā?

    Haec rota circum axem semper versātur.

    Fortūna hanc rotam possidet.

    Omnia in vītā hominum semper mūtantur.

6. Cūr prō certō scīre dēbet homō, quī dīvitiās et honōrēs habet, sē tandem illās rēs relictūrum esse?

    Fortūna omnia possidet.

    Homō, quī in rotā Fortūnae sublātus erit, posteā prō certō dēscendet et cadet.

    Hominēs putant sē rēs sibi ad tempus datās semper habitūrōs esse.

TALKING

accendō, accendere, accendī, accēnsum – to light

aperiō, aperīre, aperuī, apertum – to open

candēla, candēlae, f. – candle

celebrō, celebrāre, celebrāvī, celebrātum – to celebrate

diēs nātālis fēlīcissimus – an extremely happy birthday

diēs nātālis fēlīx – a happy birthday

diēs nātālis, m. – birthday

fasciculus, fasciculī, m. – package, parcel

Grātissimī vēnistis. "Welcome to you all ([literally] very pleasing you have come)."

lībum, lībī, n. – cake

nātālicia, nātāliciae, f. – a birthday party

nātāliciam agitāre – to put on/celebrate a birthday party

nātālicium (dōnum), n. – birthday gift

Quot annōs nāta/us es? "How old are you?"

Septendecim annōs nāta/us sum. "I am seventeen years old."

Diēs nātālis tibi fēlīx sit! "Happy birthday!"

Sit tibi Fortūna propitia! "May Fortune be kind to you!"

A BIRTHDAY PARTY

whomst've summoned me :)

HELEN OPENS THE DOOR OF HER PARENTS' HOUSE TO ADMIT MARK, CHRISTY, AND MARY, WHO BRING BRIGHTLY WRAPPED PACKAGES.

Marīa, Mārcus, Christīna: (*IN UNISON*) Salvē (*greetings*), Helena! Sit tibi Fortūna propitia nōn sōlum hōc diē nātālī sed etiam per tōtam (*whole*) vītam!

Helena: Grātissimī vēnistis! Diēs nātālis meus erit fēlīcissimus, quia (*because*) vēnistis! Bonum est nātālem diem cum amīcīs celebrāre.

Mārcus: Nātāliciam apud tē agitāre cupimus. Dōna nātālicia habēmus multa.

Helena: Sī mihi dōna erunt data tot (*so many*) et tanta, dīvitiās magnās habēbō.

Christīna: Lībum etiam habēmus.

Helena: Mox comedēmus. Prīmum (*first*) autem fasciculōs illōs pulchrōs aperīre cupiō.

Christīna: Quot annōs, Helena, hodiē (*today*) nāta es?

Helena: Hodiē septendecim annōs nāta sum.

Christīna: Itaque septendecim candēlās in lībō pōnere dēbēbimus.

Mārcus: Quis candēlās accendet?

Helena: Ego!

Mārcus: Bene. (*Fine.*) Deinde vehementer (*strongly*) efflāre (*blow out*) dēbēbis omnēsque candēlās simul (*simultaneously*) exstinguere. Tunc lībum—sed nōn candēlās—comedēmus!

Helena: Exspectāte! Prīmum fasciculōs illōs aperiam, deinde candēlās accendēmus lībumque comedēmus!

DERIVATIVES

axis – axial, axis

fortūna – fortunate, misfortune, unfortunately

honor – dishonest, dishonorable, honest, honorary

rota – around, comptroller, control, enroll, rondo, role, roller, rotary, rotation, rotund, roulette, rotunda

externus – external

futūrus – future, futuristic

dēscendō – descend, condescend, descendant, descent

errō – aberration, arrant, err, erratic, erroneous, errata

mūtō – commute, immutable, molt, mutable, mutation, mutual, transmutation

reprehendō – reprehend, reprehensible

tollō – extol, intolerable, tolerance, tolerably

circum – circumnavigate, circumference, circumcision, circumlocution, circumscribe, circumspect, circumstance, circumstantial, circumvent

VOCABULARY TO KNOW

NOUNS

adulēscēns, adulēscentis, *m./f.* – young man, young lady

axis, axis, *m.* – axle, axis

barba, barbae, *f.* – beard

carō, carnis, *f.* – meat, flesh

cōnstantia, cōnstantiae, *f.* – constancy

cor, cordis, *n.* – heart

dīvitiae, dīvitiārum, *f. pl.* – wealth, riches

fortūna, fortūnae, *f.* – fortune, the goddess Fortune

fūr, fūris, *m.* – thief

fūrtum, fūrtī, *n.*– theft

herba, herbae, *f.* – plant, vegetation

honor, honōris, *m.* – honor, public office or distinction

inīquitās, inīquitātis, *f.* – injustice, mischief

lēx, lēgis, *f.* – law

pellis, pellis, *f.* – skin, hide

pōmum, pōmī, *n.* – fruit

proelium, proeliī, *n.* – battle, combat

rota, rotae, *f.* – wheel

vestīmentum, vestīmentī, *n.* – a garment, *pl.* clothes

vulnus, vulneris, *n.* – wound

DEMONSTRATIVE PRONOUNS/ADJECTIVES

hic, haec, hoc – this, latter

ille, illa, illud – that, former

ADJECTIVES

aequus, aequa, aequum – even; **aequō animō** – indifferently

aliēnus, aliēna, aliēnum + ā/ab + *ablative* – foreign to, inconsistent with

dīvīnus, dīvīna, dīvīnum – divine

externus, externa, externum – outward, external

ferōx, ferōcis (*genitive*) – fierce, ferocious

futūrus, futūra, futūrum – about to be (*the future active participle of* sum, esse, fuī)

hūmānus, hūmāna, hūmānum – human

pauper, pauperis (*genitive*) – poor

plēnus, plēna, plēnum + *genitive* or + *ablative* – full of

terribilis, terribile – terrifying

ūllus, ūlla, ūllum – any

VERBS

abundō, abundāre, abundāvī, abundātum + *ablative* – to abound with

accipiō, accipere, accēpī, acceptum – to accept, receive

accūsō, accūsāre, accūsāvī, accūsātum + *accusative* + *genitive* – to accuse someone of something

colō, colere, coluī, cultum – to worship, cultivate

coquō, coquere, coxī, coctum – to cook

crēscō, crēscere, crēvī, —— – to grow

dēlectō, dēlectāre, dēlectāvī, dēlectātum – to delight, please

dēscendō, dēscendere, dēscendī, dēscēnsum – to descend

egeō, egēre, eguī, —— + *ablative* – to lack something

ēripiō, ēripere, ēripuī, ēreptum – to snatch away

errō, errāre, errāvī, errātum – to wander, make a mistake

lūdō, lūdere, lūsī, lūsum – to play

mūtō, mūtāre, mūtāvī, mūtātum – to change

possideō, possidēre, possēdī, possessum – to possess

pūniō, pūnīre, pūnīvī, pūnītum – to punish

recipiō, recipere, recēpī, receptum – to take back

reprehendō, reprehendere, reprehendī, reprehēnsum – to blame, rebuke

sānō, sānāre, sānāvī, sānātum – to heal

sedeō, sedēre, sēdī, sessum – to sit

terō, terere, trīvī, trītum – to wear out, rub

tollō, tollere, sustulī, sublātum – to lift up, raise; destroy

versō, versāre, versāvī, versātum – to turn

vīvō, vīvere, vīxī, vīctum – to live

vulnerō, vulnerāre, vulnerāvī, vulnerātum – to wound

ADVERBS

celeriter – swiftly

forīs – outside, in the open

noctū – during the night

paene – almost

PREPOSITIONS

circum + *accusative* – around

inter + *accusative* – between, among

CONJUNCTION

postquam – after

PREPOSITIONAL PHRASE USED ADVERBIALLY

prō certō – for certain, for sure

▶ EXERCISE 1

Conjugate the following verb in the perfect passive voice.

1. *vulnerō, vulnerāre, vulnerāvī, vulnerātum*

Conjugate the following verb in the pluperfect passive voice.

1. *mūtō, mūtāre, mūtāvī, mūtātum*

Conjugate the following verb in the future perfect passive voice.

1. *ēripiō, ēripere, ēripuī, ēreptum*

▶ EXERCISE 2

Write the perfect passive and future active participles of the following verbs and translate both forms.

Example: accūsō

accūsātus, accūsāta, accūsātum   accused *or* having been accused

accūsātūrus, accūsātūra, accūsātūrum   about to accuse *or* going to accuse *or* intending to accuse

1. coquō

2. dēlectō

3. sānō

4. terō

5. versō

▶ EXERCISE 3

Decline the following phrases.

1. *hoc pōmum*

2. *illa inīquitās*

▶ EXERCISE 4

Change the direct statement into an indirect statement using the accusative and infinitive construction. Make the tense and voice of the infinitive fit the context. Then translate the sentence.

Example: Fortūna poētae dīcit: "Multa dedī et nihil aliud iam dabō."

Fortūna poētae dīcit sē multa dedisse et nihil aliud sē esse datūram.

Fortune says to the poet that she has given many things and that she will give nothing else (other).

1. Poēta dīcit: "Sum ā fortūnā relictus et omnia bona sunt ab eā ērepta."

2. Poēta dīcit: "Fortūnam fūrtī accūsābō."

3. Nam poēta dīcit: "Omnēs rēs prō certō possidēbam."

4. Fortūna dīcit: "Omnia in vītā hominum semper mūtantur."

5. Fortūna quoque dīcit: "Hominēs vīvunt sīcut in magnā rotā."

▶ EXERCISE 5

Fill in the blanks with the correct perfect passive or future active participle of the verbs in parentheses. Make the participle agree with the noun in case, number, and gender. Translate the sentences.

Example: Faciēs _____ Hūnōrum sunt terribilēs. (vulnerō)

           Hūnī, Hūnōrum, *m. pl.* – Huns

Faciēs vulnerātae Hūnōrum sunt terribilēs.   The wounded faces of the Huns are terrible.

1. Hūnī _____ terribilēs vidērī cupiunt. (pugnō)

2. Hūnī vestīmenta ex animālium pellibus _____ gerunt. (faciō)

3. Hūnī carnem nōn _____, sed _____ comedere solent. (coquō, terō)

4. Eī nōn sōlum carnem, sed etiam herbās ex terrā _____ capiunt. (ēripiō)

5. Hūnī _____ in equīs suīs sedent. (dormiō)

▶ EXERCISE 6

Translate into Latin.

1. Augustine was blamed. For many bad things had been done by him.

   Augustīnus, Augustīnī, *m.* – Augustine

2. The tree was sought by Augustine and by his friends. Plans had been made by them about a theft.

3. All the fruits had been taken from the tree. Not many of them, however, were eaten by the thieves.

4. After Augustine is accused of theft, he will be suffering. (use the future perfect in the subordinate clause)

5. If the injustice is understood by Augustine, he will want to be punished. (use the future perfect in the subordinate clause)

Augustine wearing the headdress (miter), the cape (cope), and
the ring and holding the staff (crozier) of his bishopry.

CONSIDERING THE CLASSICAL GODS

VULCAN

The last god in the Olympian pantheon is Vulcan, known in Greek as Hephaestus. He is the son of Jupiter and Juno, although according to one myth Juno produced Vulcan without a male partner, owing to her jealousy of Jupiter for giving birth to Minerva from his head. However, Vulcan had the unfortunate physical imperfection of being lame in both feet. Upon seeing her newborn offspring, Juno, ashamed at his deformity, cast him out of heaven. Vulcan later took revenge on his mean-spirited mother by fashioning for her a special golden chair from which she could not move when she sat in it. Then he departed from Olympus, refusing to release Juno until Bacchus, god of wine, made him drunk, which caused Vulcan to return. In another ancient source, Vulcan's lameness is explained as the result of his interference in a quarrel between Jupiter and Juno. Jupiter, in a fit of rage, is said to have grasped Vulcan by the ankle and flung him down to earth.

Vulcan is also a blacksmith, and in that capacity was portrayed as making Jupiter's thunderbolts. He is the god of fire as well, and of the arts in which fire is employed. He is a highly skilled craftsman in spite of his physical handicap, and is noted for creating legendary

A modern statue of Vulcan overlooking Birmingham, Alabama.

391

works of art, such as the shields of the Greek hero Achilles and the Roman hero Aeneas. Special honor was paid to Vulcan on the Greek island of Lemnos, where he was supposed to have landed after being tossed out of heaven; the words "volcano" and "volcanic" are derived from Vulcan's Latin name.

You have now completed all the mythology readings about the pantheon of the gods and goddesses. In ancient Rome, there was a temple built to all the gods, called the Pantheon.

The Doric-style Temple of Hephaestus, once known as the Theseion, was constructed in the fifth century BCE and overlooks the agora in Athens.

The original Pantheon, a temple to all the gods, was built by Agrippa in 27 BCE after the victory at the battle of Actium in 31 BCE. Burned in the great fire of Rome, the Pantheon was rebuilt in 125 CE during the reign of the emperor Hadrian.

The Romans were known for their use of domes in architecture. The interior dome of the Pantheon features a hole, twenty-nine feet in diameter, in the roof, called the *oculus* or "eye."

READ AND TRANSLATE THE FOLLOWING PASSAGE

You have read about Aeneas in Chapter 11.

Aenēās diū per multās terrās magnā cōnstantiā errāverat et per multa maria nāvigāverat. Multae rēs ab eō erant vīsae atque factae. Terrae aliēnae perīculōrum plēnae ab eō erant petītae. Dīdō rēgīna ab eō erat amāta et posteā relicta. Tandem Aenēās in Italiā prope patriam futūram erat. Ibi hostēs terribilēs eum exspectābant. Cum iīs pugnātūrus Aenēās armīs egēbat. Eius māter Venus Vulcānum petīvit et rogāvit: "Poterisne scūtum prō filiō meō parāre?" Venus dīxit Aenēam esse hostēs victūrum et post Aenēam Rōmānōs magnam glōriam habitūrōs esse. Dīxit Vulcānum haec omnia in scūtō caelāre dēbēre. Vulcānus novum scūtum excūdit, quō armātus Aenēās in proelium intrāvit et hostēs vīcit.

Aenēās, Aenēae, *m.* – Aeneas
caelō, caelāre, caelāvī, caelātum – to engrave
Dīdō, Dīdōnis, *f.* – Dido
excūdō, excūdere, excūdī, excūsum – to forge
glōria, glōriae, *f.* – glory

Italia, Italiae, *f.* – Italy
scūtum, scūtī, *n.* – shield
Venus, Veneris, *f.* – Venus
Vulcānus, Vulcānī, *m.* – Vulcan

ROMAN EDUCATION

During the early Republic, Roman fathers taught their sons to read and write, while the education of girls was limited to spinning and weaving. But in later periods Roman parents of means entrusted the education of their children to slaves of Greek origin, known as *paedagōgoi,* "leaders of the children," and private tutors with special expertise in literature and rhetoric, usually slaves or freed slaves. While girls did not attend school outside the home, they often benefited from the presence of learned tutors in their households, and there is much evidence that Roman women were readers and writers.

A Roman primary school was called the *lūdus litterārius.* Children from elite backgrounds (sons of equestrians and senators) attended school. However, Horace's father, a freedman, had his son educated at Rome rather than at a local school. Pupils usually wrote on wax tablets, using the back of the pen to smooth the wax when they made an error they wished to erase. From this practice came the proverb *Saepe stilum vertās,* "Turn the pen often," an admonition to revise one's writings frequently. Only capital letters were used. The pace of learning was fairly slow. Teachers were allowed to inflict corporal punishment if pupils misbehaved. The first century CE Roman poet Martial complained about the classroom noise that resulted from shouting and beatings.

Boys attended Roman middle schools, or *schola grammaticī,* from the age of twelve on, where the program of study focused on Latin and Greek grammar and literature. At this level students read aloud and recited passages previously learned by heart, and also listened to the meticulous explanations of the text they were reading by the teacher, called a *grammaticus.* Enunciation was stressed because of the importance of oratory in Roman public life.

From the second to third century CE, this relief on a stele shows a student, with appropriate hand gesture, addressing his teacher.

The upper school was known as a *schola rhētoris*, and there, from age fifteen on, students concentrated on studying rhetoric from skilled experts, the rhetors. They were instructed in how to compose and arrange the six parts of a public speech: the *exordium*, beginning; *nārrātiō*, the statement of facts; *partītiō*, the outline; *cōnfirmātiō*, the proof; *refūtātiō*, the refutation; and the *perōrātiō*, summing up, or conclusion. Teachers in schools of rhetoric also gave the students exercises in writing *chrīae*, sentences proposed for grammatical and logical development in different ways. Students often were assigned to present imaginary cases, and write speeches defending both sides of a given case.

For further education especially talented and ambitious Roman males, such as Cicero, traveled to Greece, listened to the illustrious rhetoricians there, and visited the libraries, *bibliothēcae*. The most famous library in the classical world was that of Alexandria in Egypt. Built in the third century BCE, it was burned during the later part of classical antiquity. There were several libraries in Athens, as well as one on the island of Rhodes, located at the school attended by Cicero. Libraries at Rome were at first private collections, but in the latter part of the first century BCE the first public library was established on the Aventine Hill.

The facade of the library of Tiberius Julius Celsus in Ephesus.

EXPLORING ROMAN LIBRARIES

PUBLIC LIBRARIES AND THEIR BOOKS

Formal education in the Roman world had three stages: a teacher called a *magister* or *litterātor* taught the basics of reading, writing, and mathematics; the *grammaticus* taught language and literature, especially poetry; and in the final stage (the most important for those destined for or aspiring to a public career in the courts and politics) a *rhētor* supervised training in public speaking.

Before the late first century BCE, those at Rome who desired "further education" through reading had two resources available to them: booksellers' shops (which seem to have offered mostly "school books," that is, those texts most used by schoolmasters, like Vergil's *Aeneid*, and "best sellers," like elegiac poetry) and friends with book collections. Some wealthy aristocrats owned huge libraries: Sulla took "the library of Aristotle" from the conquered city of Athens in 84 BCE, and Lucullus, who became notorious for a life of luxurious retirement from political activity, used his library to attract Greek scholars to his household. The orator and author Cicero mentions a library in at least three of his residences: the *domus* on the Palatine in Rome, the country villa at Tusculum, and the seaside house at Antium. As in other areas of life, the Romans adopted the Greek name for an institution associated with Greek culture: the Greek word *bibliotheke* became the Latin *bibliothēca*.

Julius Caesar planned many improvements for the city of Rome, including "making public the largest possible Greek and Latin libraries," according to his biographer Suetonius (who was himself in charge of Rome's public libraries). Caesar may have hoped that his library would surpass the famous library at Alexandria in Egypt, established by the Macedonian dynasty of the Ptolemies in an effort to preserve all of Greek literature; at the least, Caesar's library would have put Latin literature on an equal basis with Greek literature.

Julius Caesar did not live to see the fulfillment of his plans for a "public library," but Asinius Pollio, one of Caesar's closest lieutenants, established a library between 39 and 28 BCE in the Ātrium Libertātis, a public building on the slopes of the Capitoline Hill that had previously housed a shrine of the goddess Liberty and the records of the censors. Rome soon had two more libraries, both associated with the building program of the emperor Augustus: one in the porticoes attached to the temple of Apollo, next to the emperor's house on the Palatine Hill, and another in the Porticus of Octavia in the Campus Martius. Subsequent emperors built more public libraries, including the library in the Temple of Peace built by Vespasian and the library in the Forum of Trajan.

The builders of Rome's public libraries, and the authors whose works would be in them, expected at least some members of the public to enter them. Horace and Ovid anticipated readers of their poetry in Rome's first public libraries. When an ancient author mentions by name specific users of Rome's libraries, however, they are either writers or scholars, or connected to the emperor's family, or both. Readers seem to have treated Rome's public libraries during the Empire just as readers had treated private libraries in aristocrats' homes during the Republic, as private spaces where scholars and friends gathered to discuss literature and philosophy.

The Forum of Trajan provides the best evidence available for the appearance of Rome's public libraries. Two rooms, one to either side of the courtyard around the Column of Trajan, show the plan considered characteristic of Roman libraries: wall-niches into which book cabinets were set, columns separating the niches, a low platform running around the base of the wall giving access to the book cabinets, unobstructed floor space where readers might sit, marble and other colored stone covering walls and floors, and separate rooms for the Latin and Greek collections. Libraries were decorated with large numbers of statues, portrait busts, or both, especially of authors.

Perhaps inspired by the example of the emperors in Rome, some aristocrats donated magnificent libraries to their home towns: the orator and administrator Pliny the Younger dedicated a library in Comum in northern Italy, and the consul Tiberius Julius Aquila dedicated a library to his father, the consul Tiberius Julius Celsus, in Ephesus in the province of Asia. In the interior of the library of Celsus, at the middle of the back wall, was an apse; beneath the apse lay a chamber, accessible from a passage that separated the

Trajan's libraries flanked the Column of Trajan—key components of the Forum of Trajan. Note the Renaissance period addition of a statue of St. Peter atop the column.

A close-up view of the facade of the library of Tiberius Julius Celsus in Ephesus.

inner and outer walls of the library building. This chamber held a marble sarcophagus containing a lead coffin, apparently that of Celsus. He seems to have achieved the rare privilege of burial within a city; and the library named after him served also as his tomb monument.

Some believe that the great imperial bath buildings or *thermae* of Rome included libraries, which we might take as evidence for a wide reading audience in Rome. The baths of Trajan, Caracalla, and Diocletian all contain rooms identified as libraries on the basis of their architectural form, particularly the presence of wall-niches in paired rooms. The presence of libraries fits with the general idea that the *thermae* provided facilities not only for bathing but for a wide range of athletic, social, and cultural activities. The evidence for libraries in bathing complexes, however, is weak. No literary evidence or inscription clearly proves that there were ever libraries in baths; and no archaeological remains of rooms in baths can be shown definitely to have been libraries.

The standard form of "book" for the Romans was the roll; a reader needed both hands to handle a roll, one to unroll a new section for reading, the other hand to roll up the section already read. A roll might be made up of sheets of either papyrus or animal skin. For papyrus paper, two layers of strips from the plant's soft interior, at right angles to one another, were pressed together, releasing a natural gummy substance, which bonded together the strips and layers. Animal skins (of sheep, goats, or cattle) might be tanned to produce leather, or a more complicated process of washing, depilating, soaking in lime, and stretching and drying on a frame might be used to produce parchment. Dried sheets of paper were glued together, or sheets of skin were sewn together, to form a roll. Rolls were written on only one side; but once a roll was no longer in use, pages might be cut from the roll to be reused: preserved papyrus sheets from Greco-Roman Egypt often have literary texts on one side (the original side used, or "rectō") and private documents—letters, receipts, accounts—on the other (the reused or "versō"). The usual writing implement was a reed pen with a split nib, like a modern fountain pen; black ink was made from soot or lampblack mixed with gum.

One set of "library rules" survives from the Roman Empire, on an inscription from the library of Pantainos (named after the man who donated it), which sat beside a very busy corner of the Agora in Athens: it specifies the hours of operation ("from the first hour to the sixth hour") and that no book is to be removed from the library. The inscription does not say who can enter and use the library. In a world where no more than ten percent of the population may have been literate, perhaps it was unnecessary to specify who could use the library: those with the necessary education, leisure time, and desire to visit a public library were probably few in number. Roman public libraries were monuments to literature and culture, and they demonstrated that the Romans were worthy successors to the cultural heritage and achievements of the Greeks.

T. Keith Dix
Associate Professor of Classics
University of Georgia
Athens, Georgia

PHRASES, QUOTATIONS, AND ABBREVIATIONS RELATING TO SCHOOLS, LIBRARIES, AND BOOKS

PHRASES AND QUOTATIONS

- Alma māter. "Nurturing mother." Common name for a university that a person has attended.

- Alumnus/Alumna. "A nurtured <son/daughter>." Graduate of a college or a university.

- Ex librīs. "From the books," words often found on special plates inside the cover of books indicating the owner, whose name should be in the genitive case.

- Floruit. (abbreviated *fl.*) "Flourished." An indication of the time when a certain person was most active.

- Vādemēcum. "Go with me!" A small manual or reference work.

- Verbātim. "Word by word," precisely and accurately.

Ex Librīs, a Latin phrase meaning "From the books," is sometimes found on a bookplate pasted on the inside cover of a book, followed by the name of the person who owns the book.

ABBREVIATIONS

- AD. An abbreviation for *Annō Dominī*, "in the year of the Lord," an older expression for CE, "Common Era."

- e.g. An abbreviation for *exemplī grātiā*, "for the sake of an example or illustration."

APPENDIX A

CHRONOLOGICAL LIST OF THE AUTHORS AND WORKS STUDIED

Titus Maccius Plautus (b. Sarsina, Umbria; ca. 254 BCE–184 BCE), *Menaechmī*, "The Menaechmi."

Publius Terentius Afer (b. Libya; between 195 and 185 BCE–ca. 159 BCE), *Adelphoi*, "The Brothers."

Mārcus Tullius Cicero (b. Arpinum, southeast of Rome; 106 BCE–43 BCE), *Dē officiīs*, "On Duties"; *Epistulae*, "Letters."

Gāius Iūlius Caesar (b. Rome; 100 BCE–44 BCE), *Dē bellō Gallicō*, "On the Gallic War."

Gāius Valerius Catullus (b. Verona; ca. 84 BCE–ca. 54 BCE), *Carmina*, "Poems."

Cornēlius Nepos (b. northern Italy; ca. 100 BCE–ca. 25 BCE), *Dē virīs illustribus*, "On Famous Men."

Gāius Sallustius Crispus (b. Aminternum, near Rome; 86 BCE–35/34 BCE), *Dē coniūrātiōne Catilīnae*, "About the Plot of Catiline."

Publius Vergilius Maro (b. Mantua; 70 BCE–19 BCE), *Aeneīs*, "Aeneid."

Titus Līvius (b. Padua; 59 BCE–17 CE), *Ab Urbe Conditā*, "From the Founding of the City."

Quīntus Horātius Flaccus (b. Venusia, southern Italy; 65 BCE–8 BCE), *Saturae*, "Satires."

Publius Ovidius Nāso (b. Sulmo, Italian Apennines; 43 BCE–17 CE), *Metamorphōsēs*, "Transformations."

Lūcius Annaeus Seneca (b. Corduba, Spain; ca. 4 BCE–65 CE), *Epistulae*, "Letters."

Gāius Plīnius Caecilius Secundus (b. Como, northern Italy; ca. 61 CE–ca. 112/113 CE), *Epistulae*, "Letters."

Cornēlius Tacitus (b. probably northern Italy; ca. 56 CE–116/120 CE), *Annālēs*, "Annals."

Āpulēius (b. Madaurus, North Africa; second century CE), *Metamorphōsēs*, "Transformations."

Ammiānus Marcellīnus (b. probably Antioch, Syria; ca. 330–395 CE), *Rēs gestae ā fīne Cornēliī Tacitī*, "Deeds Accomplished from the End of Cornelius Tacitus's History."

Aurēlius Augustīnus (b. Tagaste, North Africa; 354 CE–430 CE), *Cōnfessiōnēs*, "Confessions."

Anicius Manlius Sevērīnus Boēthius (b. Rome; ca. 480 CE–ca. 524 CE), *Cōnsōlātiō Philosophiae*, "Consolation of Philosophy."

APPENDIX B

ADDITIONAL STATE MOTTOES

Ad astra per aspera. "To the stars through difficulties!" Motto of Kansas

Alīs volat propriīs. "Flies with own wings." Motto of Oregon

Cēdant arma togae. "Let arms yield to the toga." Motto of Wyoming

Crēscit eundō. "It grows by going." Motto of New Mexico

Deō grātiās habeāmus. "Let us be grateful to God." Motto of Kentucky

Dīrigō. "I direct." Motto of Maine

Dītat Deus. "God enriches." Motto of Arizona

Dum spīrō spērō. "As long as I breathe, I hope." Motto of South Carolina

Esse quam vidērī. "To be rather than to seem." Motto of North Carolina

Estō perpetua! "Be eternal!" Motto of Idaho

Excelsior. "Ever upward." Motto of New York

Labor omnia vincit. "Work overcomes all things." Motto of Oklahoma

Nīl sine nūmine. "Nothing without divine will." Motto of Colorado

State seal of Arizona with the Latin phrase *Dītat Deus.*

Quae sūrsum volō vidēre. "I want to see the things that are above." Motto of Minnesota

Quī transtulit sustinet. "He who has transplanted sustains." Motto of Connecticut

Sī quaeris paenīnsulam amoenam, circumspice! "If you are seeking a lovely peninsula, look around!" Motto of Michigan

Virtūte et armīs. "With courage and with weapons." Motto of Mississippi

HISTORICAL TIMELINE

Authors and Literary Periods		Roman History and Legend
	ca. 1183 BCE	Fall of Troy
	753 BCE	Founding of Rome by Romulus and Remus
	753–509 BCE	**Monarchy**
Earliest Latin inscriptions	ca. 600 BCE	
Early Latin Literature	late sixth century–84 BCE	Mucius Scaevola attempted assassination of Porsenna
	509–31 BCE	**Roman Republic**
	480 BCE	Battle of Thermopylae
Laws of the Twelve Tables	451–450 BCE	Creation of the Twelve Tables law code
	390s–380s BCE	Gallic invasions of Rome [throughout the fourth century]
	312 BCE	Construction of the Via Appia by Appius Claudius Caecus
Livius Andronicus	284–204 BCE	
	280–279 BCE	Pyrrhus of Epirus invades Italy
	264–241 BCE	First Punic War
Plautus	254–184 BCE	
Ennius	239–169 BCE	
Cato the Elder	234–149 BCE	
	218–202 BCE	Hannibal invades Italy; Second Punic War
Terence	195 or 185–ca. 159 BCE	
	149–146 BCE	Third Punic War; destruction of Carthage
	133, 123–122 BCE	Tribunates of Tiberius and Gaius Gracchi
Cicero	106–43 BCE	
Caesar	100–44 BCE	
Cornelius Nepos	ca. 100–ca. 25 BCE	
	89 BCE	Conflict between Marius and Sulla: First Civil War

Sallust	86–35/34 BCE	
Catullus	84–54 BCE	
Golden Age Literature	83 BCE–17 CE	
	82–80 BCE	Sulla's dictatorship
	73–71 BCE	Spartacus and Slave Revolt
Vergil	70–19 BCE	
Maecenas	70–8 BCE	
Horace	65–8 BCE	
	63 BCE	Catiline conspiracy
	63/62 BCE	Pompeii earthquake
	59 BCE	First Triumvirate formed: Caesar, Crassus, Pompey
Livy	ca. 59 BCE–17 CE	
	58–51 BCE	Caesar's conquest of Gaul
Tibullus	ca. 54–19 BCE	
Propertius	ca. 50–15 BCE	
	49 BCE	Caesar crosses the Rubicon: Second Civil War
	44 BCE (March 15th)	Caesar's assassination
	43 BCE	Second Triumvirate formed: Antony, Lepidus, Octavian
Ovid	43 BCE–17 CE	
	42 BCE	Defeat of Brutus and Cassius at Philippi: Third Civil War
	39–28 BCE	Asinius Pollio builds a library on slopes of Capitoline
	31 BCE	Defeat of Antony and Cleopatra at the Battle of Actium
	31 BCE–180 CE	**Early Roman Empire**
	27 BCE–14 CE	Augustus
	27 BCE	Octavian assumes the name Augustus
	27 BCE	Agrippa builds Pantheon
	14–37 CE	Tiberius
Silver Age Literature	17–150 CE	
Petronius	first century CE	
Seneca	ca. 4 BCE–65 CE	
Pliny the Elder	ca. 23/24–79 CE	
Frontinus	ca. 30–104 CE	
	37–41 CE	Caligula
Martial	ca. 40–102 CE	

	41–54 CE	Claudius
	54–68 CE	Nero
Tacitus	ca. 56–116/120 CE	
Juvenal	ca. 60–ca. 140 CE	
Pliny the Younger	ca. 61–ca. 112 CE	
	63 CE	Earthquake in Pompeii
	64 CE (July 19th)	Great Fire in Rome
	69–79 CE	Vespasian
Suetonius	ca. 69–ca. 140 CE	
	79–81 CE	Titus
	79 CE (August 24th)	Eruption of Vesuvius
	80 CE	Colosseum is dedicated in Rome
	81–96 CE	Domitian
	96–109 CE	Nerva
	98–117 CE	Trajan
	112 CE	Forum of Trajan, column dedicated
	117–138 CE	Hadrian
Hyginus	second century CE	
	125 CE	Hadrian rebuilds Pantheon
Apuleius	second century CE	
	135 CE	Library of Celsus is completed in Ephesus
	138–161 CE	Antoninus Pius
Late Latin Literature	150–400 CE	
	161–180 CE	Marcus Aurelius
	180–476 CE	**Late Roman Empire**
	180–192 CE	Commodus
	193–211 CE	Septimius Severus
	211 CE	Geta
	211–217 CE	Caracalla
	222–235 CE	Severus Alexander
	235–284 CE	The "Military" emperors
Dio Cassius	early second century CE, late third century CE	
	284–305 CE	Diocletian
	293 CE	Instituting the Tetrarchy
	312–337 CE	Constantine
	313 CE	Edict of Milan, toleration of Christianity

	330 CE	Establishment of Constantinople as Capital of the Empire
Ammianus Marcellinus	ca. 330–395 CE	
Augustine	354–430 CE	
	361–363 CE	Julian
	386 CE	Augustine's conversion
	395 CE	Division of the Empire upon death of Theodosius I
Quintus Smyrnaeus	fourth century CE	
Medieval Latin Literature	400–ca. 1400 CE	
	410 CE	Alaric and Visigoths sack Rome
	434–451 CE	Attila the Hun's rule
	455 CE	Vandals sack Rome
	476–ca. 1400 CE	**Medieval Era**
	476 CE	Traditional date of the fall of the Roman Empire
	476 CE	Romulus Augustulus, last Roman emperor, is deposed by Odoacer
Boethius	ca. 480–ca. 524 CE	
	493 CE	Theodoric (the Ostrogoth) assumes control over Italy
	527–565 CE	Justinian
	528–534 CE	Law Code of Justinian
	1453 CE	Fall of Constantinople and the Eastern Roman Empire to the Ottoman Turks

GRAMMATICAL FORMS AND PARADIGMS

Only forms taught in the book are listed in this appendix.

DECLENSIONS OF NOUNS

First Declension

	Singular	Plural
Nominative	lupa	lupae
Genitive	lupae	lupārum
Dative	lupae	lupīs
Accusative	lupam	lupās
Ablative	lupā	lupīs
Vocative	lupa	lupae

Second Declension: *amīcus*

	Singular	Plural
Nominative	amīcus	amīcī
Genitive	amīcī	amīcōrum
Dative	amīcō	amīcīs
Accusative	amīcum	amīcōs
Ablative	amīcō	amīcīs
Vocative	amīce	amīcī

Second Declension: *puer*

	Singular	Plural
Nominative	puer	puerī
Genitive	puerī	puerōrum
Dative	puerō	puerīs
Accusative	puerum	puerōs
Ablative	puerō	puerīs
Vocative	puer	puerī

Second Declension: *ager*

	Singular	Plural
Nominative	ager	agrī
Genitive	agrī	agrōrum
Dative	agrō	agrīs
Accusative	agrum	agrōs
Ablative	agrō	agrīs
Vocative	ager	agrī

Second Declension: *vir*

	Singular	Plural
Nominative	vir	virī
Genitive	virī	virōrum
Dative	virō	virīs
Accusative	virum	virōs
Ablative	virō	virīs
Vocative	vir	virī

Second Declension: *bellum*

	Singular	Plural
Nominative	bellum	bella
Genitive	bellī	bellōrum
Dative	bellō	bellīs
Accusative	bellum	bella
Ablative	bellō	bellīs
Vocative	bellum	bella

Third Declension:
Masculine and Feminine Nouns

	Singular	Plural
Nominative	passer	passerēs
Genitive	passeris	passerum
Dative	passerī	passeribus
Accusative	passerem	passerēs
Ablative	passere	passeribus
Vocative	passer	passerēs

Third Declension: Neuter Nouns

	Singular	Plural
Nominative	tempus	tempora
Genitive	temporis	temporum
Dative	temporī	temporibus
Accusative	tempus	tempora
Ablative	tempore	temporibus
Vocative	tempus	tempora

Third Declension: *i*–stem Nouns
Same Number of Syllables (Masculine and Feminine)

	Singular	Plural
Nominative	cīvis	cīvēs
Genitive	cīvis	cīvium
Dative	cīvī	cīvibus
Accusative	cīvem	cīvēs
Ablative	cīve	cīvibus
Vocative	cīvis	cīvēs

Third Declension: *i*–stem Nouns
Different Number of Syllables (Masculine and Feminine)

	Singular	Plural
Nominative	urbs	urbēs
Genitive	urbis	urbium
Dative	urbī	urbibus
Accusative	urbem	urbēs
Ablative	urbe	urbibus
Vocative	urbs	urbēs

Third Declension: *i*–stem Nouns
(Neuters in *–al, –ar, –e*)

	Singular	Plural
Nominative	mare	maria
Genitive	maris	marium
Dative	marī	maribus
Accusative	mare	maria
Ablative	marī	maribus
Vocative	mare	maria

Third Declension: *vīs*

	Singular	Plural
Nominative	vīs	vīrēs
Genitive	—	vīrium
Dative	—	vīribus
Accusative	vim	vīrēs
Ablative	vī	vīribus
Vocative	vīs	vīrēs

Fourth Declension: Masculine and Feminine Nouns

	Singular	Plural
Nominative	tumultus	tumultūs
Genitive	tumultūs	tumultuum
Dative	tumultuī	tumultibus
Accusative	tumultum	tumultūs
Ablative	tumultū	tumultibus
Vocative	tumultus	tumultūs

Fourth Declension: Neuter Nouns

	Singular	Plural
Nominative	cornū	cornua
Genitive	cornūs	cornuum
Dative	cornū	cornibus
Accusative	cornū	cornua
Ablative	cornū	cornibus
Vocative	cornū	cornua

Fourth Declension: *domus*

	Singular	Plural
Nominative	domus	domūs
Genitive	domūs	domuum (domōrum)
Dative	domuī (domō)	domibus
Accusative	domum	domōs (domūs)
Ablative	domō (domū)	domibus
Vocative	domus	domūs

Fifth Declension: *rēs*

	Singular	Plural
Nominative	rēs	rēs
Genitive	reī	rērum
Dative	reī	rēbus
Accusative	rem	rēs
Ablative	rē	rēbus
Vocative	rēs	rēs

Fifth Declension: *diēs*

	Singular	Plural
Nominative	diēs	diēs
Genitive	diēī	diērum
Dative	diēī	diēbus
Accusative	diem	diēs
Ablative	diē	diēbus
Vocative	diēs	diēs

DECLENSIONS OF ADJECTIVES

Adjectives of the First and Second Declension: *iūstus*

	Singular			Plural		
	Masculine	**Feminine**	**Neuter**	**Masculine**	**Feminine**	**Neuter**
Nominative	iūstus	iūsta	iūstum	iūstī	iūstae	iūsta
Genitive	iūstī	iūstae	iūstī	iūstōrum	iūstārum	iūstōrum
Dative	iūstō	iūstae	iūstō	iūstīs	iūstīs	iūstīs
Accusative	iūstum	iūstam	iūstum	iūstōs	iūstās	iūsta
Ablative	iūstō	iūstā	iūstō	iūstīs	iūstīs	iūstīs
Vocative	iūste	iūsta	iūstum	iūstī	iūstae	iūsta

Adjectives of the First and Second Declension: *pulcher*

	Singular			Plural		
	Masculine	**Feminine**	**Neuter**	**Masculine**	**Feminine**	**Neuter**
Nominative	pulcher	pulchra	pulchrum	pulchrī	pulchrae	pulchra
Genitive	pulchrī	pulchrae	pulchrī	pulchrōrum	pulchrārum	pulchrōrum
Dative	pulchrō	pulchrae	pulchrō	pulchrīs	pulchrīs	pulchrīs
Accusative	pulchrum	pulchram	pulchrum	pulchrōs	pulchrās	pulchra
Ablative	pulchrō	pulchrā	pulchrō	pulchrīs	pulchrīs	pulchrīs
Vocative	pulcher	pulchra	pulchrum	pulchrī	pulchrae	pulchra

Adjectives of the First and Second Declension: *miser*

	Singular			Plural		
	Masculine	Feminine	Neuter	Masculine	Feminine	Neuter
Nominative	miser	misera	miserum	miserī	miserae	misera
Genitive	miserī	miserae	miserī	miserōrum	miserārum	miserōrum
Dative	miserō	miserae	miserō	miserīs	miserīs	miserīs
Accusative	miserum	miseram	miserum	miserōs	miserās	misera
Ablative	miserō	miserā	miserō	miserīs	miserīs	miserīs
Vocative	miser	misera	miserum	miserī	miserae	misera

Adjectives of the Third Declension: Three Nominative Endings

	Singular			Plural		
	Masculine	Feminine	Neuter	Masculine	Feminine	Neuter
Nominative	ācer	ācris	ācre	ācrēs	ācrēs	ācria
Genitive	ācris	ācris	ācris	ācrium	ācrium	ācrium
Dative	ācrī	ācrī	ācrī	ācribus	ācribus	ācribus
Accusative	ācrem	ācrem	ācre	ācrēs	ācrēs	ācria
Ablative	ācrī	ācrī	ācrī	ācribus	ācribus	ācribus
Vocative	ācer	ācris	ācre	ācrēs	ācrēs	ācria

Adjectives of the Third Declension: Two Nominative Endings

	Singular		Plural	
	Masculine / Feminine	Neuter	Masculine / Feminine	Neuter
Nominative	fortis	forte	fortēs	fortia
Genitive	fortis	fortis	fortium	fortium
Dative	fortī	fortī	fortibus	fortibus
Accusative	fortem	forte	fortēs	fortia
Ablative	fortī	fortī	fortibus	fortibus
Vocative	fortis	forte	fortēs	fortia

Adjectives of the Third Declension: One Nominative Ending

	Singular			Plural		
	Masculine	Feminine	Neuter	Masculine	Feminine	Neuter
Nominative	fēlīx	fēlīx	fēlīx	fēlīcēs	fēlīcēs	fēlīcia
Genitive	fēlīcis	fēlīcis	fēlīcis	fēlīcium	fēlīcium	fēlīcium
Dative	fēlīcī	fēlīcī	fēlīcī	fēlīcibus	fēlīcibus	fēlīcibus
Accusative	fēlīcem	fēlīcem	fēlīx	fēlīcēs	fēlīcēs	fēlīcia
Ablative	fēlīcī	fēlīcī	fēlīcī	fēlīcibus	fēlīcibus	fēlīcibus
Vocative	fēlīx	fēlīx	fēlīx	fēlīcēs	fēlīcēs	fēlīcia

DECLENSIONS OF PRONOUNS

Personal Pronouns: First and Second Person

	First singular	Second singular	First plural	Second plural
Nominative	ego	tū	nōs	vōs
Genitive	meī	tuī	nostrī/nostrum	vestrī/vestrum
Dative	mihi	tibi	nōbīs	vōbīs
Accusative	mē	tē	nōs	vōs
Ablative	mē	tē	nōbīs	vōbīs

Personal Pronoun: Third Person; Demonstrative Pronoun/Adjective: *is, ea, id*

	Singular			Plural		
	Masculine	Feminine	Neuter	Masculine	Feminine	Neuter
Nominative	is	ea	id	eī (iī)	eae	ea
Genitive	eius	eius	eius	eōrum	eārum	eōrum
Dative	eī	eī	eī	eīs (iīs)	eīs (iīs)	eīs (iīs)
Accusative	eum	eam	id	eōs	eās	ea
Ablative	eō	eā	eō	eīs (iīs)	eīs (iīs)	eīs (iīs)

Possessive Adjectives

First person singular	meus, mea, meum
Second person singular	tuus, tua, tuum
Third person singular	suus, sua, suum / eius
First person plural	noster, nostra, nostrum
Second person plural	vester, vestra, vestrum
Third person plural	suus, sua, suum / eōrum, eārum, eōrum

Relative Pronoun and Interrogative Adjective: *quī, quae, quod*

	Singular			Plural		
	Masculine	Feminine	Neuter	Masculine	Feminine	Neuter
Nominative	quī	quae	quod	quī	quae	quae
Genitive	cūius	cūius	cūius	quōrum	quārum	quōrum
Dative	cui	cui	cui	quibus	quibus	quibus
Accusative	quem	quam	quod	quōs	quās	quae
Ablative	quō	quā	quō	quibus	quibus	quibus

Interrogative Pronoun: *quis, quid*?

	Singular		Plural		
	Masculine / Feminine	Neuter	Masculine	Feminine	Neuter
Nominative	quis	quid	quī	quae	quae
Genitive	cūius	cūius	quōrum	quārum	quōrum
Dative	cui	cui	quibus	quibus	quibus
Accusative	quem	quid	quōs	quās	quae
Ablative	quō	quō	quibus	quibus	quibus

Interrogative Adjective: *quī, quae, quod*?

	Singular			Plural		
	Masculine	Feminine	Neuter	Masculine	Feminine	Neuter
Nominative	quī	quae	quod	quī	quae	quae
Genitive	cūius	cūius	cūius	quōrum	quārum	quōrum
Dative	cui	cui	cui	quibus	quibus	quibus
Accusative	quem	quam	quod	quōs	quās	quae
Ablative	quō	quā	quō	quibus	quibus	quibus

Demonstrative Pronoun/Adjective: *hic, haec, hoc*

	Singular			Plural		
	Masculine	Feminine	Neuter	Masculine	Feminine	Neuter
Nominative	hic	haec	hoc	hī	hae	haec
Genitive	huius	huius	huius	hōrum	hārum	hōrum
Dative	huic	huic	huic	hīs	hīs	hīs
Accusative	hunc	hanc	hoc	hōs	hās	haec
Ablative	hōc	hāc	hōc	hīs	hīs	hīs

Demonstrative Pronoun/Adjective: *ille, illa, illud*

	Singular			Plural		
	Masculine	Feminine	Neuter	Masculine	Feminine	Neuter
Nominative	ille	illa	illud	illī	illae	illa
Genitive	illīus	illīus	illīus	illōrum	illārum	illōrum
Dative	illī	illī	illī	illīs	illīs	illīs
Accusative	illum	illam	illud	illōs	illās	illa
Ablative	illō	illā	illō	illīs	illīs	illīs

CONJUGATIONS OF VERBS

Present Active

	First conjugation	Second conjugation	Third conjugation	Fourth conjugation	Third conjugation –iō
First person singular	parō	teneō	petō	audiō	capiō
Second person singular	parās	tenēs	petis	audīs	capis
Third person singular	parat	tenet	petit	audit	capit
First person plural	parāmus	tenēmus	petimus	audīmus	capimus
Second person plural	parātis	tenētis	petitis	audītis	capitis
Third person plural	parant	tenent	petunt	audiunt	capiunt

Present Passive

	First conjugation	Second conjugation	Third conjugation	Fourth conjugation	Third conjugation –iō
First person singular	paror	teneor	petor	audior	capior
Second person singular	parāris	tenēris	peteris	audīris	caperis
Third person singular	parātur	tenētur	petitur	audītur	capitur
First person plural	parāmur	tenēmur	petimur	audīmur	capimur
Second person plural	parāminī	tenēminī	petiminī	audīminī	capiminī
Third person plural	parantur	tenentur	petuntur	audiuntur	capiuntur

Imperfect Active

	First conjugation	Second conjugation	Third conjugation	Fourth conjugation	Third conjugation –iō
First person singular	parābam	tenēbam	petēbam	audiēbam	capiēbam
Second person singular	parābās	tenēbās	petēbās	audiēbās	capiēbās
Third person singular	parābat	tenēbat	petēbat	audiēbat	capiēbat
First person plural	parābāmus	tenēbāmus	petēbāmus	audiēbāmus	capiēbāmus
Second person plural	parābātis	tenēbātis	petēbātis	audiēbātis	capiēbātis
Third person plural	parābant	tenēbant	petēbant	audiēbant	capiēbant

Imperfect Passive

	First conjugation	Second conjugation	Third conjugation	Fourth conjugation	Third conjugation –iō
First person singular	parābar	tenēbar	petēbar	audiēbar	capiēbar
Second person singular	parābāris	tenēbāris	petēbāris	audiēbāris	capiēbāris
Third person singular	parābātur	tenēbātur	petēbātur	audiēbātur	capiēbātur
First person plural	parābāmur	tenēbāmur	petēbāmur	audiēbāmur	capiēbāmur
Second person plural	parābāminī	tenēbāminī	petēbāminī	audiēbāminī	capiēbāminī
Third person plural	parābantur	tenēbantur	petēbantur	audiēbantur	capiēbantur

Future Active

	First conjugation	Second conjugation	Third conjugation	Fourth conjugation	Third conjugation –*iō*
First person singular	parābō	tenēbō	petam	audiam	capiam
Second person singular	parābis	tenēbis	petēs	audiēs	capiēs
Third person singular	parābit	tenēbit	petet	audiet	capiet
First person plural	parābimus	tenēbimus	petēmus	audiēmus	capiēmus
Second person plural	parābitis	tenēbitis	petētis	audiētis	capiētis
Third person plural	parābunt	tenēbunt	petent	audient	capient

Future Passive

	First conjugation	Second conjugation	Third conjugation	Fourth conjugation	Third conjugation –*iō*
First person singular	parābor	tenēbor	petar	audiar	capiar
Second person singular	parāberis	tenēberis	petēris	audiēris	capiēris
Third person singular	parābitur	tenēbitur	petētur	audiētur	capiētur
First person plural	parābimur	tenēbimur	petēmur	audiēmur	capiēmur
Second person plural	parābiminī	tenēbiminī	petēminī	audiēminī	capiēminī
Third person plural	parābuntur	tenēbuntur	petentur	audientur	capientur

Perfect Active

First person singular	parāvī
Second person singular	parāvistī
Third person singular	parāvit
First person plural	parāvimus
Second person plural	parāvistis
Third person plural	parāvērunt

Perfect Passive

First person singular	parātus, parāta, (parātum) sum
Second person singular	parātus, parāta, (parātum) es
Third person singular	parātus, parāta, parātum est
First person plural	parātī, parātae, (parāta) sumus
Second person plural	parātī, parātae, (parāta) estis
Third person plural	parātī, parātae, parāta sunt

Pluperfect Active

First person singular	parāveram
Second person singular	parāverās
Third person singular	parāverat
First person plural	parāverāmus
Second person plural	parāverātis
Third person plural	parāverant

Pluperfect Passive

First person singular	parātus, parāta, (parātum) eram
Second person singular	parātus, parāta, (parātum) erās
Third person singular	parātus, parāta, parātum erat
First person plural	parātī, parātae, (parāta) erāmus
Second person plural	parātī, parātae, (parāta) erātis
Third person plural	parātī, parātae, parāta erant

Future Perfect Active

First person singular	parāverō
Second person singular	parāveris
Third person singular	parāverit
First person plural	parāverimus
Second person plural	parāveritis
Third person plural	parāverint

Future Perfect Passive

First person singular	parātus, parāta, (parātum) erō
Second person singular	parātus, parāta, (parātum) eris
Third person singular	parātus, parāta, parātum erit
First person plural	parātī, parātae, (parāta) erimus
Second person plural	parātī, parātae, (parāta) eritis
Third person plural	parātī, parātae, parāta erunt

Present Imperative

	First conjugation	Second conjugation	Third conjugation	Fourth conjugation	Third conjugation –*iō*
Second person singular positive	parā	tenē	pete	audī	cape
Second person plural positive	parāte	tenēte	petite	audīte	capite
Second person singular negative	nōlī parāre	nōlī tenēre	nōlī petere	nōlī audīre	nōlī capere
Second person plural negative	nōlīte parāre	nōlīte tenēre	nōlīte petere	nōlīte audīre	nōlīte capere

Participles

Perfect passive	parātus, parāta, parātum
Future active	parātūrus, parātūra, parātūrum

Infinitives

	Active	Passive
Present	parāre	parārī
Perfect	parāvisse	parātus, parāta, parātum esse
Future	parātūrus, parātūra, parātūrum esse	—

The Irregular Verb *sum*

	Present	Imperfect	Future	Perfect	Pluperfect	Future perfect
First person singular	sum	eram	erō	fuī	fueram	fuerō
Second person singular	es	erās	eris	fuistī	fuerās	fueris
Third person singular	est	erat	erit	fuit	fuerat	fuerit
First person plural	sumus	erāmus	erimus	fuimus	fuerāmus	fuerimus
Second person plural	estis	erātis	eritis	fuistis	fuerātis	fueritis
Third person plural	sunt	erant	erunt	fuērunt	fuerant	fuerint
Infinitive	esse	—	futūrus, -a, -um esse	fuisse	—	—

The Irregular Verb *possum*

	Present	Imperfect	Future	Perfect	Pluperfect	Future perfect
First person singular	possum	poteram	poterō	potuī	potueram	potuerō
Second person singular	potes	poterās	poteris	potuistī	potuerās	potueris
Third person singular	potest	poterat	poterit	potuit	potuerat	potuerit
First person plural	possumus	poterāmus	poterimus	potuimus	potuerāmus	potuerimus
Second person plural	potestis	poterātis	poteritis	potuistis	potuerātis	potueritis
Third person plural	possunt	poterant	poterunt	potuērunt	potuerant	potuerint
Infinitive	posse	—	—	potuisse	—	—

LATIN SYNTAX

Only syntax taught in the book is listed in this appendix.

USE OF CASES

Case	Function
Nominative	Subject. Predicate nominative (noun or adjective).
Genitive	Modifier (often possession). Partitive genitive. Objective genitive.
Dative	Indirect object. Possession.
Accusative	Direct object. Place to which. Accusative subject of indirect statement.
Ablative	Agent (with passive voice). Manner. Instrument (means). Separation. Place from which. Place where.
Vocative	Direct address.

PREPOSITIONS

Preposition	Case	Meaning
ā, ab	ablative	by, from, away from
ad	accusative	toward, to, into
ante	accusative	in front of
apud	accusative	at the house of
circum	accusative	around
contrā	accusative	against
cum	ablative	with
dē	ablative	about, concerning, down from, from
ē, ex	ablative	from, out of
in	ablative	in, on
in	accusative	into, to
inter	accusative	between, among
per	accusative	through
post	accusative	after
prō	ablative	for, on behalf of
prope	accusative	near
propter	accusative	because of
sine	ablative	without

CONJUNCTIONS

Conjuction	Meaning
atque	and
autem	however
cum	when, after
dum	while
enim	for, in fact
et	and
igitur	therefore
itaque	and so
nam	for, in fact
nec	and not, nor
nōn sōlum . . . , sed etiam . . .	not only . . . , but also . . .
postquam	after
-que	and
sed	but
sī	if
tamen	however

INTERROGATIVE WORDS

Interrogative Word	Meaning
cūr?	why?
-ne?	interrogative particle
quī? quae? quod?	which? what?
quis? quid?	who? what?

SUBJECT-VERB AGREEMENT

The subject agrees with the verb in number.

Puer currit.   The boy is running.

The predicate nominative agrees with the subject in case and number. Predicate adjectives also agree with the subject in gender.

Vīta est gaudium.   Life is joy.

Praemium est magnum.   The prize is great.

NOUN-ADJECTIVE AGREEMENT

The adjective agrees with the noun in case, number, and gender.

Ōrātiōnem longam audīvī.   I heard a long speech.

Librum celebrem legō.   I am reading a renowned book.

FUNCTIONS OF THE INFINITIVE

1. Complementary with *dēbeō, possum, soleō.*

    The infinitive can complete the meaning of these verbs. Example: in the sentence *legere dēbeō,* which means "I ought to read," the infinitive completes the meaning of "I ought."

2. Indirect statement after verbs of saying and thinking.

    In English, a subordinate statement after a verb of saying or thinking begins with the conjunction "that." In classical Latin no such conjunction is used; instead the subordinate statement expresses its subject as an accusative and its verb as an infinitive, making the subordinate indirect statement a kind of object for the verb of saying or thinking. Consider the English sentence, "I think that the book is good." In Latin the same sentence, *Putō librum esse bonum,* expresses the subject of the indirect statement in the accusative case (*librum*) and the verb of the indirect statement as an infinitive (*esse*).

3. Nominative and infinitive.

    In Latin the accusative and infinitive construction noted above is typically not used with a passive verb of saying or thinking. Instead, the subject of the indirect statement is also the subject of the verb of saying or thinking, and so appears in the nominative case (along with any predicate nouns or adjectives). The verb of the indirect statement is still expressed as an infinitive. In this case, Latin is much closer to English. Consider the English sentence, "The book is thought to be good." In Latin the same sentence, *Liber bonus esse putātur,* expresses the subject and its predicate in the nominative case (*Liber bonus*) while the verb of the indirect statement is expressed as an infinitive (*esse*).

TENSES OF THE INFINITIVE IN THE INDIRECT STATEMENT

In Latin, when the verb of an indirect statement is represented by an infinitive, the tense of that infinitive expresses time **relative to the main verb**. This is not the same as in English, where the tense of the verb within an indirect statement is not always relative to its main verb.

Infinitive	Time in relation to main verb	Example
Present Infinitive	SAME	***Putō** multōs hominēs librum **legere.*** = I **think** that many people **are reading** the book. ***Putābam** multōs hominēs librum **legere.*** = I **used to think** that many people **were reading** the book.
Perfect Infinitive	BEFORE	***Putō** multōs hominēs librum **lēgisse.*** = I **think** that many people **have read** the book. ***Putābam** multōs hominēs librum **lēgisse.*** = I **used to think** that many people **had read** the book.
Future Infinitive	AFTER	***Putō** multōs hominēs librum **lectūrōs esse.*** = I **think** that many people **will read** the book. ***Putābam** multōs hominēs librum **lectūrōs esse.*** = I **used to think** that many people **would read** the book.

EXPRESSION OF POSSESSION WITH PERSONAL PRONOUNS AND DEMONSTRATIVES

Possession is **not** indicated by the genitive of first and second person pronouns (*ego, tū, nōs, vōs*) or by the genitive of the reflexive pronoun of the third person (*suī, sibi, sē, sē*). These pronouns have corresponding possessive adjectives (*meus, tuus, noster, vester, suus*) to indicate possession.

Examples:

Librum meum habeō.	I have my book.
Librum tuum habeō.	I have your book.
Librum vestrum habeō.	I have your (plural) book.
Librum nostrum habētis.	You (plural) have our book.
Librum suum habent.	They have their (own) book.
Librum suum habet.	S/he has her/his (own) book.

However, possession **is** indicated by the genitive of the *non-reflexive* third person pronouns (*is, ea, id*).

Examples:

Librum eius habet.	S/he has her/his (someone else's) book.
Librum eōrum habent.	They have their (other people's) book.

In general, the genitive case often shows possession.

liber puellae	the book of the girl

Possession can also be expressed by a dative of possession.

Mihi sunt multī librī.	I have many books.

TRANSITIVE AND INTRANSITIVE VERBS

A transitive verb can take an accusative direct object when the subject performs an action on someone or something.

Example:

Librum teneō.	I hold a book.

Intransitive verbs **do not** take an accusative direct object, because they merely express the state or condition of the subject.

Examples:

Liber est meus.	The book is mine.
In casā meā maneō.	I am staying in my house.

SUBSTANTIVE ADJECTIVES, ESPECIALLY NEUTER PLURAL

Sometimes adjectives without an expressed noun are used to indicate generic persons or things. Gender and context make the frame of reference clear.

Examples:

Fortēs *fugere nōn solent.*	Brave people are not accustomed to flee.
Bonī mala *nōn laudant.*	Good people do not praise bad things.

CONSTRUCTION OF THE RELATIVE PRONOUN

A relative pronoun refers to a logically preceding word (called an antecedent) that is usually expressed, but sometimes only implied. A relative pronoun logically reflects its antecedent's gender and number, but the pronoun's case (again logically) is determined by its use in its own clause.

Example:

Hī sunt librī **quōs** *habēmus.*	These are the books that we have.

PARTICIPLES AS VERBS AND ADJECTIVES

A participle is both an adjective and a verb. Like an adjective, it agrees with a noun (expressed or implied). Like a verb, it relates an action and is modified by adverbial constructions.

Examples:

Librum ab amīcō datum habeō.
I have the book (having been) given by a/my friend.

Fortūna semper discessūra nihil dat.
Fortune, always being about to go away, gives nothing.

ENGLISH TO LATIN GLOSSARY

This glossary contains the **Vocabulary to Learn** from all the chapters.

LIST OF ABBREVIATIONS:

(1) = first conjugation
abl. = ablative
acc. = accusative
adj. = adjective
adv. = adverb
conj. = conjunction
dat. = dative
f. = feminine

gen. = genitive
inf. = infinitive
m. = masculine
n. = neuter
pl. = plural
prep. = preposition
sg. = singular

NOTE:

The genitive of second declension words ending in **–ius** or **–ium** is indicated with a single **–ī,** which is the genitive ending itself. Note that in the full form of the genitive there is normally a double **i**: *fīlius, –ī (= fīliī); gaudium, –ī (= gaudiī).*

A

abandon, relinquō, -ere, relīquī, relictum

abound with, abundō (1) + *abl.*

about, dē, *prep. + abl.*

about to be, futūrus, -a, -um, *participle*

accept, accipiō, -ere, -cēpī, -ceptum

accuse someone of something, accūsō (1) + *acc. + gen.*

adopt, capiō, -ere, cēpī, captum

advice, cōnsilium, -ī, *n.*

after, cum, *conj.;* postquam, *conj.*

after, post, *prep. + acc.*

afterward, posteā, *adv.*

against, contrā, *prep. + acc.;* in, *prep. + acc.*

all, omnis, -e, *adj.*

almost, paene, *adv.*

already, iam, *adv.*

also, etiam, *adv.;* quoque, *adv.*

always, semper, *adv.*

among, inter, *prep. + acc.*

and, et, *conj.;* atque, *conj.;* -que, *conj.*

and not, nec, *conj.*

and so, itaque, *conj.*

anger, īra, -ae, *f.*

animal, animal, -ālis, *n.*

another, alius, alia, aliud, *adj.*

answer, respondeō, -ēre, -spondī, -spōnsum

any, ūllus, -a, -um, *adj.*

appearance, fōrma, -ae, *f.*

argument, argūmentum, -ī, *n.*

armed, armātus, -a, -um, *adj.*

around, circum, *prep. + acc.*

ash, cinis, -eris, *m.*

ask, rogō (1)

at home, domī

at last, tandem, *adv.*

at the house of, apud, *prep. + acc.*

athlete, āthlēta, -ae, *m.*

attack, impetus, -ūs, *m.*

await, exspectō (1)

awaken, excitō (1)

away from, ā *or* ab, *prep. + abl.*

axis, axle, axis, -is, *m.*

B

bad, malus, -a, -um, *adj.*

battle, proelium, -ī, *n.*

be, sum, esse, fuī, ——

be able, possum, posse, potuī, ——

be accustomed, soleō, -ēre, solitus sum + *inf.*

be afraid, timeō, -ēre, timuī, ——

be eager for, studeō, -ēre, studuī, —— + *dat.*

be inert, iaceō, -ēre, iacuī, ——

be interested in, studeō, -ēre, studuī, —— + *dat.*

be on fire, ārdeō, -ēre, ārsī, ——

be unwilling, nōlō, *irregular verb*

beard, barba, -ae, *f.*

beautiful, pulcher, pulchra, pulchrum, *adj.*

because of, propter, *prep. + acc.*

beginning, initium, -ī, *n.*

behave, agō, -ere, ēgī, āctum;
  (s/he) behaves, sē gerit

believe somebody, crēdō, -ere, crēdidī, crēditum + *dat.*

between, inter, *prep.* + *acc.*

blame, reprehendō, -ere, -prehendī, -prehēnsum

blood, sanguis, sanguinis, *m.*

body, corpus, -oris, *n.*

book, liber, librī, *m.*

bosom, gremium, -ī, *n.*

boy, puer, puerī, *m.*

brave, fortis, -e, *adj.*

brook, rīvus, -ī, *m.*

build, aedificō (1)

burn, ārdeō, -ēre, ārsī, ——

but, sed, *conj.*

by, ā *or* ab, *prep.* + *abl.*

C

call, vocō (1)

camp, castra, -ōrum, *n. pl.*

can, possum, posse, potuī, ——

capture, capiō, -ere, cēpī, captum

care for, cūrō (1)

carry, gerō, -ere, gessī, gestum

cause, causa, -ae, *f.*

cave, spēlunca, -ae, *f.*

chain, vinculum, -ī, *n.*

change, mūtō (1)

chest, pectus, -oris, *n.*

choose, legō, -ere, lēgī, lēctum

citizen, cīvis, -is, *m./f.*

city (city of Rome), urbs, urbis, *f.*

class (of people), classis, -is, *f.*

clothes, vestīmenta, -ōrum, *n. pl.*

cloud, nūbēs, -is, *f.*

combat, proelium, -ī, *n.*

come, veniō, -īre, vēnī, ventum

concerning, dē, *prep.* + *abl.*

conflagration, incendium, -ī, *n.*

confusion, tumultus, -ūs, *m.*

conquer, vincō, -ere, vīcī, victum

consider, putō (1)

constancy, cōnstantia, -ae, *f.*

consul, cōnsul, -ulis, *m.*

consume, cōnsūmō, -ere, -sūmpsī, -sūmptum

cook, coquō, -ere, coxī, coctum

cottage, casa, -ae, *f.*

country house, vīlla, -ae, *f.*

courage, fortitūdō, -inis, *f.*

crowded, celeber, -bris, -bre, *adj.*

cruel, crūdēlis, -e, *adj.*

cultivate, colō, -ere, coluī, cultum

D

danger, perīculum, -ī, *n.*

darkness, tenebrae, -ārum, *f. pl.*

daughter, fīlia, -ae, *f.*

day, diēs, diēī, *m./f.*

deadly, fūnestus, -a, -um, *adj.*

death, mors, mortis, *f.*

deception, dolus, -ī, *m.*

decide, dēcernō, -ere, -crēvī, -crētum + *inf.*

defeat, vincō, -ere, vīcī, victum

delight, dēliciae, -ārum, *f. pl.* (*noun*)

delight, dēlectō (1) (*verb*)

descend, dēscendō, -ere, -scendī, -scēnsum

design, parō (1)

desire, cupiō, -ere, -īvī, -ītum

destiny, fātum, -ī, *n.*

destroy, dēleō, -ēre, dēlēvī, dēlētum; tollō, -ere, sustulī, sublātum

determine, dēcernō, -ere, -crēvī, -crētum

devastate, dēvastō (1)

difficult, difficilis, -e, *adj.*

disaster, clādēs, -is, *f.*

distinguished, praeclārus, -a, -um, *adj.*

divine, dīvīnus, -a, -um, *adj.*

do, agō, -ere, ēgī, āctum; faciō, -ere, fēcī, factum

down from, dē, *prep.* + *abl.*

drive, agō, -ere, ēgī, āctum

during the night, noctū, *adv.*

dwell, habitō (1)

E

each, omnis, -e, *adj.*

easily, facile, *adv.*

eat, comedō, -ere, -ēdī, -ēsum

emperor, imperātor, -ōris, *m.*

enemy, hostis, -is, *m.*

engulf, corripiō, -ere, -ripuī, -reptum

enter, intrō (1)

envy someone, invideō, -ēre, invīdī, invīsum + *dat.*

eruption, incendium, -ī, *n.*

esteem, aestimō (1)

even, aequus, -a, -um, *adj.*

even, etiam, *adv.*

ever, umquam, *adv.*

every, omnis, -e, *adj.*

everywhere, ubīque, *adv.*

example, exemplar, -āris, *n.*; exemplum, -ī, *n.*

exceedingly, valdē, *adv.*

exclaim, exclāmō (1)

expect, exspectō (1)

external, externus, -a, -um, *adj.*

extinguish, exstinguō, -ere, exstīnxī, exstīnctum

eye, oculus, -ī, *m.*

F

face, faciēs, -ēī, *f.*

fall, cadō, -ere, cecidī, cāsum

family, familia, -ae, *f.*

famous, praeclārus, -a, -um, *adj.*

far, longē, *adv.*

farmer, agricola, -ae, *m.*

fate, fātum, -ī, *n.*

father, pater, -tris, *m.*

fatherland, patria, -ae, *f.*

fear, timor, -ōris, *m.* (*noun*)

fear, timeō, -ēre, timuī, —— (*verb*)

feed, alō, -ere, aluī, altum/alitum

feel, sentiō, -īre, sēnsī, sēnsum

feel pain, doleō, -ēre, doluī, ——

ferocious, ferōx, -ōcis, *adj.*

fetter, vinculum, -ī, *n.*

few, paucī, -ae, -a, *pl. adj.*

field, ager, agrī, *m.*

fierce, ācer, ācris, ācre, *adj.;* ferōx, -ōcis, *adj.*

fight, pugnō (1)

finger, digitus, -ī, *m.*

fire, ignis, -is, *m.*

first, prīmus, -a, -um, *adj.*

flame, flamma, -ae, *f.*

flee, fugiō, -ere, fūgī, ——

fleet, classis, -is, *f.*

flesh, carō, carnis, *f.*

flow, fluō, -ere, flūxī, fluxum

for (conj.), enim, *conj.;* nam, *conj.*

for (prep.), prō, *prep. + abl.*

for a long time, diū, *adv.*

for certain, for sure, prō certō, *adverbial phrase*

force, vīs, —— *f.; pl.* vīrēs, vīrium; impetus, -ūs, *m.*

foreign to, aliēnus, -a, -um, *adj. + prep.* ā *or* ab + *abl.*

forest, silva, -ae, *f.*

form, fōrma, -ae, *f.*

former, ille, illa, illud

fortunate, fēlīx, -īcis, *adj.*

fortune, fortūna, -ae, *f.*

Fortune, the goddess Fortūna, -ae, *f.*

free someone from something, līberō (1) + *acc. + abl.*

friend, amīcus, -ī, *m.*

from, ā *or* ab, *prep. + abl.;* ē *or* ex, *prep. + abl.*

fruit, pōmum, -ī, *n.*

full of, plēnus, -a, -um, *adj. + gen.* or + *abl.*

G

garment, vestīmentum, -ī, *n.*

general, dux, ducis, *m.;* imperātor, -ōris, *m.*

geographical places, loca, locōrum, *n. pl.*

get ready, parō (1)

gift, dōnum, -ī, *n.*

girl, puella, -ae, *f.*

give, dō, dăre, dedī, dătum

go away, discēdō, -ere, -cessī, -cessum

go to, petō, -ere, petīvī, petītum

god, deus, -ī, *m.*

goddess, dea, -ae, *f.*

good, bonus, -a, -um, *adj.*

goodbye!, valē!

great, magnus, -a, -um, *adj.*

grief, dolor, -ōris, *m.*

grow, crēscō, -ere, crēvī, ——

H

hand, manus, -ūs, *f.*

happy, fēlīx, -īcis, *adj.*

hatred, odium, -ī, *n.*

have, habeō, -ēre, habuī, habitum

he, is, ea, id, *personal pronoun*

head, caput, -itis, *n.*

head for, petō, -ere, petīvī, petītum

heal, sānō (1)

hear, audiō, -īre, audīvī, audītum

heart, cor, cordis, *n.*

heaven, caelum, -ī, *n.*

help, auxilium, -ī, *n.*

her, suus, -a, -um, *possessive adj.;* eius

herself, sē, *acc. of the reflexive pronoun*

hide, pellis, -is, *f.* (*noun*)

hide, occultō (1) (*verb*)

himself, sē, *acc. of the reflexive pronoun*

his, suus, -a, -um, *possessive adj.,* eius

hold, teneō, -ēre, tenuī, tentum

home, domus, -ūs, *f.*

honor, honor, -ōris, *m.*

horn, cornū, -ūs, *n.*

horse, equus, -ī, *m.*

house, domus, -ūs, *f.*

household, familia, -ae, *f.*

however, autem, *conj.;* tamen, *conj.*

human, hūmānus, -a, -um, *adj.*

human being, homō, -inis, *m.*

hurt, doleō, -ēre, doluī, ——, (*intransitive*)

husband, marītus, -ī, *m.*

I

I, ego, *personal pronoun*

I do not care a bit, aestimō ūnīus assis

if, sī, *conj.*

immediately, statim, *adv.*

impetus, impetus, -ūs, *m.*

important, magnus, -a, -um, *adj.*

in, in, *prep. + abl.*

in fact, enim, *conj.;* nam, *conj.*

in front of, ante, *prep. + acc.*

in such a way, ita, *adv.*

in the open, forīs, *adv.*

inconsistent with, aliēnus, -a, -um, *adj. + prep.* ā *or* ab + *abl.*

indication, argūmentum, -ī, *n.*

indifferently, aequō animō

injustice, inīquitās, -ātis, *f.*

into, ad, *prep. + acc.;* in, *prep. + acc.*

it, is, ea, id, *personal pronoun*

it is allowed to, it is permitted (for someone to do something) licet + *dat. + inf.*

its, suus, -a, -um, *possessive adj.;* eius

itself, sē, *acc. of the reflexive pronoun*

J

joy, gaudium, -ī, *n.*

judge, iūdex, -icis, *m.* (*noun*)

judge, iūdicō (1) (*verb*)

just, iūstus, -a, -um, *adj.*

just as, sīcut, *adv.*

K

keen, ācer, ācris, ācre, *adj.*

kill, occīdō, -ere, occīdī, occīsum

king, rēx, rēgis, *m.*

know, sciō, scīre, scīvī, scītum

L

lack something, egeō, -ēre, eguī, —— + *abl.*

land, terra, -ae, *f.*

lap, gremium, -ī, *n.*

large, magnus, -a, -um, *adj.*

latter, hic, haec, hoc
law, lēx, lēgis, *f.*
lead, agō, -ere, ēgī, āctum; dūcō, -ere, dūxī, ductum
leader, dux, ducis, *m.*
learned, doctus, -a, -um, *adj.*
leave, discēdō, -ere, -cessī, -cessum
leave behind, relinquō, -ere, relīquī, relictum
legitimate, iūstus, -a, -um, *adj.*
letter (epistle), litterae, -ārum, *f. pl.;* epistula, -ae, *f.*
letter (of the alphabet), littera, -ae, *f.*
lie down, iaceō, -ēre, iacuī, ——
life, vīta, -ae, *f.*
lift up, tollō, -ere, sustulī, sublātum
like, similis, -e, *adj. + gen.* or + *dat.*
listen, audiō, -īre, -īvī, -ītum
literature, litterae, -ārum, *f. pl.*
little house, casa, -ae, *f.*
live (be alive), vīvō, -ere, vīxī, vīctum
live (dwell), habitō (1)
long, longus, -a, -um, *adj.*
look at, cōnspiciō, -ere, -spexī, -spectum
look for, quaerō, -ere, quaesīvī, quaesītum
look here!, ecce, *interj.*
lose, āmittō, -ere, -mīsī, -missum
love, amor, -ōris, *m.* (*noun*)
love, amō (1) (*verb*)

M

make, faciō, -ere, fēcī, factum
make a mistake, errō (1)
make a speech, ōrātiōnem habeō
make plans, cōnsilia capiō
man, vir, virī, *m.*
man (i.e., human being), homō, -inis, *m.*
many, multus, -a, -um, *adj.*
matter, rēs, reī, *f.*
meat, carō, carnis, *f.*

meet, conveniō, -īre, -vēnī, -ventum
memory, memoria, -ae, *f.*
midday, merīdiēs, -ēī, *m.*
mind, animus, -ī, *m.*
mischief, inīquitās, -ātis, *f.*
miserable, miser, misera, miserum, *adj.*
mistress, domina, -ae, *f.*
mother, māter, mātris, *f.*
mountain, mōns, montis, *m.*
mouth, ōs, ōris, *n.*
move, moveō, -ēre, mōvī, mōtum
much, multus, -a, -um, *adj.*
much, multum, *adv.*
must, dēbeō, -ēre, dēbuī, dēbitum + *inf.*
my, meus, -a, -um, *possessive adj.*

N

name, nōmen, -inis, *n.*
near, prope, *prep. + acc.*
neglect, neglegō, -ere, neglēxī, neglēctum
never, numquam, *adv.*
new, novus, -a, -um, *adj.*
nice, pulcher, pulchra, pulchrum, *adj.*
night, nox, noctis, *f.*
no, minimē, *adv.*
nor, nec, *conj.*
not, nōn, *negative adv.*
not only . . . , but also . . . , nōn sōlum . . . , sed etiam . . .
not want, nōlō, *irregular verb*
nothing, nihil, *negative pronoun*
nourish, alō, -ere, aluī, altum/alitum
now, nunc, *adv.;* iam, *adv.*

O

observe, cōnspiciō, -ere, -spexī, -spectum
often, saepe, *adv.*
old, vetustus, -a, -um, *adj.*
old age, senectūs, -ūtis, *f.*
old man, senex, -is, *m.*

on, in, *prep. + abl.*
on account of, propter, *prep. + acc.*
on behalf of, prō, *prep. + abl.*
only, tantum, *adv.*
open, iūstus, -a, -um, *adj.*
oracle, ōrāculum, -ī, *n.*
order somebody to do something, iubeō, -ēre, iussī, iussum + *acc. + inf.*
order, iussus, -ūs, *m.*
other, alius, alia, aliud, *adj.*
ought to, dēbeō, -ēre, dēbuī, dēbitum + *inf.*
our, noster, nostra, nostrum, *possessive adj.*
out of, ē *or* ex, *prep. + abl.*
outside, forīs, *adv.*
outward, externus, -a, -um, *adj.*
overcome, vincō, -ere, vīcī, victum
overwhelm, opprimō, -ere, oppressī, oppressum
owe, dēbeō, -ēre, dēbuī, dēbitum

P

pain, dolor, -ōris, *m.*
parent, parēns, parentis, *m./f.*
part, pars, partis, *f.*
particle added to the first word of an interrogative sentence, -ne
passages of a book, locī, locōrum, *m. pl.*
peace, pāx, pācis, *f.*
people, hominēs, hominum, *m. pl.*
perhaps, fortasse, *adv.*
pet, dēliciae, -ārum, *f. pl.*
place, locus, locī, *m.* (*noun*)
place, pōnō, -ere, posuī, positum (*verb*)
plan, cōnsilium, -ī, *n.*
plant, herba, -ae, *f.*
play, lūdō, -ere, lūsī, lūsum
please, dēlectō (1)
poet, poēta, -ae, *m.*
poison, venēnum, -ī, *n.*
poor, pauper, pauperis, *adj.*

possess, possideō, -ēre, possēdī, possessum

prepare, parō (1)

preserve, servō (1)

proof, argūmentum, -ī, *n.*

public office or distinction, honor, -ōris, *m.*

punish, pūniō, -īre, pūnīvī, pūnītum

put, pōnō, -ere, posuī, positum

Q

queen, rēgīna, -ae, *f.*

R

raise, tollō, -ere, sustulī, sublātum

read, legō, -ere, lēgī, lēctum

reason, causa, -ae, *f.*

rebuke, reprehendō, -ere, -prehendī, -prehēnsum

receive, accipiō, -ere, -cēpī, -ceptum

red, ruber, rubra, rubrum, *adj.*

regard, aestimō (1)

remain, maneō, -ēre, mānsī, mānsum

renowned, celeber, -bris, -bre, *adj.*

reward, praemium, -ī, *n.*

rich, dīves, dīvitis, *adj.*

riches, dīvitiae -ārum, *f. pl.*

right hand, dextra, -ae, *f.*

road, via, -ae, *f.*

rock, saxum, -ī, *n.*

Roman, Rōmānus, -a, -um, *adj.*

Rome, Rōma, -ae, *f.*

rouse, excitō (1)

rub, terō, -ere, trīvī, trītum

run, currō, -ere, cucurrī, cursum

run away, fugiō, -ere, fūgī, ——

rural, rūsticus, -a, -um, *adj.*

rush at, petō, -ere, petīvī, petītum

rustic, rūsticus, -a, -um, *adj.*

S

s/he/it, is, ea, id, *personal pronoun*

sad, miser, misera, miserum, *adj.*

sail, nāvigō (1)

sailor, nauta, -ae, *m.*

save, servō (1)

say, dīcō, -ere, dīxī, dictum

say/said, inquam, (*only introducing direct speech*); **s/he says/said,** inquit (*only introducing direct speech*)

sea, mare, maris, *n.*

search, quaerō, -ere, quaesīvī, quaesītum

see, videō, -ēre, vīdī, vīsum

seek, petō, -ere, petīvī, petītum

seem, videor

seize, corripiō, -ere, -ripuī, -reptum

send, mittō, -ere, mīsī, missum

separate, sēparō (1)

serious, sevērus, -a, -um, *adj.*

severe, sevērus, -a, -um, *adj.*

shadows, tenebrae, -ārum, *f. pl.*

she, is, ea, id, *personal pronoun*

she-wolf, lupa, -ae, *f.*

ship, nāvis, -is, *f.*

shore, lītus, -oris, *n.*

should, dēbeō, -ēre, dēbuī, dēbitum + *inf.*

show, ostendō, -ere, ostendī, ostentum

similar, similis, -e, *adj. + gen.* or *+ dat.*

sister, soror, -ōris, *f.*

sit, sedeō, -ēre, sēdī, sessum

skin, pellis, -is, *f.*

sky, caelum, -ī, *n.*

sleep, dormiō, -īre, dormīvī, dormītum

sleep, somnus, -ī, *m.*

small, parvus, -a, -um, *adj.*

smoke, fūmus, -ī, *m.*

snatch away, ēripiō, -ere, -ripuī, -reptum

so great, tantus, -a, -um, *adj.*

so, tam, *adv.*; ita, *adv.*

soldier, mīles, -itis, *m.*

son, fīlius, -ī, *m.*

soon, mox, *adv.*

soul, animus, -ī, *m.*

sparrow, passer, -eris, *m.*

speech, ōrātiō, -ōnis, *f.*

spirit, animus, -ī, *m.*

stand, stō, -āre, stetī, statum

stir up, excitō (1)

stone, saxum, -ī, *n.*

storm, tempestās, -ātis, *f.*

story, fābula, -ae, *f.*

stream, rīvus, -ī, *m.*

strength, vīs, —— *f.; pl.* vīrēs, vīrium

strengthen, firmō (1)

strict, sevērus, -a, -um, *adj.*

strong, fortis, -e, *adj.*

study, studeō, -ēre, studuī, —— + *dat.*

suddenly, subitō, *adv.*

suppress, opprimō, -ere, oppressī, oppressum

swiftly, celeriter, *adv.*

sword, gladius, -ī, *m.*

T

take, capiō, -ere, cēpī, captum; dūcō, -ere, dūxī, ductum

take back, recipiō, -ere, -cēpī, -ceptum

take care of, cūrō (1)

teach, doceō, -ēre, docuī, doctum

tear, lacrima, -ae, *f.*

tell, nārrō (1)

temple, templum, -ī, *n.*

terrifying, terribilis, -e, *adj.*

that, ille, illa, illud, *demonstrative pronoun and adj.*; is, ea, id, *demonstrative pronoun and adj.*

that, quī, quae, quod, *relative pronoun*

theft, fūrtum, -ī, *n.*

their, suus, -a, -um, *possessive adj.*; eōrum

themselves, sē, *acc. of the reflexive pronoun*

then, deinde, *adv.*; tum, *adv.*; tunc, *adv.*

there, ibi, *adv.*

therefore, igitur, *conj.*

thief, fūr, fūris, *m.*

thing, rēs, reī, *f.*

think, cōgitō (1); putō (1)

this, hic, haec, hoc, *demonstrative pronoun and adj.;* is, ea, id, *demonstrative pronoun and adj.*

through, per, *prep. + acc.*

throw, iaciō, -ere, iēcī, iactum

time, tempus, -oris, *n.*

to, ad, *prep. + acc.;* in, *prep. + acc.*

together, ūnā, *adv.*

touch, tangō, -ere, tetigī, tāctum

toward, ad, *prep. + acc.*

tree, arbor, -oris, *f.*

trickery, dolus, -ī, *m.*

true, vērus, -a, -um, *adj.*

try, temptō (1)

turn, versō (1)

U

uncle, avunculus, -ī, *m.*

understand, intellegō, -ere, intellēxī, intellēctum

uproar, tumultus, -ūs, *m.*

V

vegetation, herba, -ae, *f.*

very, valdē, *adv.*

villa, vīlla, -ae, *f.*

voyage, nāvigō (1)

W

wage war, bellum gerō

wait for, exspectō (1)

wake up, excitō (1)

walk, ambulō (1)

wall, wall-fence, mūrus, -ī, *m.*

wander, errō (1)

want, cupiō, -ere, -īvī, -ītum

war, bellum, -ī, *n.*

water, aqua, -ae, *f.*

we, nōs, *personal pronoun*

wealth, dīvitiae, -ārum, *f. pl.*

weapons, arma, -ōrum, *n. pl.*

wear out, terō, -ere, trīvī, trītum

weather, caelum, -ī, *n.*

well, bene, *adv.*

well-known, celeber, -bris, -bre, *adj.*

what?, quid?, *interrogative pronoun,* quod?, *interrogative adj.*

wheel, rota, -ae, *f.*

when, cum, *conj.*

which? quī, quae, quod?, *interrogative adjective*

which, quī, quae, quod, *relative pronoun*

while, dum, *conj.*

white, albus, -a, -um, *adj.*

who, quī, quae, quod, *relative pronoun*

who?, quis?, *interrogative pronoun*

why, cūr, *adj.*

wife, uxor, -ōris, *f.*

wind, ventus, -ī, *m.*

with, cum, *prep. + abl.*

with all one's might, prō vīribus

with me, mēcum

with you, tēcum

without, sine, *prep. + abl.*

wolf, *see she-wolf*

woman, fēmina, -ae, *f.;* mulier, -ieris, *f.*

word, verbum, -ī, *n.*

worship, colō, -ere, coluī, cultum

wound (noun), vulnus, -eris, *n.*

wound (verb), vulnerō (1)

wretched, miser, -a, -um, *adj.*

Y

yes, ita, *adv.*

you (pl.), vōs, *personal pronoun*

you (sg.), tū, *personal pronoun*

young lady, young man, adulēscēns, -entis, *m./f.*

your, yours (pl.), vester, vestra, vestrum, *possessive adj.*

your, yours (sg.), tuus, -a, -um, *possessive adj.*

LATIN TO ENGLISH GLOSSARY

This glossary contains the **Vocabulary to Learn*** as well as the **Reading Vocabulary** from all the chapters.

*All words from the **Vocabulary to Learn** are asterisked and coded, e.g., C12 means the word first appeared as **Vocabulary to Learn** in Chapter 12. In a very few instances, an additional meaning for the word is given in a later part of the text. Such additional meanings appear in the Glossary and when the additional meaning is part of the **Vocabulary to Learn**, the chapter introducing that additional meaning is also noted.

LIST OF ABBREVIATIONS:

(1) = first conjugation
abl. = ablative
acc. = accusative
adj. = adjective
adv. = adverb
conj. = conjunction
dat. = dative
f. = feminine

gen. = genitive
inf. = infinitive
m. = masculine
n. = neuter
pl. = plural
prep. = preposition
sg. = singular

NOTE:

The genitive of second declension words ending in **–ius** or **–ium** is indicated with a single **–ī**, which is the genitive ending itself. Note that in the full form of the genitive there is normally a double **i**: *fīlius, -ī (= fīliī); gaudium, -ī (= gaudiī)*.

A

ā *or* **ab**, *prep. + abl.*, by, from, away from* C5

absum, abesse, āfuī, ——, to be absent, away

abundō (1) + *abl.*, to abound with* C20

accipiō, -ere, -cēpī, -ceptum, to accept, receive* C21

accurrō, -ere, -currī, -cursum, to run up

accūsō (1) + *acc. + gen.*, to accuse someone of something* C21

ācer, ācris, ācre, *adj.,* keen, fierce* C10

ad tempus, for the time being, for a while

ad, *prep. + acc.,* toward, to, into* C4

adolēscō, -ere, adolēvī, adultum, to grow up

adulēscēns, -entis, *m./f.,* young man, young lady* C20

aedificō (1), to build* C10

Aenēās, Aenēae (*gen.*), **Aenēae** (*dat.*), **Aenēam/ān** (*acc.*), **Aenēā** (*abl.*), Aeneas, Trojan refugee, legendary founder of Roman race

aequus, -a, -um, *adj.,* even; **aequō animō,** indifferently* C20

Aeschinus, -ī, *m.,* Aeschinus

aestimō (1), to regard, esteem; **aestimō ūnīus assis,** I do not care a bit* C7

ager, agrī, *m.,* field* C3

agō, -ere, ēgī, āctum, to drive, lead, do, behave* C11

agricola, -ae, *m.,* farmer* C1

albus, -a, -um, *adj.,* white* C14

aliēnus, -a, -um, *adj. + prep.* ā/ab + *abl.,* foreign to, inconsistent with* C21

alius, alia, aliud, *adj.,* another, other* C13

alō, -ere, aluī, altum/alitum, to feed, nourish* C17

amāns, amantis, *m./f.,* lover

ambulō (1), to walk* C2

amīcus, -ī, *m.,* friend* C3

āmittō, -ere, -mīsī, -missum, to lose* C17

amō (1), to love* C2

amor, -ōris, *m.*, love* C7

Amūlius, -ī, *m.*, Amulius

angustus, -a, -um, *adj.*, narrow

animal, -ālis, *n.*, animal* C9

animus, -ī, *m.*, spirit, soul, mind* C3

ante, *prep. + acc.*, in front of* C15

antequam, *conj.*, before

Apollō, Apollinis, *m.*, Apollo, god of the sun, poetry, light, music

appropinquō (1), to approach

apud, *prep. + acc.*, at the house of* C13

aqua, -ae, *f.*, water* C1

arbor, -oris, *f.*, tree* C14

ārdeō, -ēre, ārsī, ——, to burn, be on fire* C11

argūmentum, -ī, *n.*, proof, indication, argument* C15

arma, -ōrum, *n. pl.*, weapons* C9

armātus, -a, -um, *adj.*, armed* C4

asportō (1), to carry away

at, *conj.*, but

Athēniēnsēs, Athēniēnsium, *m. pl.*, the Athenians

āthlēta, -ae, *m.*, athlete* C1

atque, *conj.*, and* C13

attonitus, -a, -um, *adj.*, astounded

auctōritās, -ātis, *f.*, authority

audiō, -īre, audīvī, audītum, to hear, listen* C9

autem, *conj.*, however* C4

auxilium, -ī, *n.*, help* C5

avunculus, -ī, *m.*, uncle* C16

axis, -is, *m.*, axle, axis* C21

B

barba, -ae, *f.*, beard* C19

bellum, -ī, *n.*, war* C4; **bellō iūstō**, through open warfare

belua, -ae, *f.*, beast

bene, *adv.*, well* C1

bonus, -a, -um, *adj.*, good* C4

bracchium, -ī, *n.*, arm

C

cadō, -ere, cecidī, cāsum, to fall* C14

caelum, -ī, *n.*, sky, heaven, weather* C16

calidus, -a, -um, *adj.*, hot

callidus, -a, -um, *adj.*, clever, cunning

capiō, -ere, cēpī, captum, to take, adopt, capture; **cōnsilia capere**, to make plans* C10

caput, -itis, *n.*, head* C9

carō, carnis, *f.*, meat, flesh* C19

Carthāgine, at Carthage, in Carthage

Carthāgō, -inis, *f.* Carthage

casa, -ae, *f.*, little house, cottage* C3

castra, -ōrum, *n. pl.*, camp* C4

Catilīna, -ae, *m.*, Catiline, a bankrupt revolutionary whose plot to overthrow the Republic was exposed by Cicero

Catullus, -ī, *m.*, Catullus, Roman poet

causa, -ae, *f.*, cause, reason* C16

celeber, -bris, -bre, *adj.*, renowned, well-known, crowded* C10

celeriter, *adv.*, swiftly* C19

cibus, -ī, *m.*, food

cicātrīx, cicātrīcis, *f.*, scar

Cicerō, -ōnis, *m.*, Cicero, Roman political figure of the first century BCE

cinis, -eris, *m.*, ash* C16

circum, *prep. + acc.*, around* C21

circus, -ī, *m.*, circus, often referring to the Circus Maximus in particular

cīvis, -is, *m./f.*, citizen* C9

clādēs, -is, *f.*, disaster* C16

clam, *adv.*, secretly

clāmor, -ōris, *m.*, shout, cry

classis, -is, *f.*, fleet* C16

claudō, -ere, clausī, clausum, to lock up

clīvus, -ī, *m.*, hill

cōgitō (1), to think* C5

cognōscō, -ere, -nōvī, -nitum, to recognize, get to know

colō, -ere, coluī, cultum, to worship, cultivate* C18

comedō, -ere, -ēdī, -ēsum, to eat* C14

coniūrātiō, -ōnis, *f.*, plot

cōnsilium, -ī, *n.*, plan* C5

cōnspiciō, -ere, -spexī, -spectum, to look at, observe* C11

cōnstantia, -ae, *f.*, constancy* C21

cōnsul, -ulis, *m.*, consul* C9

cōnsultō, *adv.*, on purpose

cōnsūmō, -ere, -sūmpsī, -sūmptum, to consume* C12

contrā, *prep. + acc.*, against* C8

conveniō, -īre, -vēnī, -ventum, to meet* C14

coquō, -ere, coxī, coctum, to cook* C19

cor, cordis, *n.*, heart* C20

cornū, -ūs, *n.*, horn* C17

corpus, -oris, *n.*, body* C9

corripiō, -ere, -ripuī, -reptum, to seize, engulf* C17

crēdō, -ere, crēdidī, crēditum + *dat.*, to believe somebody* C9

crēscō, -ere, crēvī, ——, to grow* C19

crūdēlis, -e, *adj.*, cruel* C11

Ctēsiphō, -ōnis, *m.*, Ctesipho

cum ... tum ..., both ... and ...

cum, *conj.*, when, after* C18

cum, *prep. + abl.*, with* C3

Cupīdō, Cupīdinis, *m.*, Cupid (in Greek, Eros)

cupiō, -ere, -īvī, -ītum, to desire, want* C10

cūr, *adv.*, why? * C15

cūria, -ae, *f.*, senate (building)

cūrō (1), to care for, take care of* C2

currō, -ere, cucurrī, cursum, to run* C17

D

dē, *prep. + abl.,* about, concerning, down from* C5

dea, -ae, *f.,* goddess* C18

dēbeō, -ēre, dēbuī, dēbitum + *inf.,* ought, must, should; to owe* C2

dēcernō, -ere, -crēvī, -crētum + *inf.,* to decide, determine* C8

deinde, *adv.,* then* C3

dēlectō (1), to delight, please* C20

dēleō, -ēre, dēlēvī, dēlētum, to destroy* C10

dēliciae, -ārum, *f. pl.,* delight, pet* C7

Delphicus, -a, -um, *adj.,* belonging to Delphi, Delphic

Delphīs, at Delphi

Dēmea, -ae, *m.,* Demea

dēns, dentis, *m.,* tooth

dēscendō, -ere, -scendī, -scēnsum, to descend* C21

deus, -ī, *m.,* god* C10

dēvastō (1), to devastate* C17

dextra, -ae, *f.,* right hand* C12

dīcō, -ere, dīxī, dictum, to say* C8

Dīdō, Dīdōnis, *f.,* Dido, exile from Phoenician Tyre, founding queen of Carthage

diēs, diēī, *m./f.,* day* C18

difficilis, -e, *adj.,* difficult* C15

digitus, -ī, *m.,* finger* C7

discēdō, -ere, -cessī, -cessum, to leave, go away* C13

discō, -ere, didicī, ——, to learn

diū, *adv.,* for a long time* C2

dīves, dīvitis, *adj.,* rich* C13

dīvīnus, -a, -um, *adj.,* divine* C20

dīvitiae, -ārum, *f. pl.,* wealth, riches* C21

dō, dāre, dedī, dātum, to give* C4

doceō, -ēre, docuī, doctum, to teach* C6

doctus, -a, -um, *adj.,* learned* C13

doleō, -ēre, doluī, ——, to feel pain, hurt* C5

dolor, -ōris, *m.,* grief, pain* C11

dolus, -ī, *m.,* trickery, deception* C4

domī, at home* C3

domina, -ae, *f.,* mistress* C7

domus, -ūs, *f.,* house, home* C17

dōnum, -ī, *n.,* gift* C10

dormiō, -īre, dormīvī, dormītum, to sleep* C18

Druidēs, -um, *m. pl.,* the Druids

dūcō, -ere, dūxī, ductum, to lead, take* C13

dulcissime rērum, dear fellow, literally "the sweetest of all things"

dum, *conj.,* while* C6

duo, duae, dua, *numeral,* two

dux, ducis, *m.,* leader, general* C8

E

ē *or* **ex,** *prep. + abl.,* from, out of* C4

ecce, *interj.,* look here! * C15

egeō, -ēre, eguī, —— *+ abl.,* to lack something* C20

egestās, -ātis, *f.,* lack, poverty

ego, *personal pronoun,* I* C3

ēiciō, -ere, ēiēcī, ēiectum, to throw away

enim, *conj.,* for, in fact* C13

eō diē, on that day

epistula, -ae, *f.,* letter* C5

equus, -ī, *m.,* horse* C10

ēripiō, -ere, -ripuī, -reptum, to snatch away* C21

errō (1), to wander, make a mistake* C21

et, *conj.,* and* C1

etiam, *adv.,* even, also* C15

Etrūscus, -a, -um, *adj.,* Etruscan

ēvanēscō, -ere, ēvanuī, ——, to disappear

excitō (1), to awaken, wake up, rouse, stir up* C18

exclāmō (1), to exclaim* C18

excutiō, -ere, -cussī, -cussum, to shake off

exemplar, -āris, *n.,* example* C9

exemplum, -ī, *n.,* example* C6

exeunt, they exit, go out

eximō, -ere, -ēmī, -ēmptum, to take out

exspectō (1), to wait for, await, expect* C2

exstinguō, -ere, exstīnxī, exstīnctum, to extinguish* C17

externus, -a, -um, *adj.,* outward, external* C21

F

Fābricius, -ī, *m.,* Fabricius

fābula, -ae, *f.,* story* C2

faciēs, -ēī, *f.,* face* C18

facile, *adv.,* easily* C17

faciō, -ere, fēcī, factum, to do, make* C12

familia, -ae, *f.,* family, household* C5

fātum, -ī, *n.,* fate, destiny* C18

fax, fācis, *f.,* torch

Fēlīciō, ——, *m.,* Felicio, a servant's name

fēlīx, -īcis, *adj.,* fortunate, happy* C10

fēmina, -ae, *f.,* woman* C16

femur, femoris, *n.,* the upper leg, the thigh

ferōx, -ōcis, *adj.,* fierce, ferocious* C19

ferus, -a, -um, *adj.,* wild, savage

fīlia, -ae, *f.,* daughter* C1

fīlius, -ī, *m.,* son* C3

firmō (1), to strengthen* C6

flamma, -ae, *f.,* flame* C10

flexus, -a, -um, *adj.,* curved

fluō, -ere, flūxī, fluxum, to flow* C14

folium, -ī, *n.,* leaf

forīs, *adv.,* outside, in the open* C19

fōrma, -ae, *f.,* form, appearance* C2

fortasse, *adv.,* perhaps* C15

fortis, -e, *adj.,* brave, strong* C10

fortitūdō, -inis, *f.,* courage* C8

fortūna, -ae, *f.,* fortune, the goddess Fortune* C21

frāter, frātris, *m.,* brother

fugiō, -ere, fūgī, ——, to flee, run away* C10

fūmus, -ī, *m.,* smoke* C16

fūnestus, -a, -um, *adj.,* deadly* C16

fūr, fūris, *m.,* thief* C20

fūrtum, -ī, *n.,* theft* C20

futūrus, -a, -um, *participle,* about to be* C21

G

Gallī, -ōrum, *m. pl.,* the Gauls, the inhabitants of France

gaudium, -ī, *n.,* joy* C5

gerō, -ere, gessī, gestum, to carry; **sē gerit,** s/he behaves* C9; *with clothing or articles of clothing as its object,* to wear; **bellum gerere,** to wage war* C12

gladius, -ī, *m.,* sword* C14

Graecia, -ae, *f.,* Greece

Graecus, -a, -um, *adj.,* Greek; **Graecī, -ōrum,** *m. pl.,* the Greeks

gremium, -ī, *n.,* bosom, lap* C7

gutta, -ae, *f.,* drop

H

habeō, -ēre, habuī, habitum, to have* C2

habitō (1), to live, dwell* C2

hāc nocte, tonight

herba, -ae, *f.,* plant, vegetation* C19

heus!, hey!

hic, haec, hoc, *demonstrative pronoun and adj.,* this, latter* C19

homō, -inis, *m.,* man (i.e., human being); *pl.* people* C8

honor, -ōris, *m.,* honor, public office or distinction* C21

hostis, -is, *m.,* enemy* C10

hūc atque illūc, hither and thither, to and fro

hūmānus, -a, -um, *adj.,* human* C20

Hūnī, -ōrum, *m. pl.,* the Huns

I

iaceō, -ēre, iacuī, ——, to lie down, be inert* C6

iaciō, -ere, iēcī, iactum, to throw* C17

iam, *adv.,* already* C14

iānua, -ae, *f.,* door

ibi, *adv.,* there* C12

igitur, *conj.,* therefore* C16

ignis, -is, *m.,* fire* C12

ille, illa, illud, *demonstrative pronoun and adj.,* that, former* C20

illūc, *adv.,* to that place, thither

imparātus, -a, -um, *adj.,* unprepared

impedīmentum, -ī, *n.,* impediment

imperātor, -ōris, *m.,* emperor, general* C17

impetus, -ūs, *m.,* impetus, force, attack* C17

importūnus, -a, -um, *adj.,* boorish

improbus, -a, -um, *adj.,* bad, wicked

in, *prep. + abl.,* in, on* C3

in, *prep. + acc.,* into, to* C4

incendium, -ī, *n.,* conflagration, eruption* C16

industria, -ae, *f.,* industry, care

inīquitās, -ātis, *f.,* injustice, mischief* C20

inīquus, -a, -um, *adj.,* unjust

initium, -ī, *n.,* beginning* C17

inquam, I say/I said (*only introducing direct speech*)* C15

inquit, s/he says or said (*only introducing direct speech*)* C12

intellegō, -ere, intellēxī, intellēctum, to understand* C8

inter, *prep. + acc.,* between, among* C19

intereā, *adv.,* meanwhile

intrō (1), to enter* C4

inūsitātus, -a, -um, *adj.,* strange, unusual

invideō, -ēre, invīdī, invīsum + *dat.,* to envy someone* C7

invīsō, -ere, invīsī, invīsum, to visit

ipse, ipsa, ipsum, *demonstrative pronoun and adj.,* -self

īra, -ae, *f.,* anger* C12

is, ea, id, *personal and demonstrative pronoun and adj.,* s/he/it, this, that* C12

ita, *adv.,* so, in such a way* C18; yes* C11

Italia, -ae, *f.,* Italy

itaque, *conj.,* and so* C1

iubeō, -ēre, iussī, iussum + *acc. + inf.,* to order somebody to do something* C4

iūdex, -icis, *m.,* judge* C13

iūdicō (1), to judge* C6

Iuppiter, Iovis, *m.,* Jupiter, king of gods (in Greek, Zeus)

iussus, -ūs, *m.,* order (*usually employed in the ablative singular only*)* C17

iūstus, -a, -um, *adj.,* legitimate, just, open* C4

L

lacrima, -ae, *f.,* tear* C5

laqueus, -ī, *m.,* noose, lasso

leaena, -ae, *f.,* lioness

legō, -ere, lēgī, lēctum, to read, choose* C16

lēx, lēgis, *f.,* law* C20

liber, librī, *m.,* book* C6

līberō (1) + *acc. + abl.,* to free someone from something* C8 licet + *dat.* + *inf.,* it is allowed, it is permitted for someone to do something* C13

ligneus, -a, -um, *adj.,* wooden

littera, -ae, *f.,* letter of the alphabet; litterae, -ārum, *f. pl.,* literature, letter (epistle)* C6

lītus, -oris, *n.,* shore* C16

locus, -ī, *m.,* place; locī, -ōrum, *m. pl.,* passages of a book; loca, -ōrum, *n. pl.,* geographical places* C17

longē, *adv.,* far* C5

longus, -a, -um, *adj.,* long* C5

Lūcīlius, -ī, *m.,* Lucilius, a friend of Seneca's to whom he addressed his philosophical essays in the form of letters

lūculentus, -a, -um, *adj.,* splendid

lūdō, -ere, lūsī, lūsum, to play* C20

lūmen, -inis, *n.,* light

lupa, -ae, *f.,* she-wolf* C1

M

Maecēnās, Maecēnātis, *m.,* Maecenas, friend of Augustus, patron of the arts

magnus, -a, -um, *adj.,* large, great, important* C4

maior, maius, *adj.,* bigger, greater

male, *adv.,* badly

malitia, -ae, *f.,* badness, wickedness

malus, -a, -um, *adj.,* bad* C4

maneō, -ēre, mānsī, mānsum, to remain* C6

manus, -ūs, *f.,* hand* C17

Mārcus Tullius Cicero, -ōnis, *m.,* Marcus Tullius Cicero

mare, maris, *n.,* sea* C9

marītus, -ī, *m.,* husband* C18

Mārs, -tis, *m.,* Mars, the god of war (in Greek, Ares)

māter, mātris, *f.,* mother* C16

mēcum = cum mē, with me* C13

mellītus, -a, -um, *adj.,* sweet as honey

memoria, -ae, *f.,* memory* C6

Menaechmus, -ī, *m.,* Menaechmus; Menaechmī, -ōrum, *m. pl.,* the brothers Menaechmi

mercimōnium, -ī, *n.,* merchandise

Mercurius, -ī, *m.,* Mercury, messenger god, patron of merchants, travelers, thieves (in Greek, Hermes)

merīdiēs, -ēī, *m.,* midday* C18

meus, -a, -um, *possessive adj.,* my* C7

mīles, -itis, *m.,* soldier* C8

minimē, *adv.,* no* C11

Mīsēnum, -ī, *n.,* a base for the imperial Roman navy in the Bay of Naples; Mīsēnī, at Misenum

miser, misera, miserum, *adj.,* wretched, miserable, sad* C5

mittō, -ere, mīsī, missum, to send* C11

mōns, montis, *m.,* mountain* C16

mordeō, -ēre, momordī, morsum, to bite

mors, mortis, *f.,* death* C9

mortuus, -a, -um, *adj.,* dead

moveō, -ēre, mōvī, mōtum, to move* C10

mox, *adv.,* soon* C14

Mūcius (-ī) Scaevola (-ae), *m.,* Mucius Scaevola

mulier, -ieris, *f.,* woman* C9

multum, *adv.,* much* C18

multus, -a, -um, *adj.,* much, many* C6

mūnīmentum, -ī, *n.,* protection, fortification

mūrus, -ī, *m.,* wall, wall-fence* C17

mūtō (1), to change* C21

N

nam, *conj.,* for, in fact* C5

nārrō (1), to tell* C2

nātūra, -ae, *f.,* nature

nauta, -ae, *m.,* sailor* C1

nāvigō (1), to sail, voyage* C8

nāvis, -is, *f.,* ship* C16

-ne, a particle added to the first word of an interrogative sentence* C11

nec, *conj.,* and not, nor* C10

necō (1), to kill

neglegō, -ere, neglēxī, neglēctum, to neglect* C15

nēminī, to nobody

Nerō, Nerōnis, *m.,* Nero, Julio-Claudian emperor

nihil, *negative pronoun,* nothing* C13

nisi, *conj.,* if not, unless

nōbīscum = cum nōbīs

noctū, *adv.,* during the night* C20

nōlō, *irregular verb,* not to want, be unwilling* C13

nōmen, -inis, *n.,* name* C12

nōn, *negative adv.,* not* C2

nōn sōlum . . . , sed etiam . . . , not only . . . , but also . . .* C5

nōnne?, don't you?

nōs, *personal pronoun,* we* C12

noster, nostra, nostrum, *possessive adj.,* our* C12

nōtus, -a, -um, *adj.,* known

novus, -a, -um, *adj.,* new* C11

nox, noctis, *f.,* night* C10

nūbēs, -is, *f.,* cloud* C16

nūgae, -ārum, *f. pl.,* trifles

num?, do I? (negative answer implied)

numquam, *adv.,* never* C16

nunc, *adv.,* now* C2

O

ō, *interjection,* oh!

occīdō, -ere, occīdī, occīsum, to kill* C12

occultātus, -a, -um, *adj.,* hidden

occultō (1), to hide* C18

occultus, -a, -um, *adj.,* hidden

oculus, -ī, *m.,* eye* C7

odium, -ī, *n.,* hatred* C14
oleum, -ī, *n.,* oil
omnis, -e, *adj.,* each, every, all*
C13
opprimō, -ere, oppressī,
oppressum, to overwhelm,
suppress* C16
oppugnō (1), to attack
ōrāculum, -ī, *n.,* oracle* C8
ōrātiō, -ōnis, *f.,* speech;
ōrātiōnem habēre, to make a
speech* C9
ōs, ōris, *n.,* mouth* C14
ostendō, -ere, ostendī,
ostentum, to show* C12

P

paene, *adv.,* almost* C20
papae!, wow!
parātus, -a, -um, *adj.,* prepared
(often + *inf.*)
parēns, -rentis, *m./f.,* parent* C14
pariēs, parietis, *m.,* wall
parō (1), to prepare, get ready*
C2; design* C5
pars, partis, *f.,* part* C16
parvus, -a, -um, *adj.,* small* C15
passer, -eris, *m.,* sparrow* C7
pater, -tris, *m.,* father* C18
patria, -ae, *f.,* fatherland* C2
paucī, -ae, -a, *adj.,* few* C10
paulisper, *adv.,* for a little while
pauper, pauperis, *adj.,* poor* C20
pāx, pācis, *f.,* peace* C9
pectus, -oris, *n.,* chest* C14
pellis, -is, *f.,* skin, hide* C19
per, *prep. + acc.,* through* C14
perīculum, -ī, *n.,* danger* C10
permoveō, -ēre, -mōvī, -mōtum,
to perturb
Persae, -ārum, *m. pl.,* the Persians
petō, -ere, petīvī, petītum, to
seek, head for, go to, rush at*
C8
piger, pigra, pigrum, *adj.,* lazy
pīpiō, -āre, ——, ——, to chirp
pirum, -ī, *n.,* pear (fruit)

pirus, -ī, *f.,* pear tree
plēnus, -a, -um, *adj. + gen.* or +
abl., full of* C20
pluit, -ere, pluit, ——, *an*
impersonal verb (used only in 3rd
sg.), to rain
plūs quam, more than
poena, -ae, *f.,* punishment
poēta, -ae, *m.,* poet* C1
pōmum, -ī, *n.,* fruit* C20
pōnō, -ere, posuī, positum, to
put, place* C12
porcus, -ī, *m.,* pig
porta, -ae, *f.,* gate
possideō, -ēre, possēdī,
possessum, to possess* C21
possum, posse, potuī, ——, to be
able, can* C6
post, *prep. + acc.,* after* C18
posteā, *adv.,* afterward* C1
postquam, *conj.,* after* C19
praeclārus, -a, -um, *adj.,* famous,
distinguished* C4
praefectus, -ī, *m.,* prefect,
commander, chief
praemium, -ī, *n.,* reward* C4
prīmum, *adv.,* first
prīmus, -a, -um, *adj.,* first* C14
prō certō, *adverbial phrase,* for
certain, for sure* C21
prō Iuppiter!, by Jove!
prō, *prep. + abl.,* for, on behalf of*
C13
proelium, -ī, *n.,* battle, combat*
C19
profuga, -ae, *m.,* deserter
prope, *prep. + acc.,* near* C12
propter, *prep. + acc.,* because of,
on account of* C6
Psȳchē, *(gen.)* **Psȳchēs,** *(dat.)*
Psȳchē, *(acc.)* **Psȳchēn,** *(abl.)*
Psȳchē, Psyche
puella, -ae, *f.,* girl* C1
puer, puerī, *m.,* boy* C3
pugnō (1), to fight* C10
pulcher, pulchra, pulchrum, *adj.,*
beautiful, nice* C5

pulchritūdō, pulchritūdinis, *f.,*
beauty
pūniō, -īre, pūnīvī, pūnītum, to
punish* C20
putō (1), to think, consider* C7
Pȳramus, -ī, *m.,* Pyramus
Pyrrhus, -ī, *m.,* Pyrrhus, king of
Epirus
Pȳthia, -ae, *f.,* the Pythian
priestess, responsible for
uttering the ambiguous oracles
at the shrine of Apollo at Delphi,
Greece

Q

quaerō, -ere, quaesīvī,
quaesītum, to look for, search*
C18
-que, *conj.,* and* C11
quī, quae, quod, *relative pronoun,*
which, who, that* C14
quī, quae, quod?, *interrogative*
adjective, which? what? * C15
quid agis, how are you?
quis, quid?, *interrogative pronoun,*
who? what? * C13
quō?, to what place?
quōcum = cum quō, with whom
quōmodo, how?
quondam, *adv.,* once
quoque, *adv.,* also* C11

R

rādīx, rādīcis, *f.,* root
rāmus, -ī, *m.,* branch
recipiō, -ere, -cēpī, -ceptum, to
take back* C21
rēgīna, -ae, *f.,* queen* C11
relinquō, -ere, relīquī,
relictum, to leave behind,
abandon* C11
Remus, -ī, *m.,* Remus, brother of
Romulus
reparō (1), to repair
reprehendō, -ere, -prehendī,
-prehēnsum, to blame, rebuke*
C21

rērum nātūra, rērum nātūrae, *f.,* nature

rēs, reī, *f.,* thing, matter* C18

respondeō, -ēre, -spondī, -spōnsum, to answer* C13

reveniō, -īre, -vēnī, -ventum, to return

rēx, rēgis, *m.,* king* C8

Rhēa Silvia, Rhēae Silviae, *f.,* Rhea Silvia, vestal virgin

rīvus, -ī, *m.,* brook, stream* C3

rogō (1), to ask* C13

Rōma, -ae, *f.,* Rome* C1

Rōmānus, -a, -um, *adj.,* Roman* C4

Rōmulus, -ī, *m.,* Romulus, legendary founder of Rome

rota, -ae, *f.,* wheel* C21

ruber, rubra, rubrum, *adj.,* red* C14

rūsticus, -a, -um, *adj.,* rural, rustic* C15

S

sacer, sacra, sacrum, *adj.,* holy, sacred

sacra, -ōrum, *n. pl.,* religious rites

saepe, *adv.,* often* C6

sagitta, -ae, *f.,* arrow

salūtem plūrimam dīcit + *dat.,* s/he greets (someone) (a standard formula for beginning a letter). Literally it means "(s/he) says (i.e., wishes) very much health (the best of health) to . . ."

salvē!, hello!

sanguis, sanguinis, *m.,* blood* C14

sānō (1), to heal* C19

saxum, -ī, *n.,* stone, rock* C15

scientia, -ae, *f.,* knowledge

sciō, scīre, scīvī, scītum, to know* C9

sē, *acc. of the reflexive pronoun,* herself, himself, itself, themselves* C7

sed, *conj.,* but* C4

sedeō, -ēre, sēdī, sessum, to sit* C19

sella, -ae, *f.,* seat, chair

sēmoveō, -ēre, sēmōvī, sēmōtum, to remove

semper, *adv.,* always* C5

Seneca, -ae, *m.,* Seneca, Roman author

senectūs, -ūtis, *f.,* old age* C15

senex, -is, *m.,* old man* C7

sentiō, -īre, sēnsī, sēnsum, to feel* C9

sēparō (1), to separate* C14

servō (1), to save, preserve* C6

sevērus, -a, -um, *adj.,* serious, strict, severe* C7

sī, *conj.,* if* C18

sīcut, *adv.,* just as* C15

silva, -ae, *f.,* forest* C11

similis, -e, *adj.* + *gen.* or + *dat.,* like, similar* C12

sine, *prep.* + *abl.,* without* C17

soleō, -ēre, solitus sum + *inf.,* to be accustomed* C6

sōlus, -a, -um, *adj.,* sole, only

somnus, -ī, *m.,* sleep* C18

soror, -ōris, *f.,* sister* C7

spectō (1), to look at, gaze, stare at

spēlunca, -ae, *f.,* cave* C11

statim, *adv.,* immediately* C12

stō, -āre, stetī, statum, to stand* C15

studeō, -ēre, studuī, —— + *dat.,* to study, be eager for, be interested in* C16

studiōsus, -a, -um, *adj.* + *gen.,* interested in, a student of

subitō, *adv.,* suddenly* C12

sum, esse, fuī, ——, to be* C6

summus, -a, -um, *adj.,* the top of

suus, -a, -um, *possessive adj.,* his, her, its, their* C13

Syrācūsānus, -a, -um, *adj.,* from Syracuse

T

taberna, -ae, *f.,* shop

tam, *adv.,* so* C18

tamen, *conj.,* however* C5

tamquam, *adv.,* as if

tandem, *adv.,* at last* C9

tangō, -ere, tetigī, tāctum, to touch* C14

tantum, *adv.,* only* C13

tantus, -a, -um, *adj.,* so great* C12

tēcum = cum tē, with you* C13

tempestās, -ātis, *f.,* storm* C11

templum, -ī, *n.,* temple* C8

temptō (1), to try* C17

tempus, -oris, *n.,* time* C9

tenebrae, -ārum, *f. pl.,* shadows, darkness* C6

teneō, -ēre, tenuī, tentum, to hold* C2

Terentia, -ae, *f.,* Terentia, wife of Cicero

terō, -ere, trīvī, trītum, to wear out, rub* C19

terra, -ae, *f.,* land* C1

terribilis, -e, *adj.,* terrifying* C19

tertius, -a, -um, *adj.,* third

Themistoclēs, Themistoclis, *m.,* Themistocles, Athenian general

Thisbē, Thisbēs (*gen.*), **Thisbē** (*dat.*), **Thisbēn** (*acc.*), **Thisbē** (*voc.*), *f.,* Thisbe

timeō, -ēre, timuī, ——, to fear, be afraid* C3

timor, -ōris, *m.,* fear* C8

tolerō (1), to tolerate, bear

tollō, -ere, sustulī, sublātum, to lift up, raise, destroy* C21

tonō, -āre, -uī, ——, to thunder

tōtus, -a, -um, *adj.,* whole

trāns Tiberim, on the other side of the Tiber River

trēs, tria, *numeral,* three

trīstitia, -ae, *f.,* sadness

Trōia, -ae, *f.,* Troy

Trōiānus, -a, -um, *adj.,* Trojan

tū, *personal pronoun,* you (*sg.*)* C3

tum, *adv.,* then* C13

tumultus, -ūs, *m.,* uproar, confusion* C17

tunc, *adv.,* then* C8

tuus, -a, -um, *possessive adj.,* yours, your (*sg.*)* C12

U

ubi, *adv.,* where

ubīque, *adv.,* everywhere* C15

Ulixes, Ulixis, *m.,* Odysseus, Ulysses (Latin)

ūllus, -a, -um, *adj.,* any* C21

umquam, *adv.,* ever* C15

ūnā, *adv.,* together* C11

ūnusquisque nostrum, each one of us

urbs, urbis, *f.,* city (usually the city of Rome)* C9

uxor, -ōris, *f.,* wife* C18

V

valdē, *adv.,* very, exceedingly* C3

valē!, goodbye!* C13

vectus, -a, -um, *adj.,* carried, driven

vēlāmen, vēlāminis, *n.,* veil

venēnum, -ī, *n.,* poison* C4

veniō, -īre, vēnī, ventum, to come* C9

ventus, -ī, *m.,* wind* C17

Venus, Veneris, *f.,* Venus, goddess of beauty and love (in Greek, Aphrodite)

verbum, -ī, *n.,* word* C7

versō (1), to turn* C21

vērus, -a, -um, *adj.,* true* C15

Vesta, -ae, *f.,* Vesta, goddess of the hearth (in Greek, Hestia)

vester, vestra, vestrum, *possessive adj.,* yours (*pl.*), your* C12

vestīmentum, -ī, *n.,* garment, (*pl.*) clothes* C19

Vesuvius, -ī, *m.,* (Mt.) Vesuvius

vetustus, -a, -um, *adj.,* old* C15

via, -ae, *f.,* road* C3

Via Sacra, a street in the Roman Forum

victōria, -ae, *f.,* victory

videō, -ēre, vīdī, vīsum, to see, (passive) seem* C2

vīlicus, -ī, *m.,* bailiff, steward

vīlla, -ae, *f.,* country house, villa* C15

vincō, -ere, vīcī, victum, to conquer, defeat* C8

vīnctus, -a, -um, *adj.,* bound, chained

vinculum, -ī, *n.,* chain, fetter* C4

vir, virī, *m.,* man* C3

vīs, ——, *f.,* pl. **vīrēs, vīrium,** force, strength; **prō vīribus,** with all one's might* C12

vīta, -ae, *f.,* life* C6

vīvō, -ere, vīxī, vīctum, to live* C19

vocō (1), to call* C2

vōs, *personal pronoun,* you (*pl.*)* C12

vulnerō (1), to wound* C19

vulnus, -eris, *n.,* wound* C19

vult, he wishes

X

Xerxēs, Xerxis, *m.,* Xerxes, the great king of the Persians (who invaded Greece in 480 BCE)

LATIN GRAMMAR

Allen, J. H., and J. B. Greenough. *Allen and Greenough's New Latin Grammar*. Edited by Anne Mahoney. Newburyport, MA: Focus Publishing/R. Pullins, 2001.

Gildersleeve, Basil L., and Gonzalez Lodge. *Gildersleeve's Latin Grammar*. 3rd ed. 1895. Reprint, Wauconda, IL: Bolchazy-Carducci Publishers, 2003.

LATIN COMPOSITION

Minkova, Milena. *Introduction to Latin Prose Composition*. Wauconda, IL: Bolchazy-Carducci Publishers, 2007. First published 2002 by Wimbledon Publishing Co.

Minkova, Milena, and Terence Tunberg. *Readings and Exercises in Latin Prose Composition: From Antiquity to the Renaissance*. Newburyport, MA: Focus Publishing/R. Pullins, 2004.

Mountford, James F., ed. *Bradley's Arnold Latin Prose Composition*. Rev. ed. Wauconda, IL: Bolchazy-Carducci Publishers, 2006.

LATIN DICTIONARIES

Lewis, Charlton T., and Charles Short. *A Latin Dictionary*. Oxford: Clarendon Press, 1879.

Oxford Latin Dictionary. 2nd ed. Edited by P. G. W. Glare. Oxford: Clarendon Press, 2012.

Smith, William, and Theophilus D. Hall. *Smith's English-Latin Dictionary*. Reprinted from the 1871 American Book Company edition, *A Copious and Critical English-Latin Dictionary*, with a new foreword by Dirk Sacré. Wauconda, IL: Bolchazy-Carducci Publishers, 2000.

CONVERSATIONAL LATIN

Traupman, John. *Conversational Latin for Oral Proficiency*. 4th ed.: *Audio Conversations*. Performed by Mark Robert Miner et al. Compact disks. Wauconda, IL: Bolchazy-Carducci Publishers, 2006.

LATIN LITERATURE

Albrecht, Michael von. *A History of Roman Literature: From Livius Andronicus to Boethius*. Leiden: Brill Academic Publishers, 1997.

IJsewijn, Jozef. *Companion to Neo-Latin Studies, Part I: History and Diffusion of Neo-Latin Literature*. 2nd ed. Supplementa Humanistica Lovaniensia, 5. Leuven: Leuven University Press, 1990.

IJsewijn, Jozef, and Dirk Sacré. *Companion to Neo-Latin Studies, II: Literary, Linguistic, Philological and Editorial Questions*. 2nd ed. Supplementa Humanistica Lovaniensia, 14. Leuven: Leuven University Press, 1998.

Mantello, Frank, and Arthur G. Rigg. *Medieval Latin: An Introduction and Bibliographical Guide.* Washington, DC: The Catholic University of America Press, 1996.

HISTORY OF THE LATIN SPEAKING WORLD

Boatwright, Mary T., Daniel J. Gargola, and Richard J. A. Talbert. *A Brief History of the Romans.* 2nd ed. New York: Oxford University Press, 2013.

Holmes, George. *The Oxford History of Medieval Europe.* Oxford: Oxford University Press, 2001.

Thompson, Bard. *Humanists and Reformers: A History of the Renaissance and Reformation.* Grand Rapids and Cambridge: William B. Eerdmans Publishers, 1996.

MYTHOLOGY

Colakis, Marianthe, and Mary Joan Masello. *Classical Mythology and More: A Reader Workbook.* Wauconda, IL: Bolchazy-Carducci Publishers, 2007.

Morford, Mark P. O., and Robert J. Lenardon. *Classical Mythology.* 10th ed. New York: Oxford University Press, 2013.

DAILY LIFE

Brucia, Margaret A., and Gregory Daugherty. *To Be a Roman: Topics in Roman Culture.* Wauconda, IL: Bolchazy-Carducci Publishers, 2007.

Carcopino, Jérôme. *Daily Life in Ancient Rome.* 2nd ed. New Haven and London: Yale University Press, 2003.

Newman, Paul B. *Daily Life in the Middle Ages.* Jefferson, NC: McFarland & Company, 2001.

ENGLISH ETYMOLOGY

Oxford Dictionary of English Etymology. Edited by C. T. Onions et al. New York: Oxford University Press, 1966.

INTRODUCTION
Etruscan Sarcophagus (© 2008 Jupiter Images Corp.)
Engraved Stone 1 (© 2008 Shutterstock Images LLC)
Engraved Stone 2 (© 2008 Shutterstock Images LLC)
Roman Baths (© 2008 Shutterstock Images LLC)
Tiber River (© 2008 Jupiter Images Corp.)
Ruins in Carthage (© 2008 Shutterstock Images LLC)

CHAPTER 1
Romulus and Remus (Scala/Art Resource, NY)
Capitoline Wolf (© 2008 Shutterstock Images LLC)
Pont du Gard (© 2008 Shutterstock Images LLC)
SPQR (© 2008 Shutterstock Images LLC)
SPQR Mosaic (© 2015 Shutterstock Images LLC)
Farmer with Sheep (© 2008 Jupiter Images Corp.)

CHAPTER 2
Three Actors (Erich Lessing/Art Resource, NY)
Mask of Comedy (© 2008 Shutterstock Images LLC)
Theatre in Ephesus (© 2008 Shutterstock Images LLC)
Theatre at Sabratha (© 2015 Shutterstock Images LLC)

CHAPTER 3
Choreographer (Erich Lessing/Art Resource, NY)
Bosra Theatre (© 2008 Shutterstock Images LLC)
Masks (© 2008 Jupiter Images Corp.)
Theatre of Marcellus (© 2008 Shutterstock Images LLC)
Roman Road (© 2008 Shutterstock Images LLC)

REVIEW 1
Writing Utensils (Erich Lessing/Art Resource, NY)

CLASSICAL GODS 1
Mars and Venus (© 2008 Jupiter Images Corp.)
Zeus Coin (© 2008 Shutterstock Images LLC)
Jupiter and Juno (Scala/Art Resource, NY)

Temple of Hera II (© 2008 Jupiter Images Corp.)
Mt. Olympus (© 2008 Shutterstock Images LLC)

ANCIENT WORLD 1
Butcher Shop (Alinari/Art Resource, NY)
Building a Wall (© 2008 Jupiter Images Corp.)
Mosaic of Slaves (© 2008 Jupiter Images Corp.)

EXPLORATION 1
Comedy Mask (© 2008 Jupiter Images Corp.)
Caesarea Theatre (© 2008 Shutterstock Images LLC)

MĪRĀBILE AUDĪTŪ 1
Jerash Theatre (© 2008 Jupiter Images Corp.)

CHAPTER 4
Pyrrhus (SEF/Art Resource, NY)
Roman Legionary (© 2008 Jupiter Images Corp.)
Legionary Actors (© 2008 Shutterstock Images LLC)
Centurion (© 2008 Shutterstock Images LLC)

CHAPTER 5
Porculo and Wife (Alinari/Art Resource, NY)
Bust of Cicero (© 2008 Jupiter Images Corp.)
Cicero Sign (© 2008 Shutterstock Images LLC)

CHAPTER 6
Norma and the Druids (Bildarchiv Preussischer Kulturbesitz/Art Resource, NY)
Letters on Stone (© 2008 Shutterstock Images LLC)
Julius Caesar Stamp (© 2008 Shutterstock Images LLC)
Caesar and Commentaries (Scala/Art Resource, NY)
Women during Gallic Invasion (© 2008 Jupiter Images Corp.)

REVIEW 2
Roman Weapons (National Museum of Slovenia, by Tomaz Lauko)

Basilica of Maxentius (© 2008 Shutterstock Images LLC)

CLASSICAL GODS 2

Trevi Fountain (© 2008 Shutterstock Images LLC)

Neptune Fountain (© 2015 Shutterstock Images LLC)

Charon (© 2008 Jupiter Images Corp.)

House of the Vestals (© 2008 Shutterstock Images LLC)

Triptolemus (© 2015 Jupiter Images Corp.)

ANCIENT WORLD 2

Toilette of the Bride (Alinari/Art Resource, NY)

Sabine Women (Public Domain)

EXPLORATION 2

Funerary Bust (© British Museum/Art Resource, NY)

Young Roman Boy (© 2008 Shutterstock Images LLC)

Child with Amphora (© 2008 Shutterstock Images LLC)

MĪRĀBILE AUDĪTŪ 2

Annuit coeptīs (© 2008 Shutterstock Images LLC)

Caveat ēmptor (© 2008 Shutterstock Images LLC)

Three Dimension @ (© 2008 Shutterstock Images LLC)

CHAPTER 7

Catullus Reading to Lesbia (Private Collection/ Bridgeman Images)

Coin of an *As* (© 2008 Shutterstock Images LLC)

Dove Mosaic (© 2008 Shutterstock Images LLC)

Sparrow (© 2008 Shutterstock Images LLC)

Thermopolium (© 2008 Shutterstock Images LLC)

CHAPTER 8

Themistocles (Scala/Art Resource, NY)

Greek Warship (© 2008 Shutterstock Images LLC)

Leonidas (© 2008 Jupiter Images Corp.)

Delphic Sibyl (© 2008 Shutterstock Images LLC)

Sanctuary of Athena (© 2008 Shutterstock Images LLC)

CHAPTER 9

Cicero Denounces Catiline (Scala/Art Resource, NY)

Roman Body Armor (© 2008 Jupiter Images Corp.)

Side of the Senate House (© 2008 Shutterstock Images LLC)

Mediterranean Sea (© 2008 Shutterstock Images LLC)

REVIEW 3
CLASSICAL GODS 3

Pompeiian Statue of Apollo (© 2008 Shutterstock Images LLC)

Ruins at Delos (© 2008 Shutterstock Images LLC)

Apollo and Daphne (Public Domain)

Temple of Apollo, Corinth (© 2008 Shutterstock Images LLC)

ANCIENT WORLD 3

Man Wearing a Toga (© 2008 Shutterstock Images LLC)

Bust of Roman Men and Women (© 2008 Shutterstock Images LLC)

MĪRĀBILE AUDĪTŪ 3

Ē plūribus ūnum on coin (© 2008 Shutterstock Images LLC)

Ē plūribus ūnum on stamp (© 2008 Jupiter Images Corp.)

Dollar Bill (© 2008 Shutterstock Images LLC)

State Seal of Massachusetts (Public Domain)

State Seal of Virginia (Public Domain)

CHAPTER 10

Reconstructed Wooden Horse (© 2008 Jupiter Images Corp.)

Odysseus Vase (© 2008 Jupiter Images Corp.)

Vergil Mosaic (© 2008 Jupiter Images Corp.)

CHAPTER 11

Dido and Aeneas Hunting (Bridgeman-Giraudon/Art Resource, NY)

Mercury with Caduceus (© 2008 Jupiter Images Corp.)

Ruins of Carthage (© 2008 Shutterstock Images LLC)

CHAPTER 12

Mucius's Hand in the Fire (Alinari/Art Resource, NY)

Constantine's Hand (© 2008 Shutterstock Images LLC)

Temple of Antoninus (© 2008 Shutterstock Images LLC)

Antonine Column (© 2008 Jupiter Images Corp.)

REVIEW 4
CLASSICAL GODS 4

Hermes and Apollo (Erich Lessing/Art Resource, NY)

Hermes, Grand Central (© 2015 Shutterstock Images LLC)

ANCIENT WORLD 4

Mosaic of Flagon and Goblet (© 2008 Shutterstock Images LLC)

Triclinium Diagram (© 2008 Jupiter Images Corp.)

Wooden Plates (© 2008 Shutterstock Images LLC)

Slovenian Artifacts (National Museum of Slovenia, by Tomaz Lauko)

EXPLORATION 4

Bust of Homer (© 2008 Jupiter Images Corp.)

Wooden Horse (© 2008 Shutterstock Images LLC)

Computer Screen (© 2008 Shutterstock Images LLC)

MĪRĀBILE AUDĪTŪ 4

Roman Soldier (© 2008 Shutterstock Images LLC)

CHAPTER 13

Via Sacra in Forum (Scala/Art Resource, NY)

Temple of Vesta (© 2008 Shutterstock Images LLC)

Sundial (© 2008 Shutterstock Images LLC)

Bookends (© 2008 Jupiter Images Corp.)

CHAPTER 14

Suicide of Thisbe (Bridgeman-Giraudon/Art Resource, NY)

Mulberry Branch (© 2008 Shutterstock Images LLC)

Lion Mosaic (© 2008 Jupiter Images Corp.)

CHAPTER 15

Suicide of Seneca (Erich Lessing/Art Resource, NY)

Bust of "Seneca" (© 2008 Jupiter Images Corp.)

Interior of Villa of Mysteries (© 2008 Jupiter Images Corp.)

Nero Coin (© 2008 Shutterstock Images LLC)

Villa Diagram (© 2008 Jupiter Images Corp.)

REVIEW 5

Sculpture of Augustus (© 2008 Shutterstock Images LLC)

CLASSICAL GODS 5

Athena Statue in Austria (© 2008 Shutterstock Images LLC)

Minerva Cameo (© 2008 Jupiter Images Corp.)

Statue of Diana (© 2008 Shutterstock Images LLC)

Venus of Milo (© 2008 Shutterstock Images LLC)

ANCIENT WORLD 5

Sabratha, Libya (© 2008 Jupiter Images Corp.)

Via Appia (© 2008 Shutterstock Images LLC)

Roman Milestone (© 2008 Shutterstock Images LLC)

EXPLORATION 5

Justice with Scales (© 2008 Shutterstock Images LLC)

CHAPTER 16

Eruption of Vesuvius (Réunion des Musées Nationaux/Art Resource, NY)

Vesuvius and Ruins (© 2008 Shutterstock Images LLC)

Statue of Faun (© 2008 Shutterstock Images LLC)

Pompeian Street Scene (© 2008 Shutterstock Images LLC)

CHAPTER 17

Torches of Nero (Erich Lessing/Art Resource, NY)

Cornucopia (© 2008 Jupiter Images Corp.)

Bust of Nero (© 2008 Jupiter Images Corp.)

Plan of the House of the Faun (© 2008 Jupiter Images Corp.)

Ruins in the Forum (© 2008 Shutterstock Images LLC)

CHAPTER 18

Cupid and Psyche (Manuel Cohen/The Art Archive at Art Resource, NY)

Marcus Aurelius (© 2008 Shutterstock Images LLC)

Faces with Loving Looks (© 2008 Shutterstock Images LLC)

Roman Eros (© 2008 Shutterstock Images LLC)

REVIEW 6

Bay of Naples (© 2008 Shutterstock Images LLC)

CLASSICAL GODS 6

Bacchus Mosaic (© 2008 Shutterstock Images LLC)

Bacchus Brooch (© 2008 Shutterstock Images LLC)

Feast of Bacchus (© 2008 Jupiter Images Corp.)

Bacchus and Tiger (© 2008 Jupiter Images Corp.)

ANCIENT WORLD 6

Colosseum Exterior (© 2008 Shutterstock Images LLC)

Pompeiian Amphitheatre (© 2008 Shutterstock Images LLC)

Gladiators Mosaic (© 2008 Shutterstock Images LLC)

Gladiator Poster (© 2008 Shutterstock Images LLC)

Inside of Colosseum (© 2008 Shutterstock Images LLC)

EXPLORATION 6

Active Volcano (© 2008 Shutterstock Images LLC)

Fresh Lava (© 2008 Shutterstock Images LLC)

Cast of a Dead Man (© 2008 Shutterstock Images LLC)

MĪRĀBILE AUDĪTŪ 6

View of Herculaneum (© 2008 Shutterstock Images LLC)

CHAPTER 19

Attila the Hun (© 2008 Jupiter Images Corp.)

Horsehead (© 2008 Shutterstock Images LLC)

Greek Horsemen (© 2008 Shutterstock Images LLC)

CHAPTER 20

Augustine and Monica (Réunion des Musées Nationaux/Art Resource, NY)

Augustine (© 2008 Jupiter Images Corp.)

Pear Tree Branch (© 2008 Shutterstock Images LLC)

Denarius (© 2008 Shutterstock Images LLC)

CHAPTER 21

Wheel of Fortune (Réunion des Musées Nationaux/Art Resource, NY

Woodcut of Philosophy (© 2008 Jupiter Images Corp.)

REVIEW 7

Augustine (© 2008 Jupiter Images Corp.)

CLASSICAL GODS 7

Statue of Vulcan (© 2008 Shutterstock Images LLC)

Temple of Hephaestus (© 2008 Shutterstock Images LLC)

Pantheon (© 2008 Shutterstock Images LLC)

Interior of Pantheon (© 2008 Shutterstock Images LLC)

ANCIENT WORLD 7

Child and Teacher (Erich Lessing/Art Resource, NY)

Celsus Library (© 2008 Shutterstock Images LLC)

EXPLORATION 7

Trajan's Column (© 2008 Shutterstock Images LLC)

Another View of Celsus Library (© 2008 Shutterstock Images LLC)

MĪRĀBILE AUDĪTŪ 7

Ex Librīs (© 2008 Jupiter Images Corp.)

APPENDIX B

State Seal of Arizona (Public Domain)

INDEX

Note: A reference to xxvii or 192 indicates the main text, while xxviip or 192p indicates a picture or its caption.

Online
Guided Practice
to Accompany
LATIN
FOR THE
NEW
MILLENNIUM

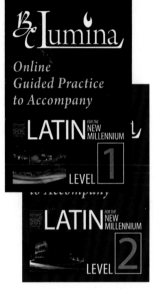

LUMINA online interactive content offers a multitude of practice exercises to support *Latin for the New Millennium*, Levels 1 and 2. Guided Language Fact sections provide immediate feedback to facilitate students' preview or review of a chapter. Mouse-over vocabulary lists allow a new format for vocabulary mastery. Infinitely replayable crossword puzzles engage students in derivative work. Automatically graded quizzes free up student-teacher interaction time for translation, oral/aural work, discussion, and other learning.

FOR STUDENTS

- Review Language Facts with immediate feedback
- Listen to audio recordings of Latin readings
- Study and practice Latin vocabulary in new formats
- Make connections between Latin and English through derivative work
- Engage with *LNM*'s Latin readings and language topics in greater depth

FOR INSTRUCTORS

- Quiz in various formats (multiple choice, fill in the blank, true/false, and matching)
- Integrate scores using your school's Learning Management Software or export scores to Excel for easy grading
- Receive new features as they are added

LUMINA FOR *LNM* CONTENTS

Each chapter in LUMINA for *LNM* begins with a **Practice Exercises** page: exercises that reinforce key concepts for each section of the textbook chapter. Many activities on this page do not allow students to enter incorrect answers; others provide detailed feedback, encouraging review of fundamentals. Replayable content allows for repeat practice.

Additional Exercises supplement the Practice Exercises and correspond to each chapter's reading, vocabulary to learn, and Language Facts. These activities continue to offer immediate feedback, but with less scaffolding, making them a flexible tool.

Each **Review** assesses students on their comprehension of the readings that appear in *LNM* review chapters. Extensive feedback clears up lingering points of confusion. Vocabulary to know is also reviewed in mouse-over format.